BASEBALL GOLD

BASEBALL GOLD

MINING NUGGETS FROM OUR NATIONAL PASTIME

DAN SCHLOSSBERG

PRESENTING SPONSOR

Library of Congress Cataloging-in-Publication Data

Schlossberg, Dan 1948–
Baseball gold : mining nuggest from our national pastime / Dan Schlossberg.
p. cm.
ISBN-13: 978-1-57243-958-0
ISBN-10: 1-57243-958-0
1. Baseball—United States—Miscellanea I. Title.

GV863.A1.S355 2007
796.357—dc22

2006033397

This book is available in quantity at special discounts for your group or organization. For further information, contact:

Triumph Books
542 South Dearborn Street
Suite 750
Chicago, Illinois 60605
(312) 939-3330
Fax (312) 663-3557

Printed in U.S.A.
ISBN: 978-1-57243-958-0
Design by Patricia Frey
Cover design by Paul Petrowsky
Front cover photo courtesy of AP/Wide World Photos

To Phyllis, whose trusty laptop saved the day when my desktop went on the D.L.

—D.S.

Contents

Foreword

During the half century that I spent in baseball as a player and broadcaster for the Baltimore Orioles, I have witnessed enormous changes. The game I loved as a kid in Little Rock, Arkansas, is hardly the same.

The biggest change has to be free agency. I don't think anybody anticipated the money being spent on players now. Maybe Marvin Miller did, but I don't think he ever foresaw what's happening now. It's great for the players to make the money, but to me the game has become more like "me, me, me, and I" than "we." That's the toughest job a manager has—to get the guys to play together as a team. Ninety percent of the players are making more money than the manager anyway. As a result, the players are a lot more independent than we were. They ask a lot more questions than we did when we started.

When I broke in under Paul Richards, I thought he was God. I would have run through a wall for him. Of course, there are more teams today. In 1961 they added two new teams and have had considerably more expansion since. When I broke in, there were 16 teams. Now there are 30.

The game has changed, too. I think the reason you see so many home runs in recent years is that the players are stronger than we were, the ballparks are smaller, and the ball is going farther than it ever did. I don't know if it's the ball, the bat, or something else. A lot of my friends are coaches or managers. But they just shake their heads. They say, "The baseball flies like a 2-iron hitting a Titleist."

The ballparks have also become hitter-friendly. Look at Camden Yards. I hear people talking about Cincinnati and Philadelphia, too. I don't know of too many pitchers' parks that are still around.

The pitching suffers, too. When I turned pro, the guys in the bullpen were the tail end of the pitching staff. Maybe four guys down there weren't as good as the other six on the staff. When someone came back from the disabled list, he went down to the pen to work himself back into shape. The advent of the closer has drastically changed the game.

Rollie Fingers, Goose Gossage, and Dennis Eckersley would come into the game in the seventh inning and close it out. They weren't

Ronnie Joyner

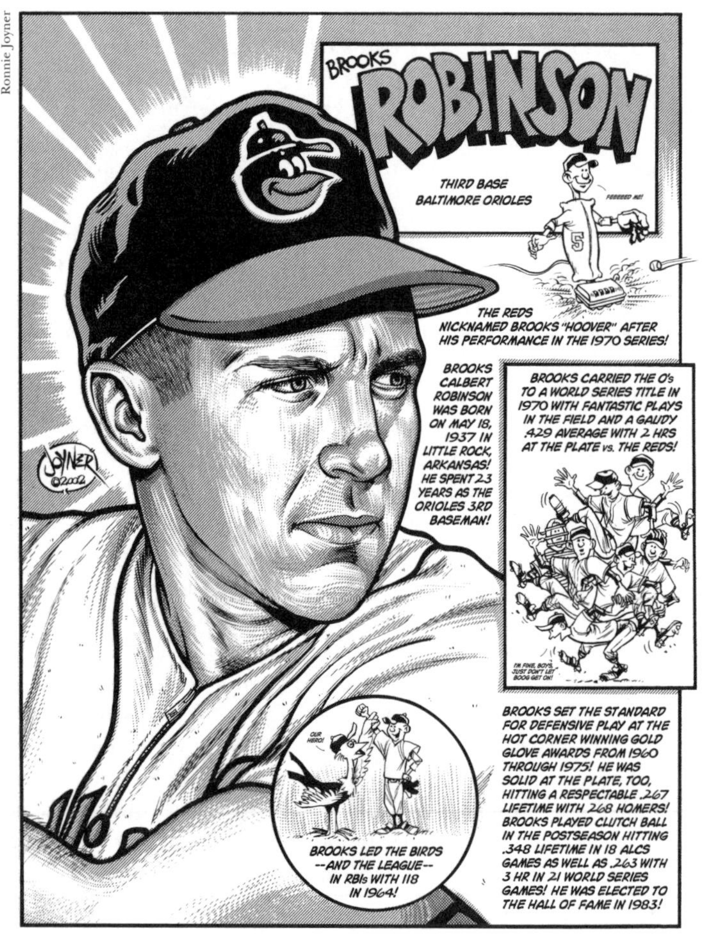

used like Mariano Rivera, who is predominantly a ninth-inning pitcher. B.J. Surhoff told me it's tougher to hit now because a left-handed pitcher always comes in to face a left-handed hitter. That wouldn't have been true 20 or 30 years ago.

I still think back to the 1966 World Series opener, when Moe Drabowsky relieved Dave McNally in the third inning and finished the game, striking out 11 Dodgers.

Everything has become so specialized. I'm surprised some managers haven't broken away from that and gone back to the old way. Now it's basically a five-and-fly. Give me five or six good innings and you've done your job. That's what coaches look for. You rarely see pitchers going eight or nine innings anymore. And money has made the difference, for both starters and closers. A top closer gets big bucks—often more than a top starter.

The Orioles played home games at Memorial Stadium during my career. There was a row of white houses behind the stadium, so it was hard to pick up the ball during day games. The team planted a row of trees and said they would block out the houses. Fifteen years later, they had grown about a foot and we were still seeing the white houses. Opposing players complained about it, too, which is why many teams placed tarps over sections of bleacher seats (for the batters' eyes).

The condition of the field was also a problem, especially after the Baltimore Colts played a couple of exhibition games in the mud right before the 1971 World Series. They had to spray the field with a green substance to make it look like grass.

The travel never bothered me at all. In the old days, we traveled by train—sometimes without air-conditioning. And we always seemed to arrive at 5:30 or 6:00 in the morning and would have to get off the train, go to the hotel, check in, and try to go back to sleep for a couple of hours.

Air travel is better. You get on the plane and sleep for a couple of hours. You arrive late but you can sleep in the next day. Flying isn't always relaxing, though. We once played an exhibition game in Aberdeen, South Dakota, and were in the plane on the tarmac, waiting to take off. There was lightning in the area and we were delayed a long time. Jim Gentile and Clint Courtney didn't like it, so they got off and took a bus to Chicago, arriving just in time for the game. I remember Jackie Jensen wouldn't fly at all and had to retire prematurely.

Even after baseball expanded to the West Coast, jet lag never bothered me. I was one of those guys who could lie down for five or six hours and that's as good as I'm going to get. We had one trip where we got into our hotel about 6:00 or 7:00 in the morning and went out and won the game pretty easily. It was more mental than anything else.

A lot of players complain about the travel, but I considered it just a part of the game. Same thing with the heat. Major league uniforms changed a lot, from heavy wool to tight-fitting double knits. In Arkansas, I played when it was hot, so the heat never bothered me. I was more concerned with how I looked in my uniform.

I wanted a low number to make me feel like I belonged in the big leagues, but I started with something like 17 or 32. I got No. 5 later on when it became available, and I was lucky enough to make it famous.

Like free agency and relief pitching, another big change I experienced was the proliferation of night games. When I broke in, we played a lot of day games, especially on the weekend, when we often had Sunday doubleheaders. I preferred to play at night. When you play six nights and then play Sunday afternoon, that's tough. Managers like to make lineup changes in those situations, to give other guys a chance.

It all came down to dollars and sense. I played in the first night game in World Series history, the second game in Pittsburgh in 1971. Now everything is under the lights because owners and advertisers know they're going to get better TV ratings.

I actually played in four World Series. We lost the two we were supposed to win and won the two we were supposed to lose.

The longer I'm out of the game, the more I appreciate the fact that I played my whole career in Baltimore. In 1977, when we went through expansion, I called Toronto and Seattle, thinking I could still play. But we always think we can play when we really can't. Things just didn't work out.

I spent more time with one team than anyone else except Carl Yastrzemski, who played 23 full seasons in Boston. I retired a month before my last season ended. I think the fans have become accustomed to players moving from team to team. The bottom line is that fans will come to the ballpark if their team wins. It is sad to see fans not being able to get attached to certain players, but that's just the way the game is now.

Growing up in Arkansas, we were big Cardinals fans because that was the only game in town, listening to their games on the radio. I could name every player from the Cardinals, every player from the Dodgers, and every player from the Giants. We fell in love with those guys and knew who was going to be there next year.

Aside from Cal Ripken Jr. and Tony Gwynn, it's not the same anymore. Free agency started just about the time I was getting out of the game and past my playing days. Then Cal became an icon in Baltimore and the team had to keep him. His dad had been a coach and manager in the organization for many years, and his brother Bill also spent some time with the team.

I'm surprised at the number of family dynasties in baseball: Bobby and Barry Bonds, the two Ken Griffeys, the Bells (Gus and Buddy), the Boones (Ray, Bob, and brothers Bret and Aaron), and the Ripkens to name a few. Gaylord and Jim Perry won Cy Young Awards, while Phil and Joe Niekro won more games than any other pitching brothers. I hit my last home run against Dave LaRoche, whose son Adam is in the big leagues now, with brother Andy on the way.

I have three sons of my own, aged 46, 44, and 43. They all went to college but weren't that interested in baseball, even though I encouraged them. Maybe they lost interest because they were around it so much. I know the Bonds and Griffey kids hung around and played, but everyone does his own thing. Bobby Bonds was a great player who batted leadoff, stole bases, and had a great throwing arm from the outfield. Then Barry came along and has been just phenomenal.

I always asked my sons whether they wanted autographs from the Hall of Fame induction weekends, but they weren't that interested. So I didn't ask anyone to sign anything for them. But I wish I had. There must have been 50 Hall of Famers who passed away since my induction in 1983—people like Ted Williams, Johnny Mize, Bill Dickey, Joe Sewell, and Cool Papa Bell. I wish I could have gotten a baseball from each one of those guys and have that collection now. It would be something I would cherish.

Like my friend Dan Schlossberg, the author of this book and more than 30 others, I do cherish the memories I have collected. I remember making $125 a week working for the Orioles in the winter of 1960. Six years later, I remember the excitement I felt when we traded for Frank Robinson, who won the Triple Crown that year and brought the World Series to Baltimore for the first time. And I remember how gratifying it was to hit a home run in my first World Series at-bat.

Throughout my career, I have always enjoyed being on a winning team. I'm sure the team that produced this project will maintain that tradition. So sit back, relax, and read about the glorious history of our national pastime. And some not-so-glorious parts, too—all saved in one lavishly illustrated volume. I'm saving a prominent spot for it on my coffee table.

—Brooks Robinson

Brooks Robinson spent his entire 23-year playing career with the Baltimore Orioles from 1955 to 1977, then broadcast for the club from 1978 to 1993. The Most Valuable Player in the 1964 American League regular season, 1966 All-Star Game, and 1970 World Series, Brooks was enshrined in the Baseball Hall of Fame in 1983.

Preface

Baseball cannot exist without the fans who follow the game, and those fans depend on the writers and announcers who cover it.

Vin Scully has probably been the best and the most versatile broadcaster. He's the only one who works alone and the only one who can get away with it. His reputation allows him to do that. And you can't argue with success.

There have been many great broadcasters: Red Barber, Mel Allen, and Ernie Harwell certainly had longevity. So did Bob Elson, who broadcast games in the 1930s, '40s, '50s, and '60s. I not only heard him as a kid when I was growing up in Iowa, but later I also got to work with him in Chicago.

In the early days of radio, broadcasters had no stat sheets. Now it takes over an hour to read the notes. Sometimes I think the PR guys are getting paid by the word. I kept my own books and hitting and pitching stats. When a reliever came in, I could say, "He's now facing us for the 10th time this year. He's had six good outings and four not-so-good and he's earned four saves." If you don't keep books, you don't know that. But there's a danger in it, too: don't use it unless it fits. That's the advice I give young broadcasters more than any other. I see them come into the booth with 25 things written across their scorecards. I tell them, "You're never going to get all that in, but don't worry because it might work tomorrow." You can't push eight pounds of feathers into a two-pound bag during a broadcast.

Guys like Elson and Rosey Rowswell pretty much reported the game as it was, but now we're more in the entertainment business. We do a lot more embellishing and talk about things that players have done more than we used to. I heard some old broadcasts of World Series games from the 1930s and 1940s and realized the announcers gave you exactly what went on at that moment and nothing more.

The guys who did the most embellishing on the air were the guys who did re-created games. One operator sat in the room next to you and another in the town where the games were. The wires might have said "B1, S1, Single," for ball one, strike one, and a single. You'd make up all the rest.

That was entertainment during the Depression.

I re-created games in the minor leagues in the early 1950s. We added sound effects, even to the point of playing the national anthem in an echo chamber or having a staff announcer stick his head in the wastebasket to make himself sound like the public address man giving the batting orders.

I really credit those re-creations with making me learn the game more and helping me reach the big leagues sooner. I even re-created Cubs games when the team was on the road. At WIND, they didn't use any sound effects, but later, on WCFL with the White Sox network, they were already using sound effects. I added some more I had used back in the old Three-I League: a great big disc with a cut for a single, double, triple, home run, staccato clapping, vendors, all kinds of things that made the game sound real.

When I re-created the Roger Maris 61st home run game in 1961, a lot of people who saw me come into the radio station the next morning asked how I got back to Chicago so fast. The game was in New York, but I was in a studio in Chicago. We had a musician who ran the sound tracks. When Maris hit his 61st, I said, "Okay, he just got it, give me all you got." We made it sound real. We had to do disclaimers before or after the re-created game—that was an FCC ruling—but the fans didn't care. They wanted to hear a game.

I also think they preferred to hear it on radio.

That's especially true for fans who can't see—they prefer radio announcers to TV announcers. I've had a great relationship with blind fans over the years. In their fan mail, they pointed out things they wanted to hear. I realized that if I could do anything to help blind fans "see" the game, I would include it in my broadcast for the other fans as well. When I spoke to the convention for the blind in Houston a few years ago, I told them how important it was to me for them to have a good word picture of every game. Blind baseball fans are good fans; they love the game and they love the radio.

The same is true for female fans—the most fanatical of all. They made me realize they wanted to be recognized as baseball fans, too. And the best place to do that is on the radio. With radio you can paint the word picture and free the fan from being glued to the TV

Milo Hamilton worked for WGN during his second stint as a Chicago Cubs broadcaster.
Chicago Cubs

set. Fans can work in the yard, fiddle around in the workshop, or run an errand and listen in the car. They have a constant flow of the game without being tied to a recliner in their living room.

The radio announcer is pretty much his own director. He can decide what fits and what doesn't. He's not tied to a strict format, and he doesn't look at stats that may not mean anything when they're up on the screen. Fans tell me all the time that they watch the game on TV with the sound turned down because they'd rather hear the radio announcer.

I try to keep the fans informed. I give the score at least once on every hitter. I do a recap at the end of three and the end of six. But

I won't mention a no-hitter in progress. There are six different ways to let people know about it, but I won't use the word. As Bob Elson used to say, "Don't ever spend your broadcast in the first part of the game because you want something left if something great happens in the ninth." If you've told people from the fifth inning on that your pitcher is throwing a no-hitter, how much mystique is left when the last out is made other than to just say it?

One of the greatest compliments I ever got was "You sound like Bob Elson with enthusiasm." That wasn't a knock at him, because times have changed. A lot of the old timers did balls and strikes. By the time I came along, we started embellishing. That started in St. Louis with Harry Caray. He wanted to make it entertaining, and he did. Caray had a big influence on the up-and-coming young announcers who heard him. He showed it was okay to be a fan on the air. He wore the game on his sleeve and let it show.

Jack Buck and I joined the Cardinals at the same time in the 1950s. He had a style and classiness in his broadcast but was not afraid to let it all hang out when it meant something. One of his most famous calls was, "Go crazy, folks, go crazy." And who can forget his description of the Kirk Gibson home run against Dennis Eckersley in the World Series: "I can't believe what I just saw." Jack was polished and creditable and a terrific announcer.

When the Ford Frick Award started in the 1970s, the voters couldn't make up their minds, so they gave it to Mel Allen and Red Barber. The next year, Bob Elson got it. At the Hall of Fame inductions every year, all the Hall of Fame players are invited back. But the broadcasters who received the Frick Award and the writers who received the J.G. Taylor Spink Award are not. Jack Brickhouse, who also worked in Chicago, didn't like that. He wanted to know whether we were in the Hall of Fame or not. Because writing and broadcasting are so important to the game, I would like to think we are in.

There are so many top guys working today: Harry Kalas in Philadelphia, Pete Van Wieren in Atlanta, Dave Van Horne in Florida, Pat Hughes with the Cubs, and the Brennamans—Marty in Cincinnati and his son Thom in Arizona. Their styles are similar and they are a credit to each other.

Dave O'Brien is the best of the young guys. He worked for the Braves and the Marlins before moving to ESPN. Gary Thorne, an attorney who became a very good broadcaster, also does a nice job for ESPN.

I always wondered how Bob Costas would do if he worked for a team, doing 200 games a year (including spring training). He did a nice job when he did network games. He was prepared, he had great knowledge of the game, and he was a fan—even carrying a picture of Mickey Mantle in his wallet.

Everyone in the media is a fan to some extent. Dan Rather once did play-by-play for the Houston Buffs. Jimmy Breslin and Scotty Reston were baseball writers before they started writing about politics. I heard George Will at a banquet and thought he gave one of the greatest in-depth talks about baseball that I have ever heard.

There were great baseball writers in every city. Grantland Rice and Damon Runyon wrote at a time when people depended on the written word. And Red Smith was one of the best of all time. I loved one of his lines: "People tell me how boring baseball is. Show me a person who says baseball is boring and I'll show you a boring person."

I liked Jimmy Cannon in New York, John Carmichael and Jerry Holtzman in Chicago, and Jim Murray in Los Angeles. Before we had computer keyboards, those guys could sit down at an old Underwood typewriter and make it sing. That's a lost art today.

The old writers just wrote stories about baseball, but the writers today cover the games differently. The columnists are now the ones who turn people on, one way or the other. Dick Young was probably the first to put a burr under someone's saddle. He was feisty, the first writer to draw the ire of fans and players.

Today's fans have so many ways to get their baseball news. In addition to all the local broadcasts, there are telecasts by ESPN, Fox, and TBS, plus radio coverage of every game by XM Satellite Radio. Although the number of daily newspapers has declined, fans have a myriad of ways to follow the game on the Internet. There's a "national" daily, *USA Today,* and several solid tabloids, including *USA Today Sports Weekly, Baseball America,* and *The Sporting News.*

As a broadcaster, I get more out of *Baseball Digest,* which is published monthly, than anything else. I love the fan letters and the way they answer them. I read the whole thing through and through. The little vignettes gave me ideas of things I could use on my shows. If I were told today that my budget was cut and I could only buy one magazine, *Baseball Digest* would be the one I'd want.

It's good to read the weeklies to find out about the young kids on their way up, but it's not necessary to read it so thoroughly because television keeps you up-to-date with replays and highlights. Every game is replayed every night on ESPN and the next morning as well. It's not like the old days, when I went over *The Sporting News* with a fine-toothed comb. Few fans have time for that—especially with so many other things going on in their lives. But I know they're as enthusiastic as ever and still have a voracious appetite for baseball. I am happy to be among those who help fill that need.

—Milo Hamilton

Milo Hamilton began his broadcast career in 1946, when still in the navy, and reached the major leagues with the St. Louis Browns seven years later. He has since done play-by-play for the Atlanta Braves, Chicago Cubs, Chicago White Sox, Pittsburgh Pirates, and St. Louis Cardinals. A mainstay in the broadcast booth of the Houston Astros since 1985, Milo won the Ford Frick Award from the Baseball Hall of Fame in 1992.

More of Milo Hamilton's thoughts on baseball media coverage may be found in chapter 8.

ACKNOWLEDGMENTS

This book would not have been possible without the generosity and cooperation of the following people: Bill Acree, Atlanta Braves; Kevin Barnes, freelance broadcaster; Bill Beck, Florida Marlins; Evelyn Begley, Society for American Baseball Research; Laura Gaynor, baseball photographer; Art Berke, *Sports Illustrated;* John Blundell, Major League Baseball; Claudette Burke, Baseball Hall of Fame; James Fiorentino, baseball artist; Sean Forman, Baseball-reference.com; Bill Goff, GoodSportsArt.com; Brad Hainje, Atlanta Braves; Brad Horn, Baseball Hall of Fame; Jeff Idelson, Baseball Hall of Fame; Lee Ivory, *USA Today Sports Weekly;* Ronnie Joyner, baseball artist; Pat Kelly, Baseball Hall of Fame; Christopher Kenneally, Copyright Clearance Center; Joseph Licata, photographer; Ed Lucas, baseball writer; Doug Lyons, baseball author; Clay Luraschi, The Topps Company; Bill Menzel, baseball photographer; Tim O'Brien, Ripley's Believe It or Not! museums; T.S. O'Connell, *Sports Collectors Digest;* Marc Okkonen, baseball author; David W. Smith, baseball author; Lyle Spatz, baseball author; Sheldon Stone, attorney at law; David Vincent, baseball author; and Lisa Washington, *USA Today.*

Fred "Houston" Arnold believed in this project from the beginning and secured the sponsorship of the Minute Maid Company.

Thanks also go to Bob Ibach, one-time publications and media relations director of the Chicago Cubs and now head of one of the country's premier sports PR firms. It was Bob who finalized details with Fred Arnold and brought Hall of Famers Brooks Robinson and Milo Hamilton into this project. An author cannot have better partners.

Nor can an author have a better team at the publishing end. Tom Bast, editorial director of Triumph Books, and his staff, including editors Linc Wonham and Jessica Paumier, have been supportive throughout this project. A special thank-you also to freelance designer Patricia Frey, who fielded a mountain of material to lay out the nuggets on these pages.

The third time's again the charm for Bob Snodgrass, the thoughtful and creative acquisitions editor with whom I worked on two books previously. I hope Bob always picks me for his team.

Thanks also to Bob Faller, director of sales and marketing at the Otesaga, my home-away-from-home in Cooperstown: thanks for putting up with me.

One big final thank-you goes to friends and family who probably never understood why their emails, phone calls, and invitations weren't always answered. A massive midsummer book project takes time away from beaches, barbecues, and parties. So thanks for letting me work in peace—for the most part, anyway.

—Dan Schlossberg

INTRODUCTION

When a prospector pans for gold, he hopes to find a few nuggets—shiny rocks certain to turn the heads of others immersed in the wading river.

So it is with this book, a project originally entitled *Baseball Bits* before the concept of solid gold came out of left field and hit the author over the head like a foam-rubber tomahawk. Like a deejay spinning solid gold records, this volume is meant not only to entertain and educate but also to delight readers—and to get them to say, "Gee, I didn't know that!"

That is exactly the reaction I had when exploring the exhibits at Ripley's Believe It Or Not! museum in St. Augustine, Florida. Although baseball is only a small fraction of the territory covered by Ripley's, the concept of finding the little-known, the unusual, and the amazing-but-true is common to both the museum and this project.

No book can cover all the bases—too much has happened in baseball's long history—but this volume does not make that attempt. It is intended solely as a fun book, filled with bits and pieces of information, illustrations, pictures, paintings, and paragraphs that present the game's great history in a format that can be read forward, backward, between innings, or during rain delays.

Information inside these pages comes from a myriad of sources, from daily newspapers, weekly tabloids, monthly magazines, and baseball libraries—including the world's finest at the Baseball Hall of Fame. But much of the material in the pages that follow comes from personal contacts, friendships with players, coaches, managers, and fellow writers forged over the past 40 years.

Calling it an offbeat history wouldn't be off base. Most fans know, for example, that Warren Spahn won more games than any left-handed pitcher; but how many know that he and Hank Aaron are the only men to homer for the Braves more than 15 years in a row, that he had 363 wins and 363 base hits, that he was one of only two pitchers to have a 20-win season after turning 40, or that he was the only player to win a battlefield commission during World War II?

Targeted for the trivia buff but broad enough for the casual fan, *Baseball Gold* is packed with little-known stories about the game: why

Harvey Haddix lost a no-hitter 36 years after he pitched it; how Hideo Nomo gave up a home run after leaving the game; who followed Mickey Mantle as the only switch-hitters with 40-homer seasons; and what team won a world championship after allowing more runs than it scored during the regular season.

Readers of *Baseball Gold* will discover the commissioner with the longest tenure, the active player selected for one league's All-Star team who played for the other, and the only man with two 60-homer seasons in the minor leagues. They will also learn that major leaguers once bought their own uniforms, that Rico Carty homered twice in the same at-bat, and that Hank Aaron was once called out for hitting a home run!

Baseball Gold begins with the Cincinnati Red Stockings and runs through the 2006 season. The emphasis is on the good old days—before unwise revenue-raising gimmicks threatened to compromise the integrity of America's national pastime. During those glory years, there were two eight-team leagues, winners went straight to the World Series, and games were played on real grass illuminated by the sun, not lights. Night games on weekends—especially in the chill of October—were taboo, and tickets were cheaper than today's ballpark franks.

It was the era of Willie, Mickey, and the Duke—not to mention Hank Aaron, Frank Robinson, Stan Musial, and Ted Williams. By today's standards, each performed Herculean feats for a mere pittance of a paycheck. Mention of Willie, Mickey, and the Duke in New York still provokes arguments.

Baseball's battles and controversies are covered, too—from Billy Martin's off-the-field fights to arguments over the real home-run king: Babe Ruth, Hank Aaron, or Barry Bonds.

This book is packed not only with anecdotes but also with box scores, cartoons, charts, graphs, pictures, and listings of spring-training sites, team nickname origins, lifetime leaders in grand slams, and much more. Many of the photographs have never been published before.

The pages that follow contain vintage art, rare photographs, original newspaper pages, and numerous reproductions of players, parks, and historic moments captured by artists commissioned by Bill Goff's GoodSportsArt.com of Kent, Connecticut. Ebbets Field and the Polo

Grounds still survive here—as do Wrigley Field, Fenway Park, and the bayside AT&T Park, where the lapping waters of McCovey Cove are filled with a flotilla of fans hoping for free souvenirs.

Lifelike portraits by Ronnie Joyner and James Fiorentino also help bring history to life in *Baseball Gold.* And the book couldn't be complete without including Topps baseball cards or material from the Baseball Hall of Fame.

As the illustrations reveal, baseball is the national pastime because it is a simple game, easy to understand, easy to follow, and different every day. No two games are alike and predictions are impossible. Joaquin Andujar was right on the money when asked to provide a one-word description of baseball: "Youneverknow."

A greeting card once received at a family gathering also applies to baseball:

To each of us you are different
To all of us you are the same

Since variety is the spice of life, it's my hope that this volume of living history will inspire older, more traditional fans and woo the younger generation back from its flirtation with faster sports like basketball and hockey.

Baseball Gold is designed to provide countless hours of reading pleasure—especially when inclement weather or the advent of the off-season makes going to the ballpark impossible. Like a utility infielder, it fits everywhere, from the coffee table to the bathroom bookshelf.

I hope the reader enjoys perusing it as much as the author enjoyed piecing it together.

—Dan Schlossberg

CHAPTER 1
IN THE BEGINNING

BROOKS ROBINSON REMEMBERS...

I was interested in baseball history at an early age. I grew up in Little Rock, and Bill Dickey grew up in a house about eight or nine blocks away. I certainly knew about Bill Dickey being with the Yankees and being from Little Rock. And Lon Warneke, the Arkansas Hummingbird. I knew all about the Gashouse Gang long before I met Paul Dean's son playing golf. I played against one of his other sons, P.D. Junior.

Too many players today do not know the history of the game. Maybe the Latin players know the history of the game in their own countries, like the importance of Roberto Clemente to Puerto Rico, Juan Marichal to the Dominican, and Minnie Minoso to Cuba, but there's no reason they should know the history of the game the way I do. I'm not even sure how much history the American guys know. When I was growing up, I knew that Johnny Vander Meer pitched back-to-back no-hitters, and I knew a lot about the very early players in baseball.

On Opening Day in Baltimore in 1957, I played third base and George Kell played first. He was always very special to me, on and off the field. In fact, I saw my first stage play in New York with George and his wife. He took me under his wing and showed me the ropes. I've always been a big admirer of his. In 1983 I was inducted into the regular phase of the Hall of Fame and George came in through the Veterans Committee. It was a big thrill to be inducted together.

Gen. Abner Doubleday's alleged invention of baseball in Cooperstown in 1839 was used as the pretext for placing the Hall of Fame in the central New York hamlet 100 years later. But none of Doubleday's 73 diaries mention the incident, and research suggests he was a plebe at West Point that year and never set foot in Cooperstown.

National Baseball Hall of Fame Library, Cooperstown, New York

BASEBALL ORIGIN?

There's a reference to baseball in the *Little Pretty Pocket Book,* a tiny handbook produced in 1787 and owned by the American Antiquarian Society in Worcester, Massachusetts. An independent research library, the American Antiquarian Society contains nearly two-thirds of all items printed in the United States from 1640 to 1821.

The key phrases from the book:

BASE-BALL.
The Ball once struck off,
Away flies the Boy
To the next destin'd Post,
and then Home with Joy.

PITTSFIELD'S PARTY

The city of Pittsfield, Massachusetts, gave baseball a 215th birthday party on September 5, 2006. The date was selected because it matched the date that the town passed a bylaw that banned baseball games within 80 yards of a newly built meeting house—not only because of noise but also out of fear windows might be broken. That ordinance was passed on September 5, 1791.

Ripley's Believe It or Not!
UMPIRES ONCE INVITED CRITICISM
BASEBALL UMPIRES IN THE 1800s WORE TOP HATS AND ASKED BOTH PLAYERS AND SPECTATORS FOR THEIR OPINIONS ON QUESTIONABLE CALLS

FIRST UNIS

The New York Knickerbockers, who began play in 1845, became the first ballclub to wear uniforms, six years later. Those suits consisted of long navy blue trousers, webbed belts, white shirts with collars, and straw hats. Although the team initially took considerable teasing from opponents, the wearing of uniforms soon became standard throughout the game.

BULLPEN ORIGIN

The word *bullpen* became part of the baseball lexicon in the 19th century. Theories for its adoption include:

- Relief pitchers warmed up near an outfield sign advertising Bull Durham tobacco
- Enclosures used by pioneers to protect themselves were called bullpens
- In bullfighting, bulls are kept in pens and let out one at a time
- Railroad worker shanties, where they rested during breaks, were called bullpens

EARLY RULES

During the 1850s, Massachusetts baseball was played on a square-shaped field that had 10 to 14 players per side and four-foot-high posts for bases. Umpires asked fans for advice and awarded victory to the first team that scored 100 runs.

PROPHETIC PIONEER

Henry Chadwick was a New York baseball writer who refined the box score for newspaper use, established the scoring system of numbering each position, and edited the *Ball Players Chronicle,* the first weekly baseball publication. The British-born Chadwick, who later spent 27 years as editor of *Spalding's Official Baseball Guide,* was named "the father of baseball" by President Theodore Roosevelt in 1904, four years before he died at age 84. Modern media guides, record books, and rosters are all the result of Chadwick's creative thinking. The one-time cricket writer began covering baseball

The 1869 Cincinnati Red Stockings, led by baseball's Wright Brothers, went undefeated.

BASE BALL AT HOBOKEN
New York, July 6, 1853. Friend P.—The first friendly game of the season, between the Gotham and Knickerbocker Base Ball Clubs, was played on the grounds of the latter. The game commenced on Friday, July 1, but had to be postponed because of weather, the Knickerbockers making nine aces to two of the Gotham.

in 1858 and published his first rule book a year later. He was the first foreign-born member of the Baseball Hall of Fame.

LINCOLN: NEWS CAN WAIT
Abraham Lincoln was playing in a closely contested baseball game in 1860 when a message arrived for him. He told the messenger not to interrupt him during the game. Afterward he found out he had been nominated for president by the Republican Party.

FIRST CLUBHOUSE
Abraham Lincoln was president of the United States when a Brooklyn ballpark became the first to boast a clubhouse. The Union and Capitoline Grounds had a clubhouse large enough to host three teams—the Eckfords, the Putnams, and the Constellations—and also had an enclosed field and graded pitcher's mound. It cost 10 cents to gain admission to the ballpark.

THROWING A CURVE
William Arthur "Candy" Cummings invented the curveball during his tenure as ace of the Brooklyn Stars, an amateur club, in 1867. He later pitched for Hartford, a charter

franchise in the National League in 1876, before becoming president of the first minor league, the International Association, at age 29 in 1877.

LOPSIDED SCORES

Early handicaps on hurlers helped hitters immensely. Forest City, based in Cleveland, beat the Brooklyn Atlantics 132–1 in a five-inning game in 1870. In another game that year Forest City scored 90 runs in the first inning and had the bases loaded with nobody out when rain halted play at Utica, New York.

WHERE TEAMS DRESSED

In the early days of the National League, teams changed into their uniforms at their hotels and rode horse-drawn wagons to the ballpark. Ballparks were not required to have visiting clubhouses until 1906.

SPALDING'S BIG YEAR

In 1875, one year before the formation of the National League (and several years before modern pitching rules were established), A.G. Spalding of Boston (National Association) posted a 57–7 record using only fastballs and curves.

SUNDAY BALL

The National League not only banned Sunday ball when it was founded in 1876 but also voted to expel clubs that violated the rule. The NL relented in 1892 after merging with the American Association, but many cities still avoided games on the Christian Sabbath. Teams tried to skirt local laws by sandwiching concerts around games, declaring that contests were exhibition games, or increasing the price of scorecards to match the price of tickets (which couldn't be sold on Sunday). Cities finally lifted their bans, with Philadelphia relenting as late as 1934 after a public referendum.

Ripley's Believe It or Not!
THE FIRST BASEBALL FINE
A PLAYER IN THE WORLD'S FIRST BASEBALL GAME PLAYED IN HOBOKEN, N.J., ON JUNE 19, 1846, WAS FINED 6 CENTS BY UMPIRE ALEXANDER CARTWRIGHT FOR SWEARING

Ripley's Believe It or Not!
THE STAR SPANGLED BANNER
WAS FIRST PLAYED PRIOR TO A BASEBALL GAME ON MAY 15, 1862 AT THE UNION GROUNDS IN BROOKLYN, N.Y., ALTHOUGH IT DIDN'T BECOME A PRE-GAME RITUAL FOR ALL GAMES — UNTIL DURING WWII.

THE WRIGHT STUFF

Baseball had its own version of the Wright Brothers. George, Harry, and Sam all played pro ball, with George the star of the first professional team, the 1869 Cincinnati Red Stockings (49 homers in 56 games). Famous for his defensive innovations, George was the first shortstop to "play in the hole" and the first to cover second base. He later became the first batter in National League history, on April 22, 1876, for Boston against Philadelphia. George served as player/manager of the Providence Grays in 1878, beating brother Harry's Boston club for the pennant; umpired games of the world tour taken by Albert Spalding's All-Stars in 1888; and helped lay the groundwork for the Baseball Hall of Fame, which admitted him in 1937.

THE NAME GAME

When Bobby M. Jones of the Rockies started against Bobby J. Jones of the Mets on May 11, 1999, they became the first pitchers with the same first and last names to start against each other in more than 100 years. There were two previous matches: John B. Taylor (Reds) against John W. Taylor (White Stockings) in 1899 and George H. Bradley (Boston) versus George W. Bradley (St. Louis) in 1876, the first year of the National League. It was hard to miss the second Bradley: he started all 64 St. Louis games that season!

ERRORS EVERYWHERE

The sloppiest baseball game ever played occurred in the inaugural season of the National League. On June 14, 1876, Boston made 24 errors and St. Louis made 16. St. Louis won the game, 20–6, before 800 fans—only half of whom stayed for the entire contest.

THE PITCHER-PRESIDENT

Candy Cummings, best known as inventor of the curveball during his amateur days, was a minor league president and major league pitcher at the same time. It happened in 1877, when the 29-year-old Cummings was named president of the first minor league, the International Association. Released after pitching poorly for the Lynn (Massachusetts) Live Oaks, Cummings hooked on with Cincinnati of the National League. He lost 14 of 19 decisions that summer and his minor league job a year later, when the International Association disbanded.

THE REAL CASEY

"Casey at the Bat," the famous baseball poem written by Ernest Thayer in 1888, was based on a real-life player. Dan M. Casey was a Philadelphia pitcher who came to bat against

Gambling was a major problem for both players and fans in the early days of baseball.
Courtesy of National Baseball Hall of Fame and Museum.

BATTING RECORD
Of Clubs Members of the National League of Professional Base Ball Clubs,
SEASON OF 1876.

NAME OF CLUB.	WHERE LOCATED.	No. of Gmes plyed.	No. of Games won.	BATTING.						
				Times at bat.	Runs scored.	Average per game.	Runs earned.	Average per game.	1st Bases.	Percentage of base hits per time at bat.
Chicago	Chicago, Ill.	66	52	2,818	624	9.45	267	4.03	926	.328
Hartford	Hartford, Conn.	69	47	2,703	429	6.22	154	2.23	711	.264
St. Louis	St. Louis, Mo.	64	45	2,536	386	6.03	109	1.70	642	.253
Boston	Boston, Mass.	70	39	2,780	471	6.73	167	2.38	723	.260
Louisville	Louisville, Ky.	69	30	2,594	280	4.06	107	1.55	641	.247
Mutual	Brooklyn, N. Y.	57	21	2,202	260	4.55	72	1.26	494	.223
Athletic	Philadelphia, Pa.	60	14	2,414	378	6.30	145	2.41	646	.267
Cincinnati	Cincinnati, O.	65	9	2,413	238	3.66	77	1.18	555	.230
	Total	520	257	20,[illegible]60	3066	5.89	1098	2.11	5338	.261

Tie Games Played—LOUISVILLE, 3; ATHLETIC, 1; HARTFORD, 1

the New York Giants in the last half of the ninth inning with two outs and men on second and third. Trailing 4–3 (the poem says 4–2), Casey took two called strikes and then swung mightily but missed, ending the August 21, 1887, game. A solid pitcher, Casey was remembered instead for his ineptitude in a single at-bat. He pitched for several other teams before becoming a streetcar conductor in Binghamton, New York.

FEARLESS INFIELDER

Bid McPhee spent 18 years with the Cincinnati Red Stockings, playing second base *without a glove.* Though the 5'8" infielder hit just .271 for his lifetime, his fielding prowess persuaded the Veterans Committee of the Hall of Fame to enshrine him in 2000.

WHITE BEAUTY

Because of his strong defense and 2,004 hits, pioneer shortstop Dave Bancroft was elected to Cooperstown in 1971. But he's best remembered for his nickname, "Beauty," applied after rivals heard him say that word whenever his pitcher threw a strike.

Switch-Pitchers

Batters didn't know whether they were facing a righty or a lefty when Tony Mullane pitched. The 19th-century star, who pitched without a glove, held both hands on the ball before throwing it with either arm. A century later, in 1995, Greg Harris of the Montreal Expos pitched a scoreless inning of relief while using both arms.

Dubious Doubleday

Abner Doubleday's credibility as the inventor of baseball wasn't helped by the 67 diaries he wrote after retiring from the U.S. Army in 1873. Neither the diaries nor the Doubleday obituary that appeared in *The New York Times* 20 years later made any reference to playing baseball in Cooperstown in 1839.

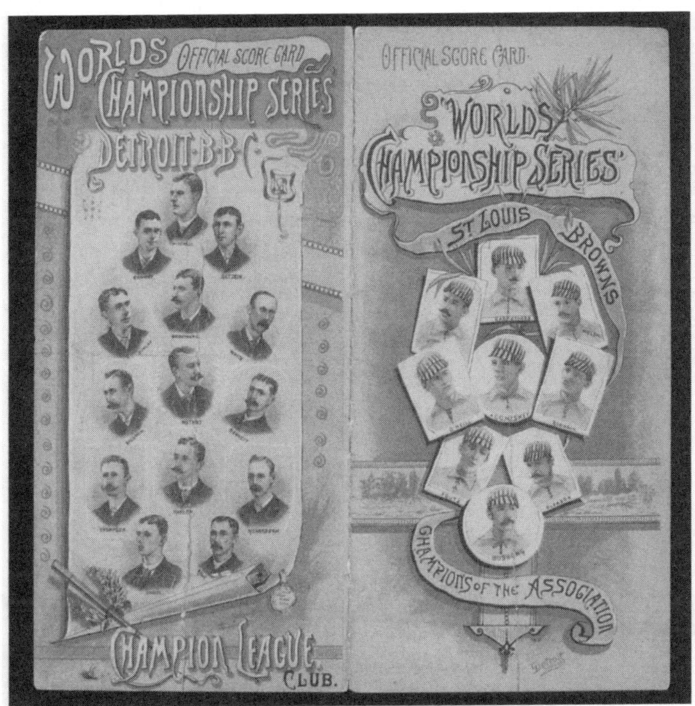

The Detroit Wolverines of the National League defeated the St. Louis Browns of the American Association in an 11-game postseason series that was the forerunner of the fall classic. Games were played in several cities, including Boston and Baltimore.

FIRST SLAM
Roger Connor, first baseman of the Troy Trojans, hit the first bases-filled homer in baseball history in 1881—five years after the establishment of the National League.

OLD HOSS POWER
Old Hoss Radbourn, who won 309 games in 11 seasons, was the winning pitcher in the most lopsided shutout of all time—a 28–0 win for Providence over Philadelphia on August 21, 1883.

ONE-ARMED BANDIT
One-armed Cleveland pitcher Hugh Daily no-hit Philadelphia, 1–0, in 1883.

GOOD OLD DAYS
The St. Louis Browns were once a good team. They won four straight pennants in the American Association, then a major league, from 1885 to 1888, and twice beat NL rivals in a forerunner of the World Series.

WHO BATS FIRST?
The home team often batted first in 19th-century games.

RAILROADED
According to Retrosheet.org, Cincinnati forfeited a game to Louisville in 1887 because the ballclub was delayed by a railroad accident and did not make it to the stadium.

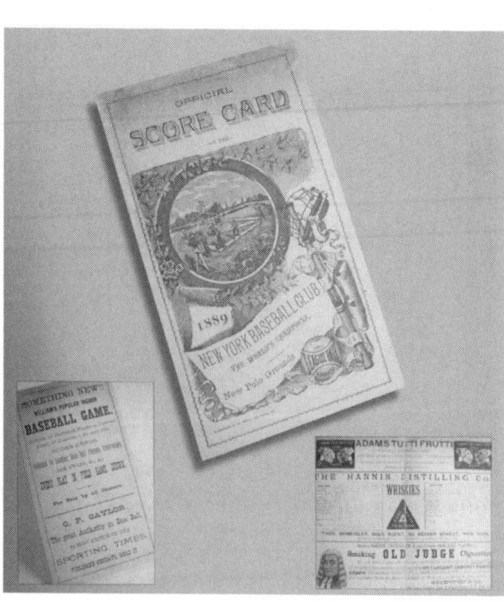

The great rivalry between the Giants and the Dodgers started in the 19th century, when the New York Giants of the National League faced the Brooklyn Bridegrooms of the American Association in a best-of-nine postseason series. In a precursor to the heartbreak of 1951, Brooklyn won the first four, then lost the last five.

Batting high!
SINCE 1894 NO ONE HAS EQUALLED HUGH DUFFY'S BATTING AVERAGE— A SIZZLING .438!

FIRST PINCH-HITTER

Catcher Jack Doyle, asked to bat for pitcher George Davies in an 1892 Cleveland Spiders game against the Brooklyn Bridgegrooms, was the first pinch-hitter in baseball history.

LONG WAY DOWN

On August 25, 1894, Chicago NL catcher William Schriver became the first player to catch a ball thrown from the top of the Washington Monument.

DISTAFF REVOLT

When the 1897 Washington Senators invited women to attend a free game pitched by handsome George Mercer, thousands accepted. But Mercer's fifth-inning ejection by umpire Bill Carpenter provoked a postgame riot. Female fans attacked the umpire, who needed a player escort to leave the field safely, and trashed National Park before police could stop them.

WAIT 'TIL NEXT YEAR

The 1899 Cleveland Spiders of the National League won 20 and lost 134 for a .130 percentage—the worst ever recorded.

FIVE SIBLINGS

The Delahanty family sent five brothers to the major leagues: Ed Delahanty, a Hall of Famer, and younger brothers Frank, Jim, Joe, and Tom.

YOUNG NEVER AGED
Though long deceased, Cy Young remains the major league leader in wins (511), complete games (749), and innings pitched (7,356$\frac{2}{3}$). Young, who lived from 1867 to 1955, was a control artist who walked only 29 while working 380 innings in 1904. He was 44 when he lost his final game in 1911 by a score of 1–0. It was his 316th defeat—by far the most losses incurred by any pitcher.

Ripley's
Believe It or Not!
"CY" YOUNG
(ORIGINALLY CALLED "CYCLONE" BECAUSE OF HIS TERRIFIC SPEED)
PITCHED 874 GAMES
WON 511 OF THEM
INCLUDING 3 NO-HIT-NO-RUN GAMES

TOO MUCH TROUBLE
Reaching Cy Young's records would require a 20-year average of 26 wins, 38 complete games, and 368 innings pitched.

CY OF RELIEF
Cy Young went 33–10 in 1901, his first season with the Boston Americans, and led the fledgling American League in wins.

FIRST EXPANSION DRAFT
In the middle of the 1902 season, New York Giants owner Andrew Freedman obtained controlling interest in the Baltimore Orioles of the American League and assigned most of its players to the Giants (plus a few to Cincinnati). Unable to field a team, Baltimore forfeited a scheduled game against St. Louis on July 17. AL president Ban Johnson removed the franchise from the league and added a new one, stocking it with surplus players from other clubs. That team moved to New York a year later and eventually became the Yankees.

Christy Mathewson had four 30-win seasons for the New York Giants.

BAD BET

Pittsburgh players matched a $10,000 bet by St. Louis owner Frank DeHaas Robison that the Pirates wouldn't repeat as National League champs in 1903. Then they smothered all opposition, wining the 1903 pennant by 27½ games.

TINKER TO EVERS, NO CHANCE

Joe Tinker and Johnny Evers, the famed double-play combination of the Chicago Cubs, had an on-field fistfight during a 1905 exhibition game and never spoke to each other again. The fight began after Evers took a taxi to the ballpark and left the rest of the team behind.

EARLY DH BOOSTER

The concept of the designated hitter was first suggested by Philadelphia Athletics manager Connie Mack in 1906.

TY RAID

The first hit ever yielded by Walter Johnson was a bunt single by Ty Cobb, on August 2, 1907. Both men were among the five charter selectees for the Baseball Hall of Fame.

DIFFERENT DRUMMER

Late in the 1908 season, rookie Philadelphia left-hander Harry Coveleski—younger brother of future Hall of Famer Stan Coveleski—defeated the New York Giants three times in five days, helping the Giants lose the NL pennant to the Chicago Cubs. Seething New York manager John McGraw spent the winter plotting to get even, then hit upon an idea during spring training. Told by a scout that Coveleski's inept drum performance in the local band soured a local lass on dating the pitcher, McGraw borrowed a tom-tom and banged on it from the third-base coaching box during Coveleski's next

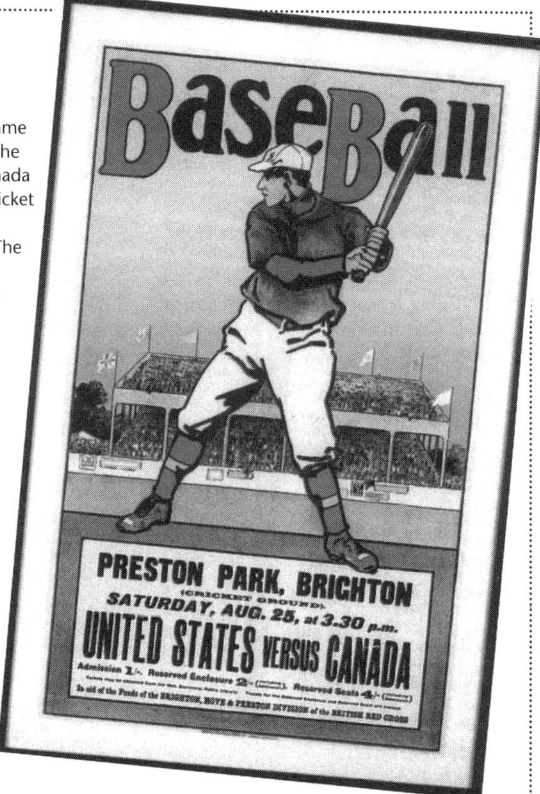

This poster helped promote a baseball game between teams from the United States and Canada at the Preston Park Cricket Grounds in Brighton, England, circa 1910. The batter is apparently a composite of Ty Cobb and Napoleon Lajoie.

outing against the Giants. Distracted and unnerved, the pitcher couldn't get the ball over the plate. He lost the game and was never able to beat the Giants again. Soon, he was back in the minors—with McGraw telling one and all how he drummed a Giant killer out of the league.

RUBE AWAKENING

Rube Waddell, a star pitcher of the dead-ball era, once woke up in a hospital covered with bandages. Asked what happened, catcher Ossie Schreckengost obliged with this story: "You said you could fly, so you opened the window and jumped." The pitcher pondered the thought, then queried his battery mate. "Why didn't you stop me?" he said. "I bet $100 you could do it," the catcher replied.

CRASH LANDING
Rube Waddell missed the 1905 World Series with a dislocated shoulder—suffered when he tried to swipe a straw hat off a teammate's head, missed his target, and crashed into a pile of luggage about to be loaded onto a waiting train. Without Waddell, the Philadelphia A's lost a five-game World Series to the New York Giants.

20-GAME QUARTET
The 1905 Boston Braves had four 20-game losers: Vic Willis (11–29), Kaiser Wilhelm (4–23), Irv Young (20–21), and Chick Fraser (14–21). No pitcher has ever lost more games in a season than Willis.

POWERFUL PITCHER
When A's manager Connie Mack needed an extra outfielder in the sixth inning of a 1906 game against the Boston Pilgrims, pitcher Chief Bender volunteered. He also responded with a pair of inside-the-park home runs.

BEWARE OF THE DOG
Umpire Brick Owens was once bitten by a dog—during a major league game in 1912. After Honus Wagner was ejected for arguing with the umpire, his pet dog sprinted from the dugout—where he spent nine otherwise-quiet seasons—and bit the arbiter's leg. Wagner said the dog, named Jason Wetherbee, was never the same after that incident.

UNFAMILIAR TERRITORY
Hall of Fame pitcher Christy Mathewson was a first baseman in the minors.

MATTY THE MAGNIFICENT
Nearly a century after he retired, Christy Mathewson still holds more than 50 pitching records. He won 373 games in 17 seasons—an average of 21.9 wins per year—and threw three shutouts in five days during the

"Baseball became the very symbol, the outward and visible expression of the drive and push and rush and struggle of the raging, tearing, booming 19th century."
—Mark Twain

1905 World Series against the Philadelphia A's. He won at least 20 games a dozen years in a row, from 1903 to 1914. The star right-hander of the New York Giants had been a football star and class president at Bucknell, where he also belonged to literary societies. Matty was nicknamed "Big Six" because his fastball was reputed to be as fast as the legendary New York City fire truck.

HISTORIC MEETING
Future Hall of Famers Christy Mathewson and Mordecai "Three-Finger" Brown met in a specially arranged Labor Day match at Chicago's Wrigley Field (then Weegman Field) on September 4, 1916. Both retired after the game.

TB KILLED MATHEWSONS
Both Christy Mathewson and his young brother Henry died from tuberculosis.

MCGRAW ON THE PHONE
John McGraw's sinusitis attacks, complicated by springtime allergies, were so severe that he often managed the Giants by telephone from the confines of the clubhouse.

NIGHT TRY FOR FEDS
The Brooklyn Tiptops, a 1915 Federal League team, planned to stage the first major league night game during a season-ending series against the Buffalo Blues. But bad weather and light installation problems intervened, canceling the experiment.

GIANT STREAKERS
John McGraw's 1916 New York Giants won a record 26 games in a row.

Chapter 2
Where They Play

Brooks Robinson Remembers...

Baltimore Memorial Stadium was my home ballpark during my entire career. It was a pitchers' park, 309 feet down the lines but 380 in a hurry and 410 to dead center. Camden Yards is player-friendly and fan-friendly.

My favorite stadiums on the road were Boston and Detroit because you could score a lot of runs there. When I went into Yankee Stadium, I was certainly in awe of the place because I knew

The National Baseball Hall of Fame and Museum's ballpark exhibit, Sacred Ground, honors ballparks of the past and present and the fan experience. Milo Stewart Jr./National Baseball Hall of Fame Library, Cooperstown, New York

the history of the stadium and the team. It was short down the line but in no time, it was 402. I'm so glad I didn't play there; the ballpark is too big for me, since I batted right-handed. I can still see those visions in my mind of Joe DiMaggio rounding first and kicking the dirt when Al Gionfriddo made that great catch in the World Series.

The place was built for left-handed hitters like the Babe and Yogi Berra. A right-handed batter could die in that ballpark. Fenway Park was the opposite, and Tiger Stadium was the opposite. There was a big center field in Detroit but left-center and right-center were pretty good areas to shoot for.

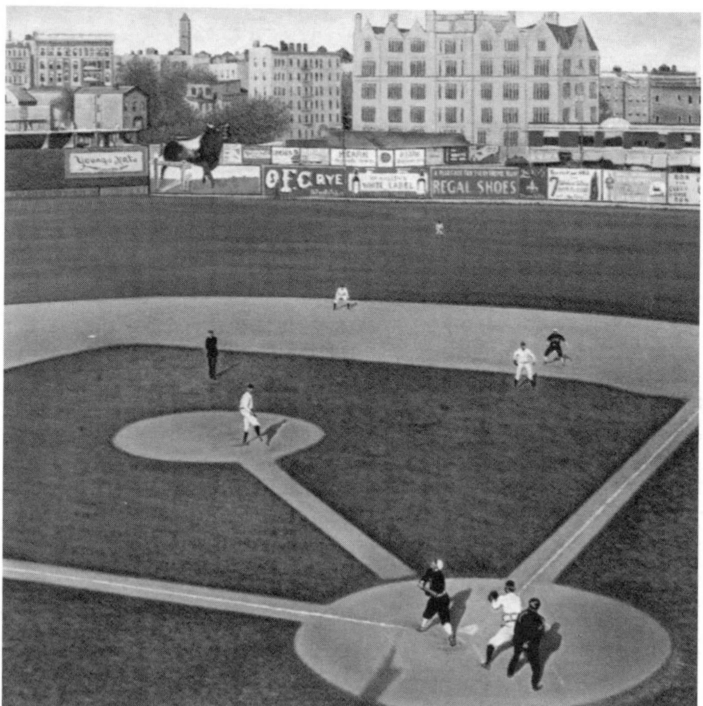

Before they became the Yankees, the New York American League team, known as the Highlanders, played home games in Hilltop Park, a field that looked like a cow pasture when compared with Yankee Stadium. Copyright 1989 by William Feldman. Reprinted with permission, Bill Goff, Inc./GoodSportsArt.com.

ANCIENT TURNSTILES
Turnstiles were used for the first time in Providence, Rhode Island, in 1878. More than 6,000 fans crammed the ballpark, many of them arriving by two special trains from Boston, and 300 carriages ringed the outfield. Boston won, 1–0.

TARPAULIN TALES
Frustrated by frequent washouts, baseball unveiled its first tarpaulin in 1884. The old, heavy tarp absorbed moisture and required drying after rain, thereby complicating the life of the ground crew. A lightweight spun-glass tarp that weighed half as much, did not absorb water, and did not need drying was introduced by Cleveland's Emil Bossard in the 1940s. By 1960, most tarps were similar to the 1,110-pound plastic-coated nylon cover used by the St. Louis Cardinals. Rolling and unrolling the tarp took nine men. Before the advent of the tarp, groundskeepers used other methods. Bill Stockstick, in St. Louis, poured gasoline over the field and burned it. If the field had excessive mud, he covered it with sawdust first, then poured on the gasoline and lit a match. Players complained of the fumes, and the method was rarely successful.

OLDEST FRANCHISE
The Chicago National League franchise is the oldest in baseball. The Cubs, once known as the White Stockings, are the only club to spend a full century in the National League, 1876–1976. The American League did not begin until 1901.

PITTSBURGH FLOOD
With water knee-deep in portions of Pittsburgh's Exposition Park on July 4, 1902, a special ground rule was created: any ball hit into the water (called Lake Dreyfuss after the Pirates owner) would be an automatic double.

BUCS' BUCKS
Total construction price of Forbes Field, opened in 1909, was $1 million. The outfield dimensions were so deep that light towers were erected inside the playing field and the batting cage was stored in left-center.

OH, NO, NOT YOU AGAIN
Among the many quirks of Detroit's Tiger Stadium was a

sign spectators couldn't see. It read: "Visitors Clubhouse. No Visitors Allowed."

GOOD HIDING PLACE
Bats, balls, and uniforms were stored in the *ceiling* of the Tiger Stadium clubhouse and brought down by an attendant when needed.

NAME CHANGES
Tiger Stadium went through three name changes during its tenure as home of the Detroit Tigers. Called Navin Field (after co-owner Frank Navin) when it opened on April 20, 1912, the park became Briggs Stadium in 1938 and Tiger Stadium in 1961.

FENWAY'S COST
The construction cost of Boston's Fenway Park, the oldest park in the big leagues, was $300,000—less than the minimum major league salary in 2007.

Double Trouble

"Every ballpark used to be unique. Now they're like breasts—if you've seen one, you've seen 'em both."

—Jim Kaat

GOOD CHOICE
Boston Mayor John "Honey Fitz" Fitzgerald, grandfather of future president John F. Kennedy, threw out the first pitch in Fenway Park history on April 20, 1912.

NO FENWAY FREEBIES
When Fenway Park opened, it had a 25-foot wooden outfield wall designed to keep kids from climbing into the ballpark without paying.

SAVING THE JUDGE
After taking the Interborough subway to the first game at Yankee Stadium, on April 18, 1923, Commissioner Kenesaw Mountain Landis got caught in a crush of fans and had to be rescued by policemen outside the ballpark.

MEGAPHONE MAN
When Yankee Stadium opened in 1923, public address announcer Jack Lenz used a giant megaphone to shout batting orders, batteries, and substitutions. Known as "the little fellow with the big voice," the mild-mannered Lenz was the Lou Gehrig of announcers, handling more than 2,000 consecutive games for both the Yankees and the

Giants (who first hired him in 1915).

FIRST P.A. SYSTEM

The New York Giants installed baseball's first public-address system on August 25, 1929, in a game against Pittsburgh. Umpire Charles Rigler had a microphone inside his mask to broadcast ball-and-strike calls.

NIGHT LID-LIFTER

The Des Moines Demons defeated the Wichita Aviators, 13–6, in the first night game in professional baseball history on May 2, 1930. Attendance at

Fenway Park has always been a nightmare for pitchers—especially left-handers, whose best pitches frequently bounce off the Green Monster, the huge left-field wall 315 feet from home. In 1950 the Sox beat the Browns 20–4 and 29–4 in consecutive games. They scored 17 runs in an inning against Detroit in 1953, winning 23–3; beat the Senators, 24–4, in 1940; and lost to the Yankees by the same score in 1923.

Fairchild Aerial Surveys

"THE FRIENDLY CONFINES OF WRIGLEY FIELD"
Hall of Fame slugger Ernie Banks, who spent his entire career with the Cubs, always lauded his home park, which he called "the friendly confines of Wrigley Field." The Wrigley family, which owned the team, spent several million dollars on beautification but refused to install lights. They maintained that the green vines on the outfield wall looked more attractive by day, when people would equate a trip to the ballpark with a picnic. "We're aiming at people not interested in baseball," Phil Wrigley once said. Copyright 1994 by Thomas Kolendra. Reprinted with permission, Bill Goff, Inc./GoodSportsArt.com.

Western League Park was 10,000—double the normal capacity.

NOVEL APPROACH

Longtime Sportsman's Park groundskeeper Bill Stockstick used a goat to help him trim the outfield grass for the St. Louis Cardinals. The goat was grazing in the outfield the morning after Frankie Frisch became the team's manager in 1933.

RUTH'S FAKE

Babe Ruth was a good defensive outfielder. When Detroit's Tiger Stadium was called Navin Field in the late 1920s, there was a board fence in left instead of double-decked stands. With one out left and Charlie Gehringer of the Tigers on second, the batter hit a long fly ball to Ruth in left. Ruth knew he could catch the ball but pretended it had cleared the wall. Watching the dejected Ruth, Gehringer left for home. The minute he left the base, Ruth came to life, caught the ball, and fired to second for the inning-ending double play.

BABE'S LAST BLAST

The first home run hit over the right-field roof at Pittsburgh's

Forbes Field was also the final home run of Babe Ruth's career. Ruth, then playing for the Boston Braves, hit the homer—his 714th—against Guy Bush on May 25, 1935.

Ruth's Receiver

Bobby Dorr, the Chicago Cubs' groundskeeper for more than 30 seasons, was Babe Ruth's first warm-up catcher with the Baltimore Orioles of the International League. Dorr later created the concept of keeping fresh baseballs in a wooden box buried near home plate. Previously, new balls were thrown out from the bench or rolled down the screen behind the plate.

Two Cleveland Parks

The Cleveland Indians had two home ballparks at the same time. They began play at League Park in 1910, opened the larger Cleveland Municipal Stadium in 1932, and then split their time between the ballparks until 1946, when the last League Park game was played. The Indians moved to Jacobs Field in 1994, condemning Cleveland Stadium to a future life as a barrier reef in Lake Erie.

Fans Flock

The Cleveland Indians had a record 455 straight sellouts at Jacobs Field from 1996 to 2000.

Mighty Mel

Mel Ott, lefty-hitting star of the New York Giants, hammered 63 percent of his 511 home runs in his home park, the Polo Grounds.

Crosley Terrace

Most ballparks, past and present, have dirt warning tracks to tell outfielders in pursuit of long flies that they are approaching the outfield wall. Cincinnati's Crosley Field (1912–1970) had an incline, known as "the Terrace." Any outfielder running uphill knew he was running out of room.

Weather Trumps History

Rain postponed the first night game in baseball history, scheduled for Cincinnati's Crosley Field on May 23, 1935, and the first night game at Chicago's Wrigley Field, slated for 8/8/88 so that people would remember when the last park was lit. Both games were played the following night.

It's October 5, 1956, Game 2 of the World Series, the Yankees versus the Dodgers at the venerable Ebbets Field. Copyright 1994 by Andy Jurinko. Reprinted with permission, Bill Goff, Inc./GoodSportsArt.com.

NIGHTTIME SLUGGER

Cincinnati's Babe Herman hit the first home run in a night game, at Crosley Field on July 10, 1935. The hit came against Brooklyn's Dutch Leonard in the fourth night game ever played.

THE HUMP

Baker Bowl, home of the Philadelphia Phillies from 1887 to 1938, had a hump in center field, where the ballpark ran over a subway tunnel. Outfielders said they could feel the rumblings of the trains below.

IN THE SWIM

Baker Bowl had a swimming pool under the clubhouse before World War I.

KILLER STADIUM

Fatalities occurred twice when parts of Baker Bowl, home of the Phillies, collapsed 24 years apart. On August 8, 1903, so many fans in the left-field stands rushed to watch a commotion on the street that the wooden Promenade Balcony buckled and fell 30 feet. Twelve fans died and 232 were hurt. On May 14, 1927, one died and 50 were injured when the right-field stands caved in under the weight of frenzied fans who had gathered there to escape a steady rain.

Wilson's Lament

During a 1934 game at Philadelphia's Baker Bowl, where the distance from home to right was only 280 feet, Dodgers pitcher Walter "Boom-Boom" Beck was getting blasted. Right fielder Hack Wilson had done the same thing in a local bar the night before. When Casey Stengel came out to replace Beck, the pitcher reacted by heaving the ball into the outfield. Wilson, with his head down and hands on his knees during the apparent pitching change, saw the ball strike the turf and reacted on instinct. He fielded the carom off the wall and threw a perfect strike to second—possibly his best defensive play of that season. But it didn't count.

Last Hurrah for Babe

Babe Ruth, then with the Boston Braves, played his last game in Philadelphia's Baker Bowl in 1935.

Ballpark Resident

Matty Schwab borrowed a minor league custom when he

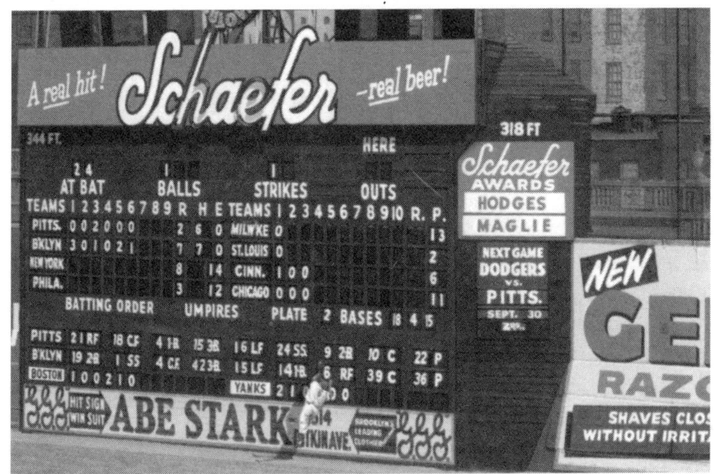

Carl Furillo climbs the Ebbets Field scoreboard to make a game-saving catch in the seventh inning of the last game of the 1956 season. The Dodgers win, 8–6, and avoid a pennant playoff with the Milwaukee Braves, who finish one game behind. Copyright 1994 by Bill Purdom. Reprinted with permission, Bill Goff, Inc./GoodSportsArt.com.

The Polo Grounds had an unusual horseshoe shape and close right-field barrier. Copyright 1994 by Andy Jurinko. Reprinted with permission, Bill Goff, Inc./GoodSportsArt.com.

persuaded Horace Stoneham, owner of the New York Giants, to build him a house under the Polo Grounds stands. The three-room cottage, under Section 31 of the left-field grandstand, was the Schwabs' summer home for many years.

WILD AND WOOLY

Sheep were used to keep grass short in Philadelphia, St. Louis, and other cities.

FENWAY FIRES

Fires damaged Fenway Park in 1926 and 1934. After the second blaze, the Red Sox replaced the wooden center-field bleachers with concrete and the wooden wall in left field with metal. A manual scoreboard was included in the new installation.

SCREEN FOR FANS

Fenway Park was the first stadium to erect a screen behind home plate to protect fans from foul balls and occasional tossed bats.

***RED* MONSTER?**

Boston's Green Monster—the 37-foot wall topped by a 23-foot screen in left field—wasn't always green. Before 1947, it was plastered with advertisements. Green paint then replaced the ads.

FENWAY FOG

Fog once interrupted the same game at Fenway Park four times.

SOUNDS FISHY

A seagull once dropped a three-pound smelt on the

Fenway Park pitcher's mound while Ellis Kinder of the St. Louis Browns watched in amazement.

FLOOD OF RUNS

Boston's 22–14 win over the Philadelphia A's in 1950 was the highest-scoring game in Fenway Park history.

CLOSE CALL

The manually operated scoreboard at Fenway Park features steel plates painted with giant numerals. But they don't go beyond the number 19. The Red Sox came close to that when they scored 17 runs, an American League record for a single frame, against Detroit in the seventh inning on June 18, 1953. The BoSox won, 23–3.

MORSE CODE MESSAGE

There's a reason for the series of dots and dashes that run vertically between the Red Sox line score and out-of-town scores on the Fenway Park scoreboard. It's Morse code for the initials of deceased Red Sox owners Thomas Austin Yawkey and Jean R. Yawkey.

TOO FAR FOR COMFORT

The distance from home plate to dead center at Braves Field in Boston was once a whopping 550 feet. Of the 38 home runs hit there in 1921, all but four stayed inside the park.

BALLPARK TROLLEY

Fans coming to games at Boston's Braves Field could ride Commonwealth Avenue streetcars directly into the ballpark.

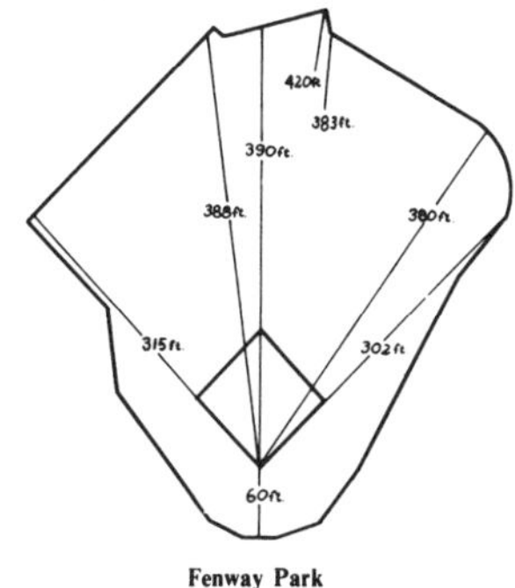

Fenway Park

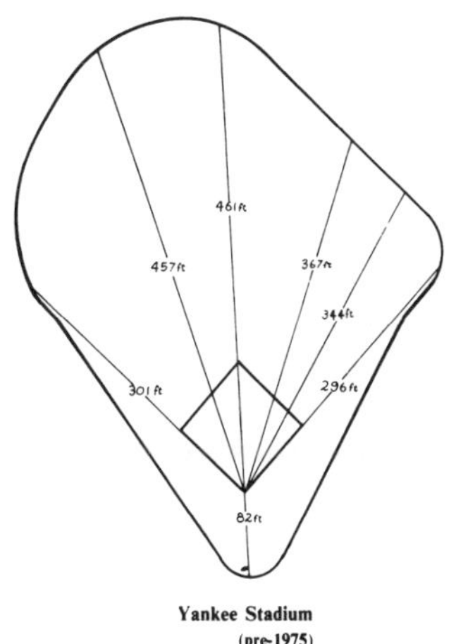

Yankee Stadium (pre-1975)

BRAVES IN FENWAY

The Boston Braves played several home games in Fenway Park, home of the Boston Red Sox. Before the larger Braves Field opened, the Braves used Fenway in 1913 to accommodate the crowd at a Memorial Day doubleheader and later in their "miracle" season of 1914 (including the third and fourth games of the World Series). Fenway, with three times the capacity of the Braves' South End Grounds, was abandoned by the Braves in 1915, when Braves Field opened in August. In fact, the Red Sox played World Series games at the larger NL park in 1915 and 1916. The Braves borrowed Fenway again in 1946, after fans attending the Braves Field opener complained that the fresh paint on the seats hadn't dried. The incident became known as "the wearing of the green" in heavily Irish Beantown. The Braves paid more than $6,000 in cleaning bills and finished the opening series in Fenway Park.

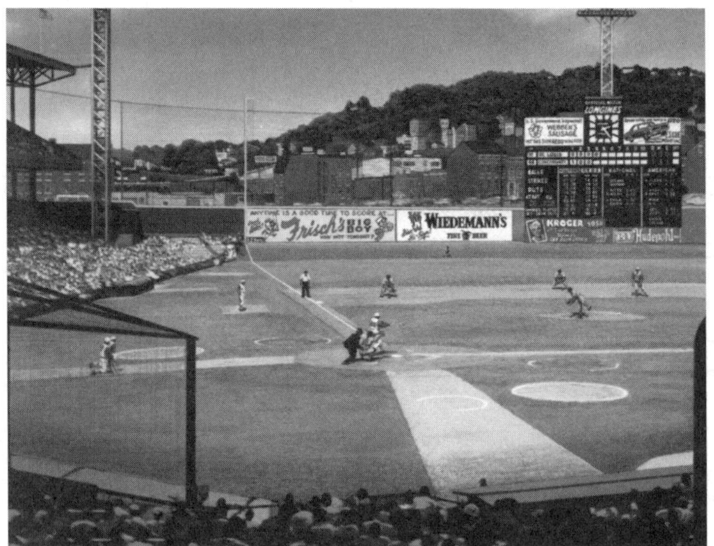

Cincinnati slugger Frank Robinson rips into a pitch at Crosley Field in 1964, two years before the Reds trade him to Baltimore. The former Redland Field features an old-time scoreboard and a sloped embankment instead of a warning track for outfielders. (Artist Bill Purdom painted this scene from a photograph he snapped at Crosley when he was 11 years old.) Copyright 1989 by Bill Purdom. Reprinted with permission, Bill Goff, Inc./GoodSportsArt.com.

BRAVES FIELD FINALE

The move of the Boston Braves to Milwaukee in March 1953 was such a surprise that only 8,822 fans turned out for the Braves Field finale, an 8–2 loss to the Brooklyn Dodgers on September 21, 1952.

NEW LIFE FOR AN OLD PARK

Boston University purchased Braves Field after the team relocated to Milwaukee in 1953.

DISTANT DIMENSIONS

Center field was so distant in Griffith Stadium that the Washington Senators kept the American flag in a small doghouse-type box in fair territory. During a game against the Athletics, a Senator's long drive buried itself in the box. Philadelphia's Socks Siebold searched feverishly but couldn't find it, allowing the batter to circle the bases with an inside-the-doghouse home run.

WASHINGTON WALLOPS

Josh Gibson hit 10 home runs out of Washington's Griffith Stadium in 1943. No big leaguer ever duplicated that feat.

TOUGH TARGETS

Since the Homestead Grays used both Washington's Griffith Stadium and Pittsburgh's Forbes Field as home parks, Josh Gibson had two of baseball's most difficult home-run targets. Center field was 457 feet from home at Forbes and 421 feet from home at Griffith, but Gibson still belted 962 career homers, including 84 in one season, and had a .391 career average. Negro Leagues manager Judy Johnson once said that if Gibson had been a big leaguer during his prime, Hank Aaron and Babe Ruth would have wound up chasing *him.*

GREENBERG GARDENS

The Pittsburgh Pirates, a bad ballclub in need of a gate attraction, shortened their home-run distances when Hank Greenberg joined the team in 1947. Left field was reduced from 365 feet from home to 335 feet, and left-center was cut by nearly 20 feet. The new section created behind the wall was called Greenberg Gardens, then changed to Kiner's Korner when Ralph Kiner became the club's top slugger. When Kiner was traded in midseason 1953, Branch Rickey wanted to tear down the short barrier at once because the Pirates had no other slugger who could reach the wall. But a league rule prevented him from restoring the original distances in midyear.

Ebbets Field Bullpen

The bullpen in Brooklyn's Ebbets Field (1913–1957) was a hazardous place to work. Squeezed between the left-field foul line and the stands, pitchers were pelted with assorted debris from the stands. Another problem was line drives from hitters; pitchers warmed up in a tiny space facing the plate, with left-handers on the outside and right-handers on the inside. An extra player stood behind bullpen catchers (who had their backs to home) to field balls hit in the pen's vicinity.

Ad Signs Pay

Woody English of the Chicago Cubs once won two suits in one game by hitting balls off an Ebbets Field outfield sign that said, "Hit sign, win suit." The sign was erected before World War II by Abe Stark, a men's clothier. The average income produced by all Ebbets Field advertising signs was $42,000 per season—enough to pay Jackie Robinson's salary.

Crazy Angles

The right-field wall at Brooklyn's Ebbets Field had 289 different angles, with concrete at the base of the wall and a wire screen atop a metal scoreboard. Duke Snider, a left-handed hitter, claimed the 40-foot height of the wall cost him many home runs.

Returning the Favor

Two players had four-homer games at Ebbets Field: Brooklyn's Gil Hodges did it against the Braves in 1950, and Joe Adcock did it for the Braves four years later.

Brooklyn Attendance

Attendance at Ebbets Field ranged from a low of 83,831 in 1918 to a high of 1,807,526 in 1947. While Brooklyn was drawing 5.5 million from 1953 to 1957, however, the Milwaukee Braves drew 10 million—causing the Dodgers to seek greener pastures.

Copycat Parks

Retro parks in Baltimore, Arlington, Milwaukee, and Tampa all have design elements taken from Ebbets Field.

A 1961 scoreless tie between the Yankees and the Red Sox is about to end with a historic home run. Roger Maris rips Tracy Stallard's 2–0 pitch for his 61st home run, making him the new single-season home-run king. Copyright 1992 by Bill Purdom. Reprinted with permission, Bill Goff, Inc./GoodSportsArt.com.

POLO GROUNDS SWING

The unusual dimensions of the Polo Grounds, longtime home of the New York Giants, perplexed pitchers and batters alike. Dusty Rhodes learned to cope by pulling the ball. "In the Polo Grounds," he said, "you either pulled the ball 260 feet and got a home run or you hit it 490 feet straightaway for an out." Rhodes went 3-for-3 as a pinch-hitter in the 1954 World Series. Two of the hits were singles, the other a three-run homer off Cleveland's Bob Lemon in the tenth inning of the opener. The ball drifted into the close right-field stands, 260 feet from home. The disgusted pitcher threw his glove; Rhodes said later he threw it farther than the ball was hit.

VANISHED PLAQUE

A Polo Grounds plaque honoring Eddie Grant, the only big leaguer killed in World War I, was pilfered by marauding fans after the last home game of the New York Giants in 1957. The plaque was never found.

FULL HOUSE

Because they played in the Los Angeles Coliseum during their first four years in Los Angeles,

Hank Aaron hits his 715th home run on April 8, 1974, against the Los Angeles Dodgers.
Copyright 1997 by Bill Purdom. Reprinted with permission, Bill Goff, Inc./GoodSportsArt.com.

the Dodgers drew some huge crowds. One of them was the largest crowd in World Series history: 92,706 for a White Sox–Dodgers game in 1959.

NO ADS, PLEASE

During their 61-year tenure at Forbes Field, the Pittsburgh Pirates refused to permit advertising billboards. The exception was a World War II recruiting sign featuring a marine sergeant.

"FRIENDLY CONFINES"

Hall of Fame slugger Ernie Banks, who spent his entire career with the Cubs, always lauded his home park, which he called "the friendly confines of Wrigley Field." The Wrigley family, which owned the team, spent several million dollars on beautification but refused to install lights. They maintained that the green vines on the outfield wall looked more attractive by day, when people would equate a trip to the ballpark with a picnic. "We're aiming at people not interested in baseball," Phil Wrigley once said.

ANSWERING VEECK

When the Yankees played at Chicago in 1960, the year Bill Veeck installed his exploding scoreboard, manager Casey

Stengel and Yogi Berra, joined by other players, brought sparklers to the ballpark. When Mickey Mantle homered and the partisan Veeck board was silent, the Yankees lit the sparklers and jumped up and down in the dugout.

FIRST ATLANTA HR

Home-run king Hank Aaron hit the most famous home run Atlanta Stadium had seen—the one that pushed him beyond Babe Ruth's career mark of 714—but not the first one. In a 1965 exhibition game against the Detroit Tigers, Tommie Aaron, Hank's younger brother, hit the first homer in the brand-new, circular ballpark. Hank hit 755 home runs in his career, Tommie 13.

FIRST AND LAST

Felipe Alou, the first Braves batter in Fulton County Stadium, managed the last regular-season game in the ballpark as an Expo 30 years later. Tony Cloninger and Joe Torre, the Opening Day battery for the 1966 Braves, appeared in the stadium's last game ever—Game 5 of the 1996 World Series—as bullpen coach and manager, respectively, of the New York Yankees.

SAD FAREWELLS

Farewell games in five different parks were downers for the home team. They included:

- Astrodome: Braves 7, Astros 5 (1999)
- Braves Field: Dodgers 8, Braves 1 (1952)
- Griffith Stadium: Twins 6, Senators 3 (1961)
- Jarry Park: Phillies 2, Expos 1 (1976)
- Polo Grounds: Phillies 5, Mets 1 (1963)

SOX TRY MILWAUKEE

Before the Seattle Pilots became the Milwaukee Brewers in 1970, the Chicago White Sox played 20 "home games" at Milwaukee County Stadium in 1968–69.

FADE TO BLACK

Do Cubs players tire more easily because of the steady diet of day games at Wrigley? On August 14, 1969, the Cubs led the Mets by nine and a half games in the NL East standings but faded so fast they finished eight games behind.

GONE WITH THE WIND

With the wind blowing out at Wrigley Field on May 17, 1979, the Philadelphia Phillies beat the Chicago Cubs, 23–22.

CHICAGO CONTRAST

One-time Minnesota third baseman Gary Gaetti hit much better at Wrigley Field, on Chicago's North Side, than he did at Comiskey Park, on the South Side. "At Wrigley, I felt like King Kong," he said. "At Comiskey, I felt like Donkey Kong."

KOUFAX ON TURF

Hall of Fame pitcher Sandy Koufax said about artificial turf: "I know one thing. I was one of those guys who pitched without a cup. I wouldn't do it on this stuff."

ASTRODOME QUIRK

Philadelphia's Mike Schmidt was deprived of a tape-measure home run when his 1974 blast in Houston struck a loudspeaker hanging from the Astrodome in center field. Under ground rules in the domed ballpark, such balls were in play; Schmidt had to settle for the longest single in baseball history.

FISK POLE

Thirty years after the fact, the Boston Red Sox named Fenway Park's left-field foul marker "the Fisk Pole" on June 14, 2005. It was named for Carlton Fisk, who waved frantically at the pole after clouting a long fly ball down the line in the twelfth inning of Game 6 in the 1975 World Series. The ball stayed fair, sending that Series into a seventh game a day later.

Yankee Stadium, opened in 1923, has hosted more World Series than any other ballpark. Bill Menzel

INVITING TARGET
The short dimensions of Boston's Fenway Park helped 5'4" shortstop Freddie Patek hit three home runs and a double during a 20–2 win by the California Angels over the Red Sox on June 20, 1980.

BOMBASTIC BEGINNING
June 27, 2003, was a good day to be in Fenway Park. En route to a 14-run first inning, which tied a 53-year-old AL record, the Boston Red Sox scored a record 10 times with nobody out. During a 25–8 win that featured 28 hits, tying a franchise mark, Boston's Johnny Damon had a three-hit inning, duplicating the feat of former Red Sox shortstop Vern Stephens 50 years earlier. Damon had a single, a double, and a triple during the big first inning.

WET GROUNDS
A 1984 Eastern League game at Burlington, Vermont, was suspended in the seventeenth inning when the automatic sprinklers came on and could not be turned off. Although 2,909 fans were there at the start, only 250 remained after the five-hour, twelve-minute marathon entered the final frame.

MONUMENT VALLEY
Yankees greats are honored with five monuments and 17 plaques, all located beyond the left-center-field fence in an area known as Monument Park. The tradition began in 1932, when a monument in memory of the late manager Miller Huggins was erected in center field. Monuments for Lou Gehrig (1941) and Babe Ruth (1949) followed. Moved beyond the fence during the 1974–75 remodeling of Yankee Stadium, they were joined by monuments to Mickey Mantle in 1996 and Joe DiMaggio in 1999. Men honored by plaques, in order of erection, are Col. Jacob Ruppert, Ed Barrow, Joe McCarthy, Casey Stengel, Thurman Munson, Elston Howard, Roger Maris, Phil Rizzuto, Billy Martin, Lefty Gomez, Whitey Ford, Bill Dickey, Yogi Berra, Allie Reynolds, Don Mattingly, Mel Allen, and Bob Sheppard.

BABE'S SMOKESTACK
The giant Babe Ruth bat that stands outside Yankee Stadium was the brainchild of Joe Garagiola Jr., then in-house lawyer for the team. Garagiola, later the first general manager of the Arizona Diamondbacks,

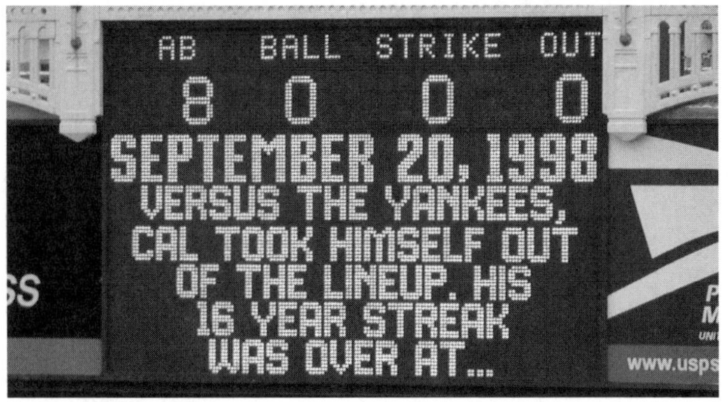
AB BALL STRIKE OUT
8 0 0 0
SEPTEMBER 20, 1998
VERSUS THE YANKEES,
CAL TOOK HIMSELF OUT
OF THE LINEUP. HIS
16 YEAR STREAK
WAS OVER AT...

The Yankee Stadium scoreboard gives a rare salute to a visiting player, the retiring Cal Ripken Jr. Bill Menzel

convinced Hillerich & Bradsby to buy the rights and paint the structure.

ORGAN GRINDER

Eddie Layton played for the Yankees, the Rangers, and the Knicks. The Yankee Stadium organist joined the team in 1967, when it began using organ music, and lasted through 2003, when he retired. He was known for playing brief renditions of "Yankee Doodle Dandy" after great plays. Layton was also a composer/performer whose 26 albums sold more than 3 million copies.

SNOW JOB

The visiting Chicago White Sox had a field day when snow fell prior to Toronto's first opener, at roofless Exhibition Stadium in 1977. They played touch football, had snowball fights, and watched Jack Brohamer ski around the infield with shin guards as skis and bats as poles. When the snow subsided, Toronto won, 9–4.

THE MOVABLE ROOF

The Toronto SkyDome was the first ballpark with a retractable roof. It opened on June 5, 1989.

TAPE-MEASURE SHOTS

Players who homered over the left-field roof at Tiger Stadium: Harmon Killebrew, Frank Howard, Cecil Fielder, and Mark McGwire.

Mistake on the Lake
During its tenure as home of the Cleveland Indians, cavernous Municipal Stadium was often called "Mistake on the Lake."

Water Show
Kauffman Stadium, part of the Harry S. Truman Sports Complex in Kansas City, features a $3 million "water spectacular" behind the wall between center field and right field. The 322-foot-wide attraction, the world's largest privately funded fountain, contains a 10-foot-high waterfall from an upper cascade pool, plus two lower pools that empty into five more 10-foot falls. Postgame water shows are accompanied by music and colored lights.

The Dirt on George
Groundskeeper George Toma worked for the Kansas City Athletics, the Kansas City Royals, and the NFL's Kansas City Chiefs in a 42-year career that ended in 1999. Born on Groundhog Day, Toma was famous for putting in 22-hour days and catching occasional naps in wheelbarrows, lockers, and press boxes. He also served as a groundskeeper at the first 39 Super Bowls.

Rockies Rock
The Colorado Rockies led the majors in attendance during their first seven seasons, starting in 1993.

Coors Concerns
Why Coors Field is unlike any other park in the majors:

- Sinkers don't sink and curves don't curve as well in Denver's thin air.
- Alpine air, with less oxygen, makes recovery from injuries more difficult.
- Playing in the Mile High City requires more energy than at sea level.
- Pitched and batted balls go straight.
- Balls seem more slick at high altitudes.
- Batted balls go farther in thinner air.

Humoring the Humidor
Does Denver's humidor help? Early in 2002, the Colorado Rockies started storing baseballs in a climate-controlled room to make them heavier, softer, and easier to grip. Thanks to preset readings of 70 degrees and 50 percent humidity, conditions at Coors Field nearly reverted to normal, with runs and homers falling by more than 10 percent.

FOSSIL FIND

A rib fragment of a Triceratops, a 10-foot-tall dinosaur that weighed 12 tons, was found by excavators during the construction of Colorado's Coors Field in 1994. The park opened a year later with a purple dinosaur named Dinger as its mascot.

HITLESS AT COORS

Hideo Nomo threw the only no-hitter at Coors Field. He also is among the handful of

West Coast baseball took on new dimensions with the openings of Seattle's Safeco Field on July 15, 1999 (top), and Pacific Bell Park, adjacent to San Francisco Bay, the following spring. In their first three seasons, both parks hosted postseason games. Top image copyright 1999 by Bill Purdom. Bottom image copyright 2000 by Bill Purdom. Reprinted with permission, Bill Goff, Inc./GoodSportsArt.com.

pitchers to hurl hitless games in both leagues.

ROCKY MOUNTAIN LOW

More than two dozen fans were hurt when a Coors Field escalator malfunctioned on July 2, 2003. Injuries ranged from broken bones to cuts and bruises.

BRICK HIGHWAY

If the bricks used to build Coors Field were laid end-to-end, they would stretch more than 200 miles—the distance from Pueblo, Colorado, to Cheyenne, Wyoming. There are 1.4 million bricks in the 50,000-seat Denver ballpark.

FOREIGN INTRIGUE

Major League Baseball opened the 1999, 2000, 2001, and 2003 seasons outside the United States.

SPLIT DOUBLEHEADER

The Mets and Yankees played a day-night doubleheader in 2003 that was split between Shea Stadium and Yankee Stadium, ballparks that are five miles apart.

FISH OUT OF WATER

The Florida Marlins hosted two "home games" against the Montreal Expos at U.S. Cellular Field in Chicago in 2004 to escape the wrath of Hurricane Ivan in the southeast. Already in town for a series with the Cubs, the Marlins served as the home team and occupied the White Sox clubhouse. It was the first time a game was played at a neutral site since the Yankees played at Shea Stadium on April 15, 1998, after a 500-pound steel joint fell from the upper deck of Yankee Stadium onto the seats below. Many of the 4,003 who attended one of the games were Cubs fans still upset that the Fish fried the Cubs in the NLCS the previous October.

CLUBHOUSE CREDO

A sign posted in many major league clubhouses reads:

> What you see here
> What you hear here
> What you say here
> Let it stay here
> When you leave here

OVERFLOW CROWDS

The 2004 Red Sox averaged 35,028 in a park that seated 33,871 officially.

A TALE OF TWO CITIES

The Marlins and Expos faced off in four different cities in

2004: Miami, San Juan, Montreal, and Chicago. Thanks to interleague play, both teams played in a record 21 stadiums that season.

KEVIN'S CLOUTS
Dodgers shortstop Kevin Elster, not known for his power, proved the point in 2000 when he hit three homers on Opening Day (the first game in San Francisco's Pac Bell Park) and then never hit three in any remaining *month* that season.

PEDAL POWER
The Giants encourage fans to ride bicycles to their ballpark by offering free use of a special room where bikes can be parked. No other club offers a similar service.

MORE THAN A SIP
The giant Coca-Cola bottle that towers over the left-field stands in Atlanta's Turner Field is 42 feet tall and decorated with 6,680 baseballs, 60 baseball shoes, 64 bases, 48 batting helmets, 18 catcher's mitts, 290 bats, 86 fielder's gloves, 24 jerseys, 71 catcher's masks, 16 chest protectors, and 24 pitching rubbers.

CATWALK NIPPED
When the Tampa Bay Devil Rays began play in 1998, balls that hit catwalks high above Tropicana Field were in play. After four such shots, however, the team asked the American League to make all catwalk clouts home runs.

MILLER PARK PROTEST
Residents of Racine, Wisconsin, recalled their representative to the state legislature after he voted for the bill that allocated state funds for the construction of Milwaukee's Miller Park. The bill, promoted by owner-turned-commissioner Bud Selig, passed by a single vote.

FOR WHOM THE BELL TOLLS
The Liberty Bell was not forgotten when the Phillies moved from Veterans Stadium to Citizens Bank Park in 2004. A 35-by-50-foot likeness of the historic bell, lit in neon, hangs 100 feet above street level, swinging and tolling whenever a Phillie hits a home run.

TRIBUTE IN TEXAS
Even though Cal Ripken Jr. spent his entire career with the Baltimore Orioles, the Texas Rangers retired the locker he used in the visiting clubhouse

in the Ballpark at Arlington. Ripken's road gray jersey and some of the equipment he used is permanently displayed.

SEATTLE TRAIN SOUNDS

Safeco Field fans may not love trains, but they must be used to them. More than 70 freights a day rumble along the Seattle-Chicago main line on the north side of the stadium and blast their horns as they approach grade crossings.

SAN JUAN SOJOURN

The Montreal Expos, dissatisfied with their draw at home, played 22 "home games" in San Juan, Puerto Rico, in 2003 and 2004.

SHAKY CEILINGS

The 1991 Montreal Expos and the 1994 Seattle Mariners made unscheduled 21-day road trips necessitated by roof repairs at their domed ballparks.

GREEN "EYE"

By stretching green tarpaulins across large chunks of seats in center field, the Oakland A's turned the Oakland Coliseum into the smallest ballpark in the major leagues. The capacity fell from 44,037 to 34,077 for baseball, dropping the Oakland

Fans flock to Oriole Park at Camden Yards, the first of a wave of new ballparks designed to blend modern amenities with historic design. This is the intersection of Eutaw and Camden Streets, just a few blocks from Babe Ruth's birthplace. Copyright 1996 by Thomas Kolendra. Reprinted with permission, Bill Goff, Inc./GoodSportsArt.com.

stadium behind Boston's Fenway Park as the American League's smallest.

Compact Park

Pittsburgh's PNC Park (capacity 38,365) is the smallest in the National League. All but 10,000 of the seats are on the first level.

Casey's Claim

Sean Casey collected the first hits at two new ballparks: Miller Park in Milwaukee and PNC Park in Pittsburgh.

Wall Honors Pirate

The right-field wall at Pittsburgh's PNC Park has a height of 21 feet because former Pirates right fielder Roberto Clemente made the number 21 famous.

Grassy Knolls

In 2005, for the first time in 40 years, all National League home games were played on natural grass—a notion Dick Allen would approve. He once said he wouldn't play on anything a horse wouldn't eat.

Dogs in the Swim

Trained dogs dive for balls hit out of AT&T Park in San Francisco. The Giants, in tandem with a local animal shelter called Pets in Need, created the Baseball Aquatic Retrieval Korps (B.A.R.K.) and even got the San Francisco Police Department to install "Water Dog Work Zone" warning signs in the water.

Looking Flushed

When the Arizona Diamondbacks opened their new Bank One Ballpark in Phoenix in 1998, women's toilets outnumbered men's, 340–55.

Model Ballparks

The Arizona Diamondbacks built more than 17 miniature replicas of their downtown Phoenix ballpark for use by local youth leagues. The parks have lights, bullpens along the foul lines, and even the dirt stripe that connects the mound with home plate.

What about BOB?

The merger between Bank One and J.P. Morgan Chase & Co. spelled the end of the line for the BOB—Bank One Ballpark in Phoenix. The domed ballpark was renamed Chase Field in 2005.

Woof

San Diego's Petco Park, which opened in 2004, is named for

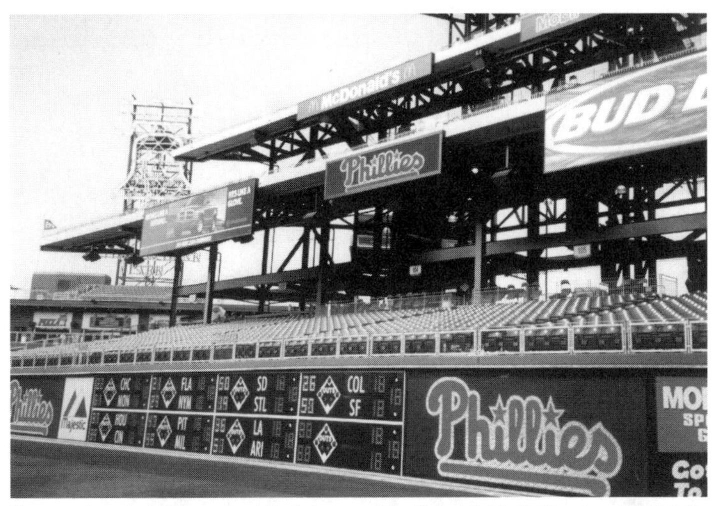

The scoreboard at Citizens Bank Park, home of the Philadelphia Phillies since 2004, tells fans not only scores of out-of-town games but also pitchers, outs per inning, and how many men are on base. Dan Schlossberg

the nationwide retailer of pet supplies. The company, based in San Diego, paid $60 million for a 22-year agreement on naming rights for the stadium.

RELIEF FOR RELIEVERS

Designers forgot to include bathrooms in the visiting bullpen at Petco Park, forcing visiting relievers to relieve themselves in public restrooms.

NAME CHANGE

Anaheim Stadium not only changed its name (to Edison International Field at Anaheim) but also its seating capacity (from 65,158 to 45,030).

RFK STADIUM REDUX

Arizona broadcaster Mark Grace thinks his last name applies to the newly resurrected RFK Stadium in Washington. "They put a lot of lipstick and makeup on her," he said. "She's still an old girl but an old girl is still a pretty girl if you ask me."

INTERNATIONAL APPEAL

Among those buying seats from old Busch Stadium in St. Louis after the 2005 campaign were residents of Australia, Canada,

Houston's Minute Maid Park hosted the 2004 All-Star Game and 2005 World Series. The locomotive, coupled to a tender full of the name sponsor's oranges, chugs along the track after an Astros home run. Dan Schlossberg

Japan, Latin America, Puerto Rico, and all 50 states.

Lots of Juice

The Houston-based Minute Maid company agreed to pay the Astros $170 million over 28 years for ballpark naming rights, plus other advertising and promotional gimmicks. The retractable-roof stadium, which opened in 2000, was previously called Enron Field and Astros Park.

Minute Maid's Design

When the Houston Astros were designing Minute Maid Park, team president Tal Smith suggested it have elements of old fields. Tal's Hill, in dead center field, features a fast-rising slope and a flagpole that is in play. The scoreboard and wall in left come from Fenway; the flagpole in center comes from Tiger Stadium; the center-field incline is borrowed from the Crosley Field terrace; and the seating on the adjacent Union Station roof was copied from Wrigley Field, where fans watch from the tops of neighboring apartment buildings. The park also has a life-sized, 48,000-pound steam locomotive that makes an 800-foot journey from center field to left after an Astros home run. The engine's tender is filled with oranges—a salute to the sponsor for whom the downtown ballpark is named.

WRIGLEY CAVE-INS

Chunks of concrete fell from the upper deck of Wrigley Field at least three times during the 2004 season, forcing the Cubs to conduct inspections and install protective netting. Maybe the venerable ball field was reacting to the team's failure to protect a 3–1 NLCS lead the previous October.

HOME-RUN HELPERS

Best home-run parks in 2004:

1. U.S. Cellular Field, White Sox
2. Wrigley Field, Cubs
3. Citizens Bank Park, Phillies
4. Coors Field, Rockies
5. Great American Ball Park, Reds

HOME-RUN KILLERS

Worst home-run parks in 2004:

1. Petco Park, Padres
2. PNC Park, Pirates
3. Kauffman Stadium, Royals
4. Miller Park, Brewers
5. Shea Stadium, Mets

LAWNMOWER WANTED

The average major league field has 9,000 square feet of grass.

WHAT'S MY LINE?

Will the real president please stand up? Oriole Park at Camden Yards has hosted twice as many Hollywood presidents as White House occupants. Real presidents who tossed out first balls were George H.W. Bush and Bill Clinton, while celluloid subs included Geena Davis, Martin Sheen, Kevin Klein, and Chris Rock.

NEW PARKS IN NEW YORK

New York City will have two new ballparks in 2009 when the Mets open their 45,000-seat Ebbets Field replica in Flushing and the Yankees open the first billion-dollar ballpark, the 53,000-seat new Yankee Stadium.

GIVING UP THE DOME

When they open their new ballpark in 2010, the Minnesota Twins will be the first team to move from a domed stadium to an open-air ballpark in the same city.

Chapter 3
How They Play

Brooks Robinson Remembers…

I go back a long time—to the days when Ed Rummill, Cal Hubbard, and Bill McKinley were active umpires. The fans used to shout, "They shot the wrong McKinley."

I always felt that Nestor Chylak was the best umpire I was ever around. I also remember Bill Valentine. Like me, he grew up in Little Rock. When I was playing in the Midget League, he was umpiring in the same league.

Major league umpires not only have to know all the rules but also have to be referees—keeping tempers cool when managers argue or benches empty. In the heat of a pennant race, that's critical.

To me, the best new rule is the DH. Adopted by the American League in 1973, three years before I retired, it allows a hitter to take the pitcher's turn at bat without forcing the pitcher out of the game. At the same time, the designated hitter doesn't play the field. I know some pitchers can hit, but most of the time they are automatic outs—at least eight times out of every ten at-bats. Many of them can't even drop a sacrifice bunt to move runners along.

I saw Dave McNally and Mike Cuellar hit grand slams in the post-season. Jim Palmer could hit, too. Great pitchers can do everything: they can hit some, they can bunt, and they don't make mistakes trying to go to second base and double up a guy. Too often, though, I see guys who give away games. They can't bunt, can't move guys over, and can't even field a bunt. Consequently, they lose games. So I'm for the DH.

Commissioner Kenesaw Mountain Landis fined top-rated umpire Bill Klem for using foul language.

National Baseball Hall of Fame Library, Cooperstown, New York

UMPIRES

HALL OF FAME UMPS

The first five umpires chosen for the Hall of Fame:

- Bill Klem, 1953
- Tom Connolly, 1953
- Billy Evans, 1973
- Jocko Conlan, 1974
- Cal Hubbard, 1976

FIRST UMPIRES

Early umpires sat in rocking chairs 20 feet behind home plate.

QUICK DECISIONS

Like umpires, batters must be quick thinkers. After the ball takes less than half a second to travel from the pitcher's hand to home plate, the batter has 1/2000th of a second to deliver the barrel of the bat into the hitting zone. The moment of impact between bat and ball consumes 1/1000th of a second, with the strongest sluggers generating 10,000 pounds of force.

LOW-PAYING JOB

The National League ordered home teams to pay umpires $5 a game in 1878.

MASKED MARVEL

NL umpire Richard Higham was the first to wear a mask. The idea went to his head, as he was later the first and only umpire expelled from the game—for collusion with gamblers.

A survivor of serious war wounds suffered during the Battle of the Bulge, Nestor Chylak joined the AL in 1954 and served 25 seasons. He was the first-base umpire during 1960 World Series Game 7, won by Bill Mazeroski's ninth-inning homer. Chylak was elected to the Hall of Fame by the Veterans Committee in 1999. National Baseball Hall of Fame, courtesy of Sue Chylak

Took Long Enough
Umpires did not wear chest protectors until 1885.

Two Umps at a Time
The Players League, a one-year venture in 1890, was the first major league to use two umpires during its games. The American League followed suit within a year or two of its achieving major league status in 1901. Box scores of 1906 indicate two umpires worked games of both the American League and the National League.

Big Brooms
Umpires did not use whisk brooms to dust off home plate until 1904. That year, a member of the Chicago Cubs was seriously injured racing from third to home when he accidentally stepped on the long-handled broom then in use. Until that incident, umpires routinely used long-handled brooms to dust the plate, then casually tossed them aside until they needed to dust again.

Workhorse Arbiters
The only umpires to work at least 5,000 games in the majors were Bill Klem and Bruce Froemming. In 2006 Froemming tied Klem's mark of longevity by an umpire. He worked his 36th season in the big leagues.

Excuses, Excuses
Ballclubs used to play 154-game schedules instead of the current 162. Managers, players, and media members joined the fans in an endless stream of second-guessing and we-should-haves. Umpire Bill Klem, a member of the Baseball Hall of Fame, explained it best when he said, "There are 154 games in a season and you can find 154 reasons why your club should have won every one of them."

British Perspective
Tom Connolly, an American League umpire from 1901 to 1931 and the league's chief umpire through 1953, was an English native who never saw baseball before age 15. Born in 1870, he came to the United States as a teenager, became a minor league ump, then moved to the National League in 1898. He umpired the first game in the new American League three years later and the first World Series in 1903.

FIRST SERIES EJECTION
Chicago Cubs manager Frank Chance was the first man ejected from a World Series game. Tom Connolly threw him out in 1910 for arguing a home run call.

UMPIRE DAY
Fans in Tacoma, Washington, held a once-in-a-lifetime promotion in 1911: Umpire Day. Tired of hearing the ridicule and abuse routinely heaped on the arbiters, the fans and players gave flowers and gifts to the umpires and agreed not to treat them with their usual callousness. When the game was over, the umpires stood outside the gates, broke up the floral bouquets they received, and handed individual flowers to female fans.

THE FIRST RE-GIFTER
Umpire Tom Connolly, who worked the first AL game in 1901, often kept historic game balls that his daughters later distributed as gifts.

UMP GOT AROUND
The first American League game had only one umpire. Tom Connolly kept moving to get the best view of the action, standing behind the plate with nobody on base, behind the pitcher with a runner on first, and behind the plate again with runners on second or third.

SHORTEST HOMER
In a 1914 Federal League game, one of two assigned umpires failed to appear. So the other, Bill Brennan, decided to stand behind the pitcher—instead of behind the catcher—for a better view of all the bases. He also stacked a pile of fresh baseballs behind the mound. Almost immediately, batter Gordon Lund lined a pitch into the pile, scattering the balls in all directions. Lund circled the bases as the confused infielders tagged him with every ball in sight. Brennan, unable to determine which ball was actually hit, awarded Lund a home run—even though the ball traveled only 70 feet.

UMPS WHO PLAYED
Four umpires played major league baseball during the modern era that began in 1901. They were George Moriarty, who played first base from 1903 to 1916; Roderick Wallace, a shortstop from 1901 to 1918; Ed Walsh, a star big-league

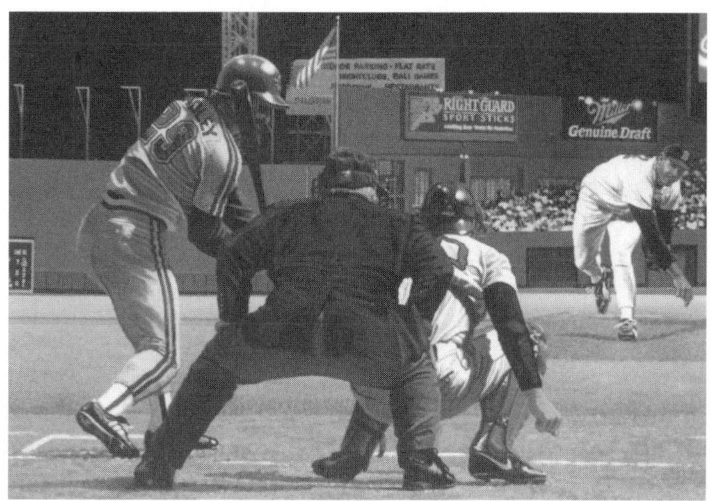

The umpire's ball-and-strike calls are vital to the success of every pitcher. Here, the ump is ready to signal a called third strike on Seattle's Phil Bradley, giving Red Sox right-hander Roger Clemens a record 20 strikeouts in a nine-inning game on April 29, 1986 (he did it again 10 years later). Clemens went on to play (and win) in the All-Star Game and received the Cy Young Award and an MVP trophy. Copyright 1996 by Bill Purdom. Reprinted with permission, Bill Goff, Inc./GoodSportsArt.com.

pitcher from 1904 to 1917; and Bill Dinneen, who threw a no-hitter for the Boston Red Sox on September 27, 1905, and called balls and strikes for five no-hitters *as an umpire* between 1910 and 1923.

No-Hit Ump

Frank O'Loughlin, an AL umpire from 1902 to 1918, called a record six no-hitters.

Evans Had Fun

Umpire Billy Evans was behind the plate when Al Schacht was pitching a game for the Senators. "Have you thrown your fastball yet?" Evans asked. "Yes," Schacht replied, "about 10 times." Evans then pressed the button letting the air out of his chest protector. "Good," he said, "I guess I won't need this."

Umpire Training

The first umpire training school opened in Hot Springs, Arkansas, in 1935.

CALM COMPLAINT

When Charlie Grimm was in one of his terms as manager of the Cubs, umpire Charlie Moran called a Cub out on a close play. Grimm led a protest posse out of the dugout. He put his hand on the umpire's head, turned to his team, and said, "The first man to bother this blind old man is fined 50 bucks!"

WRIST HITTER

Umpire George Moriarty broke his wrist during a postgame fight under the stands with four members of the Chicago White Sox. They had accused him of deliberately making bad calls during the White Sox–Indians game.

LIP STARTS RIOT

Although Brooklyn manager Leo Durocher was charged with inciting a riot after a mêlée with an umpire in 1940, Ebbets Field fans reacted by attacking a *different* umpire.

DEJECTED AND EJECTED

One day, the Cincinnati Reds were particularly rough on umpire Al Barlick. Finally, he took action, ejecting second baseman Johnny Temple. Infuriated, Temple asked why Barlick allowed the bigger stars to say the same things to him. "I don't mind taking it from the lions and tigers," Barlick replied, "but I ain't about to take it from the nits and gnats."

NEVER EJECTED

Although he was fined, benched, and booed with regularity, superstar slugger Ted Williams was never ejected from a game by an umpire.

BETTER VISION

The first umpires to wear glasses were Ed Rommel and Frank Umont in 1956.

UMPS NOT THIRSTY

In 1957 Pittsburgh manager Bobby Bragan, while arguing with the umpires, tried to make peace by offering them a drink of orange juice. He was banished to the clubhouse and, shortly thereafter, replaced by Danny Murtaugh. Murtaugh had four terms with the Pirates and became one of the club's most successful managers.

FAN ATTACKS UMP

Umpires accept derision from men in uniform and jeers from fans as part of their profession. Sometimes they have to put up with more. In 1981 Mike Reilly was tackled from behind by an irate fan during the seventh inning of the American League East Division Series between the Milwaukee Brewers and the New York Yankees. The incident was witnessed by 54,000 fans at Yankee Stadium.

FOLLOWING DAD'S FOOTSTEPS
Ed Runge and Paul Runge are the only father-and-son tandem to umpire no-hit games. Ed was behind the plate for Dave Morehead's gem on September 16, 1965, while Paul was the umpire for Charlie Lea's no-hitter on May 10, 1981.

QUICK THUMB
Padres pilot Steve Boros was booted from a 1986 game before the first pitch when he tried to give umpire Charlie Williams a videotape of a disputed call from the previous night's 4–2 loss to the Braves.

TOUGH BOOT
When umpire Drew Coble ejected soft-spoken slugger Cal Ripken Jr. from a 1989 game, he said he felt like he was ejecting God from Sunday school.

WELL-PAID UMPS
The latest contract covering umpires has a salary scale that ranged from $87,859 to $357,530 and a clause calling for annual 5 percent raises. Paid by seniority rather than merit, the umpires also received 31 paid vacation days during the season. In addition, the pact mandated the rehiring of three more umpires who lost their jobs in a 1999 labor dispute. As a result, half of the 22 fired umpires have been rehired.

FEMALE UMPIRE
Pam Postema spent some six seasons as a Triple A umpire before leaving the game. Never promoted to the majors, she later wrote a book called *You've Got to Have Balls to Make It in This League.*

Job Well Done

"When I walk off the field, there are 50 people I've tried to satisfy—the 25 players on each team. I know when I've done a good job. Just because they don't argue doesn't necessarily mean I did a good job."

—John Hirschbeck

Game of Inches

"The ball over the heart of the plate is a strike with all 68 major league umpires. The difference with umpires can be so fine. You're talking about maybe a quarter-inch, a half-inch, when the ball barely touched the black on the outside edge. [One] ump is going to give the strike to the pitcher. Others say the ball has to get the corner. If I don't know it's got the corner, I'm calling it a ball."

—John Hirschbeck

BALK-A-DAY BOB

Because of his strict interpretation of the balk rule, National League umpire Bob Davidson picked up the nickname of "Balk-a-Day Bob." He became a regular member of the NL umpiring staff in 1983.

WRONG SONG

Organist Wilbur Snapp thought he was being cute when he played *Three Blind Mice* as the umpires appeared for a 1985 Florida State League game at Jack Russell Stadium in Clearwater. They didn't agree and threw him out.

CATCHER CLEANS PLATE

After umpire John Shulock refused to clean off home plate following a Lou Piniella dirt-kicking tirade, Mariners catcher Dan Wilson had to borrow the ump's whisk broom so his pitcher would have a better target.

OWNER PAYS FINE

Yankees owner George Steinbrenner was once fined $75,000 for criticizing umpires in postseason play.

DID UMPS CHOKE?

Like players, umpires face greater scrutiny during the World Series, and sometimes, they make bad calls. Five examples:

- 1957 Game 4, Yankees at Braves. Nippy Jones leads off for Milwaukee against Tommy Byrnes. After a pitch in the dirt, Jones sprints for first base. Home-plate ump Augie Donatelli calls him back, saying he was not hit by the pitch. Jones asks for the ball and shows the ump the shoe-polish stain. Eddie Mathews hits a two-run homer with one man out and wins the game for the eventual world champions.

- 1970 Game 1, Orioles at Reds. With one out and runners at the corners in the sixth inning of a 3–3 game, Ty Cline hits an infield chopper in front of home plate. Ellie Hendricks grabs the ball and turns to tag Bernie Carbo but instead collides with umpire Ken Burkhart. Knocked to the ground, Burkhart calls Carbo out. Replays showed Hendricks tagged the runner with an empty glove—while holding the ball in his bare hand. The Orioles won, 4–3, and later won the Series.
- 1975 Game 3, Red Sox at Reds. Ed Armbrister of the Reds drops a sacrifice bunt in the bottom of the tenth inning, then hesitates while determining if the ball is fair. As he heads for first, he collides with catcher Carlton Fisk, who rushed to grab the ball. Fisk uncorks a wild throw to second, putting runners on second and third and setting up the winning rally. Plate umpire Larry Barnett refuses to call interference against Armbrister, and the Reds take the World Series in seven games.
- 1985 Game 6, Cardinals at Royals. With the Cardinals needing just three outs to clinch the Series, Don Denkinger ruled that Kansas City's Jorge Orta beat Jack Clark's toss to pitcher Todd Worrell, covering first. That sparked a Royals rally and a 2–1 win that sent the Series into a Game 7 showdown. K.C. won that one, 11–0.
- 1991 Game 2, Braves at Twins. With one on and two out in the third, Ron Gant singles but is tagged out as he returns to first after rounding the bag. Twins first baseman Kent Hrbek lifts Gant off the base as he applies the tag, but umpire Drew Coble calls the runner out, saying momentum took him off the base. The Twins win, 3–2, and eventually win a seven-game World Series.

Bad Break

Steve Palermo's 14-year career as a big-league umpire ended abruptly in 1991 when he was paralyzed by a spinal gunshot wound suffered while trying to break up an altercation outside a Dallas restaurant. Palermo, the home-plate ump for Dave Righetti's 1983 no-hitter and the first World Series game that year, later became an umpire supervisor.

FATAL OPENER
John McSherry was only 52 when he suffered sudden cardiac arrest and died two minutes into the Reds-Expos opener at Cincinnati on April 1, 1996. The popular but portly McSherry had been an umpire for 25 years.

Twilight Zone

"Umpires move around. Some guys are taller, some are shorter, so one guy's strikes might be higher than the next guy's.... The real trick [is] to find out what the top of the strike zone is from umpire to umpire. You hope to find it out before you get to two strikes. Guys will have to pay attention and do some homework to find out who's calling what."

—Tony Gwynn

SPITTIN' IMAGE
After Baltimore's Robby Alomar spit in the face of umpire John Hirschbeck on September 27, 1996, baseball needed a court order to keep the umpires from boycotting postseason games. Alomar served a five-game suspension at the start of the 1997 campaign.

WORLD UMPIRES CHIEF
Three days after the World Umpires Association was certified by the National Labor Relations Board, John Hirschbeck became its first president.

FATHER AND SON
In 1998 Harry and Hunter Wendelstedt became the first father-and-son tandem to umpire the same major league game.

STRIKE HURT UMPS
Although he worked in four championship series, two division series, one World Series, and an All-Star Game, Eric Gregg was among 22 umpires who lost their jobs in 1999 after a union-induced plan of mass resignations failed to realize their

demands. Half were later rehired.

Long Suit

Eric Gregg was such a big man that Dodgers manager Tommy Lasorda once suggested he could use his jacket as an infield tarpaulin.

Charlie's No Angel

Charlie Manuel may consider himself a mild-mannered guy, but not all umpires would agree. In two of his first three games as a major league manager (with the Cleveland Indians in 2000), Manuel was ejected for arguing.

Double Trouble

Cincinnati manager Bob Boone and his son Aaron Boone were once ejected from the same game by the same umpire—Scott Higgins.

Consistent Calls

Mike Fichter was the home-plate ump on June 11, 2003, when a record six Houston Astros no-hit the Yankees in New York. Participants in the 8–0 gem were Roy Oswalt, Pete Munro, Kirk Saarloos, Brad Lidge, Octavio Dotel, and Billy Wagner.

Squatter's Rights

Home-plate umpires made 617,294 squats during the 2003 season.

Men in Blue?

Current umpire uniforms include black windbreaker jackets with light-blue trim and black caps with the MLB silhouetted-batter logo. Charcoal-colored pants and a black shirt with white trim and the two MLB logos (behind the collar and on the front pocket) complete the ensemble. Each umpire's number is indicated on his sleeve. An alternate blue jersey was added to the uniform in 2004.

Arbiter's Argument

"Umpiring is the only occupation where a man has to be perfect on Opening Day and improve as the season goes on."

—AL umpire Nestor Chylak

RULES

FIRST AL FORFEIT
Detroit was the beneficiary of the first American League forfeit in 1901. Detroit scored five runs in the ninth to take a 7–5 lead over Chicago when a rainstorm started. Had the game been called before completion of the inning, the score would have reverted back to the end of the last full inning, when Chicago had a 5–2 lead. The umpires charged Chicago was deliberately stalling in the bottom of the ninth, hoping for a rain-shortened game, and awarded the game to Detroit by forfeit.

BLACK BALLED
Detroit won a game by forfeit in 1903 when Cleveland second baseman Napoleon Lajoie threw a discolored game ball into the stands.

FROSTY FORFEIT
Snowball-throwing fans forced a forfeit of the 1907 New York Giants opener against the Philadelphia Phillies. The barrage began in the eighth inning but increased so quickly that play had to be halted.

BRAWL = FORFEIT
The Tigers forfeited a 1924 game to the Yankees after Ty Cobb and Babe Ruth got into a brawl at home plate. The battle began after Tigers pitcher Bert Cole hit Bob Meusel with a pitch.

ALL WET IN WASHINGTON
Red Sox manager Joe Cronin, later the president of the American League, protested a 1941 Griffith Stadium game by insisting the contest could not be resumed because the uncovered field was unplayable. The Senators were leading, 6–3, at the time of the 40-minute rain delay, but AL president Will Harridge upheld the protest and forfeited the game to Boston. He ruled that Washington violated the rules because they did not have available groundskeepers to cover the field.

FAN RIOT
Unruly fans stormed onto the field in the last inning of the final game in Washington in 1971, causing the Senators to forfeit a game they were winning. The Senators became the Texas Rangers a year later.

Forfeit Rule

4.15 A game may be forfeited to the opposing team when a team

(a) Fails to appear upon the field, or being upon the field, refuses to start play within five minutes after the umpire has called "Play" at the appointed hour for beginning the game, unless such delayed appearance is, in the umpire's judgment, unavoidable;

(b) Employs tactics palpably designed to delay or shorten the game;

(c) Refuses to continue play during a game unless the game has been suspended or terminated by the umpire;

(d) Fails to resume play, after a suspension, within one minute after the umpire has called "Play";

(e) After warning by the umpire, willfully and persistently violates any rules of the game;

(f) Fails to obey within a reasonable time the umpire's order for removal of a player from the game;

(g) Fails to appear for the second game of a doubleheader within 20 minutes after the close of the first game unless the Umpire-in-Chief of the first game shall have extended the time of the intermission.

4.16 A game shall be forfeited to the visiting team if, after it has been suspended, the orders of the umpire to groundskeepers respecting preparation of the field for resumption of play are not complied with.

4.17 A game shall be forfeited to the opposing team when a team is unable or refuses to place nine players on the field.

—Official Baseball Rules

Ball Night Unravels

Dodgers fans forced the club to forfeit a game to St. Louis during a Ball Night promotion on August 10, 1995. The game was called with one out in the bottom of the ninth when rowdy spectators threw souvenir balls onto the field for the third time. It was the first forfeited game in 16 years.

COURTESY FIELDER

In the early years of baseball, opposing managers sometimes consulted during games—especially when players were injured on the field. In the first inning of a game on September 1, 1917, Cleveland's Tris Speaker broke from third while trying to steal home, but teammate Joe Evans swung away and smacked a liner into Speaker's face. Detroit manager Hughie Jennings, *as a courtesy,* allowed Speaker to sit out the second inning while he received stitches. Elmer Smith played center in the second inning, but Speaker returned in the third.

LOST HOME RUN

Babe Ruth lost a home run on July 8, 1918, because prevailing rules at the time dictated that a game would end the minute the home team scored the winning run in its last at-bat. A ball hit over the fence might be ruled a lesser hit than a home run if the winning run scored before the batter completed his circuit of the bases. Ruth, playing for the Boston Red Sox against the Cleveland Indians, was thus awarded a triple on a ball that cleared the fence. His hit scored a runner from first base. The rule was changed in 1920 so that all fence-clearing hits were home runs.

FREAK PITCH BAN

Umpires are the police officers of the diamond, charged with enforcing baseball rules. Their job became tougher in 1920, after the spitball, emery ball, and other deliveries that involved doctoring of the ball were outlawed as officials tried to "clean up" the game in the wake of the Black Sox scandal of 1919. The moguls mandated tighter winding of the ball, outlawed such trick deliveries as the spitball and emery ball, and told umpires to keep fresh, white balls in play. All three moves were designed to promote distance hitting, which Babe Ruth proved to be a great fan attraction. Team and league executives thought heavier emphasis on offense would make fans forget the scandal more quickly.

LOST RUTH HOMERS

Babe Ruth lost at least three other home runs because of fan interference or umpire rulings. In the fourth inning of a Polo Grounds game on July 5, 1921, Ruth fell victim to a fan who

After an umpire shouts "play ball," he must recognize and recall myriad rules and regulations that have been revoked, reinstated, and revised over more than a century. National Baseball Hall of Fame and Museum

reached over the fence to catch the ball. Umpires gave him a double. On April 15, 1930, umpires again gave Ruth a double—after his shot into the stands in Philadelphia struck a loudspeaker and bounced back onto the field. The exact same scenario repeated itself on September 26 of the same year.

WALKS WERE HITS

For one season—1887—walks were counted as hits. Tip O'Neill led the American Association with a .492 batting average. With the rule removed the following year, O'Neill again led the league. This time, he hit .332.

HOW MERKLE HURT

Because Christy Mathewson was deprived of a certain victory when Fred Merkle forgot to touch second base in a late-season Giants-Cubs contest in 1908, he ended his career with 373 victories, a total later equaled by longtime Phillies star Grover Cleveland Alexander. No NL pitcher ever won more. It's possible Mathewson would rank alone at the top if victory hadn't become a tie because of "Merkle's boner."

Warped Warm-Up

To speed up games in 1911, AL president Ban Johnson banned warm-up pitches between innings. On June 27, Boston pitcher Ed Karger, seeing his outfielders slow to return to their posts, lobbed a warm-up pitch to his catcher. On the second delivery, Stuffy McInnis sent a drive to right-center and raced around the bases. Red Sox outfielders refused to chase the ball and a loud argument ensued. Johnson denied the Red Sox protest and let the Philadelphia victory stand.

Triple Header

Boston's Joe Cronin lined into a 1935 triple play in a most unusual manner. His drive off the head of Cleveland third baseman Odell Hale ricocheted into the hands of shortstop Bill Knickerbocker, who completed the game-ending triple play.

Homer Title Tie

Lou Gehrig had to settle for a tie with Babe Ruth in the 1931 American League home-run race because of a base-running blunder by teammate Lyn Lary. On April 26, Gehrig hit the ball over the center-field fence in Washington for an apparent homer. But Lary, who had been on first base, thought the ball had been caught for the third out. After he rounded third, he headed straight for the dugout. Gehrig, with his head down in his home-run trot, inadvertently passed him on the base paths and was called out by umpire Bill McGowan.

Short Rain

Jocko Conlan didn't think it was funny when Pittsburgh pilot Frankie Frisch carried an umbrella to home plate before a game at Brooklyn's Ebbets Field. Frisch, trying to convince the ump to call the game because of bad weather, received an ejection instead.

Bad Pitching Change

When Leo Durocher was managing the New York Giants, his top reliever was knuckleballer Hoyt Wilhelm. One day in Pittsburgh, Durocher waved Wilhelm in from the bullpen. It wasn't a good choice. The catcher made a great save on the first pitch.

The second one almost went wild. The third pitch was just as bad. So Durocher told pitching coach Freddie Fitzsimmons to make another change. The new reliever started taking warm-ups as Wilhelm walked off into the clubhouse. After several minutes, umpire Jocko Conlan came over to the Giants' dugout. "You can't do that," he said, reminding Durocher that a pitcher has to face at least one batter. The manager conceded the point and sent one of his reserves into the clubhouse to fetch Wilhelm, who had already taken off his shirt. The pitcher put his jersey back on and threw one pitch—ball four, forcing home a Pirate with the winning run.

Bending the Rules

Free substitution is banned in baseball, but rules against it were bent during a Pirates-Cubs game in 1952. Pittsburgh catcher Clyde McCullough was forced out by an injury, and reserve receiver Ed Fitzgerald had already appeared as a pinch-hitter. Cubs manager Phil Cavarretta said he did not mind if Fitzgerald re-entered the game, and the umpires permitted the unusual maneuver. The Pirates home crowd cheered the sportsmanlike decision of the visiting manager.

Sacrifice Flies

Rules regarding the sacrifice fly have changed several times. In 1908, the present sacrifice fly rule was created: no time at bat is charged to a batter for a fly ball (with fewer than two outs) that enables a runner to score from third base. In 1926 the rule was expanded to award a sacrifice fly when any runners moved up a base. The sacrifice fly rule was abandoned in 1939, but the original (1908) version was restored in 1954.

Runs without Hits

The 1959 Chicago White Sox once scored 11 runs in an inning with only one hit—a single. The Sox received 10 walks, five of them with the bases loaded, and one hit batsmen from the generous Kansas City Athletics, who also made three errors in the 20–6 rout.

Shrinkage

After watching National League scoring increase in 1962, the first year of expansion, Baseball Commissioner Ford Frick persuaded owners to widen the strike zone to pre-1950 dimensions: top of the armpit to the bottom of the knee. The result was an increase in strikeouts, fewer walks, and the shrinkage of batting averages to their lowest since 1908.

"SAVE" RULE

The save became an official baseball statistic in 1969 after Chicago baseball writer Jerome Holtzman recommended it. Although its definition has been amended several times, the save has become as vital to a relief pitcher as the win is to a starting pitcher.

POWER PITCHERS

Between the 1973 advent of the designated hitter rule and the 1997 introduction of interleague play, no American League pitcher hit a home run. Roric Harrison of the Orioles hit the last pre-DH homer in 1972, while Bobby Witt of the Rangers hit the first homer by an AL pitcher against National League pitching in 1997.

SLUGGERS "MISSED" DH

Four sluggers who reached the Hall of Fame might not have attained stardom had the designated hitter rule applied when they played. The four—Babe Ruth, George Sisler, Ted Williams, and Stan Musial—all began their careers as pitchers.

DH "FIRSTS"

- DH first suggested by Connie Mack, 1906
- First DH, Ron Blomberg, April 6, 1973
- First DH home run, Tony Oliva, April 6, 1973
- First DH to play 162 games, Rusty Staub, 1978
- First DH in World Series, Dan Driessen, 1976
- First DH to be Rookie of the Year, Eddie Murray, 1977
- First pitcher to start game as DH, Rick Rhoden, 1988

HOYT NEEDED DH

Hoyt Wilhelm, who worked most of his 1,070 games as a pitcher in the American League, could have used a designated hitter. He homered in his first at-bat for the 1952 New York Giants but never homered again in a 21-year career.

SLUGGER CATFISH

Among pitchers who objected to the designated hitter rule

was Jim "Catfish" Hunter, who once received a $5,000 bonus from Oakland A's owner Charlie Finley for his hitting ability. The last pitcher to hit .300 and win 20 games in the same season, Hunter hit .350 while posting a 21–11 record in 1971.

RAINED-IN GAME

The only rained-in game in baseball history occurred in Houston on June 15, 1976, when torrential rains flooded the city with up to 10 inches of water. The Houston Astros and the Pittsburgh Pirates managed to get to the rainproof Astrodome, but the umpires, fans, and most stadium personnel did not.

WITNESS TO HISTORY

Rich Aurilia, later a big-league shortstop, was in the Yankee Stadium stands for George Brett's "pine tar game" on July 24, 1983. That was the game in which Brett's ninth-inning homer was nullified after the Yankees complained the pine tar on his bat extended beyond the legal 18 inches. The league later reversed the umpires' ruling and ordered the game completed.

CHANGES FOR PITCHERS

Rules and regulations regarding pitching have changed over the years. For example:

- 1865—Pitcher's box introduced
- 1877—Batters can ask pitchers to throw either high ball or low ball
- 1893—Pitching rubber introduced, along with 60'6" distance to home plate
- 1895—Pitching rubber enlarged to current standard of 6" x 24"
- 1910—Cork-centered ball introduced
- 1920—Spitball and other ball-doctoring by pitchers are banned
- 1950—Height of mound set at 15" and strike zone set from armpits to knees
- 1962—Pitchers barred from wearing oversized gloves
- 1963—Strike zone set from top of shoulders to bottom of knees
- 1973—Designated hitter bats for pitchers in American League
- 1987—Strike zone determined by batter's stance
- 2001—Strike zone from hollow of knees to midway point between belt buckle and shoulders

Crediting the Pitcher

A starting pitcher must go five innings in a game to be eligible for the victory—with one exception. Should a game be stopped after it has become an "official" game (five full innings, or four and a half with the home team ahead), but before it has gone six innings, the starter is eligible for victory after pitching four innings.

Warm-Up Pitches Rule

8.03 When a pitcher takes his position at the beginning of each inning, or when he relieves another pitcher, he shall be permitted to pitch not to exceed eight preparatory pitches to his catcher during which play shall be suspended. A league by its own action may limit the number of preparatory pitches to less than eight preparatory pitches. Such preparatory pitches shall not consume more than one minute of time. If a sudden emergency causes a pitcher to be summoned into the game without any opportunity to warm up, the Umpire-in-Chief shall allow him as many pitches as the umpire deems necessary.

—Official Baseball Rules

ERA Rule Change

When baseball rule makers realized the growing importance of relief pitching, they changed the qualifications governing the earned-run average title. Before 1950 eligible pitchers had to throw at least 10 complete games. Under the revised rule, they had to work as many innings as their team played games (currently 162). Hoyt Wilhelm became the first reliever to win the ERA crown in 1952, when he worked 159 innings under the 154-game schedule.

Top Mark, No Crown

Ted Williams twice had the AL's best batting average but failed to win the batting crown. Though he hit .345 in 1954 and .356 in 1955, rules then in effect stipulated that qualifiers for the batting title had to have 400 official at-bats. Because walks were not counted as official at-bats, Williams didn't make it. The rule was changed to apply to plate appearances in 1957.

Ted Coaxes Change

For the first 15 years of his career, Ted Williams was victimized by a rule that charged a batter with a time at bat for hitting a fly ball to the outfield—even if it scored a runner from third. The modern version of the sacrifice fly rule was adopted in 1954.

RUNNER FIELDS BALL
Don Hoak was responsible for a rule change. In 1957 the Pirates had men on first and second when the batter hit a grounder to short. Hoping to foil a double play, Hoak—running from second to third—scooped the grounder and flipped it to the shortstop. According to the prevailing rules, only Hoak was out. But the incident convinced higher powers to authorize a rule change that said both the batter and the runner would be out if a runner intentionally interfered with a batted ball.

UNLUCKY KITTEN
Harvey "the Kitten" Haddix lost a no-hitter 36 years after he pitched it! In 1991 Commissioner Fay Vincent ruled that no-hitters had to be games of nine innings or more completed without a hit. Since Haddix pitched 12 perfect innings but yielded a hit in the thirteenth on May 26, 1959, his name was removed from the list of no-hit pitchers. Although opponent Lew Burdette had yielded 12 hits to Pittsburgh, the Pirates and Braves went into the bottom half of the thirteenth scoreless. Felix Mantilla was safe on Don Hoak's error, Eddie Mathews bunted him to second, and Hank Aaron was intentionally walked. Then Joe Adcock ripped a pitch over the fence—the only hit for Milwaukee—but was called out for passing Aaron, who went from second base to the dugout after Mantilla scored. Adcock got credit for a double in a 1–0 victory.

WALKS FOR ROGER?
After failing to receive a single intentional walk while hitting 61 home runs during the 1961 season, Roger Maris had an AL-record four walks in one game against the Angels on May 22, 1962. The mark was later matched by Manny Ramirez of the 2001 Boston Red Sox.

RIPPIN' RICO
Rico Carty once hit two home runs in the same at-bat. It happened in 1963, when Carty played for Toronto of the International League. He hit a home run but was called back

because the umpire had called timeout. So Carty homered again.

NIEKRO FILE

Baseball rules prevent pitchers from scuffing, scratching, spitting, or doing anything else to a baseball that may alter its flight path. Though batters complain constantly, few pitchers are caught. One notable exception was Minnesota pitcher Joe Niekro. Niekro was once suspended for 10 days after umpires discovered a nail file in his pants pocket. Opposing Angels hitters claimed he was cutting the ball.

GHOSTLY GOPHER

Hideo Nomo gave up a home run after he left a game. It happened on April 19, 2000, when the last batter he faced, Mike Stanley, slammed a shot off the railing in left field. Nomo was sitting in the Milwaukee dugout when Stanley's shot—originally ruled a single—was changed to a home run by consensus of the umpiring crew.

THE RUNMAKER

On September 20, 2000, Ben Petrick of the Padres had four RBIs but no hits. He did have two run-scoring grounders, a sacrifice fly, and a walk with the bases loaded.

WRONG BALLS

The Houston Astros and Cincinnati Reds accidentally used batting practice balls in the first inning of a real game in 2003. After his team batted, Houston pitcher Wade Miller noticed he was given a ball stamped PRACTICE. He complained to umpire Paul Schreiber, who fished out another ball with the same blue stamp. Although batting-practice balls often have imperfections, the arbiter allowed them for the entire first inning, since the Astros had already batted. Lance Berkman didn't care: the Houston slugger hit one for a two-run homer.

SHIFTY MOVE

Marquis Grissom once stole two bases during a walk in a 2004 interleague game. Running from first on a 3–2 pitch to Barry Bonds, Grissom saw nobody guarding third because the Tampa Bay infielders had been in "the Barry Shift," with three men between first and second and the third baseman just off second. As the pitch to Bonds was called ball four, Grissom went all the way to third—with third baseman Aubrey Huff in hot pursuit.

INTERFERENCE IS RARE

Batters and catchers can be called for interference, although it doesn't happen often. Catcher's interference is called about 10 times per season, while batter's interference with a catcher is called only twice per year on average.

SMALL POTATOES

Rules govern batting leaders, with players needing minimum numbers of plate appearances to qualify for batting crowns. The difference between a .250 batting average and a .300 average is one hit per week.

ODD OUT

Hank Aaron was once called out for hitting a home run. It happened in St. Louis against an old Aaron nemesis, Curt Simmons. Aaron hit the ball out of the park, but Cardinals catcher Bob Uecker appealed to umpire Chris Pelekoudas that Aaron's foot was out of the batter's box at the time. Pelekoudas agreed and called Aaron out.

RAIN RULE

3.10 (c) The Umpire-in-Chief shall be the sole judge as to whether and when play shall be suspended during a game because of unsuitable weather conditions or the unfit condition of the playing field; as to whether and when play shall be resumed after each suspension; and as to whether and when a game shall be terminated after such suspension. He shall not call the game until at least 30 minutes after he has suspended play. He may continue the suspension as long as he believes there is any chance to resume play.

—Official Baseball Rules

THE DESIGNATED HITTER

A hitter may be designated to bat for the starting pitcher and all subsequent pitchers in any game without otherwise affecting the status of the pitcher(s) in the game. A Designated Hitter for the pitcher must be selected prior to the game and must be included in the lineup cards presented to the Umpire-in-Chief.

It is not mandatory that a club designate a hitter for the pitcher, but failure to do so prior to the game precludes the use of a Designated Hitter for that game.

Pinch-hitters for a Designated Hitter may be used. Any substitute hitter for a Designated Hitter becomes the Designated Hitter. A replaced Designated Hitter shall not reenter the game in any capacity.

The Designated Hitter may be used defensively, continuing to bat in the same position in the batting order, but the pitcher must then bat in the place of the substituted defensive player, unless more than one substitution is made, and the manager then must designate their spots in the batting order.

A runner may be substituted for the Designated Hitter and the runner assumes the role of Designated Hitter. A Designated Hitter may not pinch run.

A Designated Hitter is "locked" into the batting order. No multiple substitutions may be made that will alter the batting rotation of the Designated Hitter.

Once the game pitcher is switched from the mound to a defensive position, this move shall terminate the Designated Hitter role for the remainder of the game.

Once a pinch-hitter bats for any player in the batting order and then enters the game to pitch, this move shall terminate the Designated Hitter role for the remainder of the game.

Once the game pitcher bats for the Designated Hitter, this move shall terminate the Designated Hitter role for the remainder of the game. (The game pitcher may only pinch hit for the Designated Hitter.)

Once a Designated Hitter assumes a defensive position, this move shall terminate the Designated Hitter rule for the remainder of the game. A substitute for the Designated Hitter need not be announced until it is the Designated Hitter's turn to bat.

—Official Baseball Rules

SLUGGING PITCHERS

Some pitchers didn't need a designated hitter. Pitchers with 35 or more lifetime homers—all of whom thrived before the DH was enacted in 1973—were Wes Ferrell (Indians, Red Sox), 38; Bob Lemon (Indians), 37; Red Ruffing (Yankees), 36; and Warren Spahn (Braves), 35. Tony Cloninger, a pitcher for

3.00 Game Preliminaries

3.01 Before the game begins the umpire shall

(a) Require strict observance of all rules governing implements of play and equipment of players;

(b) Be sure that all playing lines are marked with lime, chalk, or other white material easily distinguishable from the ground or grass;

(c) Receive from the home club a supply of regulation baseballs, the number and make to be certified to the home club by the league president. Each ball shall be enclosed in a sealed package bearing the signature of the league president, and the seal shall not be broken until just prior to game time when the umpire shall open each package to inspect the ball and remove its gloss. The umpire shall be the sole judge of the fitness of the balls to be used in the game;

(d) Be assured by the home club that at least one dozen regulation reserve balls are immediately available for use if required;

(e) Have in his possession at least two alternate balls as needed throughout the game. Such alternate balls shall be put in play when

(1) A ball has been batted out of the playing field or into the spectator area;

(2) A ball has become discolored or unfit for further use;

(3) The pitcher requests such alternate ball.

The umpire shall not give an alternate ball to the pitcher until play has ended and the previously used ball is dead. After a thrown or batted ball goes out of the playing field, play shall not be resumed with an alternate ball until the runners have reached the bases to which they are entitled. After a home run is hit out of the playing grounds, the umpire shall not deliver a new ball to the pitcher or the catcher until the batter hitting the home run has crossed the plate.

—Official Baseball Rules

the Milwaukee Braves, was the first player in NL history to smack two grand slams in a game, in a 17–3 win over the San Francisco Giants on July 3, 1966 (he also had an RBI single, giving him nine RBIs). More than 20 years later, fellow pitcher Rick Rhoden hit a game-tying sacrifice fly when used as the Yankees' DH on June 11, 1988, in a game New York won 8–6.

HOLTZMAN HIT

Though he did not bat during the season because of the American League's designated hitter rule, Oakland A's pitcher Ken Holtzman hit well during World Series play in 1973 and 1974. His pair of doubles in 1973 led to rallies that helped Oakland beat the Mets, while his double and home run contributed to another world title the following fall.

MISSED CALL

Mike Schmidt, winner of back-to-back Most Valuable Player citations in the National League, was not immune to basic blunders. He was once called out after stealing second base successfully. It happened at Shea Stadium, New York, in 1979. Schmidt stole second and thought he was out, but Doug Flynn missed the tag. The umpire's "safe" call was inaudible over the roar of the crowd. Schmidt walked all the way to the third-base line before he heard his teammates yell, "Get back! Get back!" Suddenly realizing what was happening, the Philadelphia star called time and pretended he wanted a drink from the water cooler. But the ruse failed: the umpires refused to allow the deception, and the suddenly alerted Mets tagged him out.

Eight-time NL home-run king Mike Schmidt was once called out for violating base-running rules. Philadelphia Phillies

Equipment

Gloves Catch On

Pitchers, as a group, were the longest holdouts against wearing gloves during games. Catchers wore the first mitts, followed by outfielders and then infielders.

Dead-Ball Era

The period before 1920 was known as the dead-ball era. The ball had a different core than today's lively ball, moved more slowly, seldom took high bounces, and rarely reached the deepest part of the outfield. Heavier bats were used to push, rather than drive, the ball, and pitchers took short strides, emphasizing control rather than strikeouts. They let batters hit the ball and hoped fielders would catch it. At the same time, they saved wear-and-tear on their arms and were able to work often. Home runs were so rare that in 1902, National League leader Wee Tommy Leach failed to hit one out of the park. All six of his homers were inside-the-park jobs.

Colorful Suits

The 1901 Baltimore Orioles wore pink caps, black shirts with a large yellow "O" on the left front, black baggy pants with yellow belts, yellow stockings, and double-breasted jackets with wide yellow collars and cuffs and two rows of pearl buttons. Glass and metal were not prohibited from the major league uniform until 1931.

Cobb's Regimen

Ty Cobb treated bats with tobacco juice in an effort to keep dampness out of the wood. Using a chewing tobacco called Nerve navycut—an especially juicy brand—Cobb rubbed his bats for hours with the hollowed-out femur of a steer. The bone was still chained to a table in the Detroit clubhouse years after Cobb retired.

Uniform Cost

Major leaguers bought their uniforms until 1912. Price: $30.

Boston Shoestrings

The Boston National League club allowed players just one pair of shoestrings per year. If they lasted two years, the team paid the player's fare (one way only) on the horse-car to or from the park.

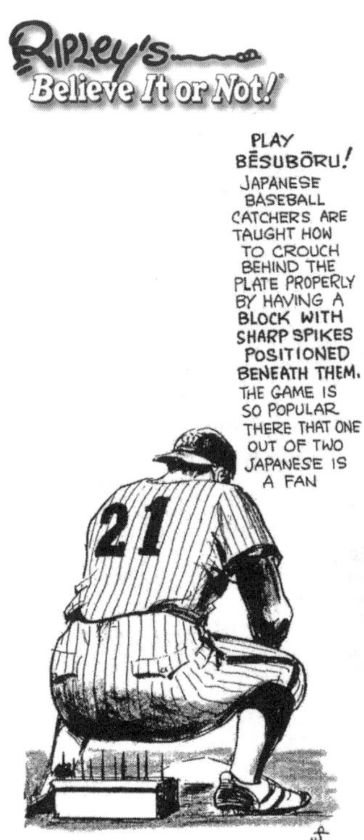

Ripley's Believe It or Not!
PLAY BĒSUBŌRU! JAPANESE BASEBALL CATCHERS ARE TAUGHT HOW TO CROUCH BEHIND THE PLATE PROPERLY BY HAVING A BLOCK WITH SHARP SPIKES POSITIONED BENEATH THEM. THE GAME IS SO POPULAR THERE THAT ONE OUT OF TWO JAPANESE IS A FAN
21

Road Grays

Connie Mack instigated the practice of dressing his players in gray uniforms away from home. His Philadelphia A's played hard, aggressive baseball before the home fans but did not wish to spoil their clean uniforms away from home. Although players refused to slide and dirty their whites, Mack reasoned they wouldn't mind so much if road uniforms were gray.

Ball Savers

On June 29, 1916, the Cincinnati Reds and the Chicago Cubs used only one ball in a nine-inning game.

Crossed Cardinals

According to *The Sporting News,* the double-bird emblem used since 1921 by the St. Louis Cardinals originated when a member of the St. Louis County Presbyterian Church looked out the window and saw two redbirds in a tree. Mrs. Clarence L. Keaton, in charge of decorating the church for a Men's Fellowship meeting featuring Branch Rickey as speaker, used two red birds. Rickey liked the look and adopted it for his team.

Lively Ball

The National League's souped-up baseball of 1930 had to be toned down after a season in which six of eight teams hit .300 and the other two topped .280. The pennant-winning Cardinals had 11 .300 hitters and the New York Giants hit a record .319. The Phils hit .315 but finished last—40 games from first—because their team earned-run average was 6.71. Pitching was hurting all around the league; a 4.07 ERA ranked as the fifth-best mark that season.

Color War
The 1937 Brooklyn Dodgers switched from blue to green caps, socks, and shirtsleeves. On the road, they went from gray to tan uniforms. They still finished sixth in an eight-team league.

Colored Balls
Larry MacPhail introduced yellow baseballs in 1938 and Charlie Finley tried orange balls 35 years later, but neither idea caught on.

Patriotic Suits
The New York Giants wore red, white, and blue uniforms during World War II fund-raising exhibition games.

Oversized Unis
Early baseball uniforms consisted of eight-ounce flannels that absorbed their weight in sweat and shrank after laundering. Players usually began the season with suits at least one size too large.

Before and After
Cliff Mapes wore No. 3 after Babe Ruth and No. 7 before Mickey Mantle. A .242 hitter with 13 homers, Mapes was wearing No. 3 when the Yankees officially retired it in 1948, the year Ruth died. When Mantle later asked for No. 7, Mapes switched again, donning No. 13.

Angry Old Bats
When the Louisville Slugger Museum posted a highway billboard bragging of "more old bats than a needlepoint convention," the Embroiders Guild of America complained. The group, also located in Louisville, has 20,000 members, some of them as old as 100.

Sandlot Bat
Two-time batting king Ferris Fain, mired in a slump, watched a sandlot slugger hit several long drives in a game, then bought his bat for three times its value. He did so well in a doubleheader the next day that he sent the bat to Louisville, where he ordered a load of exact duplicates.

Ted's Tip
Early in his career, Willie McCovey followed a tip from Ted Williams that he switch from a 38-ounce bat to a 34-ounce bat. McCovey finished with 521

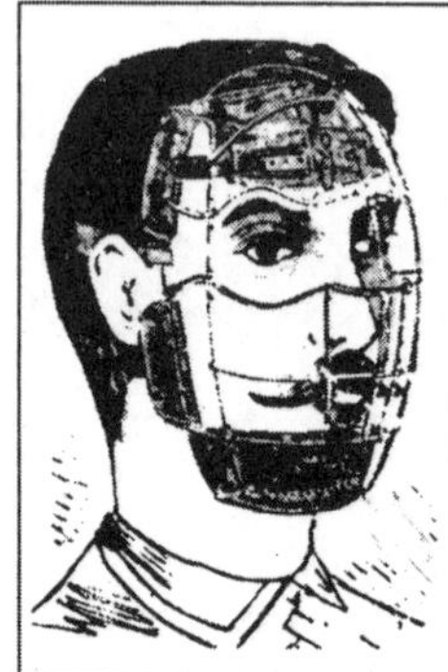

Base Ball, BATS -AND- MASKS

CHAPIN'S

Celebrated League Mask, $2

We have a large line of Fishing Tackle, Croquet, Lawn Tennis, Roller Skates, Hammocks, Playing Cards, Pocket Cutlery, Foot Balls, Boxing Gloves, Fencing Foils and Kennel Supplies.

home runs—exactly the same number hit by Williams.

SWITCHING SOX

The Chicago White Sox changed their uniform styles 57 times between 1901 and the early 1990s.

LOST BALLS

A 1994 study by STATS, Inc. revealed that 27 baseballs are hit into the stands during an average game.

BARRY'S BAT

When Barry Bonds hit a record 73 home runs in 2001, his weapon of choice was a 34-inch, 32-ounce Rideau Crusher with a red handle and a black barrel. Made of maple, the Bonds bat was crafted by Canadian carpenter Sam Holman, who emblazoned it with "SAM Bat" and the logo of a flying bat.

HOW CONLAN GOT THE JOB

Jocko Conlan, a so-so outfielder in two seasons with the White Sox in the 1930s, became an umpire by accident. Emmett Ormsby, one of the regular umpires, was overcome by heat one afternoon and Conlan, out of the lineup with a broken finger, was drafted into service. Though he was wearing his Chicago uniform, he called teammate Luke Appling out on a close play at third. The next year, American League President William Harridge got Conlan a job as a minor league ump.

TOUGH CALL

Umpire Bill Summers couldn't help being himself on a

Hollywood movie set. He got into his crouch to watch the pitch and called, "Strike one!" The director stopped the shooting and said, "Bill, that was supposed to be ball one." The arbiter answered, "Tell the pitcher that. I call 'em as I see 'em."

HIDDEN UMPIRE
No one appreciates the umpires. Few people remember that Lou Jorda was behind the plate when Bobby Thomson hit his "shot heard 'round the world" in 1951. Even fewer recall the name of the home-plate umpire when Hank Aaron hit his 715th home run. Longtime NL arbiter Doug Harvey had a theory on the anonymous role of the umpire: "When I was right," he said, "no one remembered. When I was wrong, no one forgot."

THANKLESS JOB
National League umpire Paul Pryor knew he had a thankless job. "I spoke at a banquet in Chicago and after it was over a sportswriter stood up and said he never heard of me," Pryor said. "I told him it was a compliment. Nobody likes the umpire. If your team wins, the umpire did a good job. If it loses, the umpire beat you."

SPITBALL OR SINKER?
Dodgers first baseman Norm Larker complained to umpire Frank Secory that Milwaukee pitcher Lew Burdette was throwing spitballs in a game in the early 1960s. Secory replied that they were sinkers. Larker responded, "Oh, yeah? One of them sinkers just splashed me in the right eye."

FIRST BLACK UMP
Emmett Ashford made his major league debut as the first black umpire at Washington's RFK Stadium in 1966. But it almost didn't happen. With Vice President Hubert Humphrey coming to the game, security was heavy, and stadium personnel didn't believe Ashford was an umpire. "There are no black umpires," he was told.

"There will be—if you let me into the park," the diminutive arbiter responded.

An 11-year veteran of the Pacific Coast League, the 5'7" Ashford advanced when Joe Cronin, then AL president, purchased his contract. He stayed five years, concluding with the 1970 World Series.

WEAVER'S WEB
Ron Luciano tossed Baltimore manager Earl Weaver out of so many games that he was pulled from officiating Orioles games for a year. In his first game back, he threw Weaver out again.

WEIGHT WOES
Concerned that overweight umpires might suffer physical problems, Major League Baseball provided the World Umpires Association with a medical and fitness support program in 1999. Rocky Roe, one of nearly two dozen participants who worked with trainers Mark Letendre and Mackie Shilstone, lost 34 pounds in less than three months.

ANY GAME
Although umpires may now be assigned to any game in the majors, that was not always the case. During the days when each of the two leagues had its own cadre of umps, NL arbiters were not required to run out to the outfield for a better look at foul lines, foul poles, yellow home-run stripes, and outfielders making shoestring catches. That changed with the merger.

NEXT GENERATION
Three umpires' sons officiated in the Oakland-Boston game on April 15, 2000. Jerry Crawford, Mike DiMuro, and Brian Gorman are the sons of Shag Crawford, Lou DiMuro, and Tom Gorman.

WOLF IN UMP'S CLOTHING
Philadelphia pitcher Randy Wolf is the brother of major league umpire Jim Wolf. The latter is not allowed to umpire behind home plate on nights his brother pitches.

UMPS STRIKE OUT
Calls that umpires botched in the 2005 postseason:

- ALCS, Game 2, Angels at White Sox. With the score 1–1, two outs, and the bases empty in the bottom of the ninth, A.J. Pierzynski takes a called strike three. But home-plate umpire Doug Eddings decides the ball bounced in the dirt before Josh Paul caught it—making it necessary for the catcher to complete the putout by throwing to first base. Because Eddings fails to signal his ruling, Pierzynski reaches first safely. Pinch runner Pable Ozuna then scores the

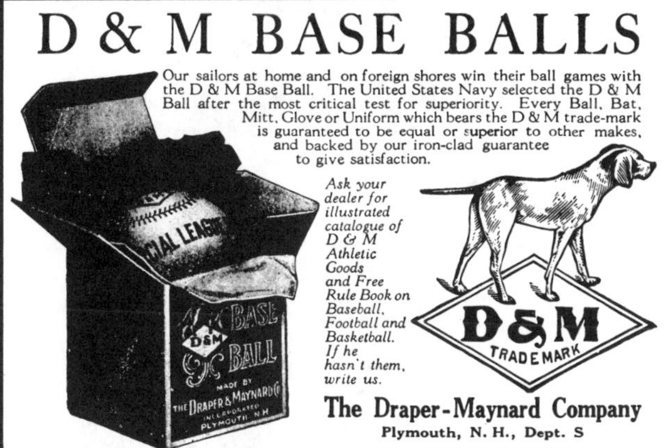

winning run on Joe Crede's double.

- ALCS, Game 4, White Sox at Angels. Nursing a 3–1 lead in the bottom of the second, the Sox get Steve Finley to hit a double-play grounder. As he runs, Finley tells home-plate ump Ron Kulpa that his bat hit Pierzynski's mitt. After the game, an 8–2 Sox win, the catcher admits Finley was right and interference should have been called.
- World Series, Game 2, Astros at White Sox. With two outs, two men on, and Houston ahead 4–2 in the bottom of the seventh, umpire Jeff Nelson waves Jermaine Dye to first base after an inside pitch from Dan Wheeler. The ball did strike something, but it was the bat, not the player. The ump didn't see it, setting the stage for Paul Konerko's grand slam. Chicago won, 7–6.

FRONTIER DAYS

The Denver Base Ball and Athletic Club, a member of the three-team Rocky Mountain League, wore red-and-gold uniforms with belts and neckties when it began play in 1885. The team played in a $900 ballpark near the present site of Coors Field and sold season tickets for $5.

SEEING GREEN

Buffalo of the Eastern League (now the International

Old uniforms on display at the Baseball Hall of Fame. Laura Gaynor

League) wore green uniforms in 1893, 75 years before Charlie Finley dressed his Kansas City Athletics in green and gold. The *Buffalo Courier* of July 29, 1893, reported that the team would wear white uniforms at home and green on the road.

PINSTRIPED POWER

Pinstripes first appeared on Yankees uniforms on April 22, 1915.

THE FIRST BLIMPIE

Balls that drop 800 feet pick up plenty of speed. Minor league catcher Joe Sprintz learned that lesson in 1939, when he broke his jaw and lost several teeth trying to catch a ball dropped from a blimp in San Francisco. And that's *without* an earthquake!

Using His Head

Negro Leaguer Willie Wells wore baseball's first pseudohelmet—a construction worker's hardhat—after he was hit in the head by a pitch in 1942.

First Helmet

Credit a traveling secretary with inventing the type of batting helmet used today. Longtime Pirates employee Charlie Muse, working with two other designers, developed the forerunner of the modern helmet in 1952 at the urging of Pittsburgh general manager Branch Rickey.

Strike Zone 'Unis

Innovative owner Bob Howsam outfitted the minor league Denver Bears in "strike zone uniforms" in 1952. The suits were white only between the knees and the chest.

Oversized Mitt

The oversized catcher's mitt, designed by Baltimore manager Paul Richards for Hoyt Wilhelm's knuckleball, lasted four years before baseball banned it. Clint Courtney was the first to wear the oversized mitt, which had a diameter of 44 inches, on May 27, 1960.

Fancy Footwear

Cleveland once protested a game because it didn't like its opponent's shoes. It happened on Opening Day 1967, when the Kansas City Athletics introduced new white shoes—the brainchild of owner Charlie Finley. After A's starter Jim Nash made his first pitch to Vic Davalillo, Indians manager Joe Adcock announced he was playing the game under protest. AL president Joe Cronin disagreed, allowing the footwear that became a staple of the A's uniform after they moved to Oakland a year later.

Daily Grind

Pitchers knew when Ted Williams was in the on-deck circle. The Red Sox slugger treated his bats with a mixture of olive oil and resin, grinding the ingredients into his bat with a dry cloth while awaiting his turn at bat. The grinding sound made a screeching noise pitchers could hear.

HOT BAT
Ted Williams once asked Mark McGwire if he smelled burnt wood when fouling a ball off.

LEFTY CATCHERS
Although catchers who throw left-handed are extremely rare, three who succeeded in the majors were Dale Long (1958), Mike Squires (1980), and Benny DiStefano (1989). One reason for the dearth of left-handed catchers: a scarcity of left-handed catcher's mitts.

KEEPING COUNT
The New Era company provides big-league teams with 2,000 hats per season.

FASHION PLATE
Yankees closer John Wetteland, a true creature of habit, wore only one hat during the 1996 season. When new hats were distributed for the World Series, he wouldn't relinquish the old one—forcing the team to stitch on a patch bearing the Series logo.

BABE'S BONNET
Yankees pitcher David Wells once took the mound wearing a cap worth $35,000. An ardent fan of Babe Ruth, Wells purchased the 1934 hat intending to wear it in a game. The idea was short-lived, as manager Joe Torre made Wells switch to a 1997-style hat after one inning. The pitcher proceeded to blow a 3–0 lead and the game.

WALKING BILLBOARDS
The Mets and Cubs were the first major league teams to wear advertising on their uniforms when they opened the 2000 season in Tokyo.

SPELLING BEE
In his April 12, 2004, start against St. Louis, Reds pitcher Aaron Harang wore a jersey that read "Cncinnati." According to equipment manager Rick Stowe, "The clubhouse guy from Arizona called me and said, 'What kindergarten did you fail?' I always check the back of the jerseys for the players' names but never thought about the front."

TOUGH HANDS
Not all modern players wear batting gloves. One of them, 2005 American League MVP Vladimir Guerrero, said he toughened his hands from pulling ropes tied to cows when he was growing up in the Dominican Republic.

Baseball Hall of Fame

The Hall of Fame's uniform display contains 60 outfits, from heavy wool flannels to modern double knits. The exhibit includes uniforms from the St. Louis Browns, the Washington Senators, the Seattle Pilots, and other defunct teams, plus the green suits worn by the Cincinnati Reds on St. Patrick's Day, satin uniforms worn by the Boston Braves for better visibility at night, and short pants tried by the Chicago White Sox.

Marc Okkonen

SPANISH UNIFORMS

The San Francisco Giants wore uniforms that read "Gigantes" on May 21, 2005, Juan Marichal Day at AT&T Park. The Spanish-language unis were later auctioned off.

TOUGH DRESS CODE

Three teams—the Mets, Astros, and Rockies—used five different uniform styles in 2005. Only seven clubs had the traditional two sets, meaning 20 additional teams wore multiple variations.

COOLER HEADS

The Coolflo batting helmets introduced in 2006 are lighter and cooler, thanks to air vents on both sides.

WHERE BIGS GET BALLS

Though China produces more than 80 percent of the baseballs used on the planet, all of those used in the major leagues are made in a Rawlings factory in Costa Rica. Pros sew 4–6 balls per hour, putting 108 stitches in each one.

ALL ABOUT BALLS

Major league teams use about 181,000 balls, weighing 29 tons, per year. (If the balls were transported in an 18-wheeler, there would still be room for a few bats and gloves.) Because the average ball stays in play for only five pitches, the typical game consumes 80 balls. Eighteen are scuffed or tossed by the ump but later used for BP. Sixty are fouled into the stands, mostly behind home or down the left-field line. Two are hit for home runs.

DISTANCE FACTORS

- Wind speed and direction
- Relative humidity
- Temperature (balls carry better in heat)
- Altitude (balls fly farther in thin air)
- Pitch speed

WHERE BALLS ARE MADE

- Cork centers: Batesville, Mississippi
- Cowhide covers: Tullahoma, Tennessee
- Yarn windings: Dolgeville, New York
- Balls assembled: Dolgeville, New York
- Samples tested: Springfield, Missouri

WEAPONS OF CHOICE

Teams routinely order about 12 dozen bats per player.

THE SIGNING DUTCHMAN
Honus Wagner was the first player whose signature appeared on a baseball bat.

BAT FACTS
Babe Ruth swung the heaviest bat (54 ounces), Al Simmons swung the longest (38 inches), and Wee Willie Keeler swung the shortest (30½ inches).

WORLD'S BIGGEST BAT
The 68,000-pound bat outside the Louisville Slugger Museum is the world's largest. The steel bat stands 120 feet tall.

BAT MUSEUM
The Louisville Slugger Museum and Visitors Center, opened in 1996, drew 400,000 people during its first two years.

THE BAT BUSINESS
Hillerich & Bradsby produces a million bats a year, including custom-made bats for more than 300 major leaguers. The Louisville-based firm, which owns 5,000 acres of timberland in New York and Pennsylvania, requires some 40,000 trees per season for its bat-making operation.

Many of baseball's superstitions and traditions involve numerology. Three of the most noted retired numbers were the single digits worn by Brooks Robinson (No. 5) of the Baltimore Orioles, Stan Musial (No. 6) of the St. Louis Cardinals, and Mickey Mantle (No. 7) of the New York Yankees.

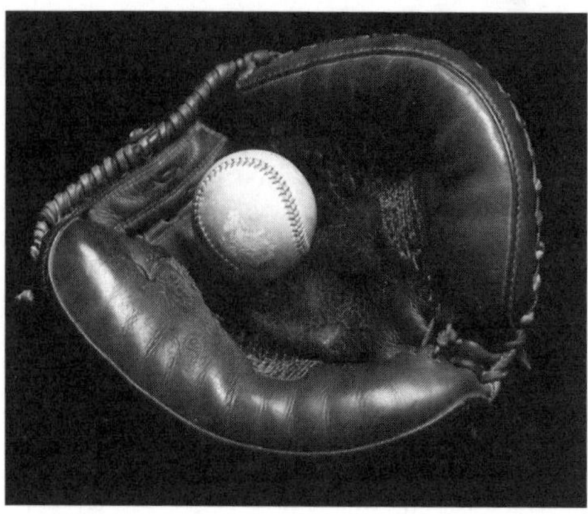

Yogi Berra's catcher's mitt and game-used ball from Don Larsen's perfect game in the 1956 World Series.
National Baseball Hall of Fame Library, Cooperstown, New York

MAPLE MAN
Joe Carter was the first player to use a bat made out of maple.

MAPLE MAGNET
The 73-homer season by Barry Bonds in 2001 convinced other players to switch to maple bats. The wood now accounts for 55 percent of the Louisville Sluggers ordered by big leaguers.

WAGON TONGUE
The 46-ounce Louisville Slugger used by Babe Ruth to hit the first homer in Yankee Stadium was sold in December 2004 for $1.26 million, the most ever paid for a baseball bat.

WHY THOMAS WEARS NO. 35
Two-time AL MVP Frank Thomas wore No. 35 with the White Sox because he wore No. 3 as a high school football player and No. 5 as a schoolboy baseball player.

MATTINGLY FAN
Texas slugger Mark Teixeira wears No. 23 to salute Don Mattingly, his schoolboy hero. Teixeira brazenly wore a Mattingly jersey to Orioles games when he was growing up in Baltimore.

SALUTE TO A MANAGER
Bob Melvin, who managed the 2006 Arizona Diamondbacks, wore No. 3 to honor Houston Astros manager Phil Garner. As the Milwaukee manager in the 1990s, Garner helped Melvin land a job as a scout, his first position after retiring as an active player.

CHAPTER 4
ON THE FIELD

BROOKS ROBINSON REMEMBERS...

The best thing that ever happened to me was signing for the minimum $4,000 and going to York, Pennsylvania, in the Class B Piedmont League to play with players of my own speed.

Paul Richards was the Orioles manager when I signed my first major league contract. He was just full of knowledge about the game. To me, he was ahead of his time. He knew every position and what made every position click. Paul had a way of taking pitchers who were over the hill, getting them back on track, and getting a lot of mileage out of them. He really put together our team. We signed a lot of young guys and gave away a lot of money.

Paul put together the White Sox team that reached the 1959 World Series and then came over to the Orioles. Our 1960 team gave the Yankees a run for their money. In '62 Billy Hitchcock came in and did a nice job for a couple of years. Then Hank Bauer came in 1964 and we almost won. He played the same team every day, but if you got into Hank's doghouse, you might not come out for a couple of weeks.

We struggled in 1965, but in '66 Frank Robinson came over and was one of three guys with 100 RBIs. That put us over the hump. We won by nine or 10 games and got into the World Series. But we didn't play well in '67 and Harry Dalton, the general manager, hired Earl Weaver. He never wanted to do anything in his life except be a big-league ballplayer. Even though he was a terrific player in the minor leagues, he didn't have enough talent. But he became a manager and worked his way up through the minors. Earl took over at the All-Star Game in '68 and we won the pennant in 1969, 1970, and 1971. It was a good run, even though we lost two of those three World Series.

I never thought a whole lot about becoming a manager; I was too consumed with playing. During my last year, though, I got calls from the White Sox and Rangers asking if I would be interested in managing. I told them I never thought about it, but they wanted to know within a couple of days. I discussed it with my wife, Connie, but we decided to wait and see what would happen.

I thought I might want to become a college baseball coach. I went down to Lafayette, Louisiana, where a friend of mine was the athletics director. I would be his assistant as well as the baseball coach. I had six months to make up my mind. Then my friend had a run-in with the school's chancellor and got fired. So I didn't have to worry about it after that.

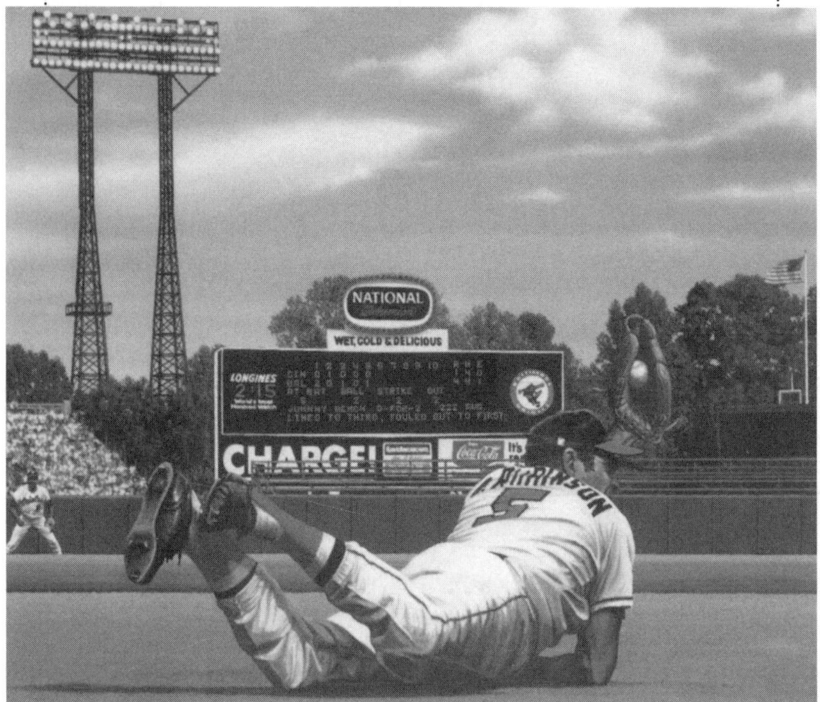

In one of several defensive gems that made him 1970 World Series MVP, Baltimore third baseman Brooks Robinson snares a Game 3 liner hit by Cincinnati's Johnny Bench.

Triple Crown Winners

Player	Year	HR	RBI	Pct.
Carl Yastrzemski	1967	44	121	.326
Frank Robinson	1966	49	122	.316
Mickey Mantle	1956	52	130	.353
Ted Williams	1947	32	114	.343
Ted Williams	1942	36	137	.356
Joe Medwick	1937	31	154	.374
Lou Gehrig	1934	49	165	.363
Jimmie Foxx	1933	48	163	.356
Chuck Klein	1933	28	120	.368
Rogers Hornsby	1925	39	143	.403
Rogers Hornsby	1922	42	152	.401
Henry Zimmerman	1912	14	98	.372
Ty Cobb	1909	9	115	.377
Napoleon Lajoie	1901	14	125	.422
Hugh Duffy	1894	18	145	.438
Tip O'Neil	1887	14	123	.442

Which O'Rourke?

Of the two O'Rourkes who starred in the pre-1900 National League, James Henry won the nickname "Orator" while Timothy Patrick was called "Voiceless."

Casey's Sparrow

Traded to Pittsburgh in 1918 after six years in Brooklyn, Casey Stengel was booed his first time up. In the outfield, he noticed a sparrow had caught itself on the fence. Seizing the opportunity, he tucked the bird under his cap. When he came up again, the crowd again booed, as expected. Stengel called time, stepped back, and gave a sweeping bow, allowing the bird to escape.

No-Whiff Kid

When Joe Sewell fanned three times during the 1930 season,

two of the three came in the same game.

BAD TIMING

Jim Tabor of the Red Sox was overlooked when he hit two grand slams in one game because he chose the same date as Lou Gehrig's famous "Luckiest Man" farewell speech: July 4, 1939.

FIELDING FLAW

Boston Bees catcher Al Lopez, later a highly successful manager, caught more than he bargained for after flubbing a foul pop during a 1939 game: an angry fan jumped out of the stands and assaulted him.

DIZZY FEELING

Cleveland catcher Rollie Hemsley was struck on the head by a thrown ball during an attempted steal of second base. Trainer Lefty Weiseman suggested he leave the game. "No way," said Hemsley. "I've started games when I've been dizzier than this!"

JIM'S JACKS

Jim Tobin of the Boston Braves was the only pitcher to hit three home runs in a game during the modern era that began in 1901. The knuckleballer turned the trick in 1942, two years before he threw two no-hitters in the same season.

BIG BAT IN BUSH LEAGUES

Joe Hauser was the only minor leaguer to have two 60-homer seasons, in 1930 and 1933.

TWO FOR ONE

No pitcher had ever thrown two no-hitters in the same season before Cincinnati's Johnny Vander Meer did it in consecutive starts during the 1938 campaign.

ONE-ARMED OUTFIELDER

Pete Gray, who reached the majors with the St. Louis Browns during wartime manpower shortages, was right-handed until he slipped while riding on the running board of a truck and his arm got caught in one of the wheels. He learned to use his left hand and continued to play ball, using a custom glove a cobbler made. He held the glove loosely on his fingertips, then discarded it quickly to field a soft fly ball with his bare hand or slide his hand fully into the fingers to catch a fly ball or line drive.

Fast Fade

"I'm throwing the ball twice as hard but it's getting there half as fast."

—Lefty Gomez

HARDLY SHAVING

Carl Scheib of the Philadelphia A's broke into the bigs in 1943 at the ripe old age of 16, making him the youngest player in American League history.

YOUTH IS SERVED

On August 20, 1945, Tommy Brown of the Brooklyn Dodgers became the youngest big leaguer to hit a home run. At 17 years, eight months, and 14 days of age, he connected against Pittsburgh's Preacher Roe.

THE MAGIC OF MIZE

Johnny Mize was the only man to finish with more home runs than strikeouts during a 50-homer season. It happened in 1947, when he had 51 home runs and 42 strikeouts.

NOT SO FUNNY

Dom DiMaggio and Sam Mele were Red Sox roommates in

Ed Walsh, who won 195 games during a 14-year career spent mainly with the White Sox, talks pitching with his son Ed Walsh Jr., who lasted four years with the Sox, from 1928 to 1932. Dad, a one-time 40-game winner who posted a record 1.82 ERA for his career, was unable to pass on his pitching talent. Chicago White Sox

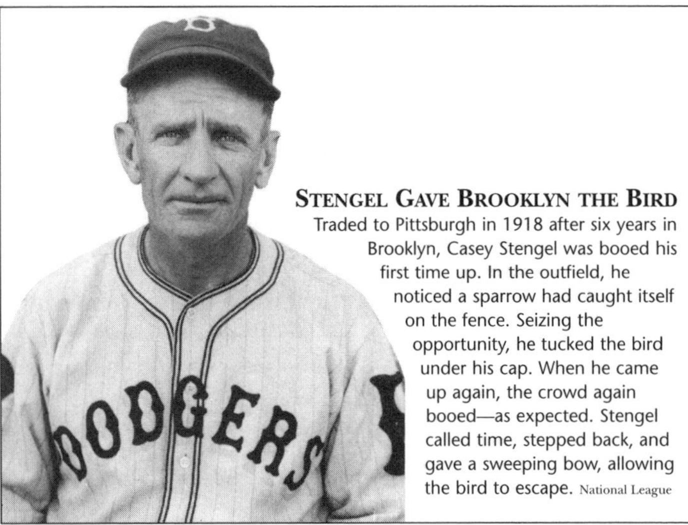

STENGEL GAVE BROOKLYN THE BIRD
Traded to Pittsburgh in 1918 after six years in Brooklyn, Casey Stengel was booed his first time up. In the outfield, he noticed a sparrow had caught itself on the fence. Seizing the opportunity, he tucked the bird under his cap. When he came up again, the crowd again booed—as expected. Stengel called time, stepped back, and gave a sweeping bow, allowing the bird to escape. National League

1947. One night in May, DiMaggio crawled into bed only to see it collapse beneath his weight. Mele laughed so heartily that he aggravated an old sacroiliac condition, forcing him to leave the next day's game in the third inning.

DOUBLE TROUBLE
Al Benton was the only pitcher to face Babe Ruth and Mickey Mantle in regular-season American League competition.

SHORT TIMER
Bobby Shantz was the shortest man ever to win an MVP award. The 5'4" southpaw won it in 1952, when he went 24–7 for the Philadelphia Athletics.

BAD BIRTHDAY
Vada Pinson fell victim to the hidden-ball trick on his birthday, August 11, 1959. The trick was executed by Milwaukee Braves first baseman Joe Adcock, known more for his batting power than his fielding prowess.

HE'S NOT CRAZY
Jimmy Piersall once hid behind the monuments in Yankee Stadium's center field when Angels pitcher Ted Bowsfield was getting shelled. Jimmy told manager Bill Rigney he had

nine children to feed and didn't want to get hurt.

PRANKSTERS, INC.
The Los Angeles Angels assigned Jimmy Piersall and Jay Johnstone to the same room. Manager Bill Rigney, explaining his reasoning, said he didn't want to screw up *two* rooms.

NOT LIKE FATHER
Tom Tresh, 1962 AL Rookie of the Year, outhomered his dad, Mike, 139–2, and also owned a big bulge in the RBI column. But they had identical .249 lifetime batting averages.

JUST A KID
Vida Blue was the youngest man to win an MVP award. He was 22 years old when he won the American League's award while pitching for the 1971 Oakland A's. He was also the last switch-hitter to win the American League MVP award.

CO-MVPS
The National League had a pair of Most Valuable Players in 1979, when Keith Hernandez of the Cardinals and Willie Stargell of the Pirates deadlocked for first place in the annual voting. It was the only tie in the history of the award, given since 1931.

CELLAR-DWELLING STARS
Most Valuable Player awards usually go to players who helped propel their teams to pennants. But not always. Andre Dawson of the 1987 Chicago Cubs and Alex Rodriguez of the 2003 Texas Rangers won MVP awards after their clubs finished last.

MVPS ANYWHERE
Robin Yount of the Milwaukee Brewers won the American League's MVP award as a shortstop in 1982 and as a center fielder in 1989. Others who won awards at different

Ronnie Joyner

positions were Stan Musial, a three-time winner, who won as a first baseman and an outfielder, and Hank Greenberg, who won as a left fielder after vacating first base, his original position, for Rudy York.

Close Race

Had either of the two Seattle voters placed him on their 1996 AL Most Valuable Player ballots, Seattle shortstop Alex Rodriguez would have beaten out Texas outfielder Juan Gonzalez. But Bob Finnigan and Jim Street placed Rodriguez third and fourth, respectively, allowing Gonzalez to win, 290–287, tying the three-point margin of Roger Maris over Mickey Mantle in 1960. The only closer vote had come in 1947, when Joe DiMaggio beat Ted Williams, 202–201.

MVP Debate

Though Pedro Martinez won All-Star MVP honors and the AL's Cy Young Award for 1999, he lost the MVP race because two writers refused to list him among their Top 10 choices. Had either George King of the *New York Post* or La Velle E. Neal III of the *Minneapolis Star* cast a first-place vote for the Red Sox star, or even placed him fourth or higher, Martinez would have won. Although he had more first-place votes than winner Ivan Rodriguez, Martinez missed becoming the fourth AL starter to win both the MVP and the Cy Young in the same season.

Tight Race

David Ortiz of the Red Sox and Alex Rodriguez of the Yankees staged a season-long battle for the 2005 American League MVP award. Although A-Rod won, presumably because he's a position player rather than a DH, a case could have been made for Ortiz. Here are the numbers:

Player	HR	RBI	BA
David Ortiz	47	148	.300
Alex Rodriguez	48	130	.321

JUAN SHORTED

With six 20-win seasons and 243 victories during a Hall of Fame career that stretched from 1960 to 1975, Juan Marichal should have been an annual contender for the Cy Young Award. But he never received a vote because of stiff competition. Here's why:

		W	L	ERA
1963	Marichal	25	8	2.41
	Sandy Koufax	25	5	1.88
1964	Marichal	21	8	2.48
	Dean Chance	25	5	1.88
1965	Marichal	22	13	2.13
	Sandy Koufax	26	8	2.04
1966	Marichal	25	6	2.23
	Sandy Koufax	27	9	1.73
1968	Marichal	26	9	2.43
	Bob Gibson	22	9	1.12
1969	Marichal	21	11	2.10
	Tom Seaver	25	7	2.21

SANDY'S SOJOURN

Sandy Koufax was the only man to win a Cy Young Award in his last season. He went 27–9 with 27 complete games, 317 strikeouts, and a 1.73 ERA in 1966 before arthritis forced him to retire at age 30. In his final five years, the Dodgers lefty went 111–34, won five straight ERA crowns, and pitched four no-hitters.

ON HIS MARK

Mark Fidrych made only $16,500 as a rookie for the 1976 Detroit Tigers but made the most of the experience. En route to the American League's Rookie of the Year award, he won 19 games, posted the league's best ERA, and started the All-Star Game. He even finished second in the voting for the annual Cy Young Award. Fidrych, felled by arm

Ripley's Believe It or Not!
BABE
RUTH
WON
MORE PRIZES
PLAYING
GOLF
THAN HE DID
PLAYING
BASEBALL

trouble as a sophomore, completed 33 of his first 43 starts.

FERNANDOMANIA

Fernando Valenzuela was the only player to win Rookie of the Year and Cy Young honors in the same season (1981).

BEST ROOKIES

The best rookies of all time performed before the Rookie of the Year award was first given in 1947. Grover Cleveland Alexander had a 28–13 record and 2.57 ERA in 1911; Shoeless Joe Jackson hit .408 with 233 hits the same year; Lloyd Waner had more hits (223) and runs (133) than any other rookie in 1927; and Ted Williams set rookie records for RBIs (145) and walks (107) in 1939.

ELUSIVE CROWNS

Stan Musial never won a home-run crown, and Willie Mays never led in runs batted in.

MCGWIRE'S MARKS

Mark McGwire hit more home runs than any other rookie, 49 in 1987, and later became the first man to hit 70 homers in a season. His record lasted three seasons.

ELITE GROUP

Hank Aaron, Willie Mays, Eddie Murray, and Rafael Palmeiro are the only players with 3,000 hits and 500 homers.

GOPHERS IN THE PARK

Sluggers like to park the ball against Chan Ho Park. In fact,

HOME-RUN KINGS

Baseball's single-season home-run leaders during the modern era that began in 1901:

Year	Record Holder	Team	Homers
1901	Sam Crawford	Reds	16
1911	Frank Schulte	Cubs	21
1915	Gavvy Cravath	Phillies	24
1919	Babe Ruth	Red Sox	29
1920	Babe Ruth	Yankees	54
1921	Babe Ruth	Yankees	59
1927	Babe Ruth	Yankees	60
1961	Roger Maris	Yankees	61
1998	Mark McGwire	Cardinals	70
2001	Barry Bonds	Giants	73

he tends to throw gopher balls that will live in history. Park was the pitcher when Barry Bonds broke Mark McGwire's record with number 71, when Bonds hit number 72, when Cal Ripken Jr. hit one in his All-Star finale, and when Fernando Tatis became the only player to hit two grand slams in the same inning!

EARLY IRON

Surprise, surprise. Cal Ripken Jr., who later became baseball's all-time Iron Man by playing in 2,632 consecutive games, played all 33 innings in the longest game in the history of professional baseball. Pawtucket beat Rochester, 3–2, in a 1981 game that also featured Hall of Famer Wade Boggs.

***THAT'S* DURABILITY**

While Cal Ripken Jr. was playing 2,632 games in a row, other players made 5,045 visits to the disabled list.

WHERE RICKEY RATES

Rickey Henderson was the ultimate leadoff man, ranking first in leadoff home runs (80),

DOUBLING UP
Players who hit into the most double plays:

Player	Number of Double Plays Hit Into
Cal Ripken Jr.	350
Hank Aaron	328
Carl Yastrzemski	323
Dave Winfield	319
Eddie Murray	316

stolen bases (1,403), walks (2,179), and runs scored (2,288). A disciplined hitter, he also reached base often enough (5,316 times) to rank third in that department.

NO WIZARD OF OZZIE
Being the identical twin brother of a baseball superstar doesn't always help. Ozzie Canseco, brother of slugger Jose, never hit a home run during a major league career that lasted only 24 games.

HUMBLE START
Calvin Griffith was a batboy for the 1924–25 Washington Senators, the team owned by his uncle and adoptive father Clark Griffith.

MY TURN
On July 5, 1935, Tony Cuccinello of the Brooklyn Dodgers and brother Al of the New York Giants became the first brothers on opposing teams to homer in the same game. Brooklyn won, 14–4.

THE ART OF SLUGGING
Art Shamsky pinch hit a home run for the Reds on August 12, 1966. He stayed in the game, homering again in both the eleventh and twelfth innings. He sat out the next day when a lefty started but was back a day later with a righty on the mound. In his first at-bat, Shamsky homered again—tying a big-league record with four consecutive home runs.

FORSCH NO-NOS
When Astro Ken Forsch pitched a no-hitter against Atlanta in April 1979, the Forsch family became the first to boast two brothers who had both pitched no-hitters. Brother Bob of the Cardinals had pitched a no-hit game in 1978.

HILL OF BENES
Brothers pitched for the same team in the same postseason game for the first time in 1996,

when Andy and Alan Benes worked for the St. Louis Cardinals versus the Atlanta Braves in Game 4 of the NLCS.

CENTURY CLUB
Mel and Todd Stottlemyre are the only father-and-son pitching tandem to both reach triple digits in victories.

REMEMBER THE ALOMAR
The San Diego Padres traded brothers Sandy Alomar Jr. and Roberto Alomar to American League teams in separate winter trades, in 1989 and 1990, respectively. In 1991 the Alomars became the first brothers to start the All-Star Game since Joe and Vince DiMaggio started for the American League in 1949.

30/30 FAMILY
Bobby and Barry Bonds, both slugging outfielders, are the only father-and-son tandem to hit 30 home runs and steal 30 bases in the same season. Barry tied Bobby's record when he did it for the fifth time in 1997. Barry and Bobby Bonds joined the same team for the first time in 1993 when the San Francisco Giants signed the son as a player and his dad as a batting coach.

A much-feared slugger who once won a Triple Crown, Jimmie Foxx had a 58-homer season en route to membership in the 500 Home Run Club. Ronnie Joyner

FATHERS AND SONS
Two father-and-son tandems have played for the same team at the same time: Ken Griffey and son Ken Jr. with the Seattle Mariners in 1999 and Tim Raines and son Tim Jr. with the Baltimore Orioles in 2001. All four were outfielders.

TRAGEDY IN MINORS
Minor leaguer Ottis Johnson was killed when hit by a pitch from Jack Clifton on June 2, 1951, more than 30 years after Ray Chapman became the only

Moe Berg...athlete, scholar, spy. American League

big leaguer to die from a HBP. Clifton went on to post a 22–6 record for Headland. Johnson had been hitting .393 with 10 homers for Dothan at the time of the incident in the Alabama-Florida League game.

SMALL BROWNIE

When the 3'7", 65-pound midget Eddie Gaedel batted for Bill Veeck's Browns on August 19, 1951, the nine-year-old St. Louis batboy was Bill DeWitt Jr., later the owner of the St. Louis Cardinals. DeWitt still owns the No. 1/8 jersey worn by Gaedel, who drew a four-pitch walk in his only at-bat.

WHY HADDIX WAS "KITTEN"

Pittsburgh lefty Harvey Haddix was nicknamed "the Kitten" because he was a disciple of Harry "the Cat" Breechen, a fellow southpaw who was his St. Louis Cardinals teammate in 1952.

PLAYING DOCTOR

After leaving the 1952 Pittsburgh Pirates, a bad ballclub for whom he hit .143 in 19 games, Johnny Berardino became a hit in Hollywood, playing *General Hospital*'s Dr. Steve Hardy for 34 years.

27 WHIFFS

Ron Necciai pitched in the major leagues for only two months, with the sad-sack Pittsburgh Pirates of 1952, and won only one game. But he'll always be remembered as the guy who struck out 27 men in a game in the minors. He did it for Pittsburgh's Bristol, Virginia, farm team in the Class D Appalachian League, also in 1952, against Welsh (West Virginia). Four men reached base (walk, hit-by-pitch, error, passed ball) but nobody got a hit. Necciai was 19 when he pitched the 27-strikeout game, 21 when he quit the game with a torn rotator cuff.

BOBO'S BEAUT

Bobo Holloman of the St. Louis Browns pitched the only complete game of his brief

U.S. Treasury Department

big-league career in his very first start. It was a no-hitter against the Philadelphia Athletics on May 6, 1953.

Good-Hitting Pitcher
Don Larsen collected seven straight hits for the St. Louis Browns in 1953. No pitcher had ever done that.

Unsung Phenom
The first pro ballplayer to hit at least 70 home runs in a season was Joe Bauman, a lefty-hitting first baseman. In 498 at-bats for Roswell, New Mexico, in the Class C Longhorn League in 1954, Bauman hit 72 home runs, knocked in 224 runs, and batted .400. Believing he was

Depletion of the ranks in the majors opened the gates for such handicapped players as one-armed Pete Gray.

Reprinted with permission, National Baseball Hall of Fame Library, Cooperstown, New York

helped by short fences, high altitude, and pitching depleted by military call-ups, big-league teams never came calling.

Too Good

Chuck Connors, who became a Hollywood star after his baseball career ended, was once sent to the minors for hitting a home run. Connors, then with the Cubs, was sent up to pinch hit with two men on and the team trailing by two runs. The count went to 3–1 and everyone, including Giants pitcher Sal Maglie, expected him to take the next pitch. Maglie threw one down the middle and Connors, seeking to cross up the logical strategy, slammed it over the right-field fence to put Chicago ahead. But manager Phil Cavarretta was steaming—Connors had ignored the "take" sign from the third-base coach. "Don't holler," Connors told the manager when he returned to the dugout. "I know you're mad and I'm probably on my way to the minor leagues." Connors was right. The next day, the Cubs shipped him out.

Hitter Too

Relief pitcher Dixie Howell homered twice while pitching 3⅔ relief innings in an 8–6 win for the Chicago White Sox against the Washington Senators in a doubleheader nightcap on June 16, 1957.

Polio Survivor

Vic Wertz, a slugging first baseman best known as the author of the World Series drive that Willie Mays turned into a game-saving catch, overcame the non-paralytic form of polio during his career.

Lew's Luck

Lew Burdette, who spent most of his career with the Braves,

not only went 5–0 against Sandy Koufax but won three of the games with home runs. The great Dodgers lefty called Burdette the toughest hitter he ever faced.

THE DIAMOND DOORMAN

Dodgers manager Walter Alston once heard Sandy Koufax and Larry Sherry sneaking in after curfew. The angry pilot pounded on

Ronnie Joyner

Sherry's door so vehemently that he cracked the diamonds in his 1955 World Series ring. The next morning Koufax kidded Sherry on the team bus. "Hey, Larry," he said, "had your door appraised for diamonds yet?"

WALKING MAN

Pat Kelly, a religious man who also happened to be a Baltimore outfielder, once had an exchange of words with fiery manager Earl Weaver. "Skip, don't you want me to walk with the Lord?" Kelly asked. Weaver's reply? "I'd rather you walk with the bases loaded."

Philadelphia A's southpaw Bobby Shantz, the 1952 AL MVP, proved good things come in small packages.
Ronnie Joyner

FOWL RESULT

Yankees coach Jim Hegan once told Mel Stottlemyre that avoiding the foul lines was a silly superstition. The pitcher agreed and stepped on one deliberately. He had immediate regrets: "The first batter was Ted Uhlaender. He hit a line drive off my left shin. It went for a hit. Rod Carew, Tony Oliva, and Harmon Killebrew followed with extra-base hits. The fifth man hit a single and scored and I was charged with five runs. I haven't stepped on a foul line since."

STEVE BLASS DISEASE

Steve Blass suffered a strange malady that struck him overnight. After leading the National League in winning percentage (.750) in 1968 and shutouts (five) in 1971, he went 2–0 in the 1971 World Series to give Pittsburgh an unexpected world title against Baltimore. Blass won a career-peak 19 games in 1972, when his ERA was a trim 2.49. Then disaster struck: his control disappeared. Unable to throw strikes, Blass had a 3–9 mark and a bloated 9.85 ERA in 1973, leading the league only in hit batsmen (12). Meditation, counseling, and changing deliveries didn't help, forcing Blass to quit after one horrendous outing in 1974 (seven walks and eight runs in five innings pitched).

Outfield Calamity
The outfield can be a dangerous place: Alfredo Edmead, a promising Pittsburgh farmhand, was killed in a collision with a teammate while chasing a fly ball in 1974.

Searing Memory
Future major leaguer Chris Reitsma, grounded by the pitching rubber, was on the mound when lightning killed the left fielder during an amateur game in Ancaster, Ontario. Every player except Reitsma was felled by the jolt.

Beware of Bat
Waiting in the on-deck circle can be hazardous to life and limb, as catcher Steve Yeager discovered in 1976. The Dodgers receiver was hurt when the jagged end of a broken bat struck him in the throat while he kneeled in the on-deck circle, awaiting his turn at bat.

New York Paranoia

"The first time I got into a bullpen cart in New York, they told me to lock the doors."
—Mike Flanagan

Redus the Raker
Gary Redus didn't do much during his five-team, 13-year career in the majors, but he did something in the minors no one will ever forget: he hit .462 for the Billings Mustangs in 1978.

Garber's Garbage
Gene Garber lost more games in a single season than any other relief pitcher. He went 6–16 for the Atlanta Braves in 1979.

Union Rejects
Not all big leaguers belong to the Major League Baseball Players Association. Kevin Millar and Damian Miller were among a handful of replacement players who cracked major league rosters after crossing picket lines during the 1994–95 strike.

Star's Sad Start
Yankees closer Mariano Rivera broke into the majors as a starter, losing his first game, 10–0, in 1995.

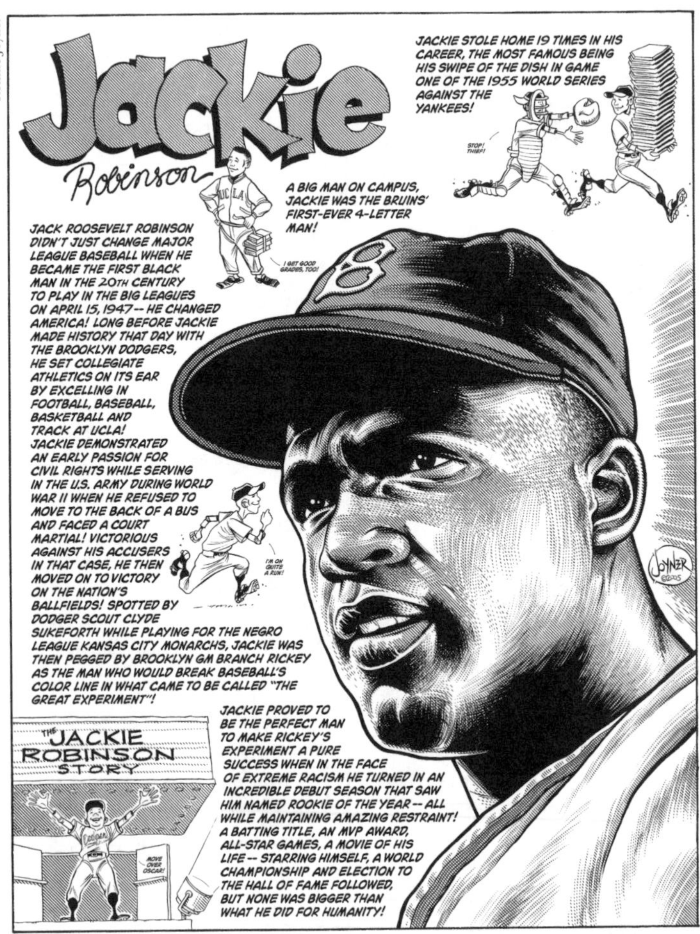

Jackie
Robinson
JACKIE STOLE HOME 19 TIMES IN HIS CAREER, THE MOST FAMOUS BEING HIS SWIPE OF THE DISH IN GAME ONE OF THE 1955 WORLD SERIES AGAINST THE YANKEES!
STOP! THIEF!
A BIG MAN ON CAMPUS, JACKIE WAS THE BRUINS' FIRST-EVER 4-LETTER MAN!
UCLA
I GET GOOD GRADES, TOO!
JACK ROOSEVELT ROBINSON DIDN'T JUST CHANGE MAJOR LEAGUE BASEBALL WHEN HE BECAME THE FIRST BLACK MAN IN THE 20TH CENTURY TO PLAY IN THE BIG LEAGUES ON APRIL 15, 1947-- HE CHANGED AMERICA! LONG BEFORE JACKIE MADE HISTORY THAT DAY WITH THE BROOKLYN DODGERS, HE SET COLLEGIATE ATHLETICS ON ITS EAR BY EXCELLING IN FOOTBALL, BASEBALL, BASKETBALL AND TRACK AT UCLA! JACKIE DEMONSTRATED AN EARLY PASSION FOR CIVIL RIGHTS WHILE SERVING IN THE U.S. ARMY DURING WORLD WAR II WHEN HE REFUSED TO MOVE TO THE BACK OF A BUS AND FACED A COURT MARTIAL! VICTORIOUS AGAINST HIS ACCUSERS IN THAT CASE, HE THEN MOVED ON TO VICTORY ON THE NATION'S BALLFIELDS! SPOTTED BY DODGER SCOUT CLYDE SUKEFORTH WHILE PLAYING FOR THE NEGRO LEAGUE KANSAS CITY MONARCHS, JACKIE WAS THEN PEGGED BY BROOKLYN GM BRANCH RICKEY AS THE MAN WHO WOULD BREAK BASEBALL'S COLOR LINE IN WHAT CAME TO BE CALLED "THE GREAT EXPERIMENT"!
I'M ON QUITE A RUN!
JOYNER ©2005
THE JACKIE ROBINSON STORY
MOVE OVER OSCAR!
JACKIE PROVED TO BE THE PERFECT MAN TO MAKE RICKEY'S EXPERIMENT A PURE SUCCESS WHEN IN THE FACE OF EXTREME RACISM HE TURNED IN AN INCREDIBLE DEBUT SEASON THAT SAW HIM NAMED ROOKIE OF THE YEAR -- ALL WHILE MAINTAINING AMAZING RESTRAINT! A BATTING TITLE, AN MVP AWARD, ALL-STAR GAMES, A MOVIE OF HIS LIFE -- STARRING HIMSELF, A WORLD CHAMPIONSHIP AND ELECTION TO THE HALL OF FAME FOLLOWED, BUT NONE WAS BIGGER THAN WHAT HE DID FOR HUMANITY!

Ronnie Joyner

SERIOUS BEANINGS

Although players have quick reflexes, not everyone is fast enough to flinch when a fastball targets the head. Baseball history is filled with such incidents. Among them:

- Ray Chapman, Cleveland shortstop, died after a pitch by submariner Carl Mays hit him in the head during a game in 1920.
- The career of Detroit player/manager Mickey

Cochrane ended in 1937 after he suffered a fractured skull from a pitched ball and lay unconscious for 10 days.

- Don Zimmer lay unconscious for 13 days after he was beaned in the minor leagues in 1953 but recovered in time to be beaned in the majors three years later.
- San Francisco slugger Jim Ray Hart was beaned twice as a rookie in 1963.
- Even after batting helmets became universal, Cubs slugger Ron Santo suffered a broken cheekbone in 1966—prompting the introduction of the helmet earflap.
- Tony Conigliaro, beaned by Jack Hamilton in 1967, missed six weeks that year and all of 1968. He returned to play well in 1969 and 1970 before his vision deteriorated as a result of the initial injury.
- Slugging shortstop Dickie Thon was never the same after Mike Torrez hit him in the face on April 8, 1984.
- Minnesota star Kirby Puckett suffered a broken upper jaw after a Dennis Martinez pitch hit him on September 28, 1995, causing him to miss the season's last week.

THE WOOD EXPRESS

During his fine 1998 rookie season, Cubs pitcher Kerry Wood struck out at least 13 men in a game five times—one more than Hall of Famer Nolan Ryan did in his first four seasons combined.

KENT'S CALAMITY

Jeff Kent was fined by the Giants for falling while riding a motorcycle—an activity prohibited by his contract. He originally claimed he suffered the injury while washing his truck.

SULKING AND SITTING

Although many players have been suspended for gambling or substance abuse, others have also been barred for bad behavior. They include:

- Bill Dickey, New York AL, 1932: punched opposing player, 30 days
- Len Randle, Texas, 1977: punched manager Frank Luchessi, 30 days
- Bill Madlock, Pittsburgh, 1980: smashed glove into umpire's face, 15 days

- Pete Rose, Cincinnati manager, 1988: shoved umpire, 30 days
- Roberto Alomar, Cleveland, 1996: spit at umpire, five games
- Juan Samuel, Detroit coach, 2000: threw punches during brawl, 15 games
- Frank Francisco, Texas, 2004: threw chair at fan, 15 games
- Kenny Rogers, Texas, 2005: shoved two cameramen, 20 games

STRAIGHT TO BIGS
Players who never set foot in the minors included Frankie Frisch, Bob Feller, Mel Ott, Ted Lyons, Ernie Banks, Al Kaline, Sandy Koufax, and Dave Winfield.

PREMATURE PASSINGS
Ten star players who died while still active in the majors:

- Darryl Kile, 33, St. Louis, coronary problems, June 22, 2002
- Thurman Munson, 32, NYY, plane crash, August 2, 1979
- Lyman Bostock, 27, California, shot by mistake, September 23, 1978
- Don Wilson, 29, Houston, carbon monoxide poisoning, January 5, 1975
- Roberto Clemente, 38, Pittsburgh, plane crash, December 31, 1972
- Ken Hubbs, 22, Chicago Cubs, plane crash, February 15, 1964
- Urban Shocker, 38, NYY, heart condition/pneumonia, September 9, 1928
- Ray Chapman, 29, Cleveland, hit in head by pitch, August 17, 1920
- Addie Joss, 31, Cleveland, tubercular meningitis, April 14, 1911
- Ed Delahanty, 35, Washington, drowned, July 9, 1903

BOBBY X BOBBY
During the 2000 season, the New York Mets had two pitchers named Bobby Jones. Bobby M. Jones, who threw left-handed, once took the roster spot of Bobby J. Jones, a righty.

FINLEY'S FOURPLAY
Chuck Finley fanned four men in an inning *three times.* No one else did it more than once.

GREAT NAME
The Atlanta Braves once had an outfield prospect named Wonderful Terrific Monds III. When his grandfather became

Future Hall of Famer Richie Ashburn eludes the tag of Dodgers catcher Rube Walker during a 1953 game at Ebbets Field. Ashburn led the National League with 14 triples that season. Copyright 1998 by Andy Jurinko. Reprinted with permission, Bill Goff, Inc./GoodSportsArt.com.

the first male child after 11 girls, his parents blurted, "Wonderful! Terrific!"

BROWN WALLBANGER

After landing on the disabled list six times in his first four years with the Dodgers, temperamental Yankees pitcher Kevin Brown found himself there again in 2004 after he punched a clubhouse wall in frustration.

UNSTEADY HELMS

During the 2004 season, Milwaukee infielder Wes Helms was waiting out a rain delay in San Juan when he went outside, slipped in the wet tunnel, and hurt his knee so badly that he needed surgery.

BUS CRASH

Pittsburgh utility man John Wehner once went on the disabled list with a shoulder injury incurred when John Vander Wal crashed into him *on the team bus.*

SUPER CYCLES

John Olerud and Bob Watson are the only men to hit for the cycle in both leagues.

BERT'S BURDEN
Bert Blyleven's bid for 300 wins was short-circuited by the fact that he often played for bad ballclubs. He won 287 times in 22 seasons but lost 74 games by one run and 41 more by two runs.

TERRIFIC TERRY
Terry Forster, a pitcher, has the highest lifetime batting average (.397) of anyone who played in at least 500 games in the big leagues.

MINOR LEAGUE FEATS
The following slugging feats from minor league annals never happened in the majors:

- Three homers in one inning (Gene Rye, 1930)
- Three grand slams in a game (John Cantley, 1914)
- Eight home runs in one game (Nig Clarke, 1902)
- Home run "cycle"—grand slam, three-run HR, two-run HR, and solo HR (Tyrone Horne, 1998)

FAMOUS FUTURE
Lou Piniella broke into pro ball in the Baltimore Orioles' farm system. At one of his minor league stops, in Aberdeen, South Dakota, the manager was Cal Ripken Sr. and the batboy was Cal Ripken Jr.

RAGGED NO-HITTER
Jim Maloney allowed a record 12 runners to reach base during a no-hitter. His 10-inning gem for the 1965 Reds over the Cubs included 10 walks, one hit batsmen, and one error.

TEEN IDOL
Tony Conigliaro hit more home runs as a teenager (24)

En route to Cooperstown, Jim Bunning pitched no-hitters in both leagues, including a 1964 perfect game on Father's Day—appropriate timing for the father of nine. Ronnie Joyner than any other player. A home-run king at 20, he took only two more years to become the youngest AL player with 100 home runs. But his bubble burst after a serious beaning by Jack Hamilton in 1967.

The Accidental Southpaw
Mickey Lolich, star pitcher for the 1968 world champion Detroit Tigers, threw left-handed because he broke his collarbone in a fall from his tricycle at age three. His doctor suggested the right-handed youngster try special exercises for the left hand.

Southpaws Succeed
Baseball has a higher percentage of lefties than the world at large. Since 1900, 27 percent of all pitchers have thrown left-handed, along with 14 percent of the position players (even though lefty throwers almost never play catcher, second base, shortstop, or third base).

"Tommy John Surgery"
Tommy John had more wins after elbow surgery (164) than before (124). Dr. Frank Jobe, who performed the pioneering operation that replaced a ligament in the pitcher's left elbow, dubbed all subsequent procedures "Tommy John surgery." A patient typically needs 12–18 months of recovery time.

Why Bother?
Since relief pitchers rarely bat, Jesse Orosco hadn't batted in nine years when he was officially disabled for pulling a muscle *during batting practice!*

Dewey Connects
Dwight Evans homered on the first pitch of the season on April 7, 1986. The Boston outfielder connected against Tigers ace Jack Morris.

Workhorse Pitchers
Pitchers who have worked at least 1,000 games in their careers:

Player	Games
Jesse Orosco	1,155
Dennis Eckersley	1,071
Hoyt Wilhelm	1,070
Kent Tekulve	1,050
Lee Smith	1,022
Goose Gossage	1,002

SURE BEATS MY RUSTY OL' '34 FORD!
Mickey Mantle
MICKEY, WHO HAILED FROM COMMERCE, OKLAHOMA, WAS KNOWN AS "THE COMMERCE COMET" BECAUSE OF HIS BLAZING SPEED!
THE BASEBALL LIFE OF MICKEY CHARLES MANTLE GOT OFF ON THE RIGHT FOOT WHEN HE WAS BORN ON OCTOBER 20, 1931 -- AND WAS THEN IMMEDIALTELY NAMED AFTER THE IMMORTAL MICKEY COCHRANE! MANTLE MADE HIS BIG LEAGUE DEBUT ON APRIL 17, 1951, AND THEN PROCEEDED TO RIDE HIS INCREDIBLE ABILITY AND BOYISH GOOD LOOKS TO ICONIC STATUS! WHILE MICKEY WAS AN EXCELLENT FIELDER WITH A STRONG AND ACCURATE ARM, IT WAS HIS AWESOME POWER AT THE PLATE THAT BECAME HIS CALLING CARD! BY 1956 MICKEY HAD ASSERTED HIMSELF AS THE GREATEST SWITCH-HITTER IN THE GAME'S HISTORY, ELECTRIFYING FANS WITH HIS TREMENDOUS BLASTS FROM BOTH SIDES OF THE PLATE! MICKEY'S POPULARITY HIT AN ALL-TIME HIGH WHEN HE TEAMED WITH ROGER MARIS IN 1961 TO MAKE THEIR LEGENDARY RUN AT BABE RUTH'S SINGLE SEASON HOME RUN MARK!
61
54
HO...
...HUM!
JOYNER ©2005
I LOVE MICKEY, I LOVE MICKEY!
ME, TOO!
MICKEY MADE THE BILLBOARD POP CHARTS IN 1956 WHEN HE PAIRED WITH TERESA BREWER ON HER HIT RECORD "I LOVE MICKEY"! THE SONG PEAKED ON SEPTEMBER 29, 1956, THE SAME DAY THAT MICKEY HIT HIS 52ND HOMER OF THE YEAR!
MICKEY'S ACHIEVEMENTS ARE NUMEROUS: 20 ALL-STAR APPEARANCES, 4 HOME RUN TITLES, 3 MVP AWARDS, A GOLD GLOVE, A TRIPLE CROWN, AND MUCH MORE! HE ALSO HELPED THE YANKEES WIN 12 PENNANTS AND 7 WORLD SERIES CHAMPIONSHIPS IN HIS FIRST 14 SEASONS! HE MADE THE MOST OF HIS WORLD SERIES APPEARANCES, TOO, ESTABLISHING MANY SERIES RECORDS, INCLUDING MOST HOME RUNS WITH 18! MICKEY RETIRED FOLLOWING THE 1968 SEASON, AND HIS TOTALS OF 536 ROUND-TRIPPERS, 2,415 HITS AND A .298 BATTING AVERAGE DEMANDED THAT HE BE A FIRST-BALLOT SELECTION TO THE HALL OF FAME IN 1974!

Ronnie Joyner

PIZZA VERSUS PEDALS

When he was a player, Angels manager Mike Scioscia had a weight problem. The Dodgers sent him to the Dominican Winter League not only with orders to lose weight but also with a stationary bike to help make it happen. Scioscia's teammate Mickey Hatcher heard noises coming from the catcher's apartment and peeked in. There was Scioscia, on the couch with a piece of pizza, while a hired Dominican kid was pumping away on the bike.

Four-Homer Games

Players who hit four home runs in one game:

American League

- Lou Gehrig, Yankees, June 3, 1932*
- Pat Seerey, White Sox, July 18, 1948, first game, 11 innings
- Rocky Colavito, Indians, June 10, 1959*
- Mike Cameron, Mariners, May 2, 2002*
- Carlos Delgado, Blue Jays, September 25, 2003*

National League

- Robert Lowe, Braves, May 30, 1894
- Ed Delahanty, Phillies, July 13, 1896
- Chuck Klein, Phillies, July 10, 1936, 10 innings
- Joe Adcock, Braves, July 31, 1954
- Willie Mays, Giants, April 30, 1961
- Mike Schmidt, Phillies, April 17, 1976, 10 innings*
- Bob Horner, Braves, July 6, 1986
- Mark Whiten, Cardinals, September 7, 1993, second game
- Shawn Green, Dodgers, May 23, 2002

* Four consecutive at-bats.

Pedro's First Pact

Superstar pitcher Pedro Martinez got $6,500 for signing his first pro contract.

Changing Stations

Cleveland teammates Kevin Mitchell and Chad Curtis tangled in the clubhouse after an argument about loud music.

Michael Jordan Plays Ball

Basketball superstar Michael Jordan quit the Chicago Bulls to spend a season in the minors with the Birmingham Barons, a Chicago White Sox affiliate. He had a bad year and returned to hoops.

Mighty Mariners

Mike Cameron and Bret Boone both homered twice in the first inning of a May 2, 2002, game. The Seattle tandem thus became the first teammates to hit two home runs apiece in the same inning. Seattle won

the game, 15–4, over the Chicago White Sox, and Cameron added two more home runs to tie another slugging record.

IN 1966,
SANDY KOUFAX
SET A NATIONAL LEAGUE RECORD BY PITCHING 323 INNINGS WITHOUT HITTING A SINGLE BATTER!
32
GRAZIANO

CENTURIES APART

Cy Young and Hideo Nomo are the only men to throw no-hitters in different centuries.

MOTOWN MISHAP

Catcher Brent Mayne, whose claim to fame was picking up a win as an emergency relief pitcher in an extra-inning game, once wrenched his back while walking through a Detroit parking lot. Turning to look for oncoming traffic, Mayne managed to hurt his back so severely that he wound up on the DL.

KNEE FOR NEWS

Eduardo Perez once missed the last game of the season because he injured his knee posing for the team picture.

BELLHORN SOUNDS

Homering from both sides of the plate in the same game is a rare feat, but Mark Bellhorn did it in the same inning—a National League record. It happened in the fourth inning of a 13–10 win against the Brewers on August 29, 2002.

MUSICAL OWNERS

Three teams changed ownership at the same time in 2002. Jeffrey Loria, owner of the Montreal Expos, purchased the Florida Marlins from John Henry, who then teamed with Tom Werner to buy the Boston Red Sox and Fenway Park for a record $660 million. Major League Baseball became the new owners of the Expos, buying the team from Loria for $120 million and promising to find it a new home. The team became the Washington Nationals in 2005.

THE RING-BEARERS

During their days as pitchers with the Oakland A's, Tim Hudson and Mark Mulder were pranksters without limits. They once applied fresh white paint to the perimeter of a white sunflower-seed bucket that pitching coach Rick Peterson had been using as a stool. They recoiled in hysteria when Peterson walked away with a white ring on the seat of his gray uniform pants.

BRAINIAC

Brainy backstop Brad Ausmus, a Dartmouth grad, never got a grade below a B.

NO SMALL FEAT

Aaron Small and Shawn Chacon, both second-half additions, gave the Yankees a combined 17 wins during the second half of the 2005 season but were gone before the second half of 2006. Small's career path went from small to big (10–0 in 2005) to small again (released in 2006 after going 0–3) as he sought to sign with the 24th different team of his professional career.

SLOW TROT

Tony Graffanino had a five-minute delay during a home-run trot for the Red Sox in 2005. Gabe Kapler, on base ahead of him, injured his heel while rounding second and had to be replaced by pinch runner Alejandro Machado before the play could be completed.

CEREAL KILLER

Coco Crisp's real name is Covelli, which his grandmother shortened to Co. His two siblings, who often shared Cocoa Krispies for breakfast, decided that little Covelli resembled the big-eared monkey on the box, so they called him Coco. The nickname stuck after the now-professional Crisp was asked to write his nickname on a questionnaire. The next thing he knew, it was posted on the scoreboard.

THE PITCHER'S WIFE

Casey Daigle's wife might be a better pitcher than he is. The journeyman right-hander, who reached the majors with the Arizona Diamondbacks, is married to Team USA softball star Jennie Finch.

Named after a President

Ted Lilly's full name is Theodore Roosevelt Lilly III. His great-grandfather rode with Teddy Roosevelt's Rough Riders around the turn of the 20th century.

Power Shortage

Fewer than half of the 16,200 players in major league history ever hit a home run.

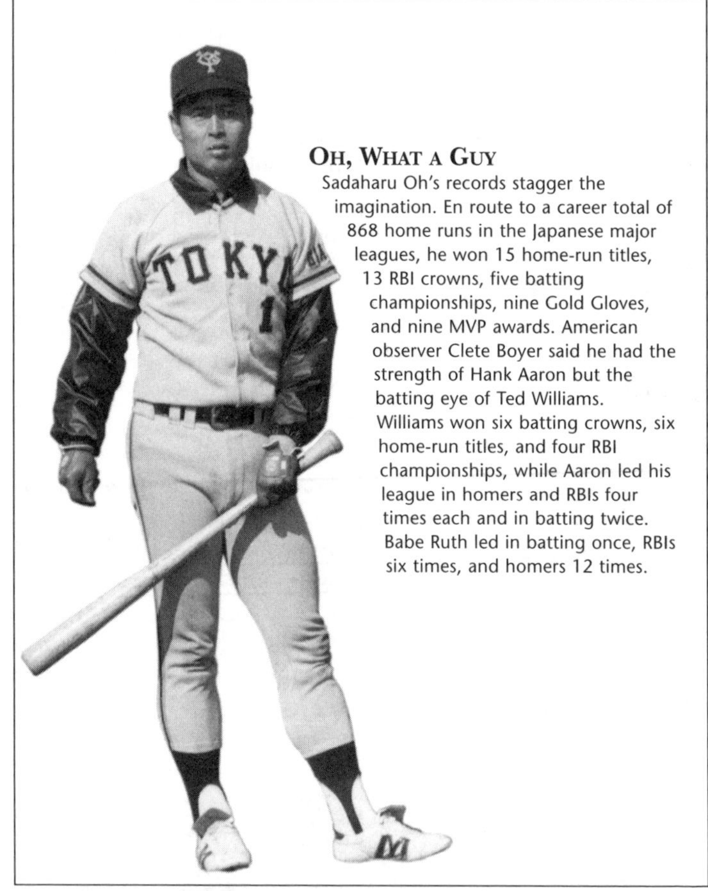

Oh, What a Guy

Sadaharu Oh's records stagger the imagination. En route to a career total of 868 home runs in the Japanese major leagues, he won 15 home-run titles, 13 RBI crowns, five batting championships, nine Gold Gloves, and nine MVP awards. American observer Clete Boyer said he had the strength of Hank Aaron but the batting eye of Ted Williams. Williams won six batting crowns, six home-run titles, and four RBI championships, while Aaron led his league in homers and RBIs four times each and in batting twice. Babe Ruth led in batting once, RBIs six times, and homers 12 times.

Not What He Ordered

Speed demons don't always produce as expected. San Diego manager Bruce Bochy called on Kerry Robinson to pinch hit with two men on, hoping to stay out of the double play. The theory worked: Robinson hit into a *triple* play.

Tony's Tough Choice

Tony Gwynn was drafted by the baseball San Diego Padres and the basketball San Diego Clippers on the same day.

Hoops to Hill

Dodgers pitcher Mark Hendrickson played four years as a forward in the NBA.

Ancient Sluggers

Home-run hitters at age 45 or more:

- Julio Franco
- Cap Anson
- Jack Quinn
- Carlton Fisk

Franco's File

Like the Energizer Bunny, Julio Franco just keeps on ticking. Franco, who turned 47 while playing for the Atlanta Braves during the 2005 season, became the oldest player to hit a grand slam, to pinch hit a grand slam, and to hit a pinch homer. He also became the oldest man to hit two home runs in a game, the oldest to steal two bases in a game, and the oldest to have at least 50 hits in a season.

Grand Slam Leaders

Player	Grand Slams
Lou Gehrig	23
Manny Ramirez	20
Eddie Murray	19
Willie McCovey	18
Robin Ventura	18
Jimmie Foxx	17
Ted Williams	17

Multiple MVPs

- Barry Bonds, 7
- Yogi Berra, 3
- Roy Campanella, 3
- Joe DiMaggio, 3
- Jimmie Foxx, 3
- Mickey Mantle, 3
- Stan Musial, 3
- Mike Schmidt, 3
- Ernie Banks, 2
- Johnny Bench, 2
- Mickey Cochrane, 2
- Lou Gehrig, 2
- Juan Gonzalez, 2
- Hank Greenberg, 2
- Rogers Hornsby, 2
- Carl Hubbell, 2
- Walter Johnson, 2

- Roger Maris, 2
- Willie Mays, 2
- Joe Morgan, 2
- Dale Murphy, 2
- Hal Newhouser, 2
- Cal Ripken Jr., 2
- Frank Robinson, 2
- Alex Rodriguez, 2
- Frank Thomas, 2
- Ted Williams, 2
- Robin Yount, 2

CY YOUNG REPEATERS

- Roger Clemens, 7
- Randy Johnson, 5
- Steve Carlton, 4
- Greg Maddux, 4
- Sandy Koufax, 3
- Pedro Martinez, 3
- Jim Palmer, 3
- Tom Seaver, 3
- Bob Gibson, 2
- Tom Glavine, 2
- Denny McLain, 2
- Gaylord Perry, 2
- Bret Saberhagen, 2

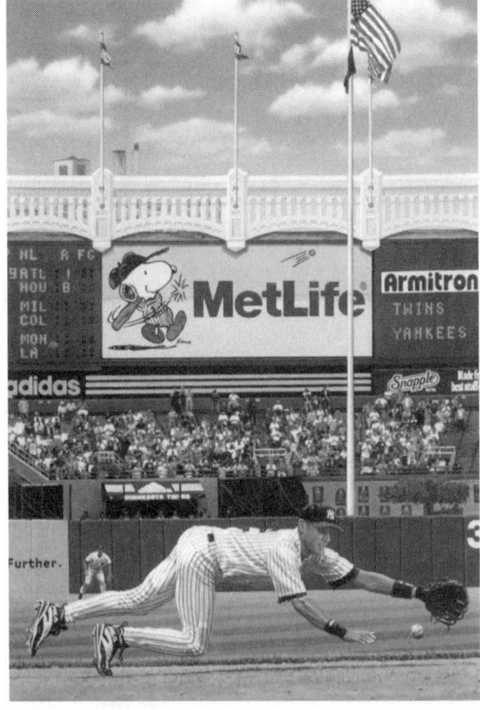

Derek Jeter won MVP awards in the All-Star Game and World Series.

Chapter 5
Teams Terrific

Brooks Robinson Remembers...

I don't like to see leagues of different sizes operate with different rules. Even the divisions are different sizes. I think things should be more uniform and maybe they will be, down the road. The designated hitter is a big bone of contention, too. I don't care which way they do it; if they want the pitchers to hit, both leagues should allow that. If they want the DH in both leagues, that's fine, too. I don't like the idea of having pitchers hit in NL parks and then going to AL parks and using the DH.

No matter what rules they use, there's nothing as good as a great pennant race.

In 1964 it went right down to the wire for the Orioles. We were in first for a while, and so were the White Sox, but the Yankees wound up winning by one game over Chicago. We lost Boog Powell with a month to go—he ran into a wall in Fenway Park and broke his wrist.

In 1967 the Twins, White Sox, Red Sox, and Tigers all had a chance to win with a week left in the schedule. I remember opening the paper in a hurry to check it out every morning. We won the World Series the year before, but Frank Robinson got hurt in '67 and we were not in the race.

Two years later, we were watching the battle between the Mets and the Cubs to see which team we might meet in the World Series. New York closed a big gap to win, blew Atlanta away in the first championship series, and beat us in a five-game Series.

I'll never forget what happened in 1978, when the Red Sox blew a big lead and finished tied with the Yankees. They had a one-game divisional playoff in Fenway Park that Bucky Dent won with a home run into the screen above the Green Monster.

TEAM NICKNAMES

Teams have changed nicknames more than 40 times since the start of the modern era in 1901. Here's the complete list:

Year	New Name	Old Name
1901	Cleveland Bluebirds	Cleveland Lake Shores
1901	Detroit Tigers	Detroit Wolverines
1902	Cleveland Broncos	Cleveland Bluebirds
1902	St. Louis Browns	Milwaukee Brewers
1903	Boston Pilgrims	Boston Somersets*
1903	Cleveland Naps	Cleveland Broncos
1903	New York Highlanders	Baltimore Orioles
1905	Washington Senators	Washington Nationals
1907	Boston Doves	Boston Beaneaters
1907	Boston Red Sox	Boston Pilgrims
1911	Boston Rustlers	Boston Doves
1911	Brooklyn Dodgers	Brooklyn Superbas
1912	Boston Braves	Boston Rustlers
1912	Cleveland Molly McGuires	Cleveland Naps
1913	New York Yankees	New York Highlanders
1914	Brooklyn Robins	Brooklyn Dodgers
1915	Cleveland Indians	Cleveland Molly McGuires
1932	Brooklyn Dodgers	Brooklyn Robins
1936	Boston Bees	Boston Braves
1941	Boston Braves	Boston Bees
1943	Philadelphia Blue Jays	Philadelphia Phillies
1944	Cincinnati Red Legs	Cincinnati Reds
1945	Philadelphia Phillies	Philadelphia Blue Jays
1946	Cincinnati Reds	Cincinnati Red Legs
1953	Milwaukee Braves	Boston Braves

1954	Baltimore Orioles	St. Louis Browns
1954	Cincinnati Red Legs	Cincinnati Reds
1955	Kansas City Athletics	Philadelphia Athletics
1958	Los Angeles Dodgers	Brooklyn Dodgers
1958	San Francisco Giants	New York Giants
1961	Cincinnati Reds	Cincinnati Red Legs
1961	Minnesota Twins	Washington Senators
1962	Kansas City A's	Kansas City Athletics
1965	California Angels	Los Angeles Angels
1965	Houston Astros	Houston Colt .45s
1966	Atlanta Braves	Milwaukee Braves
1968	Oakland A's	Kansas City A's
1970	Milwaukee Brewers	Seattle Pilots
1972	Texas Rangers	Washington Senators
1987	Oakland Athletics	Oakland A's
1997	Anaheim Angels	California Angels
2005	Washington Nationals	Montreal Expos
2005	Los Angeles Angels of Anaheim	Anaheim Angels

* The Somersets also were variously known as the Plymouth Rocks, Puritans, and Speedboys.

ROOM CHARGES

Early major leaguers were charged 50 cents per game for rooms when on the road.

BAD FORECAST

The 1909 Phillies were rained out for 10 straight days, a major league record.

KEEPING BUSY

The Phillies of the dead-ball era were so cheap that they often assigned players to take tickets.

KO'D BY LIGHTNING

New York Giants outfielder Red Murray was knocked unconscious by lightning just as

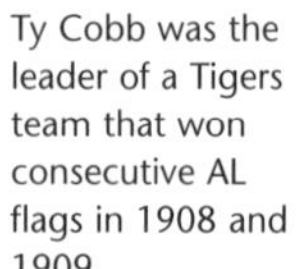

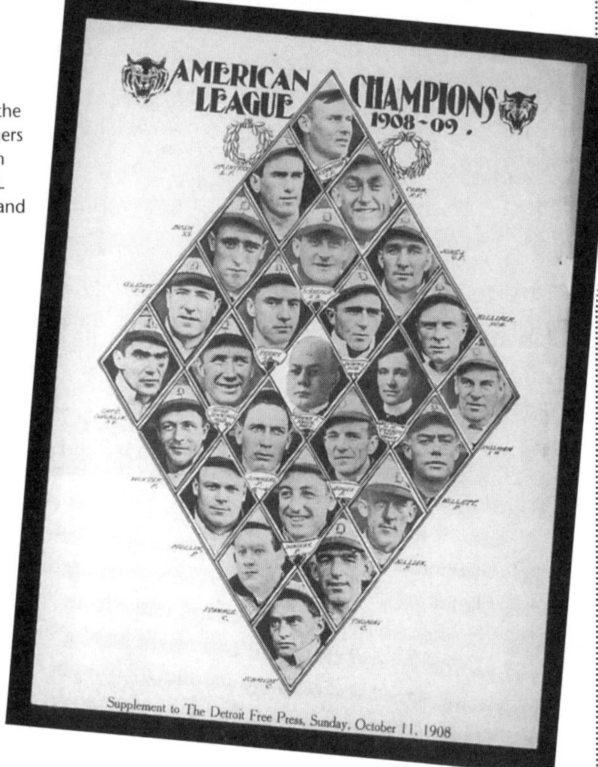

Ty Cobb was the leader of a Tigers team that won consecutive AL flags in 1908 and 1909.

he caught a game-ending fly in the twenty-first inning of a 3–1 win over Pittsburgh, July 17, 1914. Murray was otherwise uninjured.

WHAT WINNING STREAK?
Record books indicate the 1916 New York Giants won 26 games in a row. But that record streak was actually achieved in 27 games. John McGraw's men won 12 straight, tied one, then won another 14. Had the same thing happened in hockey, the team would be credited with a 14-game winning streak but a 27-game *unbeaten* streak.

BLACK SOX BACKED OUT
The 1919 Black Sox Scandal almost fell apart before its completion. Although the favored Chicago club lost four

of the first five games to Cincinnati in the best-of-nine affair, players allegedly involved in the fix were upset when the instigating gamblers failed to pay up. They won two straight before losing Game 8, 10–5, after the bettors threatened starting pitcher Claude "Lefty" Williams.

POOR CONNIE

The 1916 Philadelphia A's were a collective defensive calamity. They made 312 errors, 64 more than the next worst club, and had three 20-game losers. One of them, Jack Nabors, went 1–20.

BASEBALL PLUS FOOTBALL

Hugo Bezdek, who managed the Pirates before 1920, is the only man who managed in the majors and coached in the National Football League but never played in either.

GAME TIMES

The longest contest in big-league history, a 26-inning tie between the Dodgers and the Braves in 1920, consumed three hours and 50 minutes—exactly the time the Cubs and Giants needed for a nine-inning game in 1959.

A HUG AT THIRD

Uncle Wilbert Robinson was managing the Brooklyn Dodgers in the early 1920s. One day, with the team in a ninth-inning tie, Zack Taylor hit the ball over the center fielder's head. As he rounded third, Robinson, coaching there, grabbed him in a big congratulatory bear hug. The throw came to the base and Taylor was tagged out.

BOSTON GOES BUST

After winning five championships in 15 years, the Red Sox suffered a reversal of fortune immediately after sending Babe Ruth to the Yankees in 1920. In last place nine times over the next 13 years, the Sox watched the Yankees win their first flag and seven more during the same span. The Sox also finished second to the Yankees 14 times out of the 18 times they finished in the number two spot.

WINDY CITY

When the Chicago Cubs beat the Phillies, 26–23, at Wrigley Field on August 24, 1922, the two teams produced the most runs for a single game. Chicago took a 25–6 lead after four innings, then had to hang on for the win. In 1976 the Cubs led the Phils, 13–2, but Philadelphia came back for an 18–16 win in 10 innings—also at Wrigley.

PLAYER/MANAGER PROBLEMS
In addition to the usual job risk faced by any major league manager, player/pilots knew they could be traded at any time. Rogers Hornsby was one of several who lost their managing jobs when they were traded. Hornsby led the St. Louis Cardinals to the world championship in 1926 but was traded to the New York Giants after the season ended.

GOOD STRATEGY
The St. Louis Cardinals walked Babe Ruth 12 times in the 1926 World Series (he still hit four home runs). Ruth, frustrated when Grover Cleveland Alexander walked him with two outs in the ninth inning of Game 7 and the Yankees behind, 3–2, tried to surprise St. Louis by stealing second. He was thrown out easily—ending the World Series—in what baseball experts say was the only stupid play of his career.

IT TAKES TWO
Anticipating packed houses to see the slugging tandem of Babe Ruth and Lou Gehrig, the 1927 Yankees opened the season with a pair of public-address announcers. Jack Lenz and George Levy used megaphones to keep the Opening Day crowd of 65,000 informed. The tandem arrangement was dropped when declining attendance made it unnecessary.

FIRST CLUB TO FLY
The Hollywood Stars of the Pacific Coast League became the first professional team to fly in 1928.

MACK VERSUS GROVE
Longtime Philadelphia Athletics' manager Connie Mack did not swear, one reason he was never ejected from a game in a career that spanned more than 50 years. In 1929, when star pitcher Lefty Grove got ruffled after consecutive errors by Max Bishop and Jimmie Dykes, Mack decided to remove him from the game. "That will be all for you today, Robert," he said while the A's were batting. Grove, halfway down the bench replied, "To hell with you, Mr. Mack." With

Cincinnati went a half century between championships, then represented the National League in the World Series marred by the Black Sox Scandal. Cincinnati Reds

that, the soft-spoken pilot stood up, walked over to Grove, and pointed. "And the hell with you, too, Robert," he said. The whole bench—even Grove—laughed. The pitcher departed peacefully, laughing all the way to the clubhouse.

DYKES SHOVED MACK

Jimmie Dykes, who became manager of the Philadelphia Athletics in 1951 after Connie Mack ended a tenure that began in 1903, once pushed his predecessor into a pile of bats. It happened during the 10-run explosion of the A's in the seventh inning of the fourth game in the 1929 World Series against the Cubs. Chicago led, 8–0, before the outburst.

As the eighth run crossed for Philadelphia, the excited Dykes screamed, "We're tied; we're tied!" He pounded the man next to him so hard that he fell off the bench and into a pile of bats. Only his legs were visible. Dykes, then a 32-year-old utility infielder, suddenly realized whom he had pushed. "I pulled him out and said—very apologetically—'Gosh, Mr. Mack, I'm awfully sorry,'" Dykes recalled. "He said, 'Don't worry, Jimmie. Right now anything goes.'"

HITTERS FEAST

The ball was so lively in 1930 that the National League's eight teams combined for a .301 batting average. Six of the eight teams topped .300 and the collective

John McGraw was called "Little Napoleon" by contemporaries who respected and feared him.

earned-run average was 4.97, worst in league history. The Philadelphia Phillies were especially bad, posting a 6.70 ERA that was the worst ever recorded by a team.

FATEFUL SWITCH

Shortly after John McGraw switched Giants' third baseman Freddie Lindstrom to the outfield in 1931, the player broke his leg while making a catch. Visiting him in the hospital, McGraw blasted Lindstrom for his carelessness. "I hope you break your leg, too," the player answered. The angry McGraw stormed out of the hospital without paying attention to passing traffic. Struck by a taxi, he broke his leg, too.

FAMILY FEUD

Father and son do not always agree. Bill Veeck Sr. fired Rogers Hornsby as manager of the Chicago Cubs in 1932, but Bill Veeck Jr. hired him to manage the St. Louis Browns exactly 20 years later.

WOEFUL TURNOUT

The St. Louis Browns couldn't draw flies. During a Depression-era game in 1933, they drew *34* fans. That's no typo.

THE GASHOUSE GANG

The wild, fun-loving Cardinals of 1934 won the nickname "the Gashouse Gang" when they wore unwashed uniforms during a game in New York. With no clean suits available and no time to wash the uniforms they wore in a Boston doubleheader on Saturday, the Cards donned the same outfits for their Sunday game against the Giants. Writer Garry Schumacher, referring to the rundown Gashouse area of New

York, said, "They look like a gang from the Gashouse district! A real Gashouse gang!"

PITCHER HAD GAS
One source suggests the origin of the Gashouse Gang nickname given the Cardinals of the 1930s stemmed from Dizzy Dean's ownership of a gas station near McKechnie Field, then the club's spring training site in Bradenton, Florida.

FRISCH TOOK CUT
Frankie Frisch made $18,500 as player/manager of the 1934 St. Louis Cardinals, double the salary of any other player but considerably below his peak pay of $28,000, which he earned strictly as a player.

ELUSIVE FLAG
The Detroit Tigers won the 1940 American League pennant by one game over the Cleveland Indians. Rookie Floyd Giebell pitched the decisive game—a 2–0 victory over Indians superstar Bob Feller at Cleveland. Giebell won only two other games in his major league career.

CASUALTY OF WAR
Gene Stack of the White Sox, first American League draftee of World War II, was killed in action.

NO NIGHT GAMES
Night games were banned in 1943 because of blackout restrictions.

YOUNGEST PLAYER
Left-handed pitcher Joe Nuxhall of the Cincinnati Reds was the youngest player to appear in the majors. He made his debut on June 10, 1944, at the age of 15 years and 10 months. He pitched two-thirds

Tiny Miller Huggins, who managed such musclemen as Babe Ruth, stood just 5'4" and weighed less than 150 pounds. But he lasted 13 seasons as a player and was a well-respected manager.

Yankees teammates Babe Ruth (right) and Lou Gehrig homered in the same game 72 times—16 of them back-to-back.

of an inning in an 18–0 loss to the Cardinals.

GIRLS PLAYED TOO

The All-American Girls Professional Baseball League, immortalized by the 1992 film *A League of Their Own,* lasted 12 years (from 1943 to 1954). Founded by Cubs owner P.K. Wrigley during wartime manpower shortages, the AAGPBL paid top players $125 a week in a season of 110 to 120 games. The size of the ball, almost softball-like at the start, changed six times. Dottie "Kammie" Kamenshek, a left-handed batter who played first base for the Rockford Peaches, was considered the Babe Ruth of the distaff league. The seven-time All-Star won two batting crowns en route to a .292 career mark.

PERFECT WOMAN

The only perfect game in the history of the All-American Girls Professional Baseball League was thrown by Annabelle "Lefty" Lee, aunt of former big leaguer Bill "Spaceman" Lee. The female Lee, who also played first base in the girls' league, was the subject of a 1945 article in *Life* magazine.

LONE SENATORS HR

Power production was off sharply in the war-stripped majors of 1945. The Washington Senators hit only 27 home runs as a team and only one in their home park, Griffith Stadium. It was an inside-the-park job by Joe Kuhel.

KEEPING CLEAN

Four-time Pittsburgh Pirates pilot Danny Murtaugh played for the hapless Phillies of World War II vintage. "There was a billboard on our outfield fence that said, 'The Phillies use Lifebuoy.' One day we showed up for a game to find that a prankster had painted something below it: '...and they still stink!'"

BAAAAAAAAAD NEWS

During the 1945 season, Chicago tavern owner Billy Sianis frequented Wrigley Field with his pet goat in tow. He had tickets for both and nobody complained. But the influx of returning servicemen that followed the war's end in August convinced Cubs owner P.K. Wrigley that the goat's seat should go to a human occupant. Though he had two tickets for the Tigers-Cubs World Series, Sianis was turned away and told that the goat smelled bad. After the Cubs lost, Sianis sent Wrigley a telegram that read "Who stinks now?" and said the team would never appear in the fall classic again. In 1984 the team came close, winning the first two games of the NLCS at home against San Diego—after

Forlorn Babe Ruth, rebuffed in his bid to become a major league manager, spent some time as first-base coach for the Brooklyn Dodgers in the late 1930s.

another Sianis goat was paraded around the field before each game. The goat didn't accompany the club west, however, and the Padres won three straight to take their first NL flag. The absence of the Cubs from the World Series remains the longest drought of any of the original 16 teams.

NO MORE MIRACLES
In 29 seasons from 1917 to 1945, the Boston Braves finished fifth or worse 26 times.

LIGHTS OF GOTHAM
Night-ball pioneer Larry MacPhail installed lights when he became an executive with the Brooklyn Dodgers (1938) and the New York Yankees (1946). Cincinnati's Johnny Vander Meer pitched his second straight no-hitter in Brooklyn's first night game on June 15, 1938.

NO GUARANTEES
Before the advent of the wild-card, 100 wins in a season didn't guarantee a championship. The 1941 Brooklyn Dodgers won exactly 100 games to finish first, but the 1942 team finished second even though it had four more wins.

When the Brooklyn Dodgers played the first night game at Ebbets Field on June 15, 1938, visiting Cincinnati southpaw Johnny Vander Meer responded by throwing his second straight no-hitter. Although the Reds had been playing night games since 1935, the Dodgers were the first of the three New York clubs to light their park.

WARTIME MANEUVERS
Strange things happened during the war years, when big-league teams were strapped for players. The leagues averaged 1,500 more errors than usual, old timers were activated after years of retirement, and 32 minor league teams were forced to suspend operations. The Browns employed a one-armed outfielder, the Senators used a pitcher with a wooden

leg, and Yankees outfielder Johnny Lindell spiked teammate Herschel Martin in the nose when the pair collided in pursuit of a fly ball.

THREE-WAY GAME

In an effort to raise money for war bonds during World War II, the Brooklyn Dodgers, New York Giants, and New York Yankees played a three-way exhibition game before 50,000 fans at the Polo Grounds on June 26, 1944. Columbia University mathematics professor Paul Smith devised a formula whereby each team sat out every third inning. The Dodgers won, scoring five runs against one for the Yankees and none for the Giants.

LONG LAYOFF

Marty Marion, star shortstop for the St. Louis Cardinals, did not walk for a year after he fell off a cliff as a youngster.

TRAGIC BUS RIDE

Nine men were killed when a bus carrying the Spokane Indians of the Class B Western International League skidded on a wet roadway and crashed down a mountainside on June 24, 1946. Two years later, another minor league bus crash claimed five players from Duluth of the Class C Northern League.

GOOD TIMING

The only inside-the-park home run of Ted Williams's career clinched the 1946 AL pennant for the Boston Red Sox in Cleveland.

CLYDE'S THE GUY

Jackie Robinson's first major league manager was Clyde

The 1940 Detroit Tigers won a surprise American League pennant after first baseman Hank Greenberg moved to left field to create a spot for rookie Rudy York. Two months later, Greenberg became the first man to win an MVP award at two different positions.

Sukeforth, a coach appointed on an interim basis after the suspension of regular Brooklyn pilot Leo Durocher for the entire 1947 campaign. After two games, scout Burt Shotton took over, leading the Dodgers the rest of the way.

PIANO MAN

The Brooklyn Dodgers celebrated their 1947 NL flag by singing "It's a Beautiful Day for a Ballgame" accompanied by piano-playing infielder Bobby Bragan. The future manager often entertained players, friends, and family when a piano was present.

JACKIE'S POWER

Jackie Robinson wasn't primarily a power hitter—he twice hit 19 homers for his one-season high—but he produced when it counted. On the last day of the 1951 season, the Dodgers and the Giants were tied for the top. The Giants knocked off the Braves, and the Dodgers had to beat Philadelphia to force a playoff. Brooklyn was behind, 6–1, when word came out about the Giants win. The Dodgers tied it, 8–8, but almost lost it in the twelfth. With two outs and the bases loaded, the batter hit a low-liner to the right of second base. Jackie Robinson dove and speared it just above the ground, then crashed heavily on his shoulder. In the fourteenth, he found a fastball he liked and deposited it over the left-field wall to win the game, 9–8.

Character Builder

"Give a boy a bat, a ball, and a place to play and you'll have a good citizen."

—Manager Joe McCarthy

LIGHTING THE AL

The Cleveland Indians and the Philadelphia Athletics were the first American League teams to install lights, and the Detroit Tigers, in 1948, the last. When Tigers owner Walter O. Briggs decided to light his park, he tested several lighting systems to avoid any that might be unflattering to female fans.

SPAHN, SAIN, PRAY FOR RAIN

During the 1948 NL stretch drive, the Boston Braves banked heavily on the duo of Warren Spahn and Johnny Sain. They started 16 of 26 games at one point, winning a

10 COMMANDMENTS FOR SUCCESS IN THE MAJORS (BY JOE MCCARTHY)

1. Nobody ever became a ballplayer by walking after a ball.
2. You will never become a .300 hitter unless you take the bat off your shoulder.
3. An outfielder who throws at the back of a runner is locking the barn after the horse is stolen.
4. Keep your head up and you may not have to keep it down.
5. When you start to slide, slide. He who changes his mind may have to change a good leg for a bad one.
6. Do not alibi on bad hops. Anybody can field the good ones.
7. Always run them out. You never can tell.
8. Do not quit.
9. Do not fight too much with the umpires. You cannot expect them to be as perfect as you are.
10. A pitcher who hasn't control hasn't anything.

dozen (eight by Sain). By season's end, Sain had finished first in the league in wins (24), complete games (28), and innings pitched ($314\frac{2}{3}$). Spahn, a 15-game winner, was also among NL leaders in completions (16) and innings (257).

TED BEANED PITCHER

Ted Williams, known as a dead pull hitter, crossed up the defense one day and slammed a shot off an aluminum plate in the leg of wounded war hero Lou Brissie. The ball resounded with a loud clang, but the pitcher was not injured.

MCCARTHY ON MANAGING

Longtime manager Joe McCarthy, who left the game in 1949, usually enjoyed his job. "Sometimes I think I'm in the greatest business in the world," he said. "Then I lose four straight and want to change places with a farmer."

OLD RELIABLE

Casey Stengel won his first game as manager of the Yankees on a walkoff home run by Tommy Henrich. The date was April 19, 1949.

CASEY'S BAD GUESS

"You can't say I don't miss 'em when I miss 'em." That's how

THE WHITE HOUSE
WASHINGTON

January 15, 1942

My dear Judge:-

Thank you for yours of January fourteenth. As you will, of course, realize the final decision about the baseball season must rest with you and the Baseball Club owners -- so what I am going to say is solely a personal and not an official point of view.

I honestly feel that it would be best for the country to keep baseball going. There will be fewer people unemployed and everybody will work longer hours and harder than ever before.

And that means that they ought to have a chance for recreation and for taking their minds off their work even more than before.

Baseball provides a recreation which does not last over two hours or two hours and a half, and which can be got for very little cost. And, incidentally, I hope that night games can be extended because it gives an opportunity to the day shift to see a game occasionally.

As to the players themselves, I know you agree with me that individual players who are of active military or naval age should go, without question, into the services. Even if the actual quality of the teams is lowered by the greater use of older players, this will not dampen the popularity of the sport. Of course, if any individual has some particular aptitude in a trade or profession, he ought to serve the Government. That, however, is a matter which I know you can handle with complete justice.

Here is another way of looking at it -- if 300 teams use 5,000 or 6,000 players, these players are a definite recreational asset to at least 20,000,000 of their fellow citizens -- and that in my judgment is thoroughly worthwhile.

With every best wish,

Very sincerely yours,

Franklin D. Roosevelt

Hon. Kenesaw M. Landis,
333 North Michigan Avenue,
Chicago,
Illinois.

This letter from President Roosevelt to Commissioner Landis tells the story; the president wanted baseball to continue during the war as a morale booster.

Casey Stengel recalled his early appraisal of left-handed pitcher Warren Spahn, when both were Boston Braves in the 1940s. When Spahn refused to brush back a hitter, Stengel admonished him. "Young man," he said, "you have no guts."

SQUEEZING LEMON

Cleveland's Bob Lemon led the American League with 23 wins in 1950 but missed a chance for number 24 when he blew a 10–0 lead against the Red Sox at Fenway Park on August 28. The Sox won, 15–14.

GREAT COLLAPSES

- 1951—Dodgers, 13½ games ahead in August, collapse to tie Giants, who then win best-of-three pennant playoff on Bobby Thomson's ninth-inning homer.
- 1962—Dodgers lose six of last seven, forcing pennant playoff with Giants, who win best-of-three finale with ninth-inning rally.
- 1964—Phillies blow 6½-game lead with 12 left by dropping 10 straight. Cards win on final day, finishing one game ahead of Phils and Reds.
- 1969—Cubs blow 9½-game August lead, finish distant second to Mets in NL East.
- 1978—Red Sox blow 14-game July lead, finish tied with Yankees, then drop sudden-death divisional playoff game.
- 1980—Astros blow three-game lead in season-ending series in Los Angeles, then beat Dodgers in sudden-death NL West playoff before losing NLCS to Phillies.
- 1993—Giants blow 10-game July lead to Braves, losing NL West title on final day despite 103 victories.
- 1995—Angels blow 13-game August lead and lose sudden-death divisional playoff game to Mariners.

BIG INNINGS

Wholesale collapse of a pitching staff can result in big innings for the opposition. In 1952 the Brooklyn Dodgers scored 15 runs in the first inning against Cincinnati (final score, 19–1). A year later, the Boston Red Sox tallied 17 times in the seventh en route to a 23–3 win over Detroit.

MORE GOOD TIMING

Billy Hunter's only home run of the 1953 season made history: it was the last ever hit for the St. Louis Browns.

Calendar Check

"For the Washington Senators, the worst time of year is the baseball season."
—Roger Kahn

In their last season before moving to Baltimore, the 1953 St. Louis Browns wore an impish patch (top) on their sleeves. Far from the form that produced their only pennant in 1944, St. Louis was belittled for being "first in shoes, first in booze, and last in the American League." More respect was given the eagle insignia patch (bottom) worn by players returning from wartime service in 1945. It was sometimes called "the ruptured duck."

Hunter and Satchel Paige were the last Browns All-Stars.

BROWNS BUT NOT OUT

Although they became the Baltimore Orioles in 1954, the St. Louis Browns retain legendary status because they won only one pennant, crafted crazy promotions under maverick owner Bill Veeck, and employed such players as one-armed Pete Gray, diminutive pinch-hitter Eddie Gaedel, and legendary pitcher Satchel Paige. Their best pitcher was Ned Garver, the only man ever to win 20 games for a team that lost 100.

TRAIN LAG

Before the transplanted St. Louis Browns played their first game as the Baltimore Orioles in 1954, players rode an all-night train from Detroit and changed into their uniforms on board.

MOST AL WINS

The 1954 Cleveland Indians, playing a 154-game schedule, won 111 games, a record that lasted for 44 years.

MOST RUNS BY A CLUB

The Boston Red Sox and the Chicago White Sox both

scored a record 29 runs in separate single games during the 1950s.

HERB SCORE'S TRAGEDY
On May 7, 1957, Gil McDougald of the New York Yankees—the second batter in the first inning—hit pitcher Herb Score in the eye with a line drive. Score, a 20-game winner the previous year, suffered a broken bone and eye damage and was never again the same pitcher. McDougald, hounded by fans after the accident, retired in 1960 at age 32. Score was 29 when he finally gave it up in 1962.

TIME'S UP!
On May 18, 1957, the Baltimore Orioles and the visiting Chicago White Sox agreed in advance to a 10:20 PM curfew so that the Sox could catch a train out of town. With seconds to go, Dick Williams of the O's tied the game with a home run against Paul LaPalme—forcing the game to be replayed. Had Williams done anything else, the Sox would have won, but Baltimore laughed last, winning the replay.

BOOK 'EM, LEO
Leo Durocher was an avid reader who relaxed by reading one mystery and a more serious volume each night.

USING HIS HEAD
Charley Dressen, longtime major league manager, was a bundle of excitement during a game. Once, when Gil Hodges was at bat for his Dodgers, Dressen watched the count run to 1–2. The next pitch was high and outside—so far that the catcher missed it—but the umpire called strike three. When Hodges, assuming the pitch to be ball three, failed to run toward first on the passed ball, Dressen yelled, "Run! Run!" but the first baseman couldn't hear him. The screaming manager, jumping up and down in the dugout, banged his head on the ceiling and collapsed. Hodges finally

got the idea and made it to first. But for days afterward he avoided Dressen whenever he saw the manager rubbing the sore spot on his head.

WHY MINORS SHRUNK

The advent of air-conditioning and television reduced the minor leagues from a peak of 59 leagues in 1950 to 21 by 1960. Expansion by the majors further cut inroads into the minor league structure.

TOO OLD?

Casey Stengel was 70 when the Yankees fired him after the team lost the 1960 World Series to the Pittsburgh Pirates. During 12 years with the team, Stengel won 10 pennants and seven world championships. "I'll never make the mistake of being 70

Before Jackie Robinson broke baseball's color barrier in 1947, black baseball stars had their own leagues, teams, and superstars, some of whom later reached the Baseball Hall of Fame. Among the many standouts were Satchel Paige, Josh Gibson, Oscar Charleston, and Cool Papa Bell. JamesFiorentino.com

JACKIE HAD POWER

Jackie Robinson wasn't primarily a power hitter—he twice hit 19 homers for his one-season high—but he produced when it counted. On the last day of the 1951 season the Dodgers and the Giants were tied for the top. The Giants knocked off the Braves, and the Dodgers had to beat Philadelphia to force a playoff. Brooklyn was behind, 6–1, when word came out of the Giants win. The Dodgers tied it, 8–8, but almost lost it in the twelfth. With two outs and the bases loaded, the batter hit a low-liner to the right of second base. Jackie Robinson dove and speared it just above the ground, then crashed heavily on his shoulder. In the fourteenth, he found a fastball he liked and deposited it over the left-field wall to win the game, 9–8.

again," he told reporters at his farewell conference.

FIERY FRED

When Fred Hutchinson was managing the Cincinnati Reds, his temper occasionally got the best of him. After a doubleheader defeat against the hapless Mets at the Polo Grounds, Hutch was especially upset. Players from both teams headed for the clubhouses in center field after the game, but Hutchinson sat on the dugout bench fuming. Some 30 minutes later, he called the Cincinnati clubhouse. The clubhouse man answered. "If any of those idiots are still in there, tell them to get out," he barked. "I'm coming in." A dozen players were around when Hutch called. Three minutes later, all were gone.

CLEVER NAME

When the original Washington Senators moved to the Twin Cities of Minneapolis/St. Paul

One of the best player/managers, Lou Boudreau of the Cleveland Indians led his club's 1948 pennant drive. Reprinted with permission, National Baseball Hall of Fame Library, Cooperstown, New York

in 1961, they became the first team to identify with an entire state. The Minnesota Twins also became the first club whose hat initials were different from their team name. The "TC" on team hats stood for Twin Cities.

HEAVENLY NICKNAMES

The Angels have changed their name four times without ever leaving Southern California. They were the Los Angeles Angels from 1961 to 1964 and the California Angels from 1965 to 1996 before becoming the Anaheim Angels in 1997. Eight years later, as part of a local marketing ploy, the team started calling itself the Los Angeles Angels of Anaheim.

COLLEGE OF COACHES

The Chicago Cubs went without a manager for five years. Because owner P.K. Wrigley hated to fire managers, a rotating College of Coaches ran the team from 1961 to 1965. Unable to revive the perennial second-division club, the "college" was replaced by Leo Durocher in 1966. He promptly boasted the Cubs would not finish eighth. They didn't; they dropped to 10th, dead last in the 10-team National League.

CASEY'S QUICK QUIP

When pitcher Tug McGraw was hit hard by the opposition while working for the Mets, manager Casey Stengel came out to the mound. Pointing to the hitter, McGraw said, "I struck out this guy the last time I faced him. Let me stay in." Stengel responded, "I know you struck him out. But it was in this same inning!"

QUALITY QUARTETS

The 1961 Milwaukee Braves were the first team to hit four successive home runs; Eddie Mathews, Hank Aaron, Joe Adcock, and Frank Thomas connected against the Cincinnati Reds. Two years later, the 8-9-1-2 hitters of the Cleveland Indians—Woodie Held, Pedro Ramos, Tito Francona, and Larry Brown—duplicated that feat against the Los Angeles Angels, with Paul Foytack the victim each time. Four 1964 Minnesota Twins—Tony Oliva, Bob Allison, Jimmie Hall, and Harmon Killebrew—connected in succession against the Kansas City Athletics, but no other team hit four straight homers for 42 years. Then the Los Angeles Dodgers hit four in a row *in the ninth inning* to tie a crucial NL West game against the San Diego Padres on September 18, 2006. Jeff Kent, J.D. Drew, Russell Martin, and Marlon Anderson helped the Dodgers take a 10-inning, 11–10 game in which they hit seven home runs—after entering the game ranking last in the National League in home runs!

CLOSE BUT NO CIGAR

Though he managed for 26 years, Gene Mauch's clubs never won a pennant. Not that they didn't come close. In 1964, the Phillies blew a six-and-a-half-game lead with 12 games to play, finishing one

Because he was part owner of the team, Connie Mack managed the Philadelphia Athletics for a record 50 years, winning nine pennants and five world championships but also finishing in the basement 17 times. He was just shy of his 88th birthday when he retired in 1950. Ronnie Joyner

game behind the St. Louis Cardinals. Mauch's California Angels blew a 2–0 lead in the best-of-five ALCS in 1982 and a 3–1 lead in the expanded best-of-seven ALCS in 1986. Needing one out to nail down that elusive pennant, the 1986 Angels blew a three-run lead over Boston in Game 4 of the ALCS and then dropped three in a row. Mauch, a three-time Manager of the Year, managed one more year before retiring.

When Phils Flopped

"Asking Philadelphia to forget 1964 is like asking Chicago to forget Mrs. O'Leary's cow."

—Chuck Darrow
South Jersey Courier News

HOGGING THE FLAG
The Yankees won a record 14 pennants in 16 years from 1949 to 1964.

FINISHING THEIR STARTS
During the Dodgers' world championship season of 1965, Sandy Koufax and Don Drysdale combined for 47 complete games—seven more than the total number of *wins* produced by the New York Mets just three years earlier.

FRANCHISE LOYALTY?
Though the Milwaukee Braves announced a move to Atlanta for 1965, minority stockholder Bud Selig, a used-car dealer, blocked the move with a lawsuit that said teams should show loyalty toward their host community. Six years later, when Selig had changed his tune, his investment group purchased the one-year-old Seattle Pilots and made them into the Milwaukee Brewers.

LOYAL SERVICE
Walter Johnson and Warren Spahn were the only pitchers to start more than 600 games with one franchise.

TWIN TERRORS
The 1966 Minnesota Twins tied major league records by hitting three consecutive home runs with two outs and five home runs in one inning, all in a game against the Kansas City Athletics on June 9. Rich Rollins and Zorro Versalles started the seventh inning with home runs, then Tony Oliva, Don Mincher, and Harmon Killebrew connected with two outs. The outburst came just

two years after the Twins hit four straight home runs, a feat also accomplished by the 1961 Milwaukee Braves, the 1963 Cleveland Indians, and the 2006 Los Angeles Dodgers.

BAD PICK

The worst amateur draft choice of all time might have been Steve Chilcott, a catcher picked by the Mets in 1966. Chilcott, who never reached the majors, hit .248 in seven minor league seasons. Adding fuel to the fire was the fact that the Mets could have drafted Reggie Jackson, who went to the Oakland A's as the number two choice overall.

MAN ON THE MOVE

Eddie Mathews was the only man to play for the same team in three different cities.

BEAR FACTS

The Chicago Cubs drafted Brooks Kieschnick ahead of Billy Wagner, Torii Hunter, and Jason Varitek.

DARK PHILOSOPHY

Alvin Dark, one of a handful of managers to win pennants in both leagues, said he always relied on a *P* word while managing: *power* in San Francisco, *pitching* in Oakland, and *prayer* in Cleveland.

Doubling as third-base coach, a frenetic Leo Durocher, managing the New York Giants, whoops up a storm as Willie Mays heads for home. National League

Duke Snider hits his last home run at Brooklyn's Ebbets Field on September 22, 1957. Snider's 40th home run ties Ralph Kiner's record of five straight 40-homer seasons. It is Snider's last hurrah, as knee problems and the cavernous Los Angeles Coliseum (where the Dodgers played home games from 1958 to 1962) combined to short-circuit his power.

TIGERS LOSE STRIPES

The 1967 pennant race ended abruptly for the Detroit Tigers when they lost to the California Angels 8–5 on October 1, the last day of the season. Disgusted Tigers fans stormed the field and caused severe damage after the game.

TED WILLIAMS, MANAGER

Former Red Sox slugger Ted Williams was named Manager of the Year in the American League in 1969, his first year as a pilot, when he improved the Washington Senators' winning percentage from .404 to .531. It was the best of his four seasons with the team, including one in Dallas–Fort Worth after the Washington Senators became the Texas Rangers.

TOUGH DECISION

Preston Gomez, baseball's first Latino manager, twice pinch hit for pitchers who had completed eight no-hit innings in a game. In both cases, succeeding relief pitchers blew the no-hitters in the ninth. The luckless starters were Clay Kirby of San Diego and Don Wilson of Houston.

LAST FOR NATS

Joe Grzenda threw the last pitch in the history of the Washington Senators, on September 30, 1971, against the New York Yankees.

FOUR-MAN ROTATIONS

Big-league teams routinely used four-man pitching rotations well into the 1970s.

GOOD BUYS

George Steinbrenner paid 100 times more for the Yankees franchise in 1973 than the team paid to buy Babe Ruth from the Red Sox in 1919. But he later paid more for individual free agents than he did for the entire ballclub.

F. ROBBY'S DEBUT

Player/manager Frank Robinson—the first black manager hired and later the first fired—slammed a home run in his first at-bat in the double role. The home run, on April 7, 1975, helped the Cleveland Indians defeat the New York Yankees, 5–3.

POOR TURNOUT

No American League team drew 2 million fans in 1975—even though the pennant-winning Boston Red Sox had a red-hot rookie race between Fred Lynn and Jim Rice.

SEATTLE'S SECOND SHOT

The city of Seattle has had two major league teams. The Pilots, a 1969 expansion team, failed after one year and fled to Milwaukee. But the city sued the American League for breach of contract and won a second expansion club as compensation. When the Mariners made their debut on April 6, 1977, with entertainer Danny Kaye in the ownership group, they had similar results in a new ballpark, losing 6–0 to California in the Seattle Kingdome.

IN THE BIG INNING

The Cleveland Indians (13) and Boston Red Sox (6) combined for 19 runs, a record for a single frame, in the eighth inning of a game on April 10, 1977.

Mickey Mantle's batting feats had much to do with Casey Stengel's success as manager of the Yankees. He won 10 pennants in 12 years. American League

REVOLVING BOSSES

Dock Ellis pitched for seven different managers in 1977:

- Yankees—Billy Martin
- A's—Jack McKeon, Bobby Winkles
- Rangers—Frank Lucchesi, Eddie Stanky, Connie Ryan, Billy Hunter

GOOSE GOOSED

Goose Gossage missed the last three months of the 1979 season after he suffered a torn ligament in his left thumb during a clubhouse fight with Cliff Johnson. Without their star closer, the Yankees were unable to repeat after back-to-back world championships in 1977 and 1978.

SLUGGING SCHMIDT

Mike Schmidt hit more home runs while spending his whole career with one team (548 for the Phillies) than any other player.

STAYING POWER

Minor league managers sometimes have more longevity than their big-league counterparts. Stan Wasiak, for example, won a record 2,570 games in the minors without ever managing in the majors. Wasiak, who managed Dodgers farm clubs for 37 straight years starting in 1950, worked in 17 different cities.

MINOR LEAGUE STARS

When the big-league map had only 16 teams, minor league pitching stars were sometimes overlooked. Bill Thomas won a record 382 games in the minors without ever reaching the majors, while Tony Freitas had six straight 20-win seasons in Triple A without advancing. As late as the 1950s, Carroll Dial had consecutive seasons with 22, 27, 28, 25, and 20 wins but never got promoted. And Joe Pate had a pair of *30-win* seasons that produced only a one-year tryout with Connie Mack's Philadelphia A's.

COACH-BY-COMMITTEE

A year after winning the AL pennant in 1981, the New York Yankees endured a year of rotating coaches. Thanks to impatient owner George Steinbrenner, the team had five pitching coaches, four hitting coaches, and three managers in 1982. Pitching coaches included Jeff Torborg, Jerry Walker, Stan Williams, Clyde King, and Sammy Ellis, while hitting coaches were Mickey Vernon, Joe Pepitone, Yogi

MARTIN'S MATCHES

Billy Martin's fiery temper and burning will to win—as both player and manager—sparked numerous off-the-field encounters. Among them were:

Year	Opponent	Result
1950	Unidentified civilian	Won but fined $2,658 by U.S. Army
1952	Jimmy Piersall, Red Sox	No decision
1953	Clint Courtney, Browns	Won but fined $150 by AL
1953	Matt Batts, Tigers	Tie
1956	Tommy Lasorda, Athletics	No decision
1957	Minnie Minoso, White Sox	Draw; later traded by Yankees
1960	Gene Conley, Phillies	Lost
1960	Jim Brewer, Cubs	Won but paid $10,000 settlement
1966	Howard Fox, Twins executive	Won
1969	Dave Boswell, Twins	Won
1972	Jack Sears, Tigers fan	Won
1974	Burt Hawkins, Rangers PR man	Won
1977	Reggie Jackson, Yankees	No decision
1978	Ray Hagar, *Nevada State Journal*	Won but paid $7,500 settlement
1979	Joseph Cooper, marshmallow salesman	Won
1979	Chicago cabbie	No decision

The St. Louis Browns became the Baltimore Orioles in 1954 after years of declining attendance.
Baltimore Orioles

Berra, and Lou Piniella. Yankees managers in 1982 were Bob Lemon, Gene Michael, and King. All that maneuvering didn't help; the Yankees finished fifth in the AL East, 16 games behind the front-running Milwaukee Brewers.

HALO OR HEX?

Do the Angels suffer from a jinx? During their first 20 seasons (1961–1980), death claimed Lyman Bostock, Bruce Heinbechner, Mike Miley, Chico Ruiz, and Dick Wantz, while injury short-circuited the careers of Art Fowler, Ken Hunt, Johnny James, Ken McBride, Don Mincher, Minnie Rojas, Paul Schaal, and Bobby Valentine. One-time closer Donnie Moore, unable to cope with throwing a key playoff gopher ball in 1986, later committed suicide.

NO RHYME OR RAZOR

Because the 1986 Cincinnati Reds enforced strict rules against facial hair, future Hall of Fame reliever Rollie Fingers decided to retire rather than accept a contract offer.

POWER NO PANACEA

The 1961 Milwaukee Braves lost by a 10–8 score when four teammates hit consecutive home runs, and the 1986 Atlanta Braves lost 11–8 when Bob Horner hit four home runs in a game.

SALTY STREAK

When you're hot, you're hot: the Salt Lake City Trappers won 29 games in a row, a record for any professional sport, in 1987. The Pacific Coast League team split its first six games before starting its streak. The big-league mark is 26 straight by the 1916 New York Giants.

CENTURY MARK

Sparky Anderson and Whitey Herzog remain the only managers to guide teams to 100-win seasons in both leagues.

BIG WINNER

Sparky Anderson is the only manager to win more than 800 games in each league. In 25 years as a pilot, his teams won 2,134 games, fourth on the career list behind Connie Mack

DEAR FRIEND:

UNDOUBTEDLY YOU KNOW THAT THE NICKNAME SELECTED FOR NEW YORK'S NEW NATIONAL LEAGUE BASEBALL TEAM IS "METS".

AS WE EXPLAINED TO THE PRESS, OUR CHOICE WAS BASED ON THE FOLLOWING FIVE FACTORS:

1. IT HAS RECEIVED PUBLIC AND PRESS ACCEPTANCE.
2. IT IS CLOSELY RELATED TO OUR CORPORATE NAME—METROPOLITAN BASEBALL CLUB, INC.
3. IT IS DESCRIPTIVE OF OUR ENTIRE METROPOLITAN AREA.
4. IT HAS THE DESIRED BREVITY.
5. THE NAME HAS HISTORICAL BASEBALL BACKGROUND.

WE WANT TO THANK YOU FOR YOUR GREAT INTEREST IN OUR EFFORTS TO FIND A NAME, AND FOR THE SUPPORT THAT YOU VOICED IN OUR ENDEAVOR TO BRING YOU A TEAM IN 1962 OF WHICH WE WILL ALL BE PROUD.

METROPOLITAN BASEBALL CLUB, INC.

Charles A. Hurth

GENERAL MANAGER

Team Slumps

Teams that have lost at least 20 games in a row:

Team	League	Year	Consecutive Games Lost
Philadelphia	NL	1961	23
Baltimore	AL	1988	21
Boston	AL	1906	20
Philadelphia	AL	1916	20
Philadelphia	AL	1943	20
Montreal	NL	1969	20

(3,371), John McGraw (2,784), and Bucky Harris (2,218).

Mad Manager

After his Pirates played a sloppy game, manager Jim Leyland stormed into the clubhouse and said, "You got 10 minutes to get dressed and get out of here before the cops come in and arrest you for impersonating professional ballplayers."

Coach Longevity

Although Mel Harder was the first pitching coach, Galen Cisco had the most longevity. Harder spent 22 years with four different teams, but Cisco worked 27 years while dividing his time among five ballclubs.

Rays Remember Ripken

The Tampa Bay Devil Rays commissioned a commemorative oil painting *for a visiting player.* The $12,000 painting presented to Cal Ripken Jr. during his last visit with the Baltimore Orioles was the most expensive of all the gifts he received. Not to be outdone, the D-Rays also gave Ripken a one-year supply of free stone crab claws, valued at $700.

Youth Not Served

The first starter in the history of the Florida Marlins, Charlie Hough, was 45 years old.

Porous Pitching

The 1996 Detroit Tigers allowed more runs and earned runs and posted the worst earned-run average (6.38) in

American League history. The league's overall ERA that year was a bloated 4.99.

LONG ROAD TRIPS

To meet special circumstances, teams sometimes agree to take long road trips. The Houston Astros had a 26-game road trip in 1992, when the Republican National Convention was held in the Astrodome, while the Atlanta Braves had a 19-game journey during the 1996 Summer Olympics. The Olympics also caused both Los Angeles teams to vacate Southern California in 1984, while problems with the Olympic Stadium roof sent the Montreal Expos on the road for the last 26 games of the 1991 campaign.

BELLE'S WINDFALL

The 1997 season was the first time one player (Albert Belle) made more money than a whole team (the Pittsburgh Pirates). Belle made $10 million from the Chicago White Sox while the Pirate payroll was $9,071,667.

WORKING HIS WAY UP

White Sox co-owner Eddie Einhorn once worked in old Comiskey Park as an usher.

FISHY PRIORITIES

Shortly after the end of the 1998 World Series, reports circulated that H. Wayne Huizenga, owner of the 1997 world champion Florida Marlins, paid more for his $7.5 million house on Nantucket than he did to meet the 1998 payroll of his stripped-down team.

HELP WANTED

After winning the World Series the year before, the Florida Marlins opened the 1998 season with a pitching staff that had only 16 career victories—fewest of any staff in 100 years.

Ripley's
Believe It or Not!

WAY TO GO PERRY!
IN 1968,
SAN FRANCISCO GIANTS MANAGER ALVIN DARK TOLD REPORTERS THAT NASA WOULD "PUT A MAN ON THE MOON BEFORE GAYLORD PERRY HITS A HOME RUN."
ON JULY 20, 1969 PERRY CONNECTED FOR HIS FIRST EVER HOME RUN— 20 MINUTES AFTER NEAL ARMSTRONG WALKED ON THE MOON!

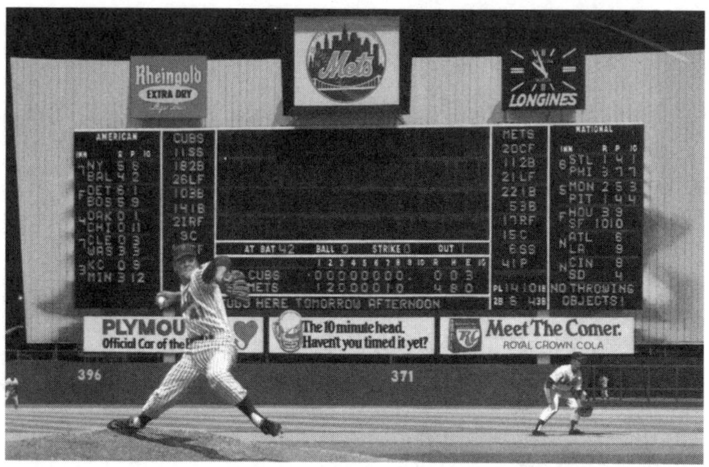

Tom Seaver comes close to throwing the first Mets no-hitter on July 9, 1969. En route to the NL's Cy Young Award, the 23-year-old right-hander retires the first 25 Cubs, fanning 11, but yields a single to 22-year-old journeyman Jim Qualls. Seaver's shutout cuts Chicago's lead over New York to three games in the NL East. It is the seventh straight win for the Mets and the fifth straight loss for the Cubs. New York maintains its momentum, romping to the divisional title, sweeping the playoffs, and winning a five-game World Series—all over favored opponents. Copyright 1997 by Bill Purdom. Reprinted with permission, Bill Goff, Inc./GoodSportsArt.com.

WORST TO FIRST

The six teams that finished last one year and first the next all played in the last decade of the 20th century. They were the Atlanta Braves and Minnesota Twins (1991), Philadelphia Phillies (1993), San Francisco Giants (1997), San Diego Padres (1998), and Arizona Diamondbacks (1999).

MORNING GLORY

The starting time of Eric Milton's no-hitter against the Angels on September 11, 1999, was 11:00 AM. The Twins had started the game early to accommodate a University of Minnesota football game slated for the same date.

ROCKIES RAMPAGE

On May 5, 1999, the Colorado Rockies became the third team of the 20th century to score in every inning, during a 13–9 win over the Chicago Cubs.

SCHOTT IN THE DARK

Marge Schott, majority owner of the Cincinnati Reds from

1984 to 1999, never strayed far from controversy. She issued a team calendar with a dozen different poses of Schottzie, her pet St. Bernard; once settled a contract dispute by flipping a coin; and ordered such arbitrary cost-cutting moves as mandating that media notes be kept to one page, printed on both sides. After she was fined and suspended for racial slurs and offensive language, she sold the team to Carl Lindner for $67 million.

ALMOST EVERYWHERE

The Milwaukee Brewers are the only team to play in four of the six divisions under baseball's 2000 format. They began life as the expansion Seattle Pilots in 1969 (AL West) but moved to Milwaukee (AL East) after one year. When the Washington Senators became the Texas Rangers in 1972, they moved from the AL East to the AL West, with the Brewers going the other way. Milwaukee was placed in the AL Central in 1994, when the leagues split into three divisions, but jumped to the NL Central in the expansion year of 1998, giving the NL 16 teams and the AL 14.

VALENTINE FOR WORKERS

Former Mets manager Bobby Valentine donated $500,000 of his own money to relief efforts following the 9/11 terrorist attack on New York City.

BAD BORAS BET

Superagent Scott Boras boasted the Texas Rangers would boost attendance by 300,000 after Alex Rodriguez, a Boras client, signed with the club. Attendance did go up, but only by 30,964—not even a towering total for a single game.

MUSICAL OWNERS

Prior to the 2002 season, Expos owner Jeffrey Loria bought the Marlins from John Henry and sold the Montreal franchise to the other 29 team owners. Henry then headed a syndicate that purchased the Boston Red Sox.

EXODUS IN MONTREAL

After Montreal Expos owner Jeffrey Loria purchased the Florida Marlins from John Henry, he invited the staff of the Expos to join him in the move. Many did—leaving the Expos with a three-man staff just prior to 2002 spring training. Loria announced a $5,000 bonus for those who elected to make the move.

A's Aces
The 2002 Oakland Athletics won an AL-record 20 consecutive games over a 24-day span from August 13 to September 6.

From Vendor to Actor
Before he went to Hollywood, Tom Hanks was a vendor in the Oakland–Alameda County Coliseum.

Three-Team Twin Bill
On September 25, 2002, the Cleveland Indians played a doubleheader at Jacobs Field *against two different teams.* They beat the White Sox, 9–2, but lost to the Twins, 4–3. It was the first three-team twin bill since September 13, 1951.

Losing Their Stripes
The 2003 Detroit Tigers lost 119 games, more than any other team in American League annals.

Good Comeback
The 2003 Florida Marlins were the first team since the 1914 Boston Braves to win a world championship after recovering from a 10-game deficit in the standings during the regular season.

April Showers
A win in April is as important as a win in September. The Red Sox finished one game out of first place in four different seasons when they lost on Opening Day.

Texas Tribute
After losing his life prematurely because of a brain tumor, Johnny Oates was honored with the retirement of the No. 26 jersey he wore while managing the Texas Rangers from 1995 to 2001.

Same City, Different Parks
On July 8, 2000, the Yankees and Mets played the first same-city, different-ballpark doubleheader since 1903. The Mets lost the afternoon game at Shea Stadium and the nightcap at Yankee Stadium. They also lost Mike Piazza, who suffered a concussion when hit by a Roger Clemens fastball.

No Whitewash
The 1932 Yankees and the 2000 Reds went full seasons without being shut out.

Anything Can Happen
Asked for a one-word description of baseball, pitcher Joaquin Andujar said,

"Youneverknow." The 2001 Cleveland Indians must have been listening; they overcame a 12-run deficit with seven outs remaining and beat the Seattle Mariners, 15–14.

HALF-DRESSED

The Los Angeles Dodgers refused a request by the San Francisco Giants that they dress in 1951-style uniforms for a promotion on the 50th anniversary of Bobby

Thomson's pennant-winning playoff home run. The Giants wore the retro suits anyway.

TORRID TWOSOME

During the 16 times that Randy Johnson and Curt Schilling pitched back-to-back for the Arizona Diamondbacks in 2001, the team never lost consecutive games. The D'backs won 25 of those 32 games, including the last two games of the World Series against the Yankees. The hard-throwing pitchers combined to fan 665 batters, topping the 1930 combination of Lefty Grove and George Earnshaw (Philadelphia A's) and the 1962 tandem of Sandy Koufax and Don Drysdale (Los Angeles Dodgers). Counting postseason play, Johnson and Schilling won 26 games each and finished first and second in earned-run average in the NL. Johnson and Schilling combined for *nine* of Arizona's 11 wins in postseason play and shared MVP honors in the World Series.

WINNING WAYS

Though the 2001 Seattle Mariners tied the 1906 Chicago Cubs for most wins in a season, the Cubs did it in the days of the 154-game schedule. Their 116–36 record was the best in baseball history.

RAGS TO RICHES

Thanks to free agency and frequent player movement, teams can rocket up or down the standings in a hurry. The 2002 Anaheim Angels were world champions one year after finishing 41 games behind in the American League West.

TEAMS WITH 110 WINS

Year	Team	W	L	Pct.
1906	Chicago Cubs	116	36	.763
2001	Seattle Mariners	116	46	.716
1998	New York Yankees	114	48	.704
1954	Cleveland Indians	111	43	.721
1909	Pittsburgh Pirates	110	42	.724
1927	New York Yankees	110	44	.714

MUSICAL MANAGERS

On February 2, 2002, Expos manager Jeff Torborg became the Marlins manager, with Frank Robinson taking over as the Expos manager. When Montreal moved to Washington three years later, Robinson went with them.

MANAGERS FIRED DURING SPRING TRAINING

- 2002—Joe Kerrigan, Red Sox (replaced by Grady Little)
- 1999—Tim Johnson, Blue Jays (replaced by Jim Fregosi)
- 1978—Alvin Dark, Padres (replaced by Roger Craig)
- 1954—Stan Hack, Cubs (replaced by Phil Cavaretta)

HOW CUBS BLEW FLAGS

- 1969—Blew big August lead to Mets in first NL East race
- 1984—Blew 2–0 NLCS lead as Padres won three straight
- 2003—Blew 3–1 NLCS lead as Marlins took four straight

PATIENCE = PENNANT

Patience paid off for the 2004 Boston Red Sox. Their hitters faced more pitches (25,592) than any other team, won 55 games at home, and had the best home offense.

CAPTAINS COURAGEOUS

Major league managers sometimes appoint team leaders to the ceremonial position of captain. Not all teams have captains and even fewer maintain the job on a continuous basis. Here are the 11 men who have filled the role for the New York Yankees:

Player	Dates
Hal Chase	1912
Roger Peckinpaugh	1914–21
Babe Ruth	May 20–25, 1922
Everett Scott	1922–25
Lou Gehrig	1935–41
Thurman Munson	1976–79
Graig Nettles	1982–84
Willie Randolph	1986–89
Ron Guidry	1986–89
Don Mattingly	1991–95
Derek Jeter	2003

INFIELD SLUGGERS

All four infielders of the 1940 Boston Red Sox and 2004 Texas Rangers hit 20 or more home runs.

PINSTRIPE POWER

The 2004 Yankees posted their 17th season of at least 100

victories and hit a team-record 242 home runs.

SCHEDULING NOT SIMPLE

Crafting the big-league schedule is no easy matter—especially when there are 30 teams, interleague play, and prearranged agreements between players and owners. The slate must be 178–183 days long, cannot include more than two day-night doubleheaders per team, and must have days off for teams traveling between Pacific and Eastern time zones. Also required, according to Major League Baseball senior vice president Katy Feeney, are fair distribution of holiday and weekend dates, a minimum of home-and-home series, and no four-series home stands or road trips. Teams submit special requests almost 18 months in advance. For 24 seasons, 1981 to 2004, the major league schedule was crafted by Henry and Holly Stephenson, working out of their home on Martha's Vineyard, Massachusetts.

JAPAN ALL-STAR SERIES

An All-Star team of 28 players from 17 big-league clubs played an eight-game series in Japan after the 2004 World Series. The ninth Japan All-Star series since 1986 drew more than 300,000 fans to games in five different cities. Toronto outfielder Vernon Wells won MVP honors with a .407 average, two home runs, and seven runs batted in. The big leaguers won five of the eight games.

Another team of U.S. All-Stars won all five games played in Japan after the 2006 World Series.

POWER SURGE

Before 1996, the only team to hit 225 home runs in a season was the 1961 Yankees. In the next nine seasons, it happened 26 times.

FANS FLOCK TO BRONX

The 2005 Yankees had the highest season attendance in baseball history.

CAPITAL REVIVAL

Washington went 34 years without major league baseball before the Montreal Expos became the Washington Nationals in 2005. After posting a 67–95 mark in their Montreal swan song, the team sold 1.9 million season tickets—more than two dozen other teams—and drew 45,596 fans to RFK Stadium for Opening Day. The

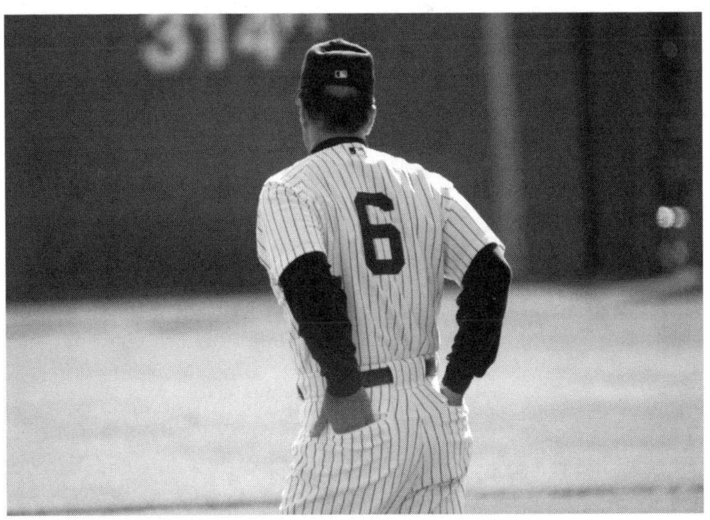

A one-time NL batting champ and MVP, Joe Torre enjoyed mixed success as manager of the Braves, Mets, and Cardinals before taking over the Yankees in 1996. The former All-Star catcher won four world championships in his first five years in the Bronx.
Bill Menzel

Nats beat Arizona, 5–3, in front of a crowd that included President George W. Bush, who threw out the first ball while wearing a red Nationals warm-up jacket. The win gave Washington undisputed possession of first place for the first time since the Washington Senators clinched their last pennant on October 1, 1933.

FIRST FOR NATS

Brad Wilkerson was the first batter for the Washington Nationals (formerly the Montreal Expos).

RAZING ARIZONA

Shortly after moving from player agent to CEO of the Arizona Diamondbacks in 2005, Jeff Moorad managed to cut the payroll from $80 million to $57 million and add 11 players to the organization.

SEPTEMBER STREAKERS

The Houston Astros believe in fast finishes; they advanced to postseason play in 2004 on the heels of a 36–10 finish and did the same in 2005 by closing with a 44–18 mark.

Against Interleague Play

"Everybody in baseball wants a balanced schedule. It's not fair otherwise. Just have the AL play the AL and have the fun of the World Series being the World Series."

—Jorge Posada

TALENTED PILOTS
Tony La Russa and Leo Durocher are the only managers to win 500 games with three different teams.

REMEMBERING BROOKLYN
The Los Angeles Dodgers celebrated Jackie Robinson Day on April 15, 2005, by wearing uniforms that said "Brooklyn" on the front. The team played there when Robinson broke baseball's color barrier in 1947.

OLD-AGE HOME
A July 2005 series between the Marlins and Giants marked the first time in the history of professional sports that opposing coaches or managers had reached their 70th birthdays. Jack McKeon, 74, managed Florida while Felipe Alou, 70, ran the Giants. Before their meeting, the pair had combined to appear in 5,794 major league games.

PEAVY'S PEEVES
Some number one pitchers can't get any respect. In 2005 San Diego ace Jake Peavy cut his left hand taking out the garbage, then cracked a rib jumping into a jubilant pile of teammates celebrating the Padres' NL West title.

HOT-LANTA
During the 15-year span from 1991 to 2005, the Atlanta Braves compiled a .606 winning percentage, easily outdistancing the runner-up New York Yankees (.579) and third-best Boston Red Sox (.539). Only the 1927–41 Yankees (.636), 1947–61 Yankees (.626), and 1903–17 New York Giants (.612) did better over any similar stretch.

BRAVES NEW WORLD
With 14 consecutive division titles from 1991 to 2005, the Atlanta Braves compiled the best streak in professional sports history. The Montreal Canadiens made 10 straight Stanley Cup appearances (1951–1960), while the Boston Celtics (1957–1965) and Los

Angeles Lakers (1982–1990) won nine straight NBA division crowns. Colorado/Quebec won nine consecutive NHL titles (1995–2003), and the New York Yankees appeared in 11 straight postseasons starting in 1995.

9 x 20

Thanks in part to longtime pitching coach Leo Mazzone, the Atlanta Braves had nine 20-game winners from 1991 to 2005.

FLORIDA FRUSTRATES BREWERS

Four Florida pitchers fanned a combined 22 Milwaukee Brewers during a 12-inning game on July 6, 2005. Perfect for more than nine innings, they retired the last 28 Brewers batters in a 5–4 victory. Tom Cheney holds the one-pitcher mark, with 21 in a 16-inning game for Washington against Baltimore on September 12, 1962.

MARGIN OF VICTORY

Although the Boston Red Sox and New York Yankees finished with identical records in 2005, the Yankees were awarded the AL East title because they won the season's series from the Sox with 10 wins in 19 games.

RICH PACT

In 1996 the three-year, $16 million contract given to Joe Torre by the Yankees made him the best-paid manager in baseball history.

METS NO-HITTERS

No-hitters are rare in the majors, nonexistent in the 45-year history of the Mets. But a dozen were thrown by former Mets after they left the team. Authors included Nolan Ryan, who threw seven, and David Cone, Doc Gooden, Hideo Nomo, Mike Scott, and Tom Seaver, with one apiece. Nomo also threw one *before* he became a Met. The Mets have played more than 7,000 games without a no-hitter.

NEW YORK ADVICE

According to research published by *USA Today* in 2005, players share the following New York survival tips:

- Find several routes to the ballpark, including the subway
- Expect unwarranted criticism
- Learn to budget your time and say no
- Prepare for hometown booing
- Never try to do too much

WINLESS WONDERS

- Chicago Cubs (last won World Series in 1908)
- San Francisco Giants (won Series in 1954)
- Cleveland Indians (won Series in 1948)
- Houston Astros (lost only World Series in 2005)
- Eight expansion franchises never won World Series

Chapter 6
Times Terrific

Brooks Robinson Remembers...

Playing in the World Series is the most exciting thing that's ever happened to me. As a youngster growing up in Little Rock, I dreamed of signing a professional contract, playing in the minor leagues, arriving in the major leagues, winning a pennant, and getting into the World Series. I always said to myself, "If those things ever happened, I would realize my life's dream." Even if it only happened once, at least you could say you were the best.

I actually played in four World Series. Going into the Dodgers series in 1966, we were underdogs. They had been there the year before. On our side, Frank Robinson had been in the 1961 World Series with the Reds. In the first game, Frank and I hit back-to-back home runs that changed the whole complexion of the Series and convinced our players they could win. The Dodgers wound up with the lowest batting average for a losing team, and we wound up with the lowest batting average for a winning team.

The 1970 World Series was unusual. The biggest thing we thought about when we went to Cincinnati was what kind of shoes we should wear. We didn't have AstroTurf in the American League. We ended up wearing our regular cleats but had to remember to pick our feet up. If you started scooting across that carpet, your cleats would almost stop you.

Before the Series started, I said to Mark Belanger, "We're going to get a lot of work in this World Series." We had Mike Cuellar, Dave McNally, and Jim Palmer, a great right-hander with a fastball and a slow curve. He got a lot of guys to pull the ball. They had Johnny Bench, Tony Perez, Lee May, and Pete Rose. Three of those guys wanted to hit it as far as they could every time they came up.

I remember the first ball that was hit to me, in the first inning of the first game. It was like a 24-hopper. I made a high throw to Boog Powell for an error. I said to myself, "Now what is coming off? The first ball you get and you make an error!" But everything after that was pretty upbeat. I got a lot of chances.

As an infielder, you can play a week and never get a chance to make an outstanding play. But in that World Series, it just seemed like every game, there were one or two chances to do something spectacular. We were hitting well and actually scored more runs than the Big Red Machine. We took advantage of their pitching staff. Wayne Simpson and Jim Merritt were hurt, and Jim McGlothlin wasn't throwing very well. Gary Nolan started a couple of games, but we hit the ball and scored a lot of runs against him.

We won and I was fortunate to win the World Series MVP award.

I also won an All-Star Game MVP—even though I played in more losing All-Star Games than anyone in the history of baseball. Even when I got the award in St. Louis, it was strange because I was on the losing team. It was the hottest day of that year, with people fainting in the stands. We went into extra innings and lost, 2–1, but I played the whole game, made a couple of good plays, and got three hits.

At Shea Stadium in 1964, I was on my way to being MVP of that game, with a triple and another base hit, before Johnny Callison changed that game with one swing of the bat against Dick Radatz in the ninth inning. Fans might not remember this, but I have more triples in All-Star history than anyone else.

Smooth-fielding Baltimore third baseman Brooks Robinson made the American League All-Star team 15 times. He was American League MVP in 1964, All-Star Game MVP in 1966—even though his team lost—and World Series MVP in 1970. Ronnie Joyner

ALL-STAR GAME

COBB NEVER AN ALL-STAR
Ty Cobb never played in an All-Star Game. His last active season was 1928, five years before the first All-Star Game was played.

DISCOUNT DUCAT
A ticket to the first All-Star Game in 1933 cost $1.10.

ALL-STAR SNUB
The all-time All-Star snub occurred in 1935, when Tigers slugger Hank Greenberg was left off the AL team by his own manager, Mickey Cochrane, even though he had 110 RBIs at the break. Greenberg finished the year with 170 RBIs as Detroit won the pennant.

STELLAR SOUTHPAW
In 1938, the year he became the only pitcher to throw consecutive no-hitters, Johnny Vander Meer was so intimidating to left-handed hitters that AL manager Joe McCarthy chose Jimmie Foxx over Lou Gehrig as his starting first baseman in the All-Star Game against the Cincinnati southpaw.

EARL THE PEARL
Earl Averill was so highly regarded as a center fielder that Joe DiMaggio moved to right during his first three All-Star Games.

ALL-STAR FAMILY
The three DiMaggio brothers made a combined 22 All-Star appearances: 13 for Joe, seven from Dom, and two for Vince. The Alomar brothers, Roberto and Sandy Jr., rank second, with 14 combined selections.

TOPPING THE MAJORS
The Negro Leagues' East-West game outdrew the All-Star Game eight times: in 1936, 1938, 1942, 1943, 1944, 1946, 1947, and 1948. Both leagues played in the same city in 1947, with the major leaguers at Wrigley Field and the Negro Leagues at the larger Comiskey Park.

BLACK ALL-STARS
The lone All-Star Game at Ebbets Field, in 1949, marked the debut of the first black All-Stars: Jackie Robinson, Roy Campanella, and Don Newcombe for the National League and Larry Doby for the American League. The AL won, 11–7.

Infielders Dick Bartell, Frankie Frisch, and Pepper Martin discuss strategy before the "Game of the Century" at Chicago in 1933. The AL prevailed, 4–2.

National League

SAGE YOGI

Prior to the 1949 All-Star Game, American League pitchers were trying to decide how to pitch to Stan Musial. With everyone offering conflicting advice, the discussion came to an end only when Yogi Berra, the All-Star catcher, piped up: "You guys are trying to stop Musial in 15 minutes while the National League hasn't stopped him in 15 years."

1953 GAME MOVED

The 1953 All-Star Game, originally scheduled for Braves Field in Boston, was moved to Cincinnati after the Braves moved to Milwaukee during spring training.

STONE WALL

Washington southpaw Dean Stone won an All-Star Game without retiring a batter. It happened on July 13, 1954, when the AL beat the NL, 11–9, at Cleveland's Municipal Stadium. Stone entered in the top of the eighth with two outs, two on, and the AL trailing, 9–8. With a 1–1 count on Duke Snider, Red Schoendienst tried to steal home. Stone's throw to catcher Yogi Berra was on target, ending the inning, and Stone was the winning pitcher when the AL scored three runs in the bottom of the eighth. The umpires rejected the National League's contention that Stone balked while making his throw.

ALL-STAR VETS

Hank Aaron, Willie Mays, and Stan Musial were selected for a record 24 All-Star Games each.

DOUBLE D DOUBLES UP

Though Don Drysdale, Robin Roberts, and Lefty Grove share the record for most All-Star Games started by a pitcher, Drysdale is the only man who did it twice in one year. It happened in 1959, the first of four years when the majors played two All-Star Games to raise money for the players' pension fund.

FOSSE'S FORTUNE

A home-plate collision between runner Pete Rose and catcher Ray Fosse in 1970 helped establish the former's reputation as "Charlie Hustle." But Fosse, saddled with a separated and fractured left shoulder because of the hit, was never the same. "I had 16 homers at the All-Star break," Fosse said, "but hit only two more that year. My career went downhill. Pete once signed a ball for me, 'Thanks for making me famous.' When he went to prison for tax evasion [in 1990], it was in my hometown of Marion, Illinois."

Rival catchers of 1933 All-Star teams were Bill Dickey (Yankees) of the American League and Gabby Hartnett (Cubs) of the National League.
National League

Carl Hubbell of the Giants fanned five straight superstars in the 1934 All-Star Game at the Polo Grounds, his home park. Reprinted with permission, National Baseball Hall of Fame Library, Cooperstown, New York

STAR POWER
Six future Hall of Famers homered in the 1971 All-Star Game: Reggie Jackson, Frank Robinson, Hank Aaron, Harmon Killebrew, Roberto Clemente, and Johnny Bench.

WRITE-IN STARTERS
Since the All-Star vote was returned to the fans in 1970, only two write-in candidates have been elected to the starting lineup: National Leaguers Rico Carty, an outfielder, in 1970 and Steve Garvey, first baseman, in 1974.

BALLOT RESPONSE
In 1976, 8,370,145 All-Star ballots were returned by fans—more than the total number of votes President Abraham Lincoln received in both his victories plus the total population of the United States at the time the Constitution was ratified.

PHANTOM SHORTSTOP
In 1974 Luis Aparicio was listed on the All-Star ballot even though he had been released by the Red Sox before the season opened.

ALL-STAR SLAM
Fred Lynn of the Boston Red Sox hit the only grand slam in All-Star history. The two-out, third-inning shot off Atlee Hammaker at Chicago's Comiskey Park came on July 6, 1983, on the 50th anniversary of the first All-Star Game.

FIRST IMPRESSION
Terry Steinbach is the only man to homer in his first major league at-bat as well as his first All-Star Game at-bat.

OLDIES BUT GOODIES
The 1989 All-Star Game featured two starters who had already celebrated their 40th

birthdays: Rick Reuschel (NL) and Nolan Ryan (AL).

CRIME DOG BARKS

With the American League nursing a 7–5 lead in the ninth inning of the 1994 All-Star Game, National League pinch-hitter Fred McGriff hit a two-out, two-run homer against Lee Smith to tie the score. The NL won in the tenth when Tony Gwynn singled and scored on a double by Moises Alou.

CHANGE OF VENUE

Closer Jeff Shaw, traded by the Reds to the Dodgers two days before the 1998 All-Star Game, made his Dodgers debut in the midsummer classic. That made him the first ballplayer to appear in the All-Star Game before making a regular-season appearance for his club. He also became the first man to pitch in an All-Star Game on his birthday.

PAST AND PRESENT

In the first All-Star vote after payroll-slashing moves destroyed the roster of the 1997 world champion Marlins, former Fish on the All-Star ballot got 6,549,643 votes while current Florida players got 962,659.

FINDING TONY

The National League couldn't take its team picture at the 1999 All-Star Game in Boston's Fenway Park because perpetual batting champ Tony Gwynn couldn't be found. Thirty minutes later, the San Diego outfielder was found eating sunflower seeds in a cool spot: inside the hand-operated scoreboard.

FOUR STRAIGHT K'S

Pedro Martinez is the only pitcher to strike out the first four opposing batters in an

Franklin D. Roosevelt was the only president who ever appeared on an All-Star program cover. Major League Baseball

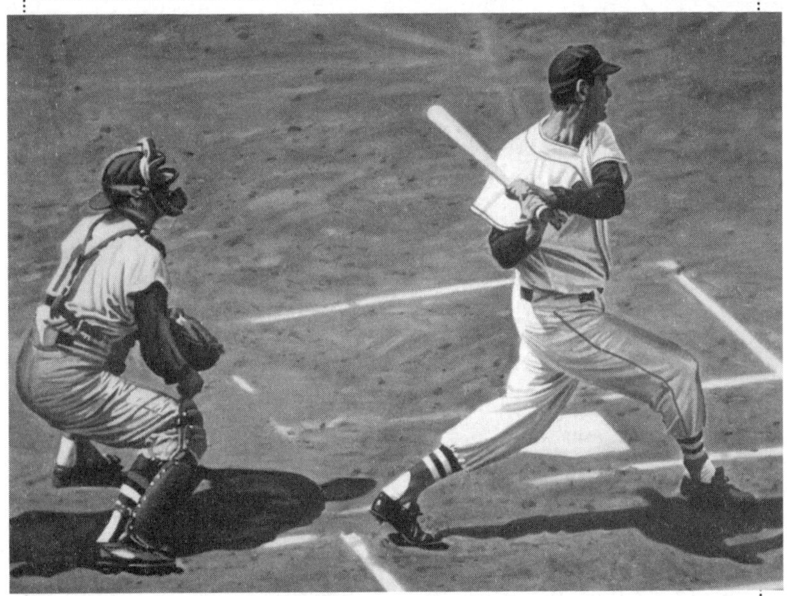

Ted Williams had a much higher batting average at Fenway Park. Copyright Andy Jurinko 1995. Reprinted with permission, Bill Goff, Inc./GoodSportsArt.com.

All-Star Game. It happened at Fenway, then his home park, in 1999.

VERSATILE ALL-STARS

Paul Molitor duplicated an earlier Pete Rose feat by playing five different positions in All-Star history. But Molitor didn't approach the record of 24 All-Star appearances, shared by Hank Aaron, Willie Mays, and Stan Musial.

ONE OF A KIND

Derek Jeter is the only man to be All-Star Game and World Series MVP in the same season (2000). No other Yankee has ever been MVP of the All-Star Game.

STAR OF STARS

Cal Ripken Jr. made a record 16 consecutive All-Star Game starts. The last man elected as the American League's starting All-Star shortstop before Ripken's streak of 16 was also a future Hall of Famer: Robin Yount.

FOND FAREWELL
In his final season, Cal Ripken Jr. was All-Star Game MVP for the second time. His homer, the second of his All-Star career, paced the AL to a 4–1 win in the 2001 Safeco Field game.

POWERFUL PITCHER
At the 2001 All-Star Game in Seattle, NL pitcher Mike Hampton had more home runs (six) than AL starters Cal Ripken Jr. (four) and Ichiro Suzuki (five).

LONG WAIT
Roger Clemens had a 15-year wait between All-Star Game starts (1986, 2001).

ALL-STAR TIES
Two All-Star Games ended in ties. The second of two games played in 1961 ended in a 1–1 tie when rain halted play after five innings, while the 2002 game wound up 7–7 when both sides ran out of pitchers after 11 innings.

NO TED TROPHY
The very first Ted Williams All-Star Game MVP award was not awarded. The legendary outfielder's name was attached to the award in 2002, when the All-Star Game ended in an 11-inning, 7–7 tie and no MVP was named.

ALL-STAR CHANGES
The All-Star Game, a tradition that started in 1933, has undergone numerous changes over the years. Among the most recent, enacted in 2003, are the following:

Dodgers flamethrower Don Drysdale started both All-Star Games for the National League in 1959.
Ronnie Joyner

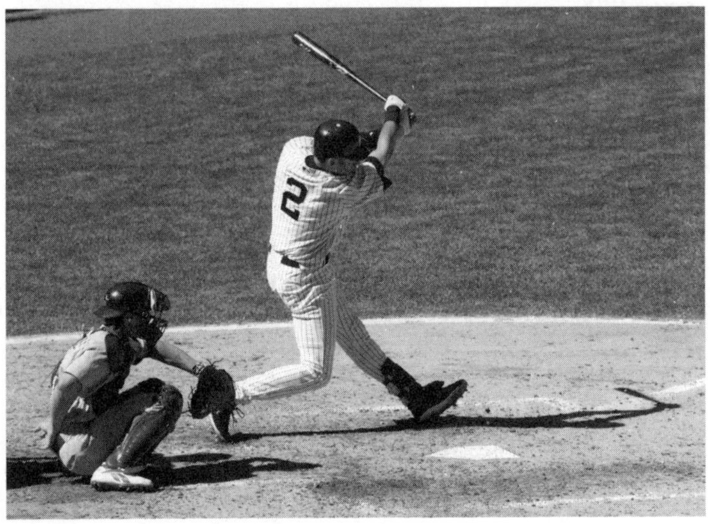

Yankees shortstop Derek Jeter was the first player to be MVP of the All-Star Game and World Series in the same season (2000). Bill Menzel

- League that wins the All-Star Game gets home-field advantage in World Series
- Roster size increased from 30 to 32 players
- Players, managers, and coaches pick nine additional AL position players and eight in the NL, plus eight pitchers from each league: five starters and three relievers
- Manager, consulting with the commissioner's office, picks final six AL spots and eight NL spots
- No pitcher is required to work more than three innings and all starting position players must receive at least one at-bat.

HOW VOTING CHANGED

The All-Star selection process has varied widely over the years. Fans picked the teams the first two years, 1933 and 1934, but the two All-Star managers took over from 1935 to 1946. Fans voted again from 1947 to 1957, but Commissioner Ford Frick stopped the practice after Cincinnati voters elected the entire Reds lineup, except for first baseman George Crowe, in 1957. Frick not only replaced Wally Post and Gus Bell with

Willie Mays and Hank Aaron but also gave the vote to players, managers, and coaches—with the stipulation they could not vote for teammates. Bowie Kuhn returned the vote to the fans in 1970, and it has stayed there since, despite several miscarriages of justice (such as .169 hitter Davey Lopes winning a spot in the lineup).

The Clemens Collapse

The worst first inning of Roger Clemens's career happened under a national spotlight—the 2004 All-Star Game at Houston's Minute Maid Park. By yielding six runs, Clemens not only gave up more than any starting pitcher in All-Star history but actually allowed the American League to hit for the cycle (single, double, triple, home run). In eight other All-Star outings, against 40 batters, Clemens had given up *one* extra-base hit. The first man to pitch for four different teams in All-Star play, Clemens had made 650 regular-season and postseason starts before his All-Star fiasco.

Good for Both

Roger Clemens and Randy Johnson are the only pitchers

who started All-Star Games for both leagues.

All-Star Anywhere

In 2004 Carlos Beltran became the first man to be chosen for one league's All-Star team but play for the other.

Star Power

Gary Sheffield was the first man to represent five different teams in the All-Star Game (Yankees, Braves, Dodgers, Padres, Brewers).

Elbowed Out

The crosstown competition between the White Sox and Cubs took another hit just before the 2006 All-Star Game when Carlos Zambrano, the top Cubs' pitcher, was conked on the pitching elbow by the bat of Joey Cora, third-base coach for the White Sox. Zambrano was being interviewed by media members from his native Venezuela when he accidentally backed into Cora's fungo bat just as the coach was completing a swing. Cora had been hitting practice grounders. Although X-rays were negative, the accident prevented Zambrano from pitching in the All-Star Game.

All-Star Rallies

Last-inning comebacks in All-Star Games:

- 2006—AL wins, 3–2, on Michael Young's two-out, two-run triple in the ninth
- 1994—NL ties in the ninth and wins in the tenth, 8–7, on a one-out double by Moises Alou
- 1987—NL wins, 2–0, on a two-run triple in the thirteenth by Tim Raines
- 1979—NL wins, 7–6, on a one-run walk in the ninth by Lee Mazzilli
- 1964—NL wins, 7–4, on Johnny Callison's three-run HR in the ninth
- 1941—AL wins, 11–9, on Ted Williams's two-out, three-run HR in the ninth

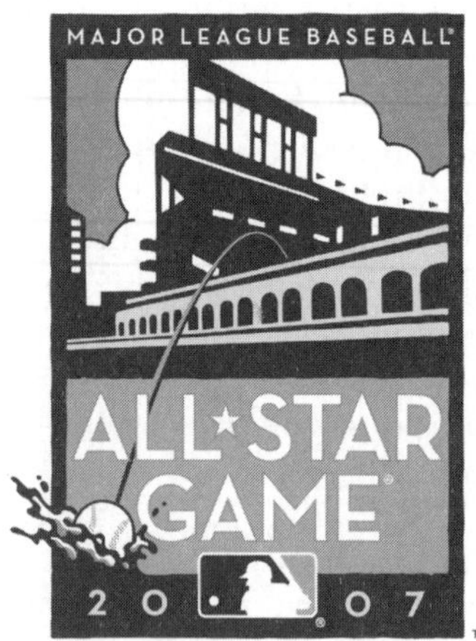

PLAYOFFS

UNEXPECTED PLAYOFFS

Before two rounds of playoffs became part of the baseball calendar, each league sent its champions directly to the World Series, unless pennant races were tied at the end of the season.

The National League, which settled ties with a best-of-three pennant playoff, needed playoffs in 1946, 1951, 1959, and 1962, while the American League, using a one-game, winner-take-all format, needed a playoff in 1948. Years later, divisional ties were broken by one-game playoffs in 1978 and 1995 (AL) and 1980, 1998, and 1999 (NL).

FRESHMAN FLASH

Facing a one-game playoff for the 1948 American League pennant, Cleveland player/manager Lou Boudreau bypassed Bob Feller and Bob Lemon to pick Gene Bearden, a rookie knuckleballer with one day of rest. To make the selection even more unlikely,

Ralph Branca, who flaunted superstition by wearing No. 13, kids nemesis Bobby Thomson (in uniform) at the 1951 World Series. New York's slugger delivered a pennant-winning homer against Brooklyn's Branca in the last inning of the National League playoff. National League

Bearden threw left-handed and was pitching in Fenway Park, where right-handed hitters drool at the proximity of the left-field wall. Boudreau must have known *something:* his team won the playoff, 8–3, and proceeded to bump off the Boston Braves in a six-game World Series.

PLAYOFF GIVEAWAY
In 1959 the Milwaukee Braves took a 5–2 lead into the ninth inning of Playoff Game 2 but could not hold on. The Los Angeles Dodgers tied it in the ninth and won, 6–5, when Felix Mantilla made a throwing error in the twelfth.

RECORDS COUNTED
Under the old playoff rules, individual statistics compiled in league playoffs were considered part of the regular season's averages. The rule allowed Milwaukee Braves third baseman Eddie Mathews to win the NL home-run crown when he hit number 46 against the Dodgers in 1959 and broke a tie with Ernie Banks.

ANOTHER MIRACLE FINISH
With star southpaw Sandy Koufax idled by a circulatory ailment in his fingers, the Los Angeles Dodgers were unable to hold the lead in the 1962 National League race. The San Francisco Giants, repeating their miracle finish of 1951, cut the lead to three games with eight to play and finally caught the Dodgers to force a playoff. In the last 13 games, the Giants were 7–6 but the Dodgers 3–10. San Francisco won the best-of-three playoff to win the right to face the Yankees in the World Series.

Leo's Lip

"I remember Leo Durocher saying to me, 'Bobby, if you ever hit one, hit one now.' I thought he was out of his mind."

—Bobby Thomson

WHY GIANTS WON
The 1951 New York Giants engineered the greatest comeback in a single season because of key player moves by manager Leo Durocher. On May 21 Whitey Lockman took over first base. On May 25 Willie Mays came up from Minneapolis to play center field. On July 20 Bobby Thomson went to third base

THE BOBBY THOMSON GAME

AT NEW YORK, OCTOBER 3, 1951

				R	H	E
Brooklyn	1 0 0	0 0 0	0 3 0	4	8	0
New York	0 0 0	0 0 0	1 0 4	5	8	0

New York	AB	R	H	RBI	Brooklyn	AB	R	H	RBI
Stanky, 2B	4	0	0	0	Furillo, RF	5	0	0	0
Dark, SS	4	1	1	0	Reese, SS	4	2	1	1
Mueller, RF	4	0	1	0	Snider, CF	3	1	2	0
Hartung*	0	1	0	0	Robinson, 2B	2	1	1	1
Irvin, LF	4	1	1	0	Pafko, LF	4	0	1	1
Lockman, 1B	3	1	2	1	Hodges, 1B	4	0	0	0
Thomson, 3B	4	1	3	4	Cox, 3B	4	0	2	1
Mays, CF	3	0	0	0	Walker, C	4	0	1	0
Westrum, C	0	0	0	0	Newcombe, P	4	0	0	0
Rigney†	1	0	0	0	Branca, P	0	0	0	0
Noble, C	0	0	0	0					
Maglie, P	2	0	0	0					
Thompson‡	1	0	0	0					
Jansen, P	0	0	0	0					
Totals	**30**	**5**	**8**	**5**	**Totals**	**34**	**4**	**8**	**4**

* Ran for Mueller in the ninth

† Struck out for Westrum in the eighth

‡ Grounded out for Maglie in the eighth

2B—Thomson, Irvin, Lockman. HR—Thomson. Sacrifice—Lockman. LOB—Brooklyn 7, New York 3.

Pitcher	IP	H	R	ER	BB	SO
Maglie	8	8	4	4	4	6
Jansen (W, 23–11)	1	0	0	0	0	0
Newcombe	8⅓	7	4	4	2	2
Branca (L, 13–12)	0	1	1	1	0	0

Branca pitched to one batter in the ninth.

Umpires—Jorda, Conlan, Stewart, Goetz. Time—2:28. Attendance—34,320.

and Don Mueller began playing right field every day.

LIGHTNING STRIKES TWICE

Before hitting the pennant-winning home run against Ralph Branca in the last inning of the last playoff game, Bobby Thomson hit *another* game-winning homer against Branca in the same series! Thomson's two-run homer in the first game gave the Giants a 3–1 win.

THIN MARGIN

The 1951 New York Giants spent only three days in first place—the shortest stay at the top of any pennant-winning team.

HISTORY'S MYSTERIES

Although Bobby Thomson and Bill Mazeroski hit the most dramatic home runs in baseball history, neither ball has been found. Thomson's "shot heard 'round the world" gave the New York Giants the 1951 NL pennant, while Mazeroski's solo shot, also in the ninth inning, was the first home run to end a World Series.

EXTRA PLAYOFFS

Baseball added scheduled playoffs when it expanded to 12-team leagues in 1969. With the leagues split into divisions, a best-of-five format was adopted to match the two winners in each league. The League Championship Series became a best-of-seven in 1985 after many clubs complained the best-of-five format was a "crapshoot." The first-round Division Series, added in 1995 after expansion to 30 teams and a three-division format that included a wild-card winner, retained the best-of-five format.

Jack Clark's three-run homer off Tom Niedenfuer gave the Cardinals a 7–5 win over the Dodgers in the decisive Game 6 of the 1985 NLCS. With first base open, Dodgers pilot Tom Lasorda could have ordered an intentional walk for Clark, the only slugger in the St. Louis lineup.
St. Louis Cardinals

Cuellar's Clout

After hitting .089 during the regular season, Baltimore pitcher Mike Cuellar got a wind-blown grand slam in Game 1 of the 1970 ALCS against Minnesota's Jim Perry. Although the Orioles won the game, 10–6, Cuellar failed to last the required five innings to pick up the win.

Chris Missed Base

Chris Chambliss never touched home plate after hitting his pennant-winning home run against Mark Littell of the Kansas City Royals on October 14, 1976. He also missed touching second. The ninth-inning leadoff shot, which snapped a 6–6 tie in the fifth and final game of the American League Championship Series, gave the Yankees their first pennant since 1964 but also ignited a riot as frenzied fans spilled onto the field. Chambliss barely made it to the Yankees dugout.

Bucky Makes a Dent

Bucky Dent hit only 40 home runs in his career, but one of them is still being felt—nearly 30 years after it happened. In a sudden-death divisional playoff between the Red Sox and Yankees at Fenway Park in 1978, Dent fouled a pitch off his foot, then feigned injury by hopping around in apparent pain. Ex-Yankees pitcher Mike Torrez, watching the spectacle, waited without throwing any warm-ups. Dent finally returned to the batter's box, swung at the next pitch he saw, and delivered a three-run homer that gave the Yankees a lead they never lost, not to mention the pennant.

After getting only 10 at-bats during the regular season, Francisco Cabrera became an Atlanta folk hero with a two-out, two-run pinch single in the ninth inning of 1992 NCLS Game 7, giving Atlanta a 3–2 win over Pittsburgh and the National League pennant. Atlanta Braves

After dreaming of postseason action for 19 years, Seattle fans get their wish as the M's steal the 1995 ALDS finale from the wild-card Yankees. Recovering from an August 15 AL West deficit of 12½ games, the Mariners manage to overcome a one-run deficit in this game on an Edgar Martinez shot into the left-field corner with two men on.

DENT IN THE NET

The Bucky Dent playoff homer that gave the Yankees the 1978 AL pennant has never been found. It was among 20 balls left in the left-field netting at Fenway Park because the Red Sox grounds crew never cleaned up after batting practice.

STICKY WICKET

In 1984, when the League Championship Series format was still best-of-five, the Chicago Cubs won the first two games at home before heading west to San Diego. The Padres won the first two in their own park but fell behind 3–0 in the finale. That was before Ryne Sandberg knocked over a jug of Gatorade that soaked the glove of first baseman Bull Durham. The Cubs had a quick inning in the last of the fifth, denying Durham's glove enough time to be properly dried. It was still sticky in the sixth when the Padres parlayed a Durham error into a three-run inning and eventual 6–3 win. The first baseman said he was unable to open the fingers of his glove in time to spear the grounder that got by.

SOUTHPAW SLUGGER

Switch-hitting shortstop Ozzie Smith had played in the majors for eight seasons before hitting a home run left-handed. The solo shot in the ninth inning gave the St. Louis Cardinals a 3–2 win over the Los Angeles Dodgers in Game 5 of the 1985 National League Championship Series. A three-run, ninth-inning homer by Jack Clark in Game 6 gave the Cardinals the pennant.

NO ANGEL HALO

In the AL Championship Series of 1986, the California Angels held a 3–1 advantage in games as they took a 5–2 lead into the ninth inning of Game 5 against the Boston Red Sox. With two outs, Don Baylor and Dave Henderson delivered two-run homers that put Boston up, 6–5, in a game they eventually won, 7–6, in 11 innings. The Red Sox won both remaining games at Fenway Park to take the pennant.

WINNING LOSERS

The only players from losing teams to win MVP honors in the League Championship Series were Fred Lynn (Angels) in 1982 and Jeffrey Leonard (Giants) in 1987.

CLARK'S BARRAGE

Will Clark of the Giants knocked in six runs, an NLCS record, in the opener of the 1989 series against the Cubs. Among his hits was a grand slam against Greg Maddux.

PLAYOFF GOPHERS

After yielding just one grand slam in 2,365⅔ regular-season innings, Greg Maddux allowed two (to Will Clark and Gary Gaetti) in 34⅔ innings of the NL Championship Series.

DONNIE'S DESPAIR

Donnie Moore, depressed after giving up the Dave Henderson homer that cost the Angels a trip to the 1986 World Series, took his own life three years later.

FIRST WILD-CARD

The 1995 Colorado Rockies finished with a 77–67 record, one game behind the Los Angeles Dodgers for the championship of the NL West but one game ahead of the Houston Astros for the NL's wild-card slot. The Rox thus became the first wild-card winner in National League history.

SLAM IN THE PINCH
Cincinnati's Mark Lewis connected for the first pinch-hit grand slam in postseason history in Game 3 of the 1995 NLDS against Los Angeles.

THOME POISONING
Jim Thome was the first player to hit two grand slams in postseason play.

CLUTCH COMEBACK
The 1996 Atlanta Braves, trailing St. Louis three games to one in the best-of-seven NLCS, posted successive 14–0, 3–1, and 15–0 wins to advance to their fourth World Series of the decade.

STRANGE ENDINGS
Game 3 of the 1997 ALCS was the first postseason game to end with a stolen base. Cleveland's Marquis Grissom scored when Omar Vizquel missed an attempted suicide squeeze and Baltimore catcher Lenny Webster missed the ball. Grissom was credited with a steal of home, giving Cleveland a 2–1 win.

RECORD SCORE
Before Boston beat Cleveland, 23–7, in Game 4 of the 1999 AL Division Series, the highest-scoring postseason game of all time was Toronto's 15–14 win over Philadelphia in Game 4 of the 1993 World Series.

GRAND SINGLE
It was the bottom of the fifteenth inning in the rain-soaked fifth game of the 1999 National League Championship Series between the Atlanta Braves and the New York Mets. The Mets tied it on three walks, sandwiched around a sacrifice bunt. Robin Ventura then hit a pitch over the wall in right-center field, ostensibly giving New York a 7–3 victory. But he only made it to first before delirious fans mobbed him, making it impossible to complete the circuit. The game-winning grand slam went into the scorebook as a single. The final score was 4–3.

THE DYE IN CAST
Oakland outfielder Jermaine Dye, later a World Series MVP with the White Sox, shattered his left kneecap in Game 4 of the 2001 ALDS between the A's and Yankees. It happened when he fouled off a pitch from Orlando "El Duque" Hernandez. Dye, idled for six months, took nearly two years to return to full health.

The first man to win two postseason games with walkoff hits, David Ortiz lived up to his "Big Papi" nickname by winning MVP honors in the 2004 ALCS. His twelvth-inning homer kept the Red Sox alive in Game 4 against the Yankees, and his fourteenth-inning RBI single the next night forced Game 6. His five homers and 19 RBIs in 14 games during the 2004 postseason helped the BoSox win eight straight postseason games, an unprecedented feat the White Sox would duplicate a year later. Bill Menzel

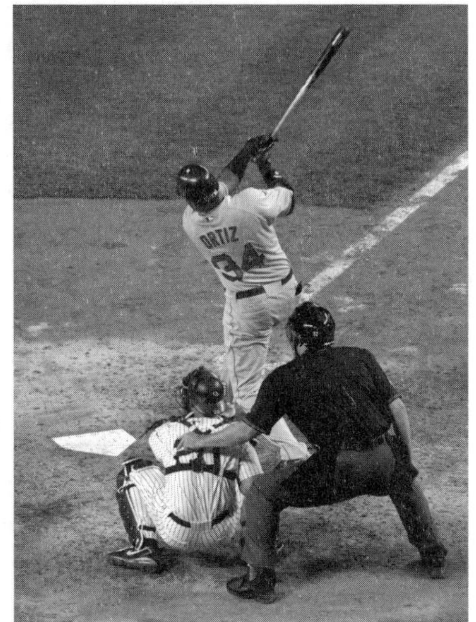

NO GUARANTEES

Teams with the best record during the 162-game regular season don't always succeed in postseason play. The Atlanta Braves were eliminated in the first-round Division Series twice (1997 and 2003) after topping the majors in wins.

GOOD MEMORY

After taking the first two NLCS games at St. Louis in 2002, the San Francisco Giants asked their bus driver to honk his horn en route to the airport. It was retribution for 1987, when the Cards beat the Giants. Said pitcher-turned-broadcaster Mike Krukow: "We couldn't get a flight out so we had to stay in the hotel and listen to people honking horns all night. It was the worst night of my life."

BULLPEN BRAWL

Yankees Jeff Nelson and Karim Garcia got into a scrap with Fenway Park groundskeeper Paul Williams during the 2003 ALCS. The fight began when Williams rooted for the Red Sox in the Yankees bullpen and refused to heed player requests to cease and desist.

BOONE-DOGGLE

The Yankees–Red Sox rivalry reached a fever pitch in Game 7 of the 2003 American League Championship Series. The teams had played a combined 324 games, 26 of them against each other, but were deadlocked after the Red Sox blew a 5–2 lead in the eighth. Each had won three games in the ALCS and scored 29 runs. One more would win it: Aaron Boone's improbable home run against erstwhile starter Tim Wakefield in the eleventh. Three months later, Boone tore a knee ligament in a pickup basketball game, found his contract voided, and signed with Cleveland. The Yankees, needing a third baseman, acquired Alex Rodriguez as Boone's replacement. Boone hit only six home runs in 54 regular-season games as a Yankee.

HELPING HIMSELF

Rookie pitcher Dontrelle Willis of the Florida Marlins had a field day in the decisive fourth game of the 2003 NL Division Series against San Francisco. With two singles and a triple, he collected five total bases—two more than Giants star Barry Bonds had in the entire series.

NL SLUGFEST

The Marlins and Cubs smacked 23 home runs, all but 10 by Chicago, in their seven-game 2003 National League Championship Series. No other NLCS has produced as many long balls.

PRIOR ARREST

Cubs pitcher Mark Prior sailed into the eighth inning of 2003 NLCS Game 6 at Wrigley Field with a 3–0 lead over Florida. He retired only one batter before disaster struck. Juan Pierre doubled on a 2–2 pitch before Luis Castillo lofted a foul fly to left that front-row Cubs fan Steve Bartman knocked away from left fielder Moises Alou. Castillo then walked, with Pierre advancing to third as the ball eluded catcher Paul Bako. Pudge Rodriguez singled in a run on an 0–2 count, but Miguel Cabrera bounced an apparent double-play grounder to sure-handed shortstop Alex Gonzalez. Proving there are exceptions to every rule, the ball hit off the heel of the infielder's glove to load the bases. Derrek Lee delivered a two-run double, tying the game and ending Prior's night. He and two relievers combined to yield eight runs in a span of 12

THE STEVE BARTMAN GAME

This is the box score of the game in which Cubs fan Steve Bartman unwittingly interfered with play, prolonging the Florida eighth inning:

GAME 6, NLCS, FLORIDA AT CHICAGO, OCTOBER 14, 2003

Marlins	0 0 0	0 0 0	0 8 0 — 8	9	0
Cubs	1 0 0	0 0 1	1 0 0 — 3	10	2

Florida	AB	R	H	RBI	Chicago	AB	R	H	RBI
Pierre, CF	5	1	3	1	Lofton, CF	5	1	1	0
Castillo, 2B	4	1	1	0	Grudzielanek, 2B	3	0	1	1
Rodriguez, C	4	1	1	1	Sosa, RF	4	1	3	1
Cabrera, RF	5	1	1	0	Alou, LF	4	0	2	0
Encarnacion, RF	0	0	0	0	Ramirez, 3B	4	0	1	0
Lee,1B	5	1	1	2	Simon, 1B	2	0	0	0
Lowell, 3B	3	1	0	0	a-Karros, 1B	1	0	0	0
Conine, LF	2	0	1	1	A.S. Gonzalez, SS	3	0	0	0
A.Gonzalez, SS	3	0	0	0	Alfonseca, P	0	0	0	0
Fox, P	0	0	0	0	Bako, C	4	1	2	0
b-Hollandsworth	0	1	0	0	Prior, P	2	0	0	0
Urbina, P	0	0	0	0	Farnsworth, P	0	0	0	0
Pavano, P	2	0	0	0	Remlinger, P	0	0	0	0
Willis, P	0	0	0	0	Martinez, SS	1	0	0	0
Mordecai, SS	2	1	1	3					
Totals	**35**	**8**	**9**	**8**	**Totals**	**33**	**3**	**10**	**2**

a walked for Simon in fifth
b walked for Fox in eighth

E—A.S. Gonzalez, Grudzielanek. DP—Florida 2, Chicago 1. LOB—Florida 6, Chicago 7. 2B—Pierre, Lee, Mordecai, Sosa. Sacrifice—Grudzielanek, Prior. SF—Conine.

Florida	IP	H	R	ER	BB	SO	Chicago	IP	H	R	ER	BB	SO
Pavano	5.2	7	2	2	1	5	Prior (L)	7.1	6	5	3	3	6
Willis	1	1	1	1	1	2	Farnsworth	0.1	1	3	3	2	0
Fox (W)	0.1	2	0	0	0	0	Remlinger	0.1	1	0	0	0	0
Urbina	2	0	0	0	0	2	Alfonseca	1	1	0	0	0	0

WP—Willis, Prior. PB—Bako.

Umpires—Reilly, Crawford, Meriwether, Culbreth, Everitt, Poncino. Time—3:00. Attendance—39,577.

pitches (not including intentional balls). Florida won the game, 8–3, and the pennant the following night.

GOAT CURSE STICKS
Blowing up the baseball that Steve Bartman deflected from Moises Alou in Game 6 of the 2003 NLCS doesn't affect the prevailing Goat Curse of Wrigley Field. So says Sam Sianis, whose family placed a hex on the Cubs for forbidding their pet goat to attend the 1945 World Series (even though it had a ticket). The curse says the Cubs will never again reach the World Series.

BELTRAN THE BLASTER
With eight home runs in his first nine postseason games, Carlos Beltran hit as many as Hank Aaron, Willie Mays, Ted Williams, and Stan Musial hit in a combined 72 postseason games.

AGE BEFORE BEAUTY?
In the fourth inning of Game 3 in the 2004 ALCS, Red Sox starter Pedro Martinez hit Yankees batter Karim Garcia in the back with a pitch. In the home half of the inning, benches emptied when Manny Ramirez glared at Roger Clemens after an inside pitch moved him back. Yankees coach Don Zimmer, 72, charged the younger, stronger Martinez, who promptly knocked him down. The Yankees eventually won the game and the series, and Zimmer apologized for his part in the fracas.

BIG BIG INNINGS
Huge innings have even more impact when they occur during the postseason. Here's a list of the biggest:

Year	Team	Opponent	Series	Game	Runs	Inning
1968	Tigers	Cardinals	WS	6	10	3rd
1929	Athletics	Cubs	WS	4	10	7th
2002	Angels	Twins	ALCS	5	10	7th
2001	Diamondbacks	Yankees	WS	6	8	3rd
1921	Giants	Yankees	WS	3	8	7th
2003	Marlins	Cubs	NLCS	6	8	8th

HOW BOSOX REBOUNDED

When the New York Yankees buried the Boston Red Sox by a 19–8 score on the night of October 16, 2004, everyone in baseball assumed the American League Championship Series was over. No team had ever rebounded from a 3–0 game deficit. But the resilient Red Sox, relying heavily on the clutch-hitting ability of David "Big Papi" Ortiz, grabbed successive extra-inning victories at Fenway Park and then maintained the momentum by winning the last two games at Yankee Stadium, 4–2 and 10–3. Reflecting on the biggest sudden collapse in baseball history, New York tabloids ran headlines that read "Damn Yankees" and "The Choke's on Us."

INTERFERENCE FOR A-ROD

In the eighth inning of ALCS Game 6 in 2004, Alex Rodriguez of the Yankees knocked the ball from the glove of Bronson Arroyo as the Boston pitcher tried to tag him along the first-base line. As the ball rolled away and Derek Jeter scored, the Yankees thought they had cut the Red Sox lead to 4–3, but the umpires cited A-Rod for interference and nullified the run. Boston won the game and the series.

RAPID ROBERTS

Although David Ortiz was the hero of Boston's comeback in the 2004 ALCS against the Yankees, the turning point of the pivotal fourth game was a stolen base by pinch runner Dave Roberts in the ninth inning. Roberts raced home on Bill Mueller's game-tying single against Mariano Rivera, and Ortiz hit a two-run homer in the twelfth to cap a 6–4 victory. With 11 RBIs, a championship series record, plus three home runs and a .387 batting average (12-for-31), Ortiz helped the Sox win four straight—and the AL flag—after overcoming a 3–0 deficit. Roberts never appeared in the World Series for the Red Sox, but he certainly helped them get there.

SHIRT SAVES SOX

A fan wearing a dark sweatshirt served a suitable backdrop when Boston's Mark Bellhorn homered in Game 6 of the 2004 ALCS at Yankee Stadium. The umpires reversed their original call, which had ruled the ball in play.

MAYHEM IN BEANTOWN
The city of Boston paid a $5.1 million settlement to the family of an Emerson College student killed by police during a boisterous celebration by Red Sox fans in 2004. Victoria Snelgrove, 21, was hit in the eye socket by a pepper-spray pellet during the October 21 riot that erupted after the BoSox rebounded from a 3–0 deficit to win the last four games of the ALCS.

PEDRO'S PAL
Star Red Sox pitcher Pedro Martinez befriended a 32-inch-tall actor named Nelson de la Rosa during the team's run to the 2004 world championship. The team seemed to win more often when Nelson was present.

COMEBACK KIDS
The Houston Astros and the Oakland A's, both 2005 playoff teams, rebounded from late-May tailspins that left them 15 games under .500.

NO RELIEF
After going 10-for-10 in save chances during the regular season, 2005 Atlanta closer Kyle Farnsworth blew a 6–1 lead in NLDS Game 4 against Houston by yielding an eighth-inning grand slam to Lance Berkman and a two-out, game-tying blow to Brad Ausmus in the bottom of the ninth. The Astros eventually won, 7–6, in an 18-inning game that featured a three-inning relief stint by erstwhile starter Roger Clemens and a game-winning homer by Chris Burke. The game, which allowed the Astros to advance to the NLCS, was the first postseason contest with two grand slams and the longest postseason match by time (5:50) as well as innings.

THE ROOF FACTOR
The Houston Astros believe closing the retractable roof at Minute Maid Park helps them win because fan noise can be deafening. In 2005 the team went 36–17 with the roof closed, 15–11 with the roof open, and 2–0 when it was used both ways. The roof was closed during NLDS games against Atlanta even though Houston weather was ideal (74 degrees and low humidity).

LONG WAIT
Eighteen years elapsed between divisional titles for the New York Mets. They were champions of the National League East in 1988 and 2006.

WORLD SERIES

WANNA PLAY NINE?

The World Series was a best-of-nine affair in 1903, its first year, and again for the three-year span from 1919 to 1921. It has been best-of-seven in all other years. Although there have been many cases of seven-game Series, no World Series ever went to a ninth game.

TRIPLE PLAY

Cleveland Indians second baseman Bill Wambsganss made an unassisted triple play to help his team defeat the Brooklyn Robins in the 1920 World Series.

FIRST SERIES SLAM

Elmer Smith of the 1920 Cleveland Indians hit the first grand slam in World Series history. No National Leaguer would hit a grand slam until 1962, when Chuck Hiller of the San Francisco Giants connected against the New York Yankees.

CASEY'S CLOUT

The hitting hero of the first 1–0 game in World Series history was better known as manager of the team he beat. Casey Stengel was with the New York Giants when his homer beat the New York Yankees on October 10, 1923.

CRAZED CUBS

The pennant-winning Chicago Cubs of 1935 won 23 in a row, and 23 of 26 (an .885 percentage) in the month of September.

The first World Series took place after the 1903 season between the Boston Americans and the Pittsburgh Pirates. Boston eventually won the best-of-nine series in eight games, played over 13 days.

PRESUMING PIRATES

When Pittsburgh built an eight-game lead over the Chicago Cubs by August 20, 1938, the Pirates anticipated participation in the World Series. The team built a new press box in Forbes Field to accommodate the expected hordes of writers. But the Cubs won 30 of their last 42 as Pittsburgh posted a 20–24 mark, and Chicago capped its drive with a September sweep of the Pirates. The highlight of that sweep—the famous "homer in the gloamin'" by Cubs player/manager Gabby Hartnett—brought victory to Chicago just before darkness would have halted play.

STOPPING THE SHIFT

Red Sox slugger Ted Williams, a notorious left-handed pull hitter, foiled the "Williams shift" by the St. Louis Cardinals when he bunted safely for one of his five hits in the 1946 World Series.

GENEROUS TED

In 1946, the only time the Red Sox reached the World Series during his tenure with the team, Ted Williams gave his entire share to the clubhouse boy as a tip.

GIONFRIDDO'S CATCH

In Game 6 of the 1947 World Series, Joe DiMaggio came to bat with two men on in the sixth inning and the Dodgers—trying to even the Series at three games each—up 8–5. Al Gionfriddo was playing near the left-field line against the right-handed batter but wouldn't stay stationary long. Joe D. sent a towering fly toward the bullpen. Gionfriddo took off in pursuit, jumped, and made a miraculous back-to-the-plate grab. DiMaggio, seeing the catch as he rounded first, kicked the dirt in a rare display of emotion. The Dodgers won that game, 8–6, but lost Game 7.

NEAT TRICK

Lou Boudreau, player/pilot of the 1948 Cleveland Indians, was the only man to manage a world champion and win the MVP award in the same season.

MICKEY'S MISHAP

Playing right field because Joe DiMaggio was in center, Mickey Mantle stepped on a drain cover, tore ligaments in his right knee, and collapsed in a heap. The injury, which plagued Mantle throughout his

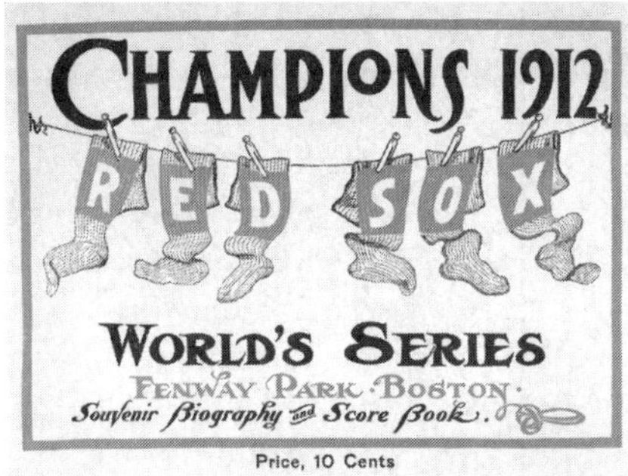

The Boston Red Sox won the AL pennant in 1912, the same year Fenway Park opened.
Boston Red Sox

career, happened in the 1951 World Series, DiMaggio's last and Mantle's first.

RELIEVERS START
Relief pitchers Jim Konstanty of the Phillies (1950) and Joe Black of the Dodgers (1952) were surprise starters for their teams in World Series openers. Konstanty lost, 1–0, while Black won, 4–2. That was the first time a black pitcher won a World Series game.

NUMBER FIVE
Game 5 of the 1952 World Series was played on October 5, Carl Erskine's fifth wedding anniversary. Erskine, working on two days' rest, yielded five runs in the fifth inning that day. He eventually won the 11-inning game, 6–5. The game ended at exactly 5:05.

WILLIE'S CATCH
His back to the plate, Willie Mays of the Giants hauled down a 460-foot drive by Vic Wertz of the Indians during the 1954 World Series at the Polo Grounds in New York. The play stifled a Cleveland rally in the eighth inning of the opening game.

DUKE DELIVERS
Duke Snider was the only man to hit four home runs in a World Series twice.

SANDY'S SNATCH
A spectacular catch by little-known outfielder Sandy Amoros in the sixth inning of Game 7 enabled the Brooklyn Dodgers to beat the New York Yankees, 2–0, and win their first world championship in 1955. Amoros, who had replaced Junior Gilliam in left at the start of the inning, easily

doubled base runner Gil McDougald after the catch. Left-handed pull hitter Yogi Berra had almost foiled the Dodgers defense by slicing the ball down the left-field line.

SPECIAL DELIVERY

Plagued by control problems throughout his career, Don Larsen switched to a new, no-windup delivery during the 1956 season. Several months later, the Yankees right-hander pitched a perfect game against the Brooklyn Dodgers in the World Series. He threw 97 pitches, only 26 of them balls, and registered all but two of his seven strikeouts on called third strikes.

COLLEGE FUND

After the 1956 World Series, perfect game author Don Larsen had his hat, glove, and ball cast in silver. He sold the items at auction in 2002, when his grandchildren needed money for college, and received $120,750.

THE REAL CULPRIT

Failure to cover first base may have cost the Yankees the 1960 world championship. With New York ahead, 7–5, and Pirates runners on first and second with nobody out, Casey Stengel replaced Bobby Shantz with Jim Coates. Bob Skinner dropped a sacrifice bunt, moving runners to second and third, but Rocky Nelson hit a short fly to right. Roberto Clemente hit a slow chopper to first that was backhanded by Moose Skowron. But Coates failed to cover the bag and Clemente reached, with Bill Virdon scoring and reducing the Yankees' lead to one run. With runners on the corners, backup catcher Hal Smith hit a 420-foot home run to put the Pirates up, 9–7. The Yankees tied it in the ninth, then lost when Bill Mazeroski led off the Pittsburgh half with a solo shot.

PREVIEW FOR MAZ

Bill Mazeroski's Game 7 home run was not the only one he hit in the 1960 World Series. He also had one in the fourth inning of the first game. "I was on Cloud 9," he said later. "A home run in the World Series! I thought it was the greatest thing that ever happened to me. It relaxed me for the rest of the Series."

SAY-WHAT KID

Jim Mason had more World Series home runs than Willie Mays.

TOP SERIES PILOTS
Joe McCarthy and Casey Stengel each won seven world championships, marks unmatched by any other manager.

JEWELRY STORE
Gene Conley is the only man to win world championship rings in two different sports. The 6'8" right-hander pitched for the 1957 world champion Milwaukee Braves and played

Ronnie Joyner

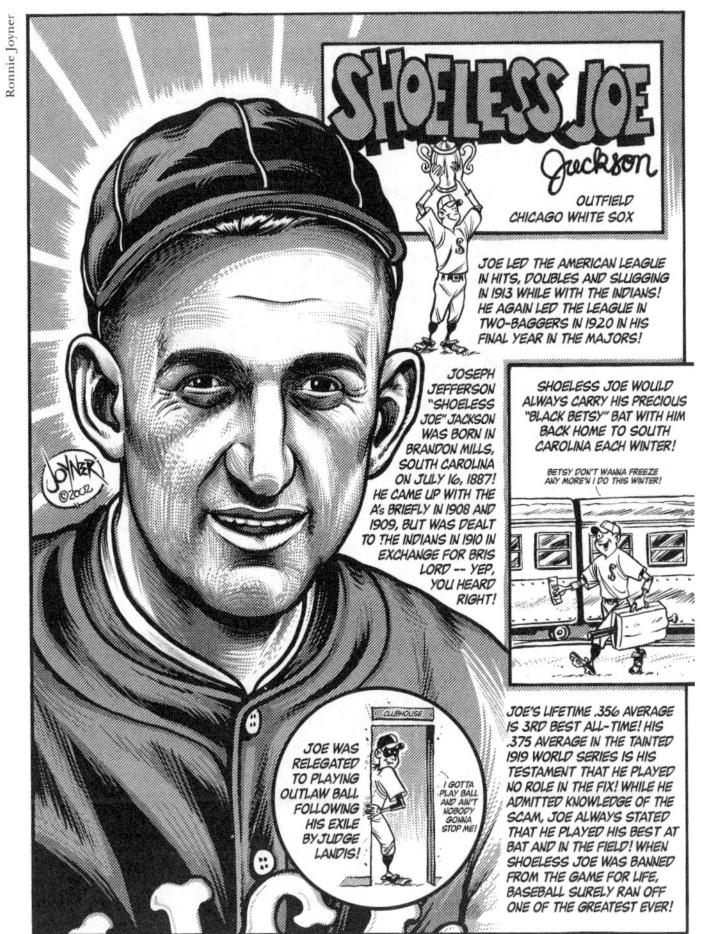

for the Boston Celtics when they won NBA titles from 1959 to 1961.

WINS BEAT RUNS

Although the New York Yankees outscored the Pittsburgh Pirates, 55–27, in the 1960 World Series, the Pirates won in seven games. New York's three wins were by scores of 10–0, 12–0, and 16–3.

SERIES SWITCHER

Not only was Billy Pierce a World Series pitcher in three

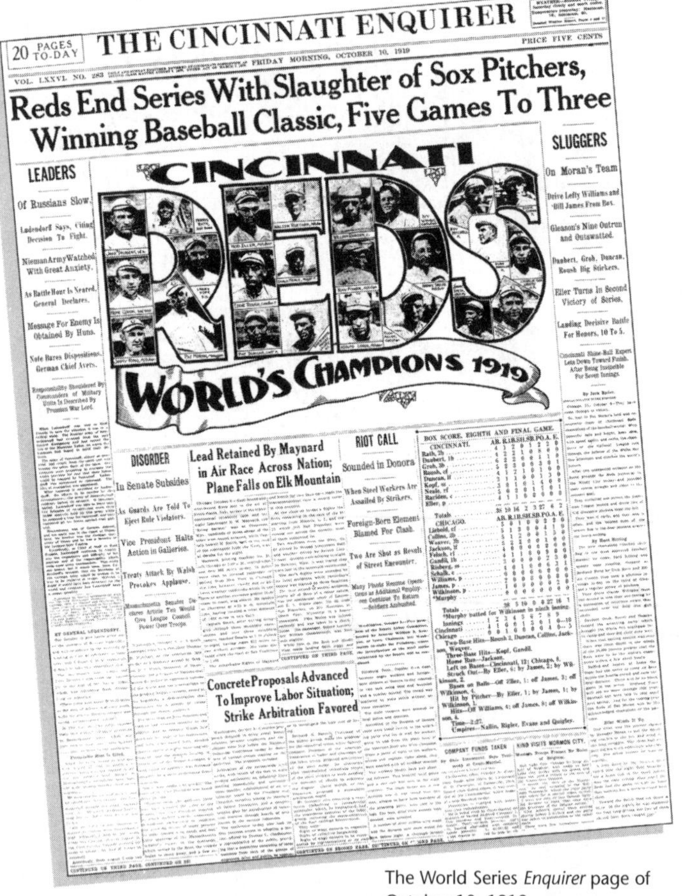

20 PAGES TO-DAY

THE CINCINNATI ENQUIRER

PRICE FIVE CENTS

VOL. LXXVI. NO. 283 — FRIDAY MORNING, OCTOBER 10, 1919

Reds End Series With Slaughter of Sox Pitchers, Winning Baseball Classic, Five Games To Three

CINCINNATI REDS WORLD'S CHAMPIONS 1919

LEADERS

Of Russians Slow.

Ludendorff Says, Citing Decision To Fight.

Nieman Army Watched With Great Anxiety.

As Battle Hour Is Neared, General Declares.

Message For Enemy Is Obtained By Huns.

Note Bares Dispositions, German Chief Avers.

Responsibility Shouldered By Commanders of Military Units Is Described By Prussian War Lord.

SLUGGERS

On Moran's Team

Drive Lefty Williams and Bill James From Box.

Gleason's Nine Outrun and Outswatted.

Daubert, Groh, Duncan, Roush Big Stickers.

Eller Turns In Second Victory of Series.

Landing Decisive Battle For Honors, 10 To 5.

Cincinnati Shine-Ball Expert Lets Down Toward Finish, After Being Invincible For Seven Innings.

DISORDER

In Senate Subsides

As Guards Are Told To Eject Rule Violators.

Vice President Halts Action in Galleries.

Treaty Attack By Walsh Provokes Applause.

Massachusetts Senator Declares Article Ten Would Give League Council Power Over Troops.

Lead Retained By Maynard in Air Race Across Nation; Plane Falls on Elk Mountain

RIOT CALL

Sounded in Donora

When Steel Workers Are Assailed By Strikers.

Foreign-Born Element Blamed For Clash.

Two Are Shot as Result of Street Encounter.

Concrete Proposals Advanced To Improve Labor Situation; Strike Arbitration Favored

COMPANY FUNDS TAKEN

KING VISITS MORMON CITY.

BOX SCORE, EIGHTH AND FINAL GAME.

CINCINNATI.	AB.	R.	1B.	SH.	SB.	PO.	A.	E.
Rath, 2b	[illegible]	[illegible]	[illegible]	[illegible]	[illegible]	[illegible]	[illegible]	[illegible]
Daubert, 1b	[illegible]	[illegible]	[illegible]	[illegible]	[illegible]	[illegible]	[illegible]	[illegible]
Groh, 3b	[illegible]	[illegible]	[illegible]	[illegible]	[illegible]	[illegible]	[illegible]	[illegible]
Roush, cf	[illegible]	[illegible]	[illegible]	[illegible]	[illegible]	[illegible]	[illegible]	[illegible]
Duncan, lf	[illegible]	[illegible]	[illegible]	[illegible]	[illegible]	[illegible]	[illegible]	[illegible]
Kopf, ss	[illegible]	[illegible]	[illegible]	[illegible]	[illegible]	[illegible]	[illegible]	[illegible]
Neale, rf	[illegible]	[illegible]	[illegible]	[illegible]	[illegible]	[illegible]	[illegible]	[illegible]
Rariden, c	[illegible]	[illegible]	[illegible]	[illegible]	[illegible]	[illegible]	[illegible]	[illegible]
Eller, p	[illegible]	[illegible]	[illegible]	[illegible]	[illegible]	[illegible]	[illegible]	[illegible]
Totals	38	10	16	2	3	27	6	2

CHICAGO.	AB.	R.	1B.	SH.	SB.	PO.	A.	E.
Liebold, cf	[illegible]	[illegible]	[illegible]	[illegible]	[illegible]	[illegible]	[illegible]	[illegible]
Collins, 2b	[illegible]	[illegible]	[illegible]	[illegible]	[illegible]	[illegible]	[illegible]	[illegible]
Weaver, 3b	[illegible]	[illegible]	[illegible]	[illegible]	[illegible]	[illegible]	[illegible]	[illegible]
Jackson, lf	[illegible]	[illegible]	[illegible]	[illegible]	[illegible]	[illegible]	[illegible]	[illegible]
Felsch, rf	[illegible]	[illegible]	[illegible]	[illegible]	[illegible]	[illegible]	[illegible]	[illegible]
Gandil, 1b	[illegible]	[illegible]	[illegible]	[illegible]	[illegible]	[illegible]	[illegible]	[illegible]
Risberg, ss	[illegible]	[illegible]	[illegible]	[illegible]	[illegible]	[illegible]	[illegible]	[illegible]
Schalk, c	[illegible]	[illegible]	[illegible]	[illegible]	[illegible]	[illegible]	[illegible]	[illegible]
Williams, p	[illegible]	[illegible]	[illegible]	[illegible]	[illegible]	[illegible]	[illegible]	[illegible]
James, p	[illegible]	[illegible]	[illegible]	[illegible]	[illegible]	[illegible]	[illegible]	[illegible]
Wilkinson, p	[illegible]	[illegible]	[illegible]	[illegible]	[illegible]	[illegible]	[illegible]	[illegible]
*Murphy	[illegible]	[illegible]	[illegible]	[illegible]	[illegible]	[illegible]	[illegible]	[illegible]
Totals	38	5	10	0	0	27	16	1

*Murphy batted for Wilkinson in ninth inning.

Two-Base Hits—Roush 2, Duncan, Collins, Jackson, Weaver.

Three-Base Hits—Kopf, Gandil.

Home Run—Jackson.

Left on Bases—Cincinnati, 12; Chicago, 8.

Struck Out—By Eller, 6; by James, 2; by Wilkinson, 2.

Bases on Balls—Off Eller, 1; off James, 3; off Wilkinson, 4.

Hit by Pitcher—By Eller, 1; by James, 1; by Wilkinson, 1.

Hits—Off Williams, 4; off James, 8; off Wilkinson, 4.

Time—2:27.

Umpires—Nallin, Rigler, Evans and Quigley.

The World Series *Enquirer* page of October 10, 1919.

different decades but he also did it with three different teams: the 1945 Detroit Tigers, the 1959 Chicago White Sox, and the 1962 San Francisco Giants.

DANDY SANDY

Sandy Koufax was the lone two-time winner of both competing World Series MVP awards. He swept the Babe Ruth Award and the Sport Magazine Award in 1963 and 1965.

DYNASTY ENDS

The 1964 World Series was the last for longtime Yankees heroes Mickey Mantle and Whitey Ford. It also marked the end of an era in which the Bronx Bombers won 10 world championships in 17 years. After losing to the St. Louis Cardinals in the seven-game 1964 Series, the Yanks did not return to Series play until 1976.

HOMERS SPARK SWEEP

Frank and Brooks Robinson hit consecutive home runs against Don Drysdale in the first inning of the 1966 World Series to start the Orioles toward a four-game sweep.

THE SECOND OF OCTOBER

October 2 favors World Series strikeout artists. In 1952

Judge Kenesaw Mountain Landis had a tough job as baseball's first commissioner: erasing the memory of the 1919 Black Sox scandal. Reprinted with permission, National Baseball Hall of Fame Library, Cooperstown, New York

Dodger Carl Erskine fanned 14 Yankees, then a single-game Series record. Exactly 11 years later, Dodgers lefty Sandy Koufax broke the mark by fanning 15 Yankees. And in 1968 Bob Gibson of the Cardinals struck out 17 Tigers.

NO SCOUTING REPORT

Baltimore Orioles superscout Jim Russo delivered advance reports on the Reds in 1970 and discussed the National League champions with all pitchers except Mike Cuellar. Asked why, Russo responded,

RUPPERT LOST HIS SHIRT

Yankees owner Jacob Ruppert literally lost his shirt during his club's World Series victory party on a train headed home from St. Louis in 1928. The players had begun to tear off each other's shirts, and team leaders Babe Ruth and Lou Gehrig—batting stars of the Series—broke into Ruppert's drawing room and ripped off his. Between them, Gehrig and Ruth got 16 hits, seven home runs, and 13 runs batted in during the four-game sweep of the Cardinals.

"You don't tell Leonard Bernstein how to conduct the New York Philharmonic and we don't tell Mike Cuellar how to pitch. He's an artist."

SURPRISE SLAM

Baltimore pitcher Dave McNally electrified the baseball world when he hit a grand slam against Cincinnati's Wayne Granger in the sixth inning of Game 3 of the 1970 World Series. He won, 9–3.

SERIES WORKHORSE

Reliever Darold Knowles of the Oakland A's appeared in all seven games of the 1973 classic against the New York Mets.

FIGHTING A'S

A pre–opening game fight involving Oakland pitchers Rollie Fingers and Blue Moon Odom didn't stop the A's from beating the Dodgers in a five-game World Series in 1974. It was the third straight world crown for the Athletics.

WINNING LOSERS

Two players from losing teams won World Series MVP awards. They were Bobby Richardson (Yankees), who received a Corvette from *Sport Magazine* in 1960, and Luis Tiant (Red Sox), who won the 1975 Babe Ruth Award in a media poll.

MR. OCTOBER

Reggie Jackson earned the nickname "Mr. October" for stellar postseason play over a period of years. He was at his best on October 18, 1977, when he hit three homers in the 8–4 Yankees win that clinched the World Series against the Dodgers. Jackson thus became the first man to hit five home runs in one fall classic.

FIRST THREE-TITLE YEAR
The 1978 New York Yankees were the first team to win three postseason series: a one-game playoff for the divisional title, a best-of-five match for the pennant, and a best-of-seven World Series.

YANKEE POODLE
George Frazier lost three World Series games in five days in 1981, when the Los Angeles Dodgers rallied from a 2–0 deficit to defeat the New York Yankees in six games.

FIVE-HIT GAMES
Paul Molitor and Marquis Grissom are the only men to produce five-hit games in postseason play. The former did it in the World Series for the 1982 Milwaukee Brewers, while the latter did it during the Division Series for the 1995 Atlanta Braves.

ROYAL REBOUND
The 1985 Kansas City Royals were the only club to overcome a 3–1 deficit twice in the same postseason. The team trailed the Toronto Blue Jays in the American League Championship Series, then came back to beat the St. Louis Cardinals in the World Series, giving Kansas City its only world championship.

TOO WILD FOR WORDS
It's Game 6 of the 1986 World Series. Red Sox at Mets. Shea Stadium, Flushing, New York. Boston leads, three games to two, and has a 5–3 lead in the tenth inning. Calvin Schiraldi retires the first two men. But

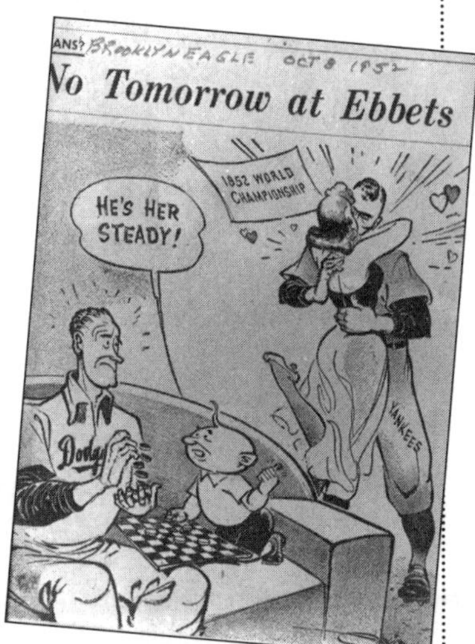

The *Brooklyn Daily Eagle* laments the Dodgers' inability to snatch the world championship from the Yankees in 1952. National Baseball Hall of Fame and Museum

With two men on, nobody out, and the score tied 2–2 in the first game of the 1954 World Series, Willie Mays turns a Vic Wertz smash into a memorable catch. The game ended when Giants pinch-hitter Dusty Rhodes lofted a tenth-inning fly ball down the right-field line but over the fence at the 257-foot mark. New York went on to sweep the series over the heavily favored Cleveland Indians.

Copyright 1993 by Bill Purdom. Reprinted with permission, Bill Goff, Inc./GoodSportsArt.com.

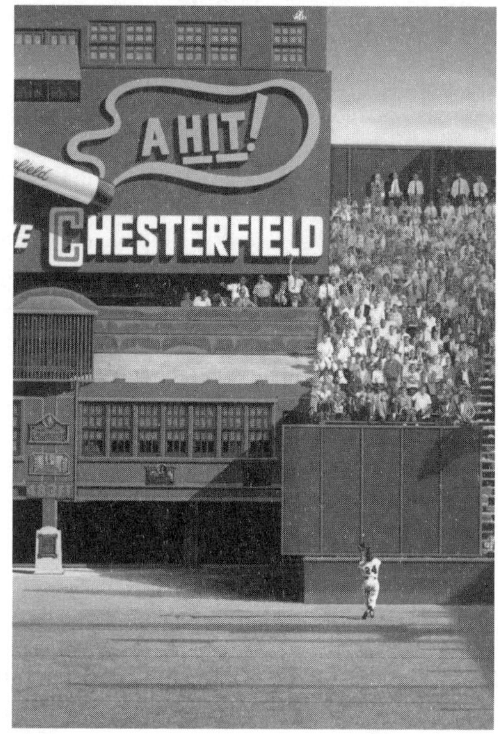

the Mets refuse to die. Three singles follow, cutting the score to 5–4 with runners on the corners. Bob Stanley relieves and gets two strikes on Mookie Wilson. Then he throws his only wild pitch of the season, plating the tying run and moving Ray Knight to second. Wilson hits a tapper to first that goes through the legs of gimpy Bill Buckner. The Red Sox have *12 pitches* in which they could end the World Series but fail to deliver. Mets win, 6–5, and take Game 7 the next night.

WEAK WORLD CHAMPS?
The 1987 Twins reached the World Series after scoring fewer runs than they allowed. No other team has ever matched that mark.

HOME COOKING
The home team won every World Series game for the first time in 1987, when the

Minnesota Twins defeated the St. Louis Cardinals.

PHOTO FINISH

A record four of the seven World Series games between the Twins and the Braves in 1991 were decided in the winning team's last at-bat, including a 10-inning, 1–0 Twins win in Game 7.

NO TRIPLE PLAY

The Toronto Blue Jays pulled off an apparent triple play during 1992 World Series Game 3 against the Atlanta Braves. According to Retrosheet.org, the Braves had runners on first and second with none out when David Justice hit a long fly to deep center. Lead runner Deion Sanders retreated toward second, not sure the ball was going to be caught, while Terry Pendleton, running from first, passed him on the base paths and was called out. Devon White caught up to the ball and threw it back to the infield, where Manuel Lee tagged Sanders out—according to the videotape. But the umpires ruled Sanders got back to the bag before the tag.

MITCH MELTS

Mitch "Wild Thing" Williams had 45 saves, including two in the playoffs, before throwing the Joe Carter gopher ball that ended the 1993 World Series with a Toronto defeat of Philadelphia in six games. The pitch he threw Carter was the last he would throw for the Phils. Williams never again saved more than six games in a season and was gone from the game within four years.

NO FALL CLASSIC

Acting commissioner Bud Selig canceled the 1994 postseason because of a player strike. The eighth work stoppage in baseball history lasted from August 12, 1994, to March 31, 1995.

ALMOST PERFECT

Tom Glavine and Mark Wohlers combined for a one-hitter to

This ring marks the only world championship in the history of the Brooklyn Dodgers, in 1955.

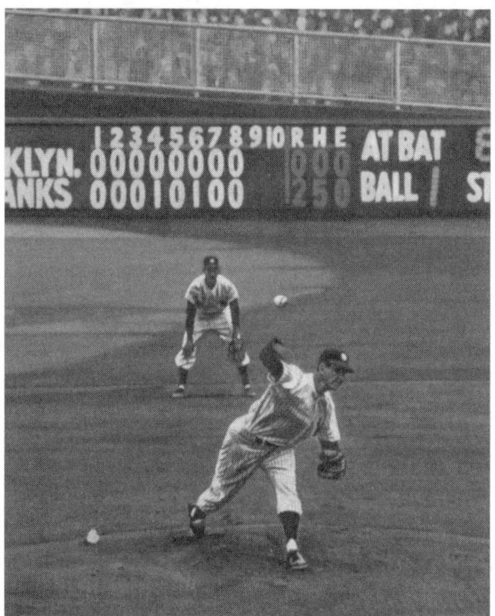

Don Larsen...brilliant against Brooklyn.

win the 1995 World Series finale for Atlanta versus Cleveland, 1–0. The only Indians hit was a bloop single by Tony Pena leading off the sixth.

HOME SWEET HOME

Three teams have came back to win the World Series after losing the first two games at home. They were the 1985 Royals, the 1986 Mets, and the 1996 Yankees.

CHILDHOOD MEMORIES

The young Tino Martinez, a future World Series hero for the Yankees, attended World Series games at Yankee Stadium with his dad, Rene.

NEXT-BEST CHAMPS

With 14 World Series appearances, the Athletics have reached the fall classic more often than any team other than the Yankees. They won nine times, second to the Yankees in the AL.

DISTANT SECOND

The Cardinals have won more world championships (10) than any team but the Yankees (26).

Power of Piazza

Mike Piazza is the only man to hit World Series homers at both Shea Stadium and Yankee Stadium.

Same Old Story

The 2000 Yankees were the first team with three straight world championships since the 1972–74 Oakland A's and only the fourth to win that many in succession. The other teams were the 1949–53 Yankees (five straight) and the 1936–39 Yanks (four in a row).

Series Streak

The New York Yankees won a record 14 straight games in the World Series (1996–2000).

Long Streak

Between 1947 and 2001, the Yankees never lost a postseason game they led after eight innings.

Nightmares in the Ninth

Arizona closer Byung Hung Kim gave up three critical late-inning homers to the Yankees on consecutive nights during the 2001 World Series. In Game 4, he gave up a two-out, two-run, game-tying homer to Tino Martinez in the ninth and a walkoff homer by Derek Jeter in the tenth. The next night, he yielded a two-run shot by Scott Brosius in the ninth to tie it; the Yankees won in 12 innings.

Old Fogey

The oldest pitcher to start the seventh game of the World Series was 39-year-old Roger Clemens, who started Game 7 for the Yankees against the Diamondbacks in 2001. He did not get a decision.

Mr. November

Derek Jeter's postmidnight, game-ending homer in Game 4 of the 2001 World Series was

Longtime Yankees catcher Yogi Berra appeared in more World Series than any other player. He reached the fall classic 14 times, winning world championships all but four times. JamesFiorentino.com

the only one ever hit in November. The fall classic had been pushed back a week by the terrorist attacks of 9/11.

SNAKES BITE YANKS

The Arizona Diamondbacks delivered 22 hits, a World Series record, while beating the Yankees, 15–2, in Game 6 of the 2001 World Series. It was the worst defeat for the Yanks in 293 postseason games at that time.

NO REST FOR RANDY

Arizona ace Randy Johnson, working in relief, was the winning pitcher in Game 7 of the 2001 World Series against the Yankees even though he started and won the night before.

PATHETIC PERFORMANCE

The .183 batting average by the New York Yankees against the Arizona Diamondbacks in 2001 was the worst ever recorded for a seven-game World Series.

OUTRAGEOUS OCTOBERS

The most runs scored by teams in postseason games:

- October 10, 1999: Red Sox defeat Indians, 23–7 (ALDS)
- October 16, 2004: Yankees defeat Red Sox, 19–8 (ALCS)
- October 2, 1936: Yankees defeat Giants, 18–4 (WS)
- October 10, 2001: Indians defeat Mariners, 17–2 (ALDS)
- October 6, 1960: Yankees defeat Pirates, 16–3 (WS)
- October 17, 1996: Braves defeat Cardinals, 15–0 (NLCS)
- October 20, 1993: Blue Jays defeat Phillies, 15–14 (WS)
- October 22, 2001: Diamondbacks defeat Yankees, 15–2 (WS)

MULTIPLE MVPS

To expedite the selection process for World Series MVP, Major League Baseball employs a small panel of voters. As a result, there were co-winners in 2001 (Randy Johnson and Curt Schilling of Arizona) and 1981 (Ron Cey, Pedro Guerrero, and Steve Yeager of Los Angeles).

SERIES FINISHER

Yankees closer Mariano Rivera is the only pitcher to be on the mound for the last out of four straight World Series (1998–2001).

TOO WILD FOR WORDS

The only time wild-card winners met in the World

Series was in 2002, when the Anaheim Angels defeated the San Francisco Giants in seven games.

FALL FRATERNITY
Brothers who played for the same team in a World Series game: Bengie and Jose Molina (Angels, 2002); Paul and Lloyd Waner (Pirates, 1927); Mort and Walker Cooper (Cardinals, 1942–44); and Felipe and Matty Alou (Giants, 1962).

SMASHING DEBUTS
Barry Bonds and Mel Ott are the only members of the 500 Home Run Club who homered in their first World Series at-bats.

WHERE BARRY BATS
Because he batted fourth for the San Francisco Giants in the 2002 World Series against the Anaheim Angels, Barry Bonds never batted in the ninth inning of any of his team's three final losses. All three ended with the leadoff or number two batters making the last out.

BONDS NOT ENOUGH
Barry Bonds hit eight postseason home runs in 2002, but the Giants still failed to win

One of the best left-right tandems in baseball history, Warren Spahn and Lew Burdette were the anchors of a pitching staff that almost produced four straight NL flags for the Milwaukee Braves from 1956 to 1959. They won all four games in the 1957 World Series and all three Milwaukee wins the following fall.
The Topps Company

the world championship, losing to the Angels in a seven-game World Series.

SNOW SHOVELS KID

J.T. Snow may be the only nonpitcher to earn a save. It happened in Game 5 of the 2002 World Series, when Snow scored a run and turned to watch teammate David Bell thundering home behind him. Snow also saw three-year-old Darren Baker, son of Giants manager Dusty Baker, dash for a dropped bat. The first baseman grabbed the batboy, whisking him out of harm's way in the nick of time, and carried him back to the dugout on his shoulders.

GIANT COLLAPSE

The San Francisco Giants needed only nine outs to close the gate on the 2002 world title. They didn't do it. Although Russ Ortiz was nursing a 5–0 lead in Game 6 at Anaheim, Dusty Baker decided to go to his bullpen. The Angels wasted no time, scoring three runs in both the seventh and the eighth innings to ice a 6–5 victory. They won again the next night, 4–1,

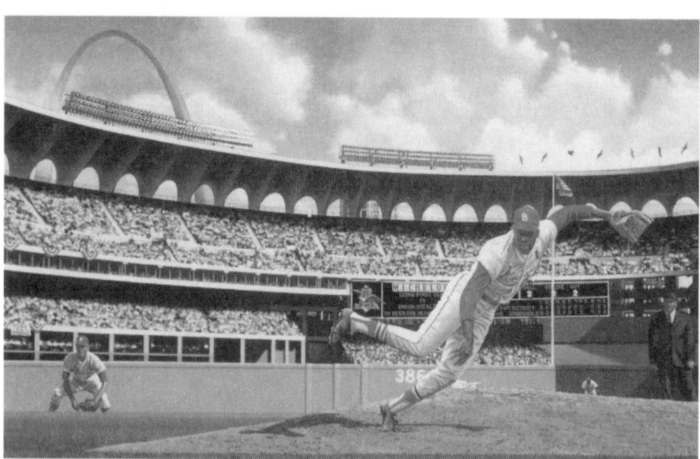

Bob Gibson pitched eight straight complete games, winning the first seven, in World Series play. The star Cardinals right-hander fanned a record 17 in a game and 35 in a seven-game Series against Detroit in 1968. Previously, Dodgers Sandy Koufax (1963) and Carl Erskine (1953) held one-game strikeout records—recorded against the Yankees—with 15 and 14, respectively. Copyright 1998 by Bill Purdom. Reprinted with permission, Bill Goff, Inc./GoodSportsArt.com.

depriving the Giants of their first world championship since 1954 and parlaying their first pennant into their first title.

WILD ABOUT WILD CARD

Wild-card winners can go far in postseason play, as the Anaheim Angels proved in 2002. After finishing four games behind Oakland in the AL West, Mike Scioscia's club won a four-game ALDS from the Yankees, a five-game ALCS from the Twins, and a seven-game World Series that matched wild-cards for the first time (Anaheim versus San Francisco). The heavenly hitting Angels even tied a postseason mark with a 10-run seventh inning in the ALCS finale against Minnesota.

QUICK TURNAROUND

The only teams to win the World Series after hitting rock-bottom in the standings during the season were the 1914 Boston Braves and 2003 Florida Marlins.

IN-SEASON REBOUND

The 2003 Florida Marlins were the first team since the 1914 Boston Braves to win a world championship after recovering from a 10-game deficit in the standings during the regular season.

RHYME OF THE ANCIENT MANAGER

Jack McKeon became the oldest manager in World Series history in 2003. At 72 years and 303 days old when that Series opened, McKeon was more than two and a half years older than Casey Stengel had been in 1960, his last World Series year.

BECKETT'S BEST

The oldest man to manage in a World Series, Jack McKeon of the 2003 Florida Marlins, banked his fortunes on a man nearly 50 years his junior, 23-year-old right-handed pitcher Josh Beckett. Asked to pitch on short rest in front of partisan Yankee Stadium fans in the seventh game of the World Series, Beckett responded with a 2–0 shutout—exactly the same result that Johnny Podres, also working on three days of rest, had given the Brooklyn Dodgers at Yankee Stadium in 1955.

TWO-SIDED PENNY

Brad Penny of the 2003 Florida Marlins was the only pitcher to win a World Series opener as a starter after also winning the final League Championship Series game.

HIDDEN BALL TRICK

Josh Beckett kept the ball he used to end the 2003 World Series in a glove under his bed.

THE CLEANUP KID

Miguel Cabrera of the 2003 Florida Marlins was the youngest man to hit cleanup in a World Series game.

BIG HAUL

Rookie stars Dontrelle Willis and Miguel Cabrera made more money with their postseason World Series shares than they did during the 2003 regular season. Willis, called up May 9, earned $234,426 during the season, while Cabrera, promoted June 20, got $165,574. A winning share for the world champion Marlins that year was $305,361.77.

CHAMPS WITHOUT TITLES

The Florida Marlins twice won world championships (1997, 2003) without ever finishing first in a division.

HOW TIME FLIES

Between the Red Sox world championships of 1918 and 2004, the price of a World Series ticket jumped from $3.30 to $140. There were also 15 presidents, 11 Boston mayors, and seven popes.

NO MOONSHINE

A lunar eclipse occurred on the night the 2004 Boston Red Sox won their first world championship in 86 years.

ST. LOUIS SWOON

The 2004 St. Louis Cardinals were the seventh team to post the best record during the regular season before suffering a World Series sweep. Part of the problem was a sudden power vacuum. After leading the 2004 National League in both batting (.278) and runs scored (855), the Cards suddenly turned frigid for the fall classic. Their fourth, fifth, and sixth batters combined to go 1-for-39 (.026). The team scored one run in their last 19 innings and never led at any point. As a team, St. Louis hit only .190, the lowest Series average by an NL team since the 1985 Cards hit .185 in a seven-game loss to Kansas City. The 2004 Redbirds had only 24 World Series hits, worst by any club in a four-game set since the 1966 Dodgers managed only 17 while being swept by the Baltimore Orioles.

Carlton Fisk of the Boston Red Sox pleads with the ball he just hit against Cincinnati's Pat Darcy in Game 6 of the 1975 World Series. The twelfth-inning drive stays fair, sending the Series into a seventh game the next night.

PAINFUL MEMORY

Theo Epstein, general manager of the 2004 world champion Boston Red Sox, was a 12-year-old fan watching on TV when Bill Buckner missed the grounder that cost the Red Sox the 1986 World Series.

EARLY BIRD GETS WORM

The 2004 Boston Red Sox won their first world title in 86 years by winning their last eight postseason games—four against the Yankees in the ALCS (after trailing 3–0) and four against the St. Louis Cardinals in the World Series. No other team had ever won four straight elimination games in a postseason series. The Sox never trailed in any game of the World Series.

BON APPETIT

During the 2004 World Series, Boston manager Terry Francona said one of his toughest jobs was keeping Kevin Millar from eating too much junk food. Games at National League parks had no designated hitter, so David Ortiz moved from DH to first base, sending Millar to the bench.

YOU SAID IT!

During the world championship parade of the Boston Red Sox on October 30, 2004, slugger Manny Ramirez held a sign that read, "Jeter is playing golf today. This is better."

SWEEPS WEEK

Tony La Russa and Bill McKechnie were the only

managers to finish on the wrong end of World Series sweeps twice. La Russa did it with the 1990 A's and the 2004 Cardinals while McKechnie did it with the 1928 Cards and the 1939 Reds.

Loser to Winner

Edgar Renteria is the only player to be the final out of a World Series (St. Louis Cardinals) and start the next season in the lineup of the team that beat them (Boston Red Sox).

Mo's Bid

Mariano Rivera's bid for the Baseball Hall of Fame received a bigger boost from his 34 saves in postseason play (prior to 2006) than his 400-plus regular-season saves. The Yankees closer moved closer to Lee Smith, owner of a record 478 saves, when he notched his 400th save in July 2006.

Low-Hit World Series Games

No-hitters

- Don Larsen (Yankees vs. Dodgers), World Series, October 8, 1956*

* perfect game

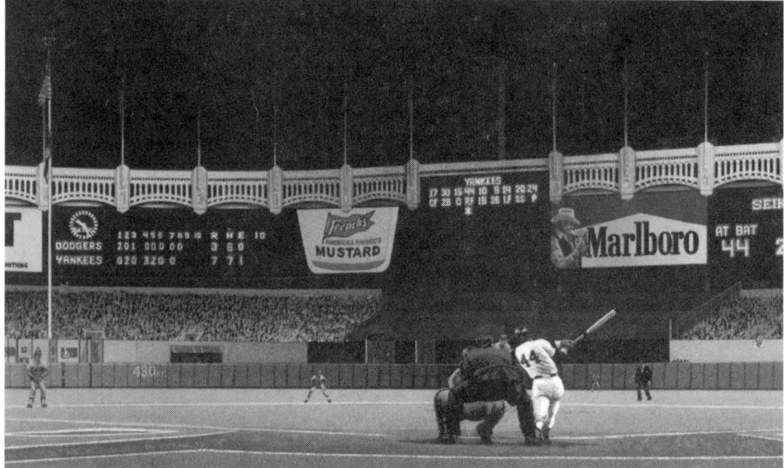

Reggie Jackson lives up to his Mr. October nickname by powering his third home run of the night during 1977 World Series Game 6 at Yankee Stadium. Only Babe Ruth, who did it twice, also had a three-homer game in the fall classic. Jackson needed only three pitches for his three homers.

One-hitters

- Ed Reulbach (Cubs vs. White Sox), World Series, October 10, 1906
- Claude Passeau (Cubs vs. Tigers), World Series, October 5, 1945
- Floyd Bevens (Yankees vs. Dodgers), World Series, October 3, 1947
- Jim Lonborg (Red Sox vs. Cardinals), World Series, October 5, 1967
- Tom Glavine and Mark Wohlers (Braves vs. Indians), World Series, October 28, 1995

Payroll Parity

Money doesn't always buy happiness in baseball. The 2005 World Series pitted the Houston Astros, with the 11th-highest payroll, against the Chicago White Sox, who ranked 13th.

Experience Counts

When the White Sox and Astros met for the 2005 World Series, Chicago's manager, general manager, and coaches had almost three times more at-bats against Houston's Roger Clemens than their 25 active players.

1977 World Series, Game 6

Los Angeles	AB	R	H	PO	A	E
Lopes,2b	4	0	1	0	4	0
Russell,ss	3	0	0	1	4	0
Smith,rf	4	2	1	1	0	0
Cey,3b	3	1	1	0	1	0
Garvey,1b	4	1	2	13	0	0
Baker,lf	4	0	1	2	0	0
Monday,cf	4	0	1	3	0	0
Yeager,c	3	0	1	4	2	0
bDavalillo	1	0	1	0	0	0
Hooton,p	2	0	0	0	0	0
Sosa,p	0	0	0	0	0	0
Rau,p	0	0	0	0	0	0
aGoodson	1	0	0	0	0	0
Hough,p	0	0	0	0	0	0
cLacy	1	0	0	0	0	0
Totals	34	4	9	24	11	0

New York	AB	R	H	PO	A	E
Rivers,cf	4	0	2	1	0	0
Randolph,2b	4	1	0	2	3	0
Munson,c	4	1	1	6	0	0
Jackson,rf	3	4	3	5	0	0
Chambliss,1b	4	2	2	9	1	0
Nettles,3b	4	0	0	0	0	0
Piniella,lf	3	0	0	2	1	0
Dent,ss	2	0	0	1	4	1
Torrez,p	3	0	0	1	2	0
Totals	31	8	8	27	11	1

Los Angeles ....2 0 1 0 0 0 0 0 1—4
New York ....0 2 0 3 2 0 0 1 x—8

a Struck out for Rau in seventh.
b Bunted safely for Yeager in ninth.
c Popped out for Hough in ninth.

Runs batted in: Garvey 2, Smith, Davalillo, Chambliss 2, Jackson 5, Piniella.
Double: Chambliss.
Triple: Garvey.
Home runs: Chambliss, Smith, Jackson 3.
Sacrifice fly: Piniella.
Double plays: Dent, Randolph and Chambliss; Dent and Chambliss.
Passed ball: Munson.
Left on bases: New York 5, Los Angeles 2.

Los Angeles	IP	H	R	ER	BB	SO
Hooton (L)	3	3	4	4	1	1
Sosa	1⅔	3	3	3	1	0
Rau	1⅓	0	0	0	0	1
Hough	2	2	1	1	0	3

New York	IP	H	R	ER	BB	SO
Torrez (W)	9	9	4	2	2	6

Hooton pitched to three batters in fourth.

Umpires: McSherry, Chylak, Sudol, McCoy, Dale, Evans.
Time: 2:18. **Attendance:** 56,407.

The box score is the result of scorekeeping decisions as well as game action.

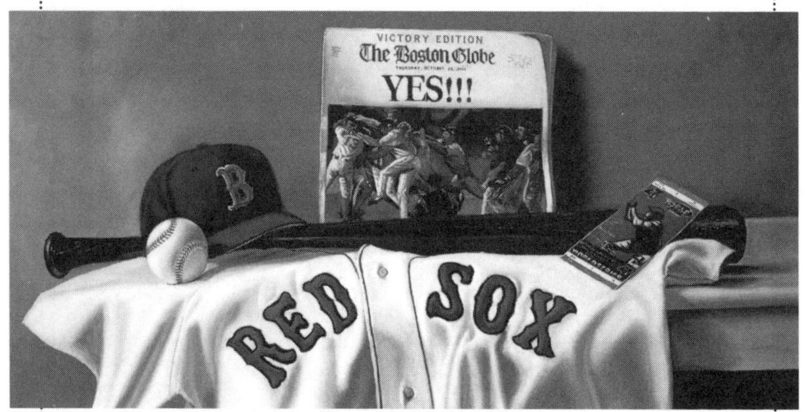

The *Boston Globe* headline says it all. The Red Sox have ended 86 years of futility with the 2004 world championship. Copyright 2005 by Bill Williams. Reprinted with permission, Bill Goff, Inc./GoodSportsArt.com.

LIDGE LICKED

Closers don't always close. Houston's Brad Lidge was the losing pitcher in Games 2 and 4 of the 2005 World Series sweep by the White Sox.

CLOSER CALAMITY

Houston closer Brad Lidge allowed no home runs in his first 20⅓ innings of postseason play. That ended when Albert Pujols beat him with a ninth-inning homer that won NLCS Game 5 for St. Louis in 2005. Nine pitches later, Lidge threw another game-ending gopher—to spray-hitting White Sox leadoff man Scott Podsednik. Podsednik was homerless in 507 at-bats during the regular season.

MARATHON MAN

Geoff Blum's game-winning, two-run homer in 2005 World Series Game 3 gave him his first RBIs in 55 days. The blow ended the longest World Series game (5:41) with a 7–5 White Sox victory over the Houston Astros. Marks were made for most pitchers (17), most pitches (482), most walks (21), most players used (43), and most men left on base (30). Sox leadoff man Scott Podsednik also became the first man to have eight at-bats in one Series game. Blum and Podsednik, whose home run had won Game 2 two days earlier, had combined for one previous home run in their White Sox careers. Podsednik had more home runs (one) and more triples (two) in the four-game World Series sweep of the Astros than he had during the regular season (no homers and one triple).

PERFECT PAUL

After winning MVP honors in the 2005 American League Championship Series, Paul Konerko of the White Sox hit a dramatic World Series grand slam against the Astros and caught the final out of Chicago's first world championship since 1917. Konerko's five home runs helped the White Sox win all but one of their 12 postseason games in 2005. Their only loss was a 3–2 defeat by the Angels in the ALCS opener.

BURLY BUEHRLE

During the 2005 World Series, White Sox ace Mark Buehrle became the first pitcher to start one game and earn a save in the next one. Catfish Hunter almost did it in the 1974 World Series, but it was not in consecutive games.

SCOTT'S SURPRISE

Among players who qualified for the batting title (502 plate appearances), Scott Podsednik of the 2005 White Sox was the only one who had no home runs on the season but then clubbed a pair in postseason play.

GOT HIS NUMBER

Bobby Jenks, the White Sox closer in the 2005 World Series, wore the same uniform number (45) that Michael Jordan had during his brief stay with the ballclub in the mid-1990s.

TRUE CHAMPIONS

The 1927 Yankees and the 2005 White Sox were the only teams in baseball history to keep first place from wire-to-wire, lead their league in victories, and sweep the World Series.

GOOD BALANCE

The 2005 White Sox and the 1997 Florida Marlins were the only world champions without a 20-game winner or a .300 hitter.

THIN MARGINS

The 1962 Yankees and the 2005 White Sox were the only teams to clinch a World Series by winning a 1–0 game on the road. But the Sox were the first team to get game-deciding homers in the ninth inning or later twice in the same postseason series.

SERIES DUCATS

The cheapest ticket for the 2006 World Series sold for $75, while the price of a premium box seat was $250.

NO WORLD SERIES

Teams that never played in the World Series:

- Texas Rangers
- Washington Nationals (formerly Montreal Expos)
- Seattle Mariners
- Colorado Rockies
- Tampa Bay Devil Rays

SERIES-ENDING HOMERS

Six players hit home runs that ended postseason series. They are:

- Chris Burke, Astros—beats Braves in eighteenth inning of 2005 NLDS Game 4
- Aaron Boone, Yankees—eleventh-inning shot tops BoSox in 2003 ALCS Game 7
- Todd Pratt, Mets—tenth-inning blast in 1999 NLDS Game 4 beats D'backs
- Joe Carter, Blue Jays—ninth-inning shot versus Phils wins 1993 World Series in six games
- Chris Chambliss, Yankees—tops Kansas City with leadoff HR in ninth inning of 1976 ALCS Game 5
- Bill Mazeroski, Pirates—leads off ninth with Series-winning HR in 1960 Game 7

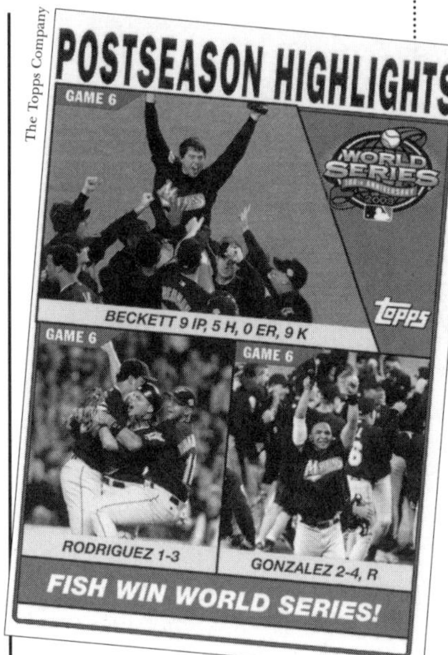

The Topps Company

WHERE SERIES BALLS WENT

- 2004—Loaned to Red Sox museum by Doug Mientkiewicz
- 2003—Ball and glove displayed in home of Josh Beckett
- 2002—In box at home of Darin Erstad
- 2001—Given to Arizona owner Jerry Colangelo by Luis Gonzalez

- 2000—Autographed ball sits in Bernie Williams's trophy case
- 1999—Held by Yankee Stadium security guard Dan Weiss
- 1998—Ball and glove in Tino Martinez's safe deposit box
- 1997—Unknown
- 1996—On display in Charley Hayes's living room
- 1995—Unknown
- 1993—Displayed in Joe Carter's home
- 1992—Shoes, glove, hat, jersey, tickets, and ball in Mike Timlin's office
- 1991—Unknown
- 1990—Loaned to Reds Museum by Todd Benzinger

FIVE-HIT GAMES

Players with five hits in a postseason game:

World Series

- Paul Molitor, Milwaukee (AL), October 12, 1982

League Championship Series

- Paul Blair, Baltimore (AL), October 6, 1969
- Hideki Matsui, New York (AL), October 16, 2004

Division Series

- Marquis Grissom, Atlanta (NL), October 7, 1995

Yankee Stadium, seen here from the air, has hosted more World Series than any other ballpark. Copyright 1989 by Andy Jurinko. Reprinted with permission, Bill Goff, Inc./GoodSportsArt.com.

- Mike Stanley, Boston (AL), October 10, 1999
- Derek Jeter, New York (AL), October 3, 2006

MANAGING TO WIN

Tony La Russa (2006 Cardinals and 1989 Athletics) and Sparky Anderson (1984 Tigers and 1975 and 1976 Reds) are the only managers who have won world championships in both leagues.

IN THE CARDS

The 2006 St. Louis Cardinals had the worst regular-season record (83–78) of any world champion.

POWER VACUUM

One of the reasons the Detroit Tigers lost the 2006 World Series was the sudden silence of Placido Polanco, who went 0-for-17 against the St. Louis Cardinals after winning AL Championship Series MVP honors against the Oakland Athletics.

HOME SWEET HOME

The 2006 St. Louis Cardinals were the first team to win the World Series in a new ballpark since the 1923 New York Yankees beat the New York Giants in the brand-new Yankee Stadium.

CHAPTER 7
THE SWAP SHOP

BROOKS ROBINSON REMEMBERS...

Getting Frank Robinson before the 1966 season was the best move the Orioles ever made. It turned around the Orioles' fortunes. Frank came over here with a little chip on his shoulder. The Reds said he was "an old 30" and that's why they were willing to let him go. We didn't know what to expect, since he had had some negative publicity in Cincinnati.

I had the best first half of my career that year, with 70-something RBIs at the All-Star break. Then I was the All-Star Game MVP. I went downhill a little after that, but Frank kept putting numbers up on the board. He had something to prove and certainly made our team better than anyone else.

It's always exciting to see what's going to happen before the July 31 trade deadline. Salaries enter into it, free agency enters into it, and so many teams think they're in the wild-card race that sometimes fewer trades are made.

Mike Cuellar coming to the Orioles from Houston was a fantastic trade. For three or four years, he ranked right up there with Jim Palmer and Dave McNally. But we made some clunkers, too, like giving up Curt Schilling, Steve Finley, and someone else for Glenn Davis.

Babe Ruth was sold to the Yankees by the Red Sox for $125,000 on January 3, 1920, then returned to Boston with the National League Braves at the end of his career.

DOZEN DARING BLOCKBUSTERS

Blockbuster trades can be best evaluated by calculating the value of players involved at the time. The following trades figure to find a place on anyone's list:

1. Rogers Hornsby (Cardinals) for Frankie Frisch and Jimmy Ring (Giants), 1926
2. Rocky Colavito (Indians) for Harvey Kuenn (Tigers), 1960
3. Frank Robinson (Reds) for Milt Pappas, Jack Baldschun, and Dick Simpson (Orioles),1966
4. Alex Rodriguez and cash (Rangers) for Alfonso Soriano and Joaquin Arias (Yankees), 2004
5. Gaylord Perry and Frank Duffy (Giants) for Sam McDowell (Indians), 1971
6. Bobby Bonds (Giants) for Bobby Murcer (Yankees), 1974
7. Orlando Cepeda (Cardinals) for Joe Torre (Braves), 1969
8. Fred McGriff and Tony Fernandez (Blue Jays) for Joe Carter and Robby Alomar (Padres), 1990
9. Chuck Klein (Phillies) for Mark Koenig, Ted Kleinhans, Harvey

One of the worst trades in baseball history occurred in 1901, when Cincinnati traded Christy Mathewson to the New York Giants for injured 19th-century standout Amos Rusie. Mathewson went on to a Hall of Fame career, while Rusie was forced to retire right after the trade.

Hendrick, and $65,000 (Cubs), 1933

10. Joe Morgan, Cesar Geronimo, Jack Billingham, Denis Menke, and Ed Armbrister (Astros) for Lee May, Tommy Helms, and Jimmy Stewart (Reds), 1971
11. David Justice and Marquis Grissom (Braves) for Kenny Lofton and Alan Embree (Indians), 1997
12. Randy Johnson (Diamondbacks) for Javier Vazquez, Brad Halsey, Dioner Navarro, and cash (Yankees); D'backs then trade Navarro, William Juarez, Danny Muegge, and Beltran Perez to Dodgers for Shawn Green (Dodgers), 2005.

BoSox Buy Babe

Babe Ruth reached the majors in 1914 when Jack Dunn, owner of the Baltimore team (International League), sold him to the Boston Red Sox with Ernie Shore and Ben Egan. The price for the trio was $25,000. The Philadelphia A's had declined to purchase Ruth earlier.

Rich Paperwork

The 1919 contract that transferred Babe Ruth from the Red Sox to the Yankees sold at auction for $996,000 in 2005.

Two Teams in a Day

In 1922 Max Flack of the Cubs was traded for Cliff Heathcote of the Cardinals between games of a morning-afternoon

Ruth Fooled Defense in Final Flurry

Babe Ruth's last great home-run display—three in a game for the Boston Braves at Pittsburgh's Forbes Field on May 25, 1935—also featured a solid single through the shortstop hole. The Pirates shortstop had shifted to the right side of second in a common shift used against the aging left-handed pull hitter.

doubleheader on Memorial Day. They were the first two major leaguers to play for two different teams on the same day.

LEAVING THE GROVE
Lefty Grove spent five years with the minor league Baltimore Orioles because club owner Jack Dunn was reluctant to sell him to a big-league team. Dunn relented in 1925 when the Philadelphia Athletics offered $100,600—some $600 more than the Yankees had paid the Boston Red Sox for Babe Ruth five years earlier.

TRADING SPACES
When player/manager Joe Cronin was sold from the Washington Senators to the Boston Red Sox after the 1934 season, the transaction included not only a $250,000 payoff from Tom Yawkey to Clark Griffith but also a five-year, $30,000 pact for Cronin as Boston's player/manager. Incumbent Red Sox pilot Bucky Harris took the vacant manager's job in Washington.

MISTAKEN IDENTITY
Hank Greenberg's Hall of Fame career in Detroit ended when Tigers owner Walter

Although the St. Louis Browns became the Baltimore Orioles in 1954, Don Larsen lasted longer than any of his fellow Brownies. Along with fellow pitcher Bob Turley, a future World Series MVP, Larsen was part of the 17-player trade between the Orioles and Yankees before the 1955 season. He authored the only World Series no-hitter—a perfect game—one year later. Ronnie Joyner

Briggs saw a photo of the slugger in a Yankees uniform—worn by Greenberg in a wartime fund-raiser because no other available uniform would fit him. Detroit traded him to Pittsburgh, where he tutored young Ralph Kiner and encouraged Jackie Robinson in 1947 before retiring.

BURDETTE FOR SAIN
The Braves made a successful waiver deal with the pennant-

hungry Yankees in 1951 when they sent Johnny Sain, 33, to New York for Lew Burdette, 24. Burdette went on to win 179 games for the Braves and teamed with southpaw Warren Spahn to give the team an even more formidable left-right punch than the old Spahn-Sain tandem.

VEECK'S PITCH

During his tenure as boss of the Browns, Bill Veeck always needed money for basic expenses. He tried to convince Cleveland's Hank Greenberg, a close friend, to buy first baseman Hank Arft, but the Indians already had Luke Easter at the position. In his final plea, Veeck's teletype jammed and printed "ARFARFARFARFARF." Greenberg wired back, "I CAN'T STOP LAUGHING. KEEP THAT DOG IN ST. LOUIS."

BOBO THE HOBO

To say Bobo Newsom was a well-traveled pitcher is an understatement. From 1935 to 1952 he played for, in order, the Browns, the Senators, the Red Sox, the Browns, the Tigers, the Senators, the Dodgers, the Browns, the Senators, the A's, the Senators, the Yankees, the Giants, the

Hank Aaron and Willie Mays, representing the cities (but not the teams) of their big-league births, enjoy a nostalgic meeting at Hall of Fame Day in Cooperstown. Bob Bartosz

Senators, and the A's. He won 211 games and lost 222.

KINER FEEDBACK
New York Mets broadcaster Ralph Kiner, who witnessed the angry backlash of fans upset with the Mets for dealing Tom Seaver in 1977, recalled a similar reaction by Pirates fans when Branch Rickey traded him to the Cubs in 1953. Kiner, Joe Garagiola, and two others became Cubs in exchange for six players and $100,000.

JUSTIFIED HOLDOUT
Don Larsen had an 11–5 record and a World Series perfect game for the 1956 Yankees but was offered only a $1,000 raise to $14,000 a year. Unwilling to take the offer, he eventually signed for $18,000—a raise of $5,000. Three years later, he was traded to the Kansas City Athletics in the deal that made Roger Maris a Yankee.

The 1964 midseason swap that sent Lou Brock from Chicago to St. Louis for Ernie Broglio may have been the most one-sided trade in baseball history. Baseball Hall of Fame

Trader's Temperament

"Gabe Paul, Bill Veeck, and Frank Lane will make a deal and not regret the after-effects in the least. If it turns out bad, they'll go ahead and make another one. That is the attitude you must take if you're going to trade. You've got to wipe it off and keep going. You gamble every time you make a deal. You always know what you've got, but you don't always know what you're getting. The best traders are the ones with the most patience and perseverance."

— Paul Richards

HARSH(MAN) VERDICT
Jack Harshman lost three games to the Yankees in 1959 but did it in a unique way—by

pitching for three different teams (Orioles, Red Sox, Indians).

NOT SO FAST

After the Cubs acquired erstwhile 20-game winner Ernie Broglio from the St. Louis Cardinals during the 1964 season, the *Chicago Tribune* said, "Thank you, thank you, oh you lovely St. Louis Cardinals. Nice doing business with you." The paper should have waited. Broglio wilted, losing 19 of 26 decisions, while fleet Lou Brock, the young outfielder Chicago sent to St. Louis, not only helped the Cards win the world title that year but also blossomed into a Hall of Famer. After the trade, Brock's .418 batting average helped St. Louis win its first flag in 18 years.

Roger Maris, acquired from the Kansas City A's, first donned Yankees pinstripes in 1960, then hit 61 homers a year later.
Reprinted with permission, National Baseball Hall of Fame Library, Cooperstown, New York

LOU BROCK FOR WHOM?

Ernie Broglio was a right-handed pitcher with promise when he was traded by the Cardinals for outfielder Lou Brock on June 15, 1964. Broglio had gone 18–8 with a 2.99 ERA in 1963 and was only 28 years old. Not long after the swap, however, the pitcher reported that his elbow had "locked." In two and a half Chicago seasons, Broglio went 7–19 and retired. Brock, on the other hand, stole his way to Cooperstown.

TORRE, SADECKI, AND CEPEDA

In 1966 the San Francisco Giants traded first baseman Orlando Cepeda to the St. Louis Cardinals for pitcher Ray Sadecki. Three years later the Cardinals traded Cepeda to the Atlanta Braves for catcher/first baseman Joe Torre. In 1974 they sent Torre to the New York Mets for Ray Sadecki. Cepeda and Torre won MVP awards for St. Louis in 1967 and 1971.

QUICK SWITCH

In 1982, with travel time shortened by air travel, Joel Youngblood became the first player to appear for different teams in different cities on the same day. After playing a day game in Chicago with the Mets, he joined the Expos for a night game in Philadelphia. Youngblood also got a hit for both of his teams that day.

Frank Howard won two American League home-run crowns after the Dodgers sent him to the Senators for pitcher Claude Osteen after the 1964 campaign. Ronnie Joyner

HOW MATHEWS HEARD

Third baseman Eddie Mathews, the only man to play for the Braves in Boston, Milwaukee, and Atlanta, was told of his 1966 trade to Houston by a sportswriter. A subsequent letter of apology from the team was addressed to Edward—rather than Edwin—Mathews.

WHY BRAVES WON

With five of the six NL West teams in contention on Labor Day 1969, the Atlanta Braves pulled a coup by acquiring 45-year-old knuckleball reliever Hoyt Wilhelm from the California Angels. In eight appearances, he had a 2–0 record, four saves, and 0.75 earned-run mark as the Braves won the division by three games. As payment for Wilhelm, Atlanta sent minor league outfielder Mickey Rivers to the Angels after the season.

TAKE MY WIFE, PLEASE

Yankees teammates Fritz Peterson and Mike Kekich swapped families after the 1972 season. Peterson traded his wife, Marilyn, their two kids, and his pet poodle for Susanne Kekich, her children, and their Bedlington terrier. Fritz and

Susanne lasted much longer than Mike and Marilyn, whose match proved to be a mismatch. Kekich's career also collapsed soon after news of the family swap became public during 1973 spring training.

NO SALE

Hall of Fame reliever Rollie Fingers and outfielder Joe Rudi wore Red Sox uniforms for three days during the 1976 season before Commissioner Bowie Kuhn vetoed their sale from the Oakland A's to Boston

Ronnie Joyner

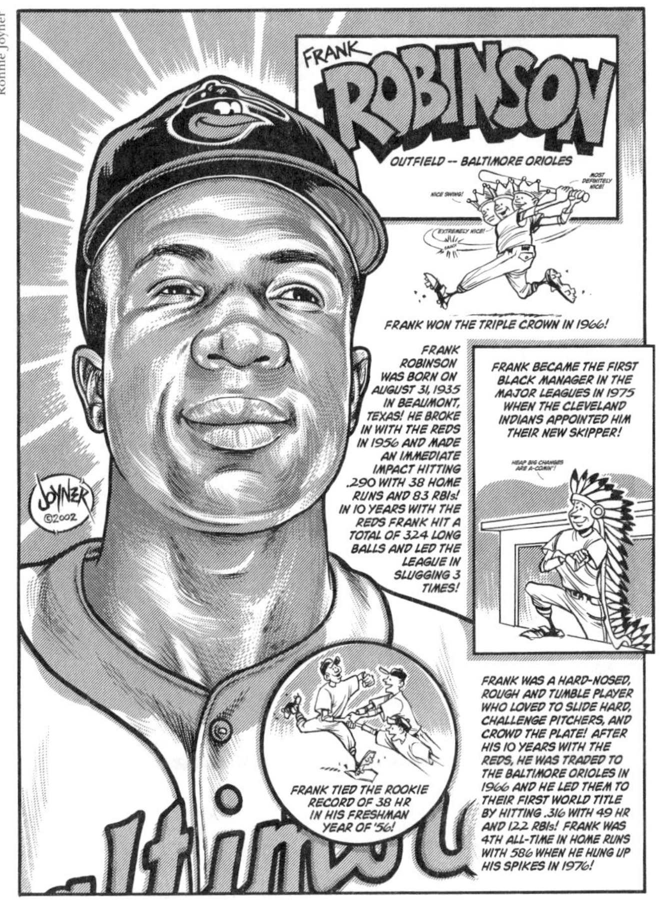

FRANK
ROBINSON
OUTFIELD -- BALTIMORE ORIOLES
NICE SWING!
MOST DEFINITELY NICE!
EXTREMELY NICE!
FRANK WON THE TRIPLE CROWN IN 1966!
FRANK ROBINSON WAS BORN ON AUGUST 31, 1935 IN BEAUMONT, TEXAS! HE BROKE IN WITH THE REDS IN 1956 AND MADE AN IMMEDIATE IMPACT HITTING .290 WITH 38 HOME RUNS AND 83 RBIs! IN 10 YEARS WITH THE REDS FRANK HIT A TOTAL OF 324 LONG BALLS AND LED THE LEAGUE IN SLUGGING 3 TIMES!
FRANK BECAME THE FIRST BLACK MANAGER IN THE MAJOR LEAGUES IN 1975 WHEN THE CLEVELAND INDIANS APPOINTED HIM THEIR NEW SKIPPER!
HEAP BIG CHANGES ARE A-COMIN'!
JOYNER ©2002
FRANK TIED THE ROOKIE RECORD OF 38 HR IN HIS FRESHMAN YEAR OF '56!
FRANK WAS A HARD-NOSED, ROUGH AND TUMBLE PLAYER WHO LOVED TO SLIDE HARD, CHALLENGE PITCHERS, AND CROWD THE PLATE! AFTER HIS 10 YEARS WITH THE REDS, HE WAS TRADED TO THE BALTIMORE ORIOLES IN 1966 AND HE LED THEM TO THEIR FIRST WORLD TITLE BY HITTING .316 WITH 49 HR AND 122 RBIs! FRANK WAS 4TH ALL-TIME IN HOME RUNS WITH 586 WHEN HE HUNG UP HIS SPIKES IN 1976!

Nine-time Milwaukee Braves All-Star Eddie Mathews was traded to the Houston Astros after the 1966 season. The National Baseball Library and Archive, Cooperstown, New York

for $1 million apiece. Both returned to the A's, then left after the season via free agency.

BEST FREE AGENT SIGNINGS

1. Barry Bonds, Giants, 1993
2. Greg Maddux, Braves, 1993
3. Reggie Jackson, Yankees, 1977
4. Catfish Hunter, Yankees, 1975
5. Terry Pendleton, Braves, 1991
6. Carlos Beltran, Mets, 2005
7. Roger Clemens, Astros, 2004
8. Manny Ramirez, Red Sox, 2000
9. Pete Rose, Phillies, 1980
10. Pedro Martinez, Mets, 2005

HITS AND MISSES

The Yankees of the George Steinbrenner era always spend heavily in the free-agent market. But they don't always succeed. Among their best acquisitions were Jason Giambi, Goose Gossage, Catfish Hunter, Reggie Jackson, Tommy John, Gary Sheffield, David Wells, and Dave Winfield. On the miss list were Dave Collins, Steve Kemp, Pascual Perez, Henry Rodriguez, Kenny Rogers, and Ed Whitson.

BAT WASN'T RUSTY

Rusty Staub, Le Grand Orange in Montreal, was the only player to get 500 hits with four different teams: the Astros, Expos, Tigers, and Mets.

FORCED TRADES

The era of free agency, financial finagling, and often-frivolous contracts caused a number of teams to trade big-name stars. Some examples:

Although he led the American League in slugging during his one year with the Baltimore Orioles in 1976, Reggie Jackson was quick to capitalize on the advent of free agency, signing a lucrative long-term pact with the Yankees. Jackson, who spent his first nine seasons with the Athletics, later moved on to the California Angels, also via free agency, and spent five years there before returning to Oakland for a last hurrah in 1987. The Topps Company

- Tom Seaver, Mets to Reds, for Doug Flynn, Steve Henderson, Dan Norman, and Pat Zachry (June 1977)
- Mark McGwire, A's to Cards, for Eric Ludwick, T.J. Mathews, and Blake Stein (July 1997)
- Mike Piazza and Todd Zeile, Dodgers to Marlins, for Manuel Barrios, Bobby Bonilla, Jim Eisenreich, Charles Johnson, and Gary Sheffield (May 1998)
- Randy Johnson, Mariners to Astros, for Freddy Garcia, Carlos Guillen, and John Halama (July 1998)
- Roger Clemens, Blue Jays to Yankees, for Homer Bush, Graeme Lloyd, and David Wells (February 1999)

CHANGE OF SOX

Carlton Fisk became a free agent in 1980 because the Boston Red Sox missed the deadline for sending him a contract by two days. After signing with the Chicago White Sox, Fisk reversed his famous No. 27 and, wearing No. 72, played a dozen more years and finished with the most home runs by a catcher (351) and most games caught (2,226). Mike Piazza later topped his long-ball mark.

During a salary dispute in 1972, the St. Louis Cardinals traded Steve Carlton to Philadelphia for fellow pitcher Rick Wise. Carlton proceeded to become the first man to win four Cy Young Awards—all with the Phils. JamesFiorentino.com

Timely Trade

Rick Sutcliffe, who went 16–1 for the 1984 Cubs after arriving from Cleveland, is the only pitcher to be traded in the middle of a season in which he won the Cy Young Award.

Marlin Massacre

After winning the 1997 World Series against Cleveland, the money-losing Florida Marlins decided to dump salary. Twenty of the 25 players on the fall classic roster were traded, including Kevin Brown, Al Leiter, Livan Hernandez, Moises Alou, Bobby Bonilla, Edgar Renteria, and Gary Sheffield. Not surprisingly, the 1998 Marlins finished dead last in the NL East.

Cook's Quip

After the Florida Marlins shipped southpaw set-up man Dennis Cook to the New York Mets for two minor leaguers on December 18, 1997, the pitcher wondered aloud whether the cost-conscious world champs were really saving money. "It's going to cost them more to ship our rings with UPS than it would have cost them to keep the team together," he said.

Brown = Bad Investment

Dumb, dumb, dumb. The Los Angeles Dodgers gave Kevin Brown a seven-year, $105 million contract in 1998. He repaid the favor with a yearly average of 10 wins and 154 innings pitched.

Traveling Man

Mike Morgan played for a record 12 teams during his 22-year career.

Sluggers for Rent

Manny Ramirez, Mark McGwire, and Rafael Palmeiro are the only players to hit at

Rickey Henderson, the single-season and career leader in stolen bases, was traded several times during his long career. He stole most of his bases during four stints with the Oakland Athletics but also played for the Yankees, the Blue Jays, the Padres, the Angels, and the Mets. Michael Zagaris

least 200 home runs for two different teams.

POSTSWAP SLUGGERS

The A's twice traded players who became baseball's single-season home-run champions after they left. Roger Maris broke Babe Ruth's record after joining the Yankees, and Mark McGwire topped Maris after joining the Cardinals.

GRIFFEY SWAP

Before the 2000 season, the Seattle Mariners sent Ken

Manny Ramirez spent eight years in Cleveland before moving to the Boston Red Sox as a free agent in 2001. He later teamed with David Ortiz, signed by Boston after Minnesota released him in 2002, to give the Red Sox a fearsome 1-2 punch in the heart of the lineup. Bill Menzel

Griffey Jr. to the Cincinnati Reds for Mike Cameron, Brett Tomko, Antonio Perez, and Jake Meyer. Griffey agreed to a nine-year, $116.5 million contract with his hometown team.

Pedro Martinez reached the majors with the Dodgers, went to Montreal in a straight-up swap for Delino DeShields, and then crossed league lines when the Expos sent him to the Red Sox for Carl Pavano and Tony Armas Jr. The star pitcher used free agency to return to the NL in 2005 with the New York Mets. The Topps Company

SUDDEN MOVE

Players move often and unexpectedly. On July 29, 2000, the Milwaukee Brewers gave Bob Wickman posters to the first 30,000 fans who passed through their turnstiles. Their timing was a bit off, though: one day earlier, Wickman had been traded to the Cleveland Indians.

PRICEY PICKUP

The Texas Rangers paid $2 million more to sign free-agent shortstop Alex Rodriguez in 2001 than owner Tom Hicks paid for the franchise when he bought it from George W. Bush and Rusty Rose three years earlier. Rodriguez signed a 10-year, $252 million pact, richest in sports history.

BOSTON BARGAIN

One of the biggest bargains in baseball history, David Ortiz signed a one-year, $1.25 million contract with Boston after Minnesota released him in 2002. Fellow Dominican Pedro Martinez, then the top Red Sox starter, convinced the team to take a flier on the big first baseman.

HIGHWAY ROBBERY

Anxious to land Tampa native Lou Piniella as manager, the Tampa Bay Devil Rays sent outfielder Randy Winn to Seattle in exchange for the rights to Piniella on October 28, 2002.

PREMATURE STANDING "O"
Thinking he was leaving the mound for the last time, Roger Clemens received a standing ovation from the rival Florida Marlins during Game 4 of the 2003 World Series. Three months later, however, he changed his mind after Andy Pettitte left the Yankees via free agency to sign with his hometown Houston Astros. Clemens, also from Houston, decided to follow suit.

PRIME MOVER
Roger Clemens is the only man to win awards from the Baseball Writers Association of America (BBWAA) while with four different teams. He won Cy Young Awards with the Red Sox, Blue Jays, Yankees, and Astros—joining Randy Johnson, Pedro Martinez, and Gaylord Perry as the only men to win the award in both leagues.

THE SOSA SWAP
When the Chicago Cubs traded Sammy Sosa to the Baltimore Orioles after the 2004 season, they agreed to kick in $16.15 million of the $25 million the slugger was still owed in a four-year, $72 million pact. The Cubs got Jerry Hairston, Mike Fontenot, and Dave Crouthers in exchange.

No star is immune from trades. Although Roger Clemens won a record seven Cy Young Awards, he did it for four different teams: the Red Sox (three times), the Blue Jays (twice), and the Yankees and Astros (once each). Clemens began his career in Boston, moved to Toronto via free agency, went to the Yankees in a trade, and continued his career after signing with Houston as a free agent in 2004. Copyright 1999 by Bill Purdom. Reprinted by permission, Bill Goff, Inc./GoodSportsArt.com.

RED INK FOR RANGERS

The February 16, 2004, swap that sent Alex Rodriguez from the Texas Rangers to the New York Yankees for Alfonso Soriano and a minor leaguer included a provision that Texas pay $67 million of the $179 million remaining on the shortstop's 10-year contract. The three years A-Rod spent in Texas cost the club $140 million, or an average of $46.7 million per season.

MILLIONS FOR BORAS

Agent Scott Boras got a $12.6 million commission when Alex Rodriguez signed with the Texas Rangers in 2000. That represented 5 percent of the 10-year contract's total value. The pact's average annual value was $25.2 million, considerably less than the Minnesota team payroll of $23.4 million during the previous season.

TOUGH LOSSES

The 2004 New York Yankees lost three pitchers who had won at least 15 games the year before: Andy Pettitte (21), Roger Clemens (17), and David Wells (15). The last team that lost three 15-game winners was the 1902 Brooklyn Superbas (later known as the Dodgers).

Even two-time AL batting kings can get traded, as Nomar Garciaparra discovered with three moves in as many years. The longtime shortstop of the Boston Red Sox joined the Chicago Cubs after a four-team midseason swap in 2004, then moved to the Los Angeles Dodgers via free agency in 2006, making a smooth transition to first base. Copyright 1999 by Bill Purdom. Reprinted with permission, Bill Goff, Inc./GoodSportsArt.com.

TRADE HELPS

Boston's trading-deadline acquisition of shortstop Orlando Cabrera and first baseman Doug Mientkiewicz allowed the team to advance to the 2004 world championship—even though the four-team trade, unpopular at the time, sent longtime star Nomar Garciaparra to the Cubs. Also

Once friendly rivals, Alex Rodriguez and Derek Jeter became teammates when the Yankees pulled off a blockbuster trade with the Texas Rangers just before 2004 spring training. Because they played the same position, A-Rod agreed to slide over to third base. The move paid big dividends a year later, when Rodriguez won his second MVP award in three seasons. Bill Menzel

involved in the four-way deal were the Expos and Twins.

CARLOS THE COLLECTOR

Carlos Beltran is the only player to drive in 50-plus runs in both leagues during the same season. He did it in 2004 for the Kansas City Royals of the American League and the Houston Astros of the National League. Beltran spent only half a season in Houston, bolting for New York via free agency after the Mets offered him a lucrative seven-year contract.

Carlos Beltran started his career with the Kansas City Royals, went to the Houston Astros in a 2004 midseason trade, then moved to the New York Mets via free agency in 2005. One year later, the star center fielder joined the handful of switch-hitters who produced 40 home runs in a season. Bill Menzel

Like Randy Johnson and Alex Rodriguez, Ken Griffey Jr. was a Seattle superstar who later found greener pastures elsewhere. The star center fielder spent 11 seasons with the Mariners before he requested and received a trade to his hometown team, the Cincinnati Reds.

Bill Menzel

The only man to have successive 60-homer seasons, Sammy Sosa suffered a sudden power vacuum after the Cubs traded him to the Orioles before the 2005 season. He played only one year in Baltimore before retiring. Sosa previously played for the Rangers and White Sox.

Wanda Chirnside

WRONG JERSEY?

Derek Lowe, the only pitcher to win three clinchers in the same postseason, caused a stir when he wore a Red Sox jersey when receiving his 2004 World Series ring. Although the ceremonies took place in Fenway Park, Lowe had crossed league lines months earlier by signing a four-year, $36 million deal with the Los Angeles Dodgers.

THE SHOVE THAT ROARED

A year after Tigers fans booed him at the Comerica Park All-Star Game, Kenny Rogers moved from Texas to Detroit via free agency and quickly became a local hero, helping the Tigers advance all the way to the World Series. Rodgers had been a fan target because he incurred a $50,000 fine and 20-game suspension for shoving two cameramen during a

With free agency and high salaries often prime reasons for player movement, even superstars switch teams with surprising frequency. Greg Maddux moved from the Braves to the Cubs to the Dodgers, while Carlos Beltran bounced from the Royals to the Astros to the Mets. Manny Ramirez moved, too, from the Cleveland Indians to the Boston Red Sox. The Topps Company

pregame workout. The suspension was reduced to 13 games upon appeal.

HE'S A MENCH

In 2006 Kevin Mench of the Rangers became the first right-handed hitter to homer in seven straight games—and was traded to the Brewers two months later.

JACKPOT FOR CARLOS

Carlos Delgado is the only man in baseball history to have three straight 30-homer seasons for three different teams. He did it for the 2004 Blue Jays, the 2005 Marlins, and the 2006 Mets.

COMPLICATED SWAP

The January 2005 trade that sent Randy Johnson from Arizona to the Yankees also involved the Los Angeles Dodgers. In exchange for Johnson, the D'backs got Brad Halsey, Javier Vazquez, Dioner Navarro, and $8 million in cash. Arizona then sent Navarro and William Juarez to Los Angeles for Shawn Green and $8 million to offset Green's salary.

RICH BLOOD

The trade that brought Randy Johnson to the Yankees gave the team a rotation that would cost them $64 million—more than the total payrolls of almost half the teams in the majors.

CHAPTER 8
COVERING THE GAME

BROOKS ROBINSON REMEMBERS...

I grew up listening to Bob Elson in Chicago, Harry Caray in St. Louis, and a few other guys who were around forever. I even got to meet Mel Ott when he was doing the games in Detroit. Meeting him was an exciting moment for me.

After I had retired as a player, getting into broadcasting was a good way for me to stay in the game. I still got to go to the same ballparks, see the same people, and hang around the baseball end of the game. After playing for 23 years, being isolated from the game would have been a tough row to hoe. But I learned to do my homework, doing a lot of reading and taking notes.

As a broadcaster, I worked with great people and had a lot of fun. Chuck Thompson used to correct my English all the time. I would say '"hisself," until I found out there was no such word. Or "thesselves" when it was "themselves."

During my first couple of years, I worked with a lady in Baltimore who would critique my work. I saw her more than a dozen times, learning things I should or shouldn't say. She corrected my grammar, too. It didn't hurt my feelings because I knew I was a real amateur. But I knew the history of the Orioles; there were only one or two guys I never met during my time with the team as a player and broadcaster. When things happened on the field, they often jarred my memory of something that happened when I played, so I would share that story on the air.

Working with Chuck Thompson, Bill O'Donnell, Jim Simpson, and Jon Miller really helped. Chuck and Jim had a way of leading me into things, and Jon might say, "Hey, Brooks, you have to get more involved." I was amazed at how they could come up with the right words at the right time. The night after Thurman Munson got killed, the Orioles played in New York and Chuck said all the right things. I thought to myself, "How do those guys do it?" They had the right words at the right moment. It amazes me to this day.

The thing I hated most as a broadcaster was a rain delay. I filled time by interviewing players. I had five questions. I'd ask my first question and didn't care what he said. Then I'd ask my second question. Anyone who knew anything about interviewing would have played off what the guy said. I was scared to death when I had to do an interview or rain fill. Fortunately, the guys liked to talk and we had lots of laughs. But I was in trouble if the delay lasted too long and I ran out of questions.

One of the reasons I stopped doing Orioles games after so many years (from 1978 to 1993) was being away from home with nothing to do. At the time, we televised only 60 games, 50 on the road and 10 at home. We'd be on a road trip for 10, 11, 12 days but do only five or six games. I hated off-days on the road, so I'd fly home to Baltimore, spend a couple of days there, and then fly out to the next city. I'd do another game and then fly back.

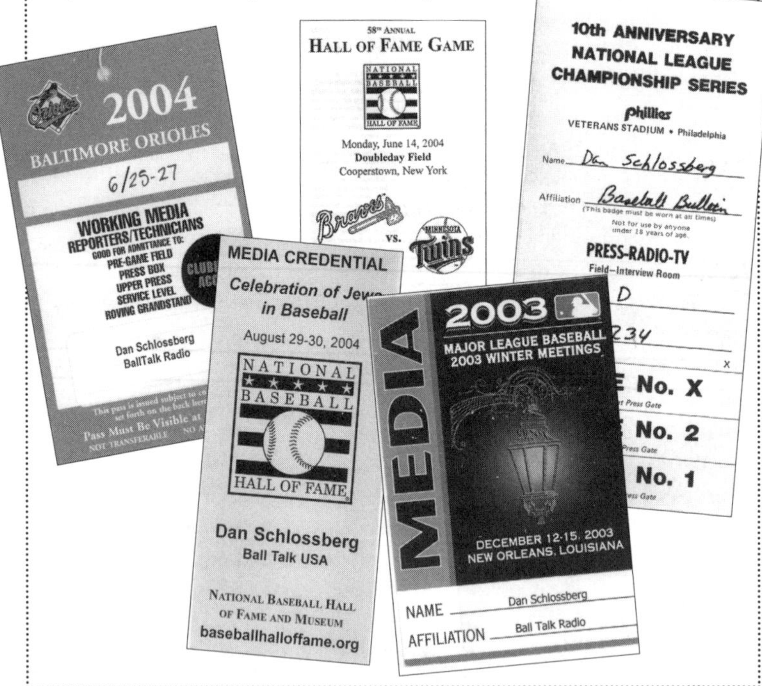

"FATHER" CHADWICK

English-born Henry Chadwick, who took on the nickname "Father" for his many pioneering efforts in the game, is the only baseball writer enshrined in the Hall of Fame. He wrote the first rule book in 1858, invented the box score, introduced many rules changes, and wrote about baseball for 50 years, starting just before the Civil War.

HOW FANS "WATCHED"

Before the advent of radio and the much-later addition of television, fans in big cities often followed World Series action by watching mechanical displays attached to downtown buildings. Megaphone men made announcements after receiving game information by Western Union wire, a system similar to what was used for the radio re-creations later done by Ronald Reagan and many others. Outdoor crowds became so big that theaters, armories, and sports arenas began to host fans willing to pay admission (25 cents at New York's Madison Square Garden for the 1912 World Series). A *Salt Lake Tribune* display nicknamed "Old Ironsides" was so popular that it remained in use until 1952.

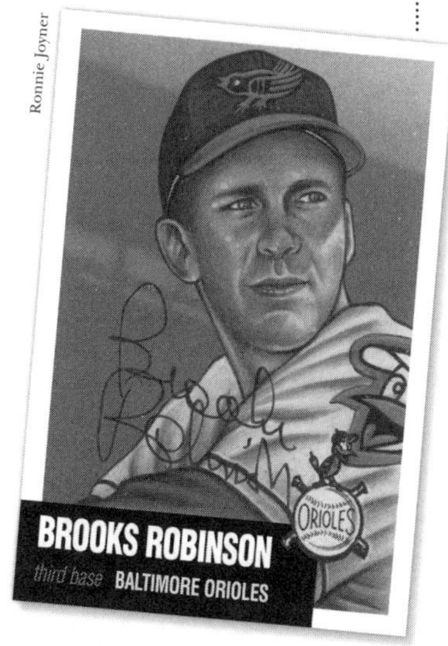

Ronnie Joyner
BROOKS ROBINSON
third base
BALTIMORE ORIOLES
ORIOLES

FROM WRITERS TO EXECUTIVES

Ban Johnson and Ford Frick were executives who began as baseball writers. Johnson was the first president of the American League, while Frick was National League president before he became commissioner of baseball. Frick had been Babe Ruth's ghostwriter when newspapers wanted Ruth's account of World Series games.

SECRET SCORER

In 1911 American League president Ban Johnson suggested the identity of scorekeepers be secret so they

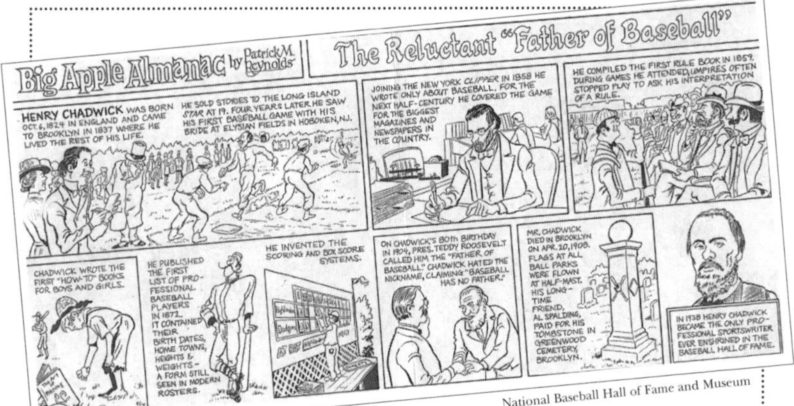

National Baseball Hall of Fame and Museum

could not be influenced by players to change their decisions. Chicago of the National League employed a mysterious "E.G. Green" as scorer from 1882 to 1891. Only team president A.G. Spalding knew that Mrs. Elisa Green Williams, mother of team treasurer C.G. Williams, was scoring the games.

PRESS PIN HISTORY
Media members first received press pins in 1911. Originally intended as press box admission badges for World Series games, pins were first issued for the All-Star Game in 1938. Though no All-Star pin was coined in 1939, a special pin was produced to honor Lou Gehrig for his feat of playing in 2,130 consecutive games. The All-Star pin resumed regular production after World War II.

LIEB'S LONG TENURE
Fred Lieb covered baseball for more than 65 years, beginning at age 21 with the 1911 *New York Press.* Lieb, who saw his first major league games in 1904, worked for several newspapers, including *The Sporting News,* before retiring to St. Petersburg, Florida, in 1948. Lieb wrote more than a dozen baseball books, including *Baseball as I Have Known It,* a review of his long sportswriting career.

ED SULLIVAN, SPORTSWRITER
Famous television host Ed Sullivan was sports editor of *The New York Graphic* in the 1920s.

The Sporting News.

VOL. 1, NO. 1 — ST. LOUIS, MO., MARCH 17, 1886. — SINGLE COPIES 5 CENTS.

THE GAME IN GOTHAM.

Esterbrook to Leave New York and Locate in Washington.

The Coming Base Ball Season to be the Liveliest the Metropolis has ever known—True Inwardness of the Squabble over Burch.

A GENUINE SENSATION

IS CRACKED UP TO BE

AT PRESENT THE LEAGUE

A ROYAL GOOD FELLOW

HARRY WRIGHT'S TEAM.

He Says the Phillies Will Be Among the Leaders This Year.

CARUTHERS COMING.

A Cablegram From Paris Announces His Departure for St. Louis.

THE NORTHWESTERN LEAGUE.

A Letter From Duluth Explaining the Prospects of the New Association.

THE WHITE STOCKINGS.

Chicago's Great Team Getting Ready for the Trip to Hot Springs.

Gore, Williamson, Pfeffer, Dalrymple, Flint, McCormick, Clarkson, Kelly and all the Champions to be given a Swim.

JOHN S. CLARKSON

CAPTAIN ANSON

MIKE KELLY

THE CHICAGO BLUES

The Pittsburgs Coming.

MATSADA SORIKICHI

The Japanese Wrestler Talks of His Wife, His Diamonds and His Money.

DIAMONDS AND PRECIOUS STONES

TEN THOUSAND SPECTATORS

THE UTICA TEAM'S TRIP.

Joe Hornung Moves His Family From New York State to the Hub.

READY FOR THE ROAD.

The Gentlemen's Driving Club Waiting for the Word.

A Brilliant Season Looked Forward to—The St. Louis Roadsters Preparing for Their Summer Campaign.

THE BANG TAILS

FINE ROADSTERS

The first edition of *The Sporting News* appeared in 1886.

Take Me Out to the Ballgame

Take me out to the ballgame,
Take me out to the crowd.
Buy me some peanuts and
Cracker Jack;
I don't care if I never get
back.
So let's root, root, root for the
home team,
If they don't win it's a shame.
For it's 1, 2, 3 strikes you're
out
At the old ballgame.

—Jack Norworth

BEFORE SOUNDPROOFING
Early radio men broadcast right from the press box, without the soundproofing provided by booths. During the 10-run uprising by the Philadelphia Athletics in Game 4 of the 1929 World Series against the Cubs, Graham McNamee was at the mike when a writer accidentally played his foil: "McNamee, will you please pipe down?"

REAGAN'S RE-CREATIONS
Before entering politics, Ronald "Dutch" Reagan broadcast baseball games for the Chicago Cubs over WHO Des Moines and played Grover Cleveland Alexander in a movie called *The Winning Team.*

QUIRKY WIRE
When Ronald Reagan re-created games for Des Moines radio station WHO, the wire carrying the play-by-play occasionally went silent. Recounting one such incident, Reagan said, "I had just announced that a pitch was on its way to Billy Jurges when the telegrapher signaled the wire went dead. I knew Wheaties [the sponsor] wouldn't stand for silence, so I had Jurges foul off the pitch. Still no report, so I had him foul off another one, this time killing time by 'describing' a fight by two fans for the foul ball. I even had Jurges just missing a home run with another long foul. Finally, the telegrapher nodded. The play-by-play was back. I found out Jurges had popped up on the first pitch!"

GOOD CALL
Cincinnati radio announcer Harry Hartman was the first broadcaster to use the phrase "Going, going, gone" to describe a home run in flight. He was on the air in the 1930s.

Sporting Life was the major competition for *The Sporting News* early in the 20th century. National Baseball Hall of Fame and Museum

RADIO WARS

When Bob Elson began broadcasting big-league games in Chicago, stations did not have exclusive rights. Up to a half-dozen stations often broadcast the same game.

HOT SPOT FOR ELSON

Bob Elson was in the right place at the right time to advance his career. He worked out of Chicago, where baseball commissioner Kenesaw Mountain Landis had his office. Because Landis liked Elson's work, he tabbed him to do dozens of All-Star and World Series games.

INROADS FROM DIXIE

Red Barber started a national trend toward giving baseball broadcasts a southern flavor.

He told stories and spun yarns rather than just doing balls and strikes. Barber started in Cincinnati before joining the Brooklyn Dodgers and eventually the New York Yankees.

Baseball's Sad Lexicon

These are the saddest of possible words:
"Tinker to Evers to Chance."
Trio of bear cubs, and fleeter than birds,
Tinker and Evers and Chance.
Ruthlessly pricking our gonfalon bubble,
Making a Giant hit into a double—
Words that are heavy with nothing but trouble:
"Tinker to Evers to Chance."

—Franklin P. Adams

THE OLD EGGHEAD

Red Barber used an egg timer to let him know when he should give the score to his Brooklyn radio audience.

FIRST FRICK AWARD

When the Hall of Fame established the Ford Frick Award, to be given annually to the top baseball broadcaster, voters had a hard time choosing the initial recipient. They decided to name both Red Barber and Mel Allen, longtime mikemen in the New York market.

HOW HARWELL STARTED

Ernie Harwell's big-league career began when Brooklyn general manager Branch Rickey heard him announcing games for the minor league Atlanta Crackers. Needing an announcer to fill in for the ailing Red Barber, Rickey requested Harwell's release. But Atlanta owner Earl Mann,

This pass was used by writers covering the World Series between the Yankees and Pirates in 1927. Before batting practice of the first game, Pittsburgh players watching Yankees sluggers hit pitch after pitch over the fence hung the "Murderers Row" nickname on the team because it "murdered" rival pitchers.

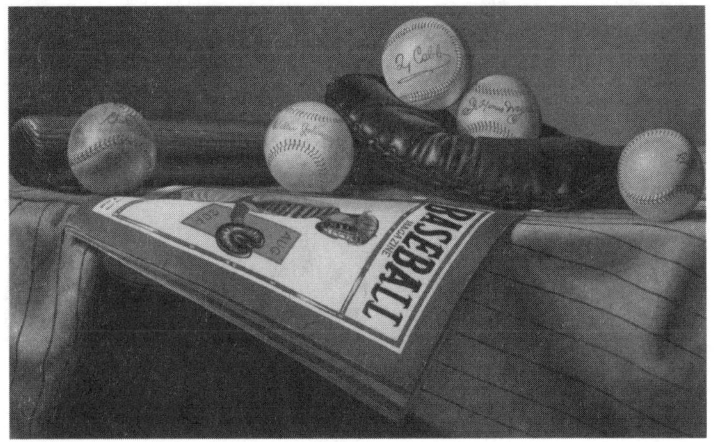

With radio the rage but television still a pipe dream, *Baseball Magazine* supplemented newspaper coverage of baseball during the first half of the 20th century. Copyright 1994 by Bill Williams. Reprinted with permission, Bill Goff, Inc./GoodSportsArt.com.

always a shrewd businessman, made the release conditional. He wanted catcher Cliff Dapper transferred to his team from Brooklyn's Montreal farm club. That made Harwell the only announcer ever traded for a catcher.

ERNIE'S ECHO

Ernie Harwell called Bobby Thomson's "shot heard 'round the world" for the 1951 New York Giants. Nobody remembers it because Harwell did it on television, which was still in its infancy. No tape was made of that telecast. On the other hand, a fan taped the Russ Hodges radio version, which became the most famous sports broadcast of all time. According to Harwell, who broadcast big-league baseball from 1948 to 2004, he and Hodges alternated between television and radio duty. It was Harwell's turn to do television for the final playoff game between the Dodgers and

Broadcasting = New Fans

"Broadcasting brought baseball directly into the home. By personalizing the players, it created new fans."

—Red Barber

NEGRO WORLD SERIES PITS NEWARK VS. KANSAS CITY

(Story on Page 29)

Scenes: K. C. and Newark Clinch Pennants

The 1946 Newark Eagles, featuring such sluggers as Monte Irvin (second from left), contended with Satchel Paige and the Kansas City Monarchs for bragging rights in the Negro Leagues. Laura Gaynor

Giants. "I thought I had the better assignment," Harwell said. "For the first time in the history of television, that series was going to be telecast coast-to-coast. There were five radio broadcasts. Poor old Russ was going to get lost on the radio and I'd be on TV."

AUNT MINNIE'S WINDOW

Pittsburgh mikeman Rosey Rowswell was known for creative re-creations of games. When Ralph Kiner or another Pirate pounded a potential home run, he yelled, "Open the window, Aunt Minnie, here it comes!" His sound effects guys broke a small pane of glass to make it sound like Aunt Minnie didn't get her window open in time.

FIRST JOCK MIKEMAN

Although he is best known as the first ex-player to become a broadcaster (1932), Jack Graney was also the first to come to bat wearing a number (1916) and the first to face a hard-throwing Red Sox southpaw named George Herman Ruth (1914). Graney, leading off for the Cleveland Indians, singled to center in that at-bat.

VOICE OF THE ANGEL

John Forsythe, future star of *Bachelor Father* and future voice of Charlie in *Charlie's Angels,* was the Ebbets Field public-address announcer in 1937–38.

RADIO DAYS

Although the Cincinnati Reds broadcast 40 games over WLW

radio during the 1929 season, new owner Sidney Weil thought the practice hurt attendance and eliminated all broadcasts in 1930. Harry Hartman, field announcer at Redland Field, persuaded the owner to restore the games the next season and did the announcing himself. Readers of *The Sporting News* twice named Hartman the nation's most popular radio broadcaster.

PAST TENSE

Hall of Fame pitcher Waite Hoyt had a memorable career as a broadcaster for the Cincinnati Reds. His specialty was broadcasting games in the past tense. He would watch a play and wait until it was over before telling his audience what happened. Hoyt was also famous for filling dead time during rain delays and even produced a record album called *Waite Hoyt in the Rain.* He was singin' in the rain long before Gene Kelly.

WAITE LISTED

When Waite Hoyt disappeared for two days during the 1945 season, the Cincinnati *Enquirer* revealed that the former pitcher was prone to spells of amnesia. Asked about the problem, former Hoyt teammate Babe Ruth replied, "Amnesia must be a new brand of Scotch."

Red Barber interviews Dodgers manager Leo Durocher before baseball's first televised game, on August 24, 1939, in Brooklyn's Ebbets Field. National League

Young Mel Allen was at the mike for the Yankees in 1950. New York Yankees

Ernie Harwell's career as a big-league broadcaster began in 1948 after the minor league Atlanta Crackers traded him to the Brooklyn Dodgers for catcher Cliff Dapper. Detroit Tigers

DIPLOMACY IN WASHINGTON

When he announced games for the Washington Senators, Bob Wolff never said who was winning or losing; he just gave the score. "It wasn't that the Senators weren't playing well," he said, "but that the other club was always playing better."

THE CARAY WAY

Harry Caray became an announcer for the St. Louis Cardinals by writing the radio station manager that he could do a better job than the incumbent. Caray and partner Gabby Street won exclusive air rights over several rivals in 1947 and, after the team was purchased by Anheuser-Busch, went to Bavaria to research beer commercials. Always anxious to find a new perspective on the game, Caray was broadcasting from the bleachers (and sitting with the fans) when he provided a graphic description of Curt Flood's "spectacular catch" at the base of the center-field wall. Caray could not actually see the play because it was out of his line of vision.

FAN ON THE AIR

Harry Caray started the tradition of acting like a fan

during his broadcasts. During a long career that started with the St. Louis Cardinals in the 1940s, Caray influenced legions of young announcers with his unabashed cheerleading at the mike. According to Milo Hamilton, who worked with Caray in both St. Louis and Chicago, "Caray wore the game on his sleeve and let it show. That became a popular way to do it in St. Louis and affected the way some young broadcasters did their games. They realized they didn't have to be afraid to show some emotion when doing a game."

CANADIAN CLUB

Harry Caray broadcast the first National League game in Canada and the first American League game in Canada. He was with the Cardinals when they opened against the Montreal Expos on April 14, 1969, and with the White Sox when they visited the Toronto Blue Jays on April 7, 1977. Both of Caray's clubs lost.

BUCK'S RÉSUMÉ

Before becoming a longtime Cardinals broadcaster, Jack Buck worked as a porter on a Great Lakes iron ore freighter, a riveter, a waiter, a factory hand, a newspaper hawker, and a soda jerk. Then he bluffed his way into Ohio State and found a way to get his voice on the air.

Russ Hodges carved his niche in broadcast lore on October 3, 1951. He was on the radio when Bobby Thomson hit a three-run, pennant-winning homer that turned a 4–2 deficit into a 5–4 win for the New York Giants over the Brooklyn Dodgers. He yelled, "The Giants win the pennant!" nine times.

National League

JUST LIKE DAD

Joe Buck joined his father, Jack, during Cardinals radio broadcasts in 1991. Fourteen years later, Chip Caray joined his father, Skip, on the Braves broadcast crew.

THE PRINCE OF PITTSBURGH

Longtime Pittsburgh broadcaster Bob Prince, who

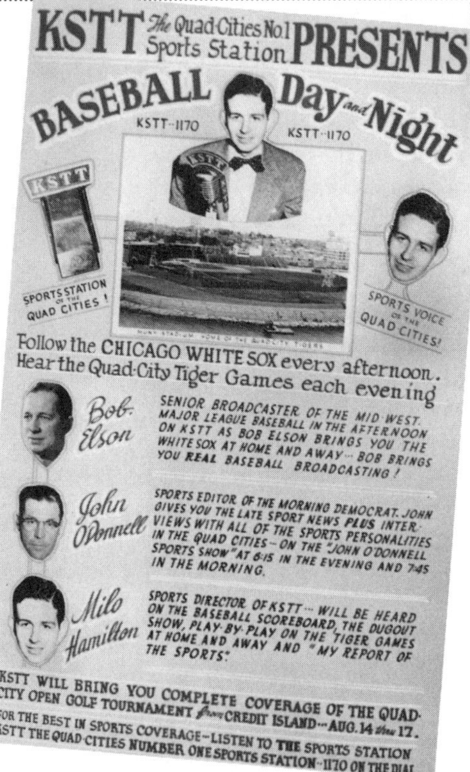

Milo Hamilton's first professional job as a broadcaster was with WQUA of Moline, Illinois, in 1950. Three years later, he reached the big leagues with the St. Louis Browns. Milo Hamilton collection

joined the Pirates as a $50-a-week assistant to Rosey Rowswell in 1948, soon won widespread recognition for his slow, nasal twang, coupled with his knowledge and passion for the game. Equally colorful off the air, Prince was known not only for his broadcasts but also for his loud sport coats and off-the-field escapades—including a three-story jump into the Chase Hotel pool in St. Louis. He openly rooted for the Pirates, encouraging them to collect "a bloop and a blast" when they were trailing.

NO NEWS FOR PRINCE

Pittsburgh broadcaster Bob Prince missed the Bill Mazeroski homer that ended the 1960 World Series against the Yankees. He was en route to the Pirates clubhouse in the ninth inning of a 9–9 tie when

Maz became the first man to end a Series with a home run. Prince found the clubhouse in pandemonium but did not know why. Standing on an equipment trunk to do live interviews, he even interviewed Mazeroski—but did not realize until later that the second baseman had hit the game-winning homer.

MIKEMEN MUST SCORE

Keeping score is part of the broadcaster's job. Since there are many different scoring systems, not all members of a broadcast team can read their partners' scorecards. Ex-player Ralph Kiner did not know how to score when he began in the booth. Fellow announcer Bob Prince taught him.

DOUBLE DUTY

Milo Hamilton and Curt Gowdy were the only men who broadcast record-breaking home runs for both Roger Maris and Hank Aaron. Hamilton re-created the Maris game from the Western Union ticker, using suitable sound effects, but witnessed the Aaron game as the voice of the Braves over WSB radio. Gowdy watched Maris hit number 61 on October 1, 1961, from the Red Sox broadcast booth at Yankee Stadium, then broadcast the Aaron game from Atlanta for the NBC network on April 8, 1974.

AARON'S CALL

Milo Hamilton's radio version of Hank Aaron's 715th home run, broadcast over Atlanta station WSB, is heard far more frequently than Vin Scully's Dodgers broadcast or Curt Gowdy's account for NBC-TV. Among other things, it's featured in the multimedia show at the Baseball Hall of Fame. "I never had anything

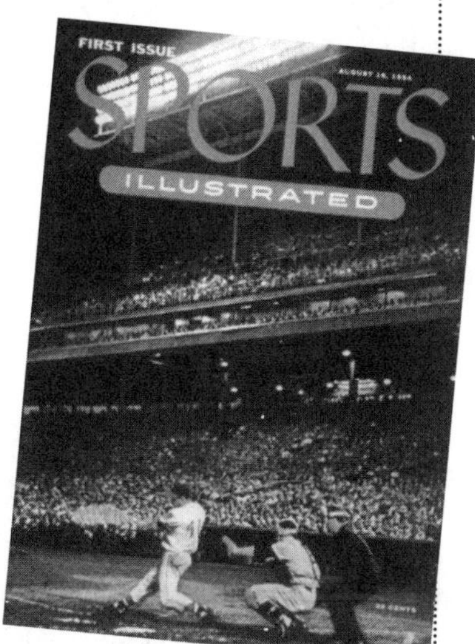

Milwaukee Braves slugger Eddie Mathews graced the cover of the first *Sports Illustrated* in 1954. *Sports Illustrated*

Milo Hamilton and Jack Buck broadcast games for the 1954 St. Louis Cardinals.
Milo Hamilton collection

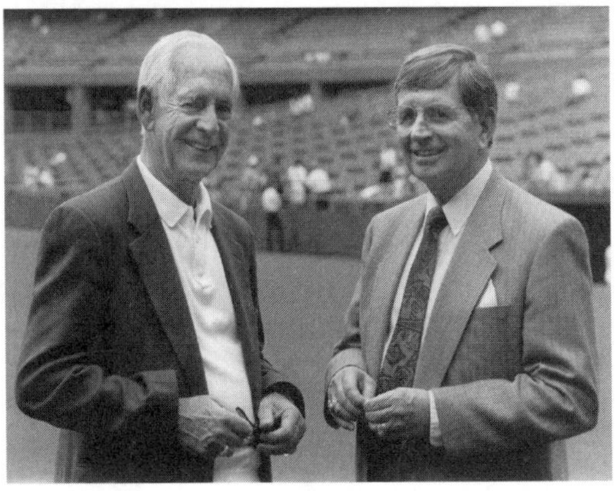

planned," said Milo. "What made the call stand up historically is the fact that the ball barely made it. Until the last split-second, when Bill Buckner leaped and almost caught it, nobody was sure the ball would clear the fence. I always thought being spontaneous was my long suit and I wanted to keep it that way. So I didn't have anything planned in advance. I didn't want it to sound like it was planned."

ANTI-INTERNET VOTE

Some broadcasters believe the Internet should not be involved in selection of the Ford Frick winner because fans are able to cast multiple votes. According to Milo Hamilton, who received the Ford Frick Award under a different system in 1992, "People can sit on those keys and run those totals up. The same thing happens with voting for the All-Star Game. Once people can pad the vote totals, it just isn't healthy."

MILO'S MAGIC MOMENTS

Highlights of Milo Hamilton's 60-year broadcast career:

- Hank Aaron hits 715th home run
- Six Astros pitchers combine for Yankee Stadium no-hitter
- Chris Burke wins NLDS with eighteenth-inning homer
- Roy Oswalt's win over Cards sends Astros to World Series
- Pirates win 1979 World Series

RADIOS AT THE PARK

Dodgers fans brought radios to the cavernous Los Angeles Coliseum because they were seated far from the field and had trouble seeing the action. They continued the tradition after the team moved to Dodger Stadium in 1962. Announcer Vin Scully tested the number of radios by asking fans to shout "Happy Birthday, Frank" to umpire Frank Secory.

HOW DRYSDALE MADE IT

Pitcher Don Drysdale became an excellent broadcaster after preparing for the transition by "announcing" games while sitting in the bullpen between starting assignments.

HUMBLE START

Dan Rather did play-by-play for the minor league Houston Buffs before becoming a reporter and anchorman for CBS News.

Radio versus TV

"When you're doing radio, you use the power of description more because you're doing everything. On TV, I feel I have to show restraint and let the picture pretty much tell it."

—Vin Scully

LUCKY GUY

Al Michaels, who broadcast games for the Reds and Giants in the 1970s before joining the ABC-TV network, once picked the women who appeared on *The Dating Game.*

During his short stay in St. Louis, Milo Hamilton visits J.G. Taylor Spink, powerful editor and publisher of *The Sporting News,* then an all-baseball publication. Milo Hamilton collection

Ralph Kiner, still an active broadcaster in 2006, was the last survivor of the three original Mets mikemen. The former Pittsburgh home-run king shared the Flushing booth with Lindsey Nelson and Bob Murphy.
Ronnie Joyner

NO LOCAL COLOR?
Local announcers were once included on national broadcasts of World Series games. The practice was dropped in 1979—the only year Milo Hamilton was affiliated with a world champion (Pittsburgh Pirates). "I think fans across the country got a kick out of hearing Red Barber and Mel Allen when they were radio announcers for the Dodgers and Yankees. You lose a lot of personal touch and insight to those teams when the local guys are left out. You just don't get that with the network announcers. You don't have to be on all the time but maybe just do three innings. But do *something* to add some local flavor. And the same goes for the city that hosts the All-Star Game."

Fans Like Radio

"There are a lot of good TV announcers, but radio is where the announcer becomes a dramatist, a companion. Baseball might be the only sport that people prefer on radio, not TV."

—Bob Costas

QUAKE COVERAGE
Baseball broadcaster Al Michaels won an Emmy Award for his coverage of the Bay Area earthquake that interrupted the 1989 World Series. Michaels, a San Francisco native, was on the air when the tremor hit just prior to the start of the third game

between the Oakland Athletics and the San Francisco Giants.

MARATHON MAN
Toronto broadcaster Tom Cheek worked 4,306 consecutive games, plus 41 in the postseason. The streak ended after 27½ seasons because of his father's death.

THREE GENERATIONS
Harry Caray, son Skip Caray, and grandson Chip Caray made broadcast history in 1992 when they all broadcast the same game, between the Chicago Cubs and the Atlanta Braves.

UNTIMELY MIKE FAILURE
Fans listening on radio missed hearing the call of Barry Bonds's 715th home run when Dave Flemming's handheld mike failed. It happened in the fourth inning of the game, broadcast on KNBR. Fans heard Flemming say, "Three-and-two. Finley runs. The payoff pitch. A swing and a drive to deep cen..."

THE TRAVAILS OF TELEVISION
When WGN started televising ballgames in 1948, Jack Brickhouse kept one eye on the field and the other on his monitor. He also placed his trust in the hands of an inexperienced cameraman. During one game, a batter hit a long fly. Brickhouse described the ball in flight and the fielder catching it—but the camera followed the ball over the wall, over rooftops, and on. The cameraman finally realized he wasn't following the ball at all but a bird in flight.

Milo's Take on Jerry Coleman

"He's as comfortable as a pair of old bedroom slippers, easy to listen to, entertaining, and credible because he played for so long."

— Milo Hamilton

SOLO SAGA CONTINUES
Longtime Dodgers broadcaster Vin Scully is the only modern broadcaster who works alone. He began his long career with Brooklyn in 1950.

STAR POWER
Many broadcasters have their own methods of communicating with fans at the ballpark. Jerry Coleman, longtime voice of the Padres, kept a long stick with a giant paper star on the end of it. Whenever San Diego made a

Milo Hamilton and Ernie Johnson called games for the Braves when they arrived in Atlanta in 1966. Atlanta Braves

great play, he waved that stick from the broadcast booth.

THE SCOOTER

According to Milo Hamilton, "Phil Rizzuto had the luxury of broadcasting in a town where he was a hero as a player. He played in so many World Series and even won an MVP award. He was in the perfect place at the perfect time. I don't know if he would have survived in another market. Scooter had a lot to bring to the game—even though he often left early and was on the George Washington Bridge when the game went into extra innings."

UECKER'S YUCKS

Longtime Milwaukee Brewers broadcaster Bob Uecker has parlayed his sense of humor into a second career. Uecker, a catcher with a career batting average of .200, made more than 100 appearances with Johnny Carson, wrote two books, and became a star of Miller Beer commercials with his self-deprecating repartee. "One time I was batting against the Dodgers in Milwaukee," he said. "They led, 2–1. It was the bottom of the ninth, bases loaded, two outs, and the pitcher has a full count on me. I looked over at the Dodger dugout and they were all in street clothes."

FRAN'S FLOCK

Fran Healy was in the Yankees broadcast booth less than a month when a flock of ducks landed on the field during a game in Toronto. "That's the first time I've ever seen a fowl in fair territory," he told his audience.

ANALYZE THIS

Milo Hamilton's favorite analysts were Lou Boudreau and Andy Ashby. "Lou may not have had the polish or smoothness that some critics demand, but he had great insight," said Hamilton, who worked with Boudreau with the Cubs and Ashby with the Astros. "I enjoyed working with him and Ashby more than any other analysts."

WHAT'S THE SCORE?

How often should radio announcers give the score? Milo Hamilton does it during every at-bat. He also does a recap after three innings and six innings. "Baseball listeners are tuners in and tuners out," he says. "I'd love to say people turn on the radio when I come on the air and never turn it off. But they're doing other things, or they've been out to dinner and are on the way home, joining the game in the fifth inning. They want to know what is going on and what went on. That's why I keep giving the score and recap the game."

MILO'S ADVICE

Advice Milo Hamilton gives young sportscasters:

- Take all the English classes you can.
- Learn how to write.
- Learn how to communicate.
- Go to a college where you can be on the air.
- Develop a style and see if you can make it your own.

BIG BUCKS FOR MILO

Milo Hamilton's first broadcast job out of the University of Iowa paid him $42.50 a week in 1950. "I always say that in those first two years, I got my master's, my Ph.D., and $50 a week," he said. "After three years, I was in the big leagues."

Former Yankees pitcher Jim Bouton shocked the baseball world in 1970 with *Ball Four,* a behind-closed-doors look at big-league ballplayers. The book became a best-seller when Baseball Commissioner Bowie Kuhn condemned it.
Laura Gaynor

SYRACUSE CHIEFS

Star sportscasters who attended Syracuse University:

- Marv Albert
- Len Berman
- Bob Costas
- Marty Glickman
- Hank Greenwald
- Sean McDonough
- Andy Musser
- Greg Papa
- Dick Stockton
- Mike Tirico

UNIVERSAL COVERAGE

The advent of XM Satellite Radio, which began carrying home feeds of all big-league broadcasts in 2005, allowed fans across the country to tune into games of their choice.

BOX SCORE EVOLUTION

Most fans follow their favorite players and teams by reading baseball box scores. Here's how they've changed over the years:

- 1845—First box score, in *New York Morning News,* shows game's cricket roots
- 1850—Box scores expand to show fielding and base running
- 1887—Henry Chadwick starts keeping won-lost records for pitchers

Sports Collectors Digest is an oversized weekly tabloid that covers the growing world of cards and collecting.

- 1898—Inning-by-inning line scores included in box scores
- 1912—Earned-run average for pitchers introduced by NL exec John Heydler
- 1920—Runs batted in becomes an official baseball statistic
- 1958—Vertical runs-batted-in column added to official box scores
- 1960—AP streamlines box scores to save space in papers
- 1964—AP starts including seasonal HR totals in box scores
- 1969—Saves become official statistic for relief pitchers

- 1990—STATS, Inc. adds batting averages to box scores
- 1992—*L.A. Times* starts using more comprehensive box score

Official Scorers

Writers usually serve as official scorers. The job is not easy. After Sacramento official scorer Steve George awarded Joe DiMaggio a questionable hit that extended his minor league hitting streak to 60 games in 1933, angry fans stormed the press box. George needed a police escort to leave safely. Forty years later, a scorer's decision deprived Nolan Ryan of the California Angels of a no-hitter. The New York Yankees made just one hit that day—a pop fly that dropped between two infielders. Both called for it, then both backed away, fearing collision.

Tired of Ted

Longtime writers who belong to the Baseball Writers Association of America (BBWAA) vote for major awards—but sometimes they let personal opinions cloud their judgment. Ted Williams outranked Joe DiMaggio in every hitting category in 1947 but lost the American League MVP voting because a Boston writer, who detested the Red Sox slugger, failed to list Williams on his ballot. Had the writer placed Williams even 10th, the Boston left fielder would have won the award.

The Mahatma

Branch Rickey's nickname, "the Mahatma," was a creation of well-known writer Tom Meany. The journalist had been reading *Inside Asia,* wherein John Gunther described Mohandas "Mahatma" Ghandi as "an incredible combination of Jesus Christ, Tammany Hall, and your father." Meany noted that Rickey was part paternal, part political, and part pontifical. He applied the Ghandi moniker, and it stuck.

Poetic Prose

"Willie Mays's glove is where triples go to die."

—Jim Murray

The Perfect Name

Longtime Yankees PA man Bob Sheppard always insisted Mickey Mantle had a perfect name. "I just loved announcing his name," Sheppard said. "One day, we were both being interviewed on television. He turned to me and said, right there on the air, that every time he heard me announce his name, he got goose bumps. I felt the same way about announcing him."

Cannon Fires

"Ballplayers who are first into the dining room are usually last in the averages."

—Jimmy Cannon

SHEPPARD'S TENURE

Bob Sheppard spent more than a half-century as public-address announcer for the Yankees. Since his debut on April 17, 1951, he announced the lineups for more than 4,000 baseball games, including nearly 100 postseason contests.

Redford's Swing

"When I made *The Natural,* I had not played baseball for 27 years. And so, 27 years later, I discovered what I liked about baseball. Let's face it: once in a lifetime, everyone would like to take a bat in his hand."

—Robert Redford

"Most men go to work, but I go to a game," he said.

***SPORTS ILLUSTRATED* JINX**

Rumors of a *Sports Illustrated* jinx grew so prevalent in 2002 that researchers reviewed 47 years of covers—only to find substance to the story. Some 913 out of 2,456 cover subjects up to that time (37.2 percent) soon experienced something negative. An uncanny 12 percent suffered death or injury. The first cover subject, Eddie Mathews, hurt his hand and missed a week as his Milwaukee Braves fell out of first place. Hall of Fame pitcher Nolan Ryan, who was 10–3 for the California Angels when he appeared on a 1975 cover, immediately lost eight games in a row. Even Ted Williams fell victim, tripping over his dog and breaking a hip within weeks of a postcareer cover appearance in 1996.

SAN DIEGO SAVIORS

After National League owners decided to place an expansion team in Montreal for the 1969 season, they needed a second city to balance the schedule. San Diego eventually beat out Seattle and Denver because Jack Murphy, sports editor of the *Union-Tribune,* and baseball writer Phil Collier proved too persuasive.

BOUTON'S BOOSTER
Pitcher-author Jim Bouton received unexpected help in promoting his tell-all book *Ball Four* in 1970: it rocketed to the top of the best-seller charts after Baseball Commissioner Bowie Kuhn denounced it.

OBVIOUS ANSWER
During his last season with the Yankees in 1981, Reggie Jackson spent 45 minutes explaining the art of hitting to blind sportswriter Ed Lucas. Jackson showed him how to hold his hands on the bat, how to position his feet, and other tricks of the trade. The next day, Lucas said to Jackson, "You forgot to tell me one thing." The surprised slugger couldn't believe his ears. "You forget to tell me to keep my eye on the ball!"

TEXAS HOLD 'EM
Covering baseball isn't an easy job—for any member of the media. Two Texas cameramen were on the wrong end of a shove from Texas pitcher Kenny Rogers early in the 2005 season. Rogers received a

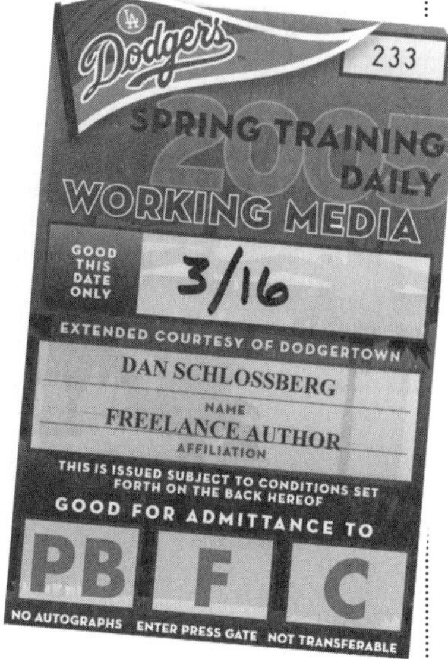

20-game suspension and a $50,000 fine for an altercation. The suspension was reduced to 13 games upon appeal.

ARTISTIC LICENSE
To play the left-handed Lou Gehrig in *Pride of the Yankees,* right-handed Gary Cooper wore hats and uniforms with logos that were deliberately reversed. The negatives were flipped for the final version of the film.

CLEANING THEIR CLOCK
Bama Rowell of the Boston Braves hit a memorable Memorial Day home run in

The Baseball at the Movies exhibit at the National Baseball Hall of Fame and Museum in Cooperstown, New York. Milo Stewart Jr./National Baseball Hall of Fame Library, Cooperstown, New York

1946. In fact, his glass-shattering blast off the Ebbets Field clock inspired Brooklyn native Bernard Malamud to re-create the incident in *The Natural.*

TRUE STORY

The character Geena Davis portrayed in the 1992 film *A League of Their Own* was Pepper Paire, a catcher for the Rockford Peaches.

TYPECAST FOREVER

Felix Mantilla's name appears in the credits of the film *Ruthless People,* created by Hollywood satirists David and Jerry Zucker and Jim Abrahams. It reads, "Utility infielder…Felix Mantilla."

FIVE FABULOUS FILMS

1. *Eight Men Out*
2. *The Natural*
3. *A League of Their Own*
4. *Field of Dreams*
5. *Fever Pitch*

Chapter 9
Talents and Traditions

Brooks Robinson Remembers...

Every time somebody mentions the Hall of Fame, the name of Pete Rose comes up. Unfortunately, Pete has burned all his bridges. Because he was banned, his name was never on the ballot. Even if he's reinstated, Pete doesn't have much support among the Hall of Famers. I don't know what to believe, but I do know he bet on baseball and that's a no-no. I remember going through the clubhouse doors in York, Pennsylvania, and seeing a sign on the door that said, "If you bet, you're out." You can do anything else, but don't bet. That was the understanding of every person who ever played.

I loved Pete, but what's killing him more than anything else is that he knows he's not going to get into the Hall of Fame. He still wants to put on that uniform and be a coach, manager, or instructor. He's just consumed by baseball. No one thought about baseball as much as Pete did.

As for Shoeless Joe Jackson and the Black Sox scandal, he's in the same boat with Pete. You still hear conflicting reports: whether he knew about the fix or took the money without knowing what it was.

By and large, I think the Hall of Fame voting is fair. It's the same as voting for the All-Star team—somebody's always going to get slighted. The best way to do it is the way they do it now: the writers vote in the regular election and players already in the Hall of Fame vote on the Veterans Committee.

The list is condensed to 25 guys every year. I always vote for Gil Hodges and Ron Santo. We vote for executives, too, and Marvin Miller was on the list. I thought he'd be a shoo-in, but he didn't get 75 percent of the vote. When Marvin took over as head of the Players Association, he must have offended a lot of people. Some of the veteran guys told me he could do anything he wanted as long as he didn't call for a strike against baseball. I was part of the first strike in 1972, and it wiped out three or four days of spring training and four or five days of the regular season. The players' pension plan was the main issue.

The Players Association has brought good fortune and good luck to its members. A lot of them think about their luck a lot. I was not superstitious but played with plenty of men who were. Luis Aparicio had to step on third base every time he went on to shortstop. Mike Cuellar never stepped on the chalk lines. Pat Dobson talked to the same sportswriter when he pitched. And Earl Weaver wore the same clothes when we were winning. We also had Chico Salmon, who believed in ghosts. He was from Panama and was superstitious in a strange way, talking about ghosts he's seen. It was kind of scary.

FLASHBACK: 1936

70 Years Later:

The Hall of Fame's 'First Five'

BY DAN HOLMES

"A player's record, playing ability, integrity, sportsmanship, character and contributions to the teams on which he played."

Those were the qualities baseball writers were asked to consider at their annual meeting in December 1935, when they received the first ballots for the National Baseball Hall of Fame.

The results of that election, though reported widely in newspapers throughout the country at the time, have become even more noteworthy as the years have passed. The electees on the 1936 ballot – "The First Five" – are revered by many as the measuring stick for Hall of Fame induction. Today, in the Museum, their bronze plaques hang together at the head of the Hall of Fame Gallery. At the time of the election, no one doubted their worthiness. One scribe wrote of their election: "Wouldn't anyone have selected them from all the ball players down to the present?"

The concept of a Hall of Fame to honor the game's greatest players dates to 1903, when National League President Harry Pulliam began gathering artifacts for the purpose of establishing a "Hall of Fame" to create "pride in the game."

At various times in baseball history, when a player accomplished a rare feat or hurled a no-hit game, it would be said that he had entered the "Hall of Fame" of the sport. But no such place or honor existed until 1936. To coincide with the baseball centennial celebration to be observed in 1939, and in large part due to the cooperative efforts of N.L. President Ford C. Frick and noted local resident and philanthropist Stephen C. Clark, a Hall of Fame and Museum was to be created in Cooperstown.

The Museum would not open until June 12, 1939, but the first official act of the Hall of Fame was the inaugural election, announced on Feb. 2, 1936. Members of the Baseball Writers' Association of America (BBWAA), under the direction of secretary Henry Edwards, were given the responsibility of voting.

Voters were instructed to select up to 10 players and active players were eligible. Thus, eight active players received votes, though none were elected. After the first 100 ballots were recorded, both Ty Cobb and Babe Ruth had appeared on every one. According to an Associated Press report, vote counting stopped momentarily when Ruth's name did not appear on a ballot for a discussion on how anyone could leave Ruth off the list.

After all 226 ballots had been tallied, the top vote-getter was Cobb, who was named on all but four. Ruth received 215 votes, as did Honus Wagner. Legendary hurlers Christy Mathewson (205) and Walter Johnson (189) also received the necessary 75% support.

Babe Ruth   Honus Wagner

24 MEMORIES AND DREAMS / INDUCTION 2006

Reprinted with permission from *Memories & Dreams*, Induction 2006, Vol. 28, No. 4

In the first vote for the Baseball Hall of Fame, Ty Cobb (bottom right) led with 222 of 226 votes, Babe Ruth and Honus Wagner tied for second with 215 each, and Christy Mathewson (bottom left) got 205. Against such competition, Cy Young (top left), who won more games than any other pitcher, couldn't even score the required 75 percent of the vote.

FIRST HALL VOTE

In the first vote for the Hall of Fame, on February 3, 1936, Ty Cobb drew 222 of 226 votes, Babe Ruth and Honus Wagner finished second with 215 each, and Christy Mathewson followed with 205. Walter Johnson, with 189, was the only other man to have the required three-quarters majority for election in the voting, then conducted by players and writers.

THE BIG TRAIN

Walter "the Big Train" Johnson threw such a lively fastball that its speed was compared to steam locomotives, the fastest form of transportation in the 1920s.

THE 3,000 EXPRESS

Ty Cobb reached 3,000 hits more quickly than any other player. He was 34 in 1921 when his single against Boston's Elmer Myers put him over the plateau.

HIGHEST PERCENTAGE OF HALL VOTES

Rank	Year	Player	Ballots Cast	Votes Rec'd	Omitted	Pct.
1.	1992	Tom Seaver	430	425	5*	98.8
2.	1999	Nolan Ryan	497	491	6	98.7
3.	1936	Ty Cobb	226	222	4	98.2
4.	1999	George Brett	497	488	9	98.2
5.	1982	Hank Aaron	415	406	9	97.8
6.	1995	Mike Schmidt	460	444	16	96.5
7.	1989	Johnny Bench	447	431	19	95.8
8.	1936	Honus Wagner	226	215	11	95.1
9.	1936	Babe Ruth	432	409	23	94.7
10.	1962	Bob Feller	160	150	10	93.8
11.	1993	Reggie Jackson	423	396	27	93.6
12.	1966	Ted Williams	302	282	20	93.4

* Seaver was named on 425 of 427 completed ballots for 99.53 percent, but three voters returned blank ballots to protest the exclusion of the suspended Pete Rose by Hall of Fame directors.

POWER PITCHER

Hall of Fame slugger George Sisler was no slouch as a college pitcher at Michigan: he once fanned 20 men in seven innings.

THE RAJAH

Rogers Hornsby used a stance suggested by Honus Wagner to win seven batting crowns during the Roaring '20s. Among them was a .424 season that ranks as the best average by any player of the modern era. Hornsby later gave Ted Williams advice that he treasured: "Get a good ball to hit."

GOPHER BROTHERS

Rogers Hornsby was the first man to homer against two brothers in one game. He did it for the St. Louis Cardinals on September 24, 1922, against Jesse and Virgil Barnes of the New York Giants.

DID PLAYERS LISTEN?

As a manager, Rogers Hornsby had many rules, regulations, and quirks. Among the things he believed:

- Air-conditioning freezes up the body and is not good for ballplayers.
- Swimming is bad for players because it requires use of the wrong muscles.
- Players should avoid golf because they should conserve energy.
- Reading and watching movies hampers players' vision.

NEW VET COMMITTEE

The Hall of Fame's Veterans Committee was revamped in 2001 to include all living Hall of Fame members (players, managers, and executives) plus writers and broadcasters honored with the Spink and Frick awards, respectively. Candidates must still receive 75 percent of the vote.

The 10 living inductees gather at the 1939 opening of the National Baseball Hall of Fame. Back row (left to right): Honus Wagner, Grover Cleveland Alexander, Tris Speaker, Nap Lajoie, George Sisler, Walter Johnson. Front row (left to right): Eddie Collins, Babe Ruth, Connie Mack, Cy Young. The 11th inductee, Ty Cobb, missed the photo due to travel delays. National Baseball Hall of Fame, Cooperstown, New York

SURPRISE ENTRY

Although he never drew more than a single vote from writers voting for the Hall of Fame, Rick Ferrell was enshrined by the Veterans Committee.

HALL OF FAME GAME

Each summer, two major league teams hook up in an exhibition contest at Cooperstown's Doubleday Field on the day of the Hall of Fame inductions. In the first such contest, on June 12, 1939, two players from each of the 16 clubs journeyed to Cooperstown. Honus Wagner and Eddie Collins chose up sides, with leagues mixing, and Babe Ruth, long retired as a player, fouled out in his only at-bat.

COOPERSTOWN PREVIEW

NL president John Heydler umpired the first inning of the first game ever played at Cooperstown's Doubleday Field—on September 6, 1920. According to local legend, the same site was the cow pasture used by Abner Doubleday when he "invented" the game in 1839.

RULE WAIVED

To be eligible for the Hall of Fame, a player must have performed in 10 major league seasons. The requirement was waived for Addie Joss, who was one game short when stricken by tubercular meningitis just as he was to pitch the first game of the 1911 season for Cleveland. Joss, who died a week later at age 31, had 160 victories and a 1.88 lifetime ERA, second only to Ed Walsh's 1.82. The wily right-hander had an uncanny ability to predict the score ahead of time. Before his perfect game against Walsh and the White Sox on October 2, 1908, he announced, "They ain't gonna score." They didn't.

SLAMLESS STARS

More than a dozen members of the Baseball Hall of Fame never homered with the bases loaded.

QUITE A COLLECTION

In the archives of the Baseball Hall of Fame are more than 35,000 hats, bats, balls, gloves, uniforms, spikes, tickets, pins, and trophies. Another 2.6 million items, from photos to recorded media, reside in the Hall's library. All have been donated.

NEW LOOK

The Baseball Hall of Fame was rededicated in 2005 after a three-year, $20 million renovation.

The Hall of Fame Plaque Gallery at the National Baseball Hall of Fame and Museum in Cooperstown, New York. Milo Stewart Jr./National Baseball Hall of Fame Library, Cooperstown, New York

FIRST ELECTED EXPO

Before Gary Carter's Hall of Fame plaque featured a Montreal Expos logo, no player had ever made the Hall of Fame under the logo of a team no longer in existence.

SIX BEST HALL CLASSES

- 1936—Ty Cobb, Babe Ruth, Honus Wagner, Christy Mathewson, Walter Johnson
- 1937—Napoleon Lajoie, Tris Speaker, Cy Young
- 1939—Eddie Collins, Wee Willie Keeler, George Sisler, Lou Gehrig
- 1972—Sandy Koufax, Yogi Berra, Early Wynn, Josh Gibson, Dutch Leonard
- 1982—Hank Aaron, Frank Robinson
- 1999—George Brett, Robin Yount, Nolan Ryan

THE SENATOR

Jim Bunning is the only member of the Baseball Hall of Fame who was also a member of the United States Senate.

NO .300 FOR YAZ

Carl Yastrzemski was the only man to win more than two batting crowns but still hit under .300 for his career.

HOW WADE LEARNED SWING

Wade Boggs learned his inside-out swing from his dad, Winfield Boggs, a fast-pitch softball star. A .328 career hitter, Boggs was the only player of the modern era with seven straight 200-hit seasons. He had 15 seasons of .300 or better.

HAPPY BIRTHDAY

Hall of Famers Wade Boggs and Joe Morgan homered on their 40th birthdays.

Ronnie Joyner

WALTER
JOHNSON
FOR A $100 BONUS, TRAIN FARE, AND THE PROMISE OF $350 A MONTH, THE WASHINGTON SENATORS WERE ABLE TO SIGN A MAN WHO MANY BELIEVE TO BE THE GREATEST PITCHER OF ALL TIME -- WALTER JOHNSON! BORN ON NOVEMBER 6, 1887, IN HUMBOLDT, KANSAS, JOHNSON WAS JUST 19 WHEN THE NATS DISCOVERED HIM MOWING DOWN BATSMEN IN A SEMI-PRO LEAGUE IN IDAHO IN 1907! RUSHED TO THE NATION'S CAPITAL, THE KID WAS ABLE TO POST 5 WINS WITH A 1.87 ERA IN 14 STARTS FOR THE LAST PLACE NATS DESPITE LITTLE OR NO RUN SUPPORT!
JOHNSON SPENT HIS ENTIRE 21 BIG LEAGUE SEASONS WITH THE PERENNIAL LAST-PLACE NATS! STILL, THE BIG TRAIN WAS ABLE TO LEAD THE LEAGUE IN WINS 5 TIMES! HIS PERSERVARENCE PAID OFF WHEN THE NATS FINALLY REACHED THE WORLD SERIES AND WON IT IN '24 WITH JOHNSON GETTING THE WIN IN A THRILLING GAME 7!
JOYNER ©2004
JOHNSON THREW WITH A SMOOTH SIDEARM MOTION! HIS BLAZING FASTBALL WAS SAID TO BE THE FASTEST IN THE GAME AND INVISIBLE TO BATTERS, STREAKING TO THE CATCHER WITH AN AUDIBLE "SWOOSH" AND SLAMMING INTO THE MITT WITH A LOUD "BOOM"!
WHAT WAS THAT SOUND, MUDDY?
UMMM, THAT WAS A STRIKE, BUB!
JOHNSON IS 2ND ALL-TIME IN WINS WITH 417; 1ST ALL-TIME IN SHUTOUTS WITH 110, AND 7TH ALL-TIME IN LIFE-TIME ERA AT 2.17! ADMIRED FOR HIS MILD, MODEST AND DECENT PERSONA, WALTER JOHNSON WAS A MEMBER OF THE 1939 INAUGURAL CLASS OF THE HALL OF FAME IN COOPERSTOWN!

WHY JUAN?

Juan Pierre's dad was a Juan Marichal fan who decided to give his son the same first name as the Hall of Fame pitcher.

MR. SCOREBOARD

There's a scoreboard operator in the communications section of the Hall of Fame. Louis Adamie, known as Mr. Scoreboard to legions of St. Louis fans, operated the Sportsman's Park and Busch Stadium scoreboards for the Cards and Browns from 1941 to 1982. He kept score and tracked every pitch in 4,350 games.

BABE'S BACKGROUND

St. Mary's Industrial School for Boys, now called Cardinal Gibbons High School, was once called "the House that Built Ruth." Babe Ruth had shown his first baseball skills while attending the Baltimore vocational school.

BABE'S PINCH-HITTER

In Babe Ruth's major league debut on July 11, 1914, he pitched the Boston Red Sox to a 4–3 win over Cleveland, but was lifted for pinch-hitter Duffy Lewis in the seventh inning. A single by Lewis led to the winning run.

BABE'S FIRST BLAST

Babe Ruth's first major league home run came *against* the Yankees, the team for whom he later hit 60 in a season. He did it for the Boston Red Sox on May 6, 1915.

EARLY HR KINGS

When Babe Ruth hit 29 home runs in 1919, he broke Gavvy Cravath's single-season record of 24, set in 1915. Ruth replaced Roger Connor as the all-time home-run king when he socked number 138 in 1921.

Christy Mathewson of the New York Giants was widely considered the best pitcher of his time. From 1903 to 1914, he never won fewer than 22 games in a season. This card is from the 1915 set.

GREAT FIRST IMPRESSION

Babe Ruth pulled a power trifecta in 1920, his first year with the Yankees. He became the first player to hit 30 homers in a season, 40 homers in a season, and 50 homers in a season—all in the same season.

SCORING DEMON

Babe Ruth scored more runs in one season (177 in 1921) than any other player.

BABE WINS BET

Babe Ruth won a $10 bet from teammate Tony Lazzeri when he hit his 60th home run in 1927.

RUTH'S ROOMIE

Ping Bodie, in his first year with the Yankees, drew Babe Ruth as his road roommate. Ruth was seldom in the room, however. When a young writer asked Bodie who his roomie was, he replied, "Babe Ruth's suitcases."

Ty Cobb's 4,000th hit was almost ignored in the media. Reprinted with permission, National Baseball Hall of Fame Library, Cooperstown, New York

BABE'S NL DEBUT

Babe Ruth had two hits, including a home run, in four at-bats against Carl Hubbell in his National League debut in 1935.

BABE'S DOZEN

Babe Ruth led his league in home runs 12 times—more than Barry Bonds, Albert Pujols, Manny Ramirez, Gary Sheffield, Jason Giambi, Vlad Guerrero, Jim Thome, David Ortiz, Andruw Jones, and Carlos Delgado *combined.* Mike Schmidt won eight home-run crowns to rank as Ruth's runner-up, while Ralph Kiner was third with seven—all in consecutive seasons.

SLUGGER SUPREME

Babe Ruth's .690 career slugging percentage tops the lifetime list.

BABE'S PATSY

Babe Ruth loved facing Rube Walberg. He reached him for 17 homers, more than he hit against any other pitcher.

BATBOY PLAYED BABE

William Bendix, who played the title role in *The Babe Ruth Story,* actually served as Ruth's batboy

Signed as a pitcher, Babe Ruth carved his niche as a home-run slugger of Herculean dimensions. In both 1920 and 1921, he hit 35 more home runs than anyone else in the American League. Ruth went on to hit 714 career home runs, a record that stood until 1974.

during the early 1920s at the Polo Grounds.

THE BIG TRAIN

During a 21-year career spent entirely with the Senators, Walter Johnson won 416 games—110 of them shutouts.

FOR OPENERS

Walter Johnson pitched the most Opening Day shutouts (seven), while Robin Roberts pitched the most consecutive openers for the same team (12). Tom Seaver had the most Opening Day starts (16).

SUPERSTITIOUS STAR

Future Hall of Famer Kiki Cuyler was suspended and traded by the 1927 Pittsburgh Pirates because he thought it was bad luck to move from third to second in the batting order.

KLEIN-UP MAN

Chuck Klein was the only player in the 20th century to

Babe Ruth connects for his 60th home run on September 30, 1927. The Bambino held the single-season and career home-run records for 34 years. Copyright 1995 by William Feldman. Reprinted with permission, Bill Goff, Inc./GoodSportsArt.com.

reach 1,000 hits in fewer than 700 games.

JUICED BALL?

Was the ball juiced in 1930? Chuck Klein of the Phillies had a .386 average, 250 hits, 40 home runs, and 170 RBIs but failed to lead the NL in any of those departments.

NO CHANCE

Jimmie Foxx drew six straight walks during a 12–8 win by his Boston Red Sox against the St. Louis Browns on June 16, 1938.

LOU'S LAST YEAR

Lou Gehrig played his last opening game at Yankee Stadium on April 20, 1939. He had no hits and was charged with an error. On May 1, he played the last game of his 2,130-game consecutive playing streak. It was also the last game of his career.

NIGHT OWLS

Lefty Gomez was a Hall of Famer not only for his pitching but also for his sense of humor. He once got into an argument with Jimmie Dykes over how to pitch to a hitter with two men on base. They decided to have Mike Kelly settle the dispute. They marched up to Kelly's room, where they pounded on the door and roused Kelly from a deep sleep. "Go away, I'm sleeping," he stammered. "I can't wait," Gomez shrieked. "Two men are on base!"

$500 APART

Ted Williams came within a whisker of sharing the same outfield with Joe DiMaggio or Stan Musial. The Yankees offered Williams a $500 signing bonus but refused to give in to his mother's demand for a grand. Williams, who had earlier rejected overtures from the St. Louis Cardinals because he didn't wish to get lost in their giant farm system, signed with his hometown San Diego Padres of the Pacific Coast League for $150 a month.

HOW SOX GOT TED

The best trade in Red Sox history? It happened on December 1, 1937, when the Sox sent five players plus $25,000 to the San Diego Padres of the Pacific Coast League for a skinny outfielder named Ted Williams.

TED WOULDN'T SIT

The last man to hit .400, Ted Williams did it after deciding to play in a season-ending doubleheader in 1941. With his average at .3995 going in, Williams could have sat—which Boston manager Joe Cronin suggested. Insisting on playing, the Red Sox slugger went 6-for-8 to finish at .406.

NO STREAK FOR TED

Ted Williams might have been the last man to hit .400 and the owner of a .344 career average, but he never had a batting streak longer than 23 games.

FISHING FIEND

Ted Williams is a member of not only the Baseball Hall of Fame but also the Game Fish

Miller Huggins of the Yankees and Tris Speaker of the Indians were rival managers in 1921, when New York finished four and a half games in front of Cleveland. The former had a trump card in Babe Ruth, who hit a then-record 59 home runs—17 more than the entire Indians lineup. American League

Rogers Hornsby compiled the best lifetime batting average of any National League player. His .358 mark ranked second to Ty Cobb of the American League (.367). Reprinted with permission, National Baseball Hall of Fame Library, Cooperstown, New York

Hall of Fame in Dania Beach, Florida. A student of both baseball and fishing, Williams once caught a 1,235-pound black marlin off the coast of Peru. It would be another 39 years before the Florida Marlins carved their niche on the big-league map.

TED'S TOTALS

Marine captain Ted Williams flew 39 combat missions in Korea—many with future astronaut John Glenn. Williams also served 39 months in World War II. Had he not lost nearly five full years to military service, Williams would most likely have finished with 686 home runs and 2,242 RBIs, according to computer analysis.

BOUDREAU SHIFT

Ted Williams was such a pull hitter that Cleveland player/ manager Lou Boudreau developed the "Boudreau Shift," with all four infielders stationed between first and second.

TRIPLE CROWN TRIPLE?

The only man to win the Triple Crown twice, Ted Williams missed his third by $^{1}/_{1000}$th of a percentage point. In 1949 he led the AL in home runs and was tied for first in RBIs but trailed George Kell in batting, .342756 to .342911.

OLDIES BUT GOODIES

Ted Williams won a batting title at age 40, Stan Musial hit .330 at age 41, and Carlton Fisk hit 72 home runs between the ages of 40 and 45. Hank Aaron, 40 years old when he passed Babe Ruth in career home runs, hit 40 more before retiring.

BOOKEND HOMERS

Ted Williams is the only 500-home-run hitter who

connected in his first and last at-bats.

HISTORIC GOPHERS
Baltimore pitcher Jack Fisher was the victim of the last home run hit by Ted Williams, in the Boston slugger's last career at-bat in 1960, and the 1961 Roger Maris home run that tied Babe Ruth's record of 60 home runs in a season.

THE FRISCO STREAKER
Joe DiMaggio's record 56-game hitting streak in 1941 wasn't his longest; he had a 61-game streak for the San Francisco Seals of the Pacific Coast League in 1933.

HARD TO IGNORE
Joe DiMaggio won three MVP awards but only led the majors in home runs once.

CONTACT MAN
Joe DiMaggio is the only player with more than 300 home runs (361) but fewer than 400 strikeouts (369).

FIRST "BIG CAT"
Hall of Famer Johnny Mize earned his "Big Cat" nickname when Giants teammate Bill Rigney saw him lounging in the sun and said, "Look at him. He looks just like a big cat."

STAN THE MAN
Stan Musial was the first man to hit five home runs in one day, but he never led his league in home runs.

IT'S ONLY FAIR
Citing his own disappointing season, Stan Musial requested and received a $20,000 salary cut from the 1960 St. Louis

When Dizzy Dean predicted, during 1934 spring training, that he and brother Paul would combine for 45 wins, skeptics laughed. Paul had yet to pitch a big-league inning. But Dizzy was prophetic: the Deans won 49—30 for Dizzy and 19 for Paul. One of Paul's wins was the only no-hitter by a member of the Dean family.
National League

Cardinals. He had been making $100,000—big money at the time.

FELLER'S FAST START

Bob Feller was 17 in 1936 when he fanned eight of nine St. Louis Browns during a three-inning exhibition game outing for the Cleveland Indians. Two weeks later, he fanned 15 men in his big-league debut and 17, then an AL record, in another game. Third on the all-time strikeout list when he retired, Feller would have ranked higher had he not enlisted in the navy on December 8, 1941, the day after the Japanese attacked Pearl Harbor. He won eight battle stars as a tail gunner on the U.S.S. *Alabama.*

Josh Gibson, best hitter in the Negro Leagues, was an exceptional all-around player who consistently won All-Star catching honors over Roy Campanella.

Reprinted with permission, National Baseball Hall of Fame Library, Cooperstown, New York

BOUDREAU'S BIG YEAR

Lou Boudreau not only managed the 1948 Indians to the AL flag but also contributed one of the best batting seasons of any shortstop: a .355 average, 98 walks, 18 homers, and 106 RBIs. He struck out only *nine* times.

OH MY JOSH!

Although Negro Leagues records sometimes included exhibition games and were often kept in a haphazard format, historians believe Josh Gibson batted .517 for the 1943 Homestead Grays and hit at least 75 home runs in two different seasons (1931 and 1936). Gibson also feasted on big-league pitching during postseason barnstorming tours. His batting average against major league (white) pitchers was a robust .412.

THE DOOR FINALLY OPENED

Satchel Paige was the first black pitcher in the World Series (1948) and the first player from the Negro Leagues inducted into the Hall of Fame.

HOW PAIGE STAYED YOUNG

Satchel Paige was at least 62 years old when he pitched one inning of an exhibition game in Atlanta Stadium and retired Hank Aaron, Ken Boyer, Junior Gilliam, and three other hitters with 12 pitches—only two of them called balls.

Paige, whose career included 2,500 games (153 of them in one season) attributed his longevity to his rules for staying young. "If you're over six years of age, follow these rules closely," he said.

1. Avoid fried meats, which anger up the blood.
2. If your stomach disputes you, lie down and pacify it with cool thoughts.
3. Keep the juices flowing by jangling around gently as you move.
4. Go very light on the vices, such as carrying on in society—the social ramble ain't restful.
5. Avoid running at all times.
6. And don't look back. Something might be gaining on you.

DOUBLE DUTY

Ted "Double Duty" Radcliffe earned his nickname as a catcher/pitcher in the Negro Leagues. An All-Star three times as a pitcher and three times as a catcher, he played for more than 30 teams over four decades. His unofficial records include 4,000 hits and 400 home runs as a hitter plus 500 wins and 4,000 strikeouts as a pitcher.

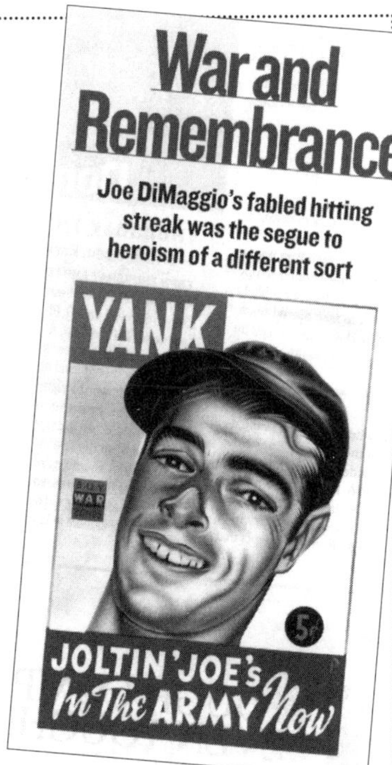

War and Remembrance
Joe DiMaggio's fabled hitting streak was the segue to heroism of a different sort
YANK
5¢
JOLTIN' JOE's In The ARMY Now

Joe DiMaggio was among many top major leaguers who wore a different kind of uniform during World War II.

Yank Magazine

WAR HERO WARREN

Warren Spahn was the only major leaguer to earn a

Cleveland player/manager Lou Boudreau talks to the ump while rubber-armed reliever Satchel Paige waits. The 42-year-old rookie—marooned for years in the Negro Leagues—was a key man in his club's 1948 pennant drive. His pitching repertoire was extraordinary. Reprinted with permission, National Baseball Hall of Fame Library, Cooperstown, New York

battlefield commission during World War II.

AMAZING COINCIDENCE

Warren Spahn believed in symmetry: he had 363 wins and 363 base hits.

CONSISTENCY COUNTS

Warren Spahn had six straight 20-win seasons from 1956 to 1961, working at least 260 innings in each of them.

HUSHED-UP HURT

Future Hall of Famer Warren Spahn worked with torn cartilage in his knee during the 1953 season. "They'd have let me go in a minute if I went on the disabled list," said the lefty, who still posted a 23–7 record that included five shutouts and a 2.10 earned-run average.

GOING ALL THE WAY

Warren Spahn completed more of his starts than any other pitcher of the postwar era. He went all the way 382 times in 665 career starts, a 57.4 percentage, and won at least 20 games in a season 13 times. His bat helped, since Spahn homered in 17 consecutive seasons—a record for a pitcher—and was often used as a pinch-hitter. He finished with 363 wins and a matching 363 base hits.

FINISHING THE JOB

Warren Spahn led his league in complete games 16 times

during a career that spanned 1942–65.

THE CASEY FACTOR

Warren Spahn said he worked for Casey Stengel "before and after he was a genius." Spahn broke in with the 1942 Boston Braves and pitched the first half of his final season with the 1965 New York Mets. But he was not part of the teams that won 10 pennants in 12 years for Stengel with the Yankees.

SANDY'S SHOT

A notoriously weak-hitting pitcher, Sandy Koufax picked a good time for his first home run. It beat Warren Spahn, 2–1. Spahn got the last laugh, however: when Koufax sent the bat to the Braves' clubhouse for Spahn's signature, the Milwaukee lefty broke it in half.

TRIPLE FAMERS

Three Hall of Fame pitchers worked in the final NL playoff game of 1959, when the Los Angeles Dodgers defeated the Milwaukee Braves, 6–5, in 12 innings at Memorial Coliseum. Don Drysdale started for the Dodgers, while Sandy Koufax (Dodgers) and Warren Spahn (Braves) both pitched a fraction of an inning in relief.

WHY KOUFAX QUIT

Star pitcher Sandy Koufax of the Los Angles Dodgers took the advice of doctors and retired at age 30 in November 1966. Though he had just won 27, lost nine, and posted a 1.73 earned-run average, Koufax revealed that continued pitching could result in permanent disability because of an arthritic left elbow.

Ted Williams finishes with a flourish, jolting a Jack Fisher pitch into the right-field seats in the final at-bat of his career. The shot gave the 42-year-old Red Sox star 521 home runs and a .344 lifetime batting average. Baltimore's third baseman at the time was another future Hall of Famer, Brooks Robinson.

EARLY ENTRY
Sandy Koufax was the youngest inductee in the history of the Hall of Fame.

JACKIE'S NUMBER RETIRED
Fifty years after Jackie Robinson broke baseball's color barrier in 1947, Major League Baseball honored him by ordering all clubs to retire Robinson's No. 42. Those players, coaches, and managers already wearing the number were allowed to keep it for the duration of their careers.

Three-time MVP Yogi Berra was reliable on both offense and defense. He helped the Yankees win 14 pennants in 16 years during his playing days, then became one of a handful of pilots to win pennants in both leagues. He won a combined 39 rings from All-Star appearances, the World Series, and the Hall of Fame.

FIRST IMPRESSION
Jackie Robinson was not only the first black player in the major leagues but also the first to be NL Rookie of the Year (1947) and Most Valuable Player (1949).

HEROIC HOYT
Future Hall of Fame reliever Hoyt Wilhelm fought at the Battle of the Bulge, earned a Purple Heart for his World War II service, and later became the first pitcher to lead each league in ERA.

HOYT'S HEX
The knuckleball is so difficult to hit that Minnesota manager Bill Rigney hated to see Hoyt Wilhelm pitch against his club. "They swing three times before the first knuckleball is halfway to the plate," he said.

LATE BLOOMER
Because he threw a knuckleball that was easy on the arm, Hoyt Wilhelm extended his career to within 16 days of his 50th birthday. He started the best five-year run of his career at age 38 and had 129 saves after age 40.

Warren Spahn won more games than any pitcher who performed after World War II. He won 20 or more 13 times—including a remarkable 23–7 season at age 42. National League

KNUCKSIE'S NICHE

With an 8–0 win over Toronto on October 6, 1985, Yankees knuckleballer Phil Niekro became the 18th 300-game winner as well as the oldest man (at age 46) to throw a shutout.

MAZ PITCHED TOO?

Future World Series hitting hero Bill Mazeroski, an Ohio native, was the only high school *pitcher* to defeat future Hall of Famer Phil Niekro.

FINGERS'S FATE

One year before winning election to Cooperstown in 1992, Rollie Fingers filed for bankruptcy and bought a $150 car at auction. After the Hall called, he was able to make $10,000 a day signing his autograph.

NEW NUMBERS

One of baseball's time-honored traditions is saluting other players by switching uniform numbers. Seattle superstars Ken Griffey Jr. and Randy Johnson, better known for usually wearing Nos. 24 and 51, respectively, wore other jerseys in one-game tributes. Griffey honored Jackie Robinson by wearing 42 on April 15, 1997,

Sandy Koufax became a star when he learned to throw his fastball more slowly. Second-string catcher Norm Sherry, later a manager, suggested he master the curve, shorten his stride, and conceal his intentions from batters and coaches. National League

Hoyt Wilhelm, the first reliever to win the ERA crown, was king of the knuckleballers. He floated his way to more than 1,000 career appearances—leaving the major leagues just short of his 49th birthday. National League

while Johnson saluted Nolan Ryan by wearing 34 the day he got his 300th strikeout in 1993. In 1998 Orel Hershiser switched from his customary No. 55 to No. 53 while pitching for the San Francisco Giants as a tribute to the late Don Drysdale, who pitched for the Los Angeles Dodgers.

NOLAN'S NUMBERS

Nolan Ryan is the only man whose number was retired by three different teams: the Astros and Rangers, for whom he wore No. 34, and the Angels, for whom he wore No. 30.

EXPLAIN THIS

Roger Clemens, Greg Maddux, and Steve Carlton combined for 15 Cy Young Awards without ever throwing a no-hitter while Nolan Ryan threw seven no-hitters without ever winning a Cy Young Award.

GOOD NEWS, BAD NEWS

Nolan Ryan holds major league marks for strikeouts, no-hitters, years of service, and grand slams allowed to opposing hitters (10).

BETTER IN BETWEEN

Bob Gibson started and ended his Hall of Fame career with the

St. Louis Cardinals by giving up home runs. Jim Baxes, the first man he faced, greeted Gibson, working in relief, with a leadoff seventh-inning homer on April 15, 1959, while Pete LaCock hit the only grand slam of his career against Gibson on September 13, 1975. The LaCock home run knocked Gibson out of the game.

NINTH-INNING BLUES

Though no Met ever pitched a no-hitter, Tom Seaver came close three times. In 1969, 1972, and 1975, he held rivals hitless into the ninth inning. Seaver pitched his only complete no-hitter in 1977, after he had been traded to the Reds.

HAPPY HUNTER

Oakland ace Catfish Hunter had three singles and three RBIs during his 1968 perfect game against Minnesota.

ROBERTS RIPPED

Because he was always around the plate, Hall of Famer Robin Roberts yielded a record 505 home runs.

ROBBIN' ROBERTS

Duke Snider loved facing Robin Roberts. That wasn't surprising, since he reached him for 19 home runs—the most any one hitter has collected against any one pitcher.

One-time Oakland World Series hero Rollie Fingers, a newcomer to the 1981 Milwaukee Brewers, was the first relief pitcher to win Most Valuable Player and a Cy Young Award in the same season and the second enshrined in Cooperstown (after Hoyt Wilhelm). His record of 341 career saves stood until 1992, when both Jeff Reardon and Lee Smith surpassed it.

THE GREAT ESCAPE

Though he yielded 303 home runs in his long career, Jim Palmer never allowed one with the bases loaded.

FINGERS IS FINE

Hall of Fame reliever Rollie Fingers averaged 120 innings

pitched per season over a seven-year stretch of his career.

DENNIS THE MENACE

Dennis Eckersley, who later made the Hall of Fame as a reliever, not only threw a shutout in his first major league start but also started his career by pitching a record 23⅔ innings without yielding an earned run. Two years later, in 1977, he threw a no-hitter in the middle of the longest hitless streak (21 innings) since Cy Young in 1904.

NERVOUS NELLIE

Though he seemed supremely confident, Dennis Eckersley admitted he was "petrified" in every one of his appearances—and that he missed that feeling after he retired.

RICKEY'S FEET

Rickey Henderson, famous for headfirst slides, promised he'd deliver a feetfirst slide when he passed Ty Cobb as the career leader in runs scored. It happened on October 4, 2001, when the 42-year-old outfielder homered for the San Diego Padres against the Los Angeles Dodgers. Henderson delivered as advertised after completing the circuit of the bases on his 2,998th career hit.

The No-Hit Games display at the National Baseball Hall of Fame and Museum contains a game-used ball from every no-hitter thrown in major league baseball since the museum's opening in 1939. Milo Stewart Jr./National Baseball Hall of Fame Library, Cooperstown, New York

Puerto Rico native Roberto Clemente leaps to make a catch amid the outfield ivy of Chicago's Wrigley Field in 1960. The rifle-armed right fielder of the Pittsburgh Pirates compiled exactly 3,000 hits before losing his life in a New Year's Eve plane crash while ferrying earthquake relief supplies to Nicaragua. He became the first Latino member of the Baseball Hall of Fame when he was posthumously enshrined in 1973.

Prolific Paul

Paul Molitor's career firsts:

- First to get five hits in a World Series Game, October 12, 1982
- First to get his 3,000th hit with a triple, September 16, 1996
- First Hall of Famer who was more DH (1,174 games) than position player
- One of two players (with Pete Rose) to play five positions in All-Star Games
- Oldest man to register first 100-RBI season (age 37)
- Author of longest AL hitting streak (39 games) since DiMaggio's 56-game streak
- Only Hall of Famer to play at least 50 games at six different positions
- Only player with 3,000 hits, 600 doubles, 500 steals, and 200 homers

What's Left?

Players reporting to the Yankees have a hard time finding jerseys because the team has retired so many numbers. The list includes 1 (Billy Martin),

HENRY "HANK" L. AARON
MILWAUKEE N.L., ATLANTA N.L.,
MILWAUKEE A.L., 1954-1976
HIT 755 HOME RUNS IN 23-YEAR CAREER TO
BECOME MAJORS' ALL-TIME HOMER KING. HAD
20 OR MORE FOR 20 CONSECUTIVE YEARS, AT
LEAST 30 IN 15 SEASONS AND 40 OR BETTER
EIGHT TIMES. ALSO SET RECORDS FOR GAMES
PLAYED (3,298), AT-BATS (12,364), LONG HITS
(1,477), TOTAL BASES (6,856), RUNS BATTED
IN (2,297). PACED N.L. IN BATTING TWICE
AND HOMERS, RUNS BATTED IN AND SLUGGING
PCT. FOUR TIMES EACH. WON MOST VALUABLE
PLAYER AWARD IN N.L. IN 1957.

This plaque, hanging in the Hall of Fame gallery, honors the career home-run king.

Baseball Hall of Fame

3 (Babe Ruth), 4 (Lou Gehrig), 5 (Joe DiMaggio), 7 (Mickey Mantle), 8 (Bill Dickey and Yogi Berra), 9 (Roger Maris), 10 (Phil Rizzuto), 15 (Thurman Munson), 16 (Whitey Ford), 23 (Don Mattingly), 32 (Elston Howard), 37 (Casey Stengel), 44 (Reggie Jackson), 42 (retired by all teams in 1997 as a salute to Jackie Robinson), and 49 (Ron Guidry).

ANOTHER MICKEY

One Hall of Famer was actually named for another. Mickey Mantle's dad named his son after his own personal favorite, Mickey Cochrane.

HENRY'S FOUR-PLAY

When Hank Aaron hit his record 715th home run on April 8, 1974, it was a case of No. 44 (Aaron) succeeding against No. 44 (pitcher Al Downing). The event occurred in the fourth inning of the fourth game in the fourth month of a year ending in four. Aaron matched his uniform number in home runs four times and led the National League in home runs and runs batted in four times each.

MEASURING AARON

How great was Hank Aaron? According to Baseball-reference.com, he led his league in extra-base hits 13 times and total bases eight times. Both are major league records.

Character Builder

"Give a boy a bat, a ball, and a place to play and you'll have a good citizen."

—Manager Joe McCarthy

THE MATHEWS FILE

Eddie Mathews was the only man to play for the Braves in Boston, Milwaukee, and

Atlanta. He was also the first rookie to hit three home runs in a game, the first *Sports Illustrated* cover man, and half of the best 1-2 slugging tandem in baseball history (he and Hank Aaron hit a record 863 home runs when they were teammates). The only man to play for, coach, and manage the Braves, Mathews was Atlanta manager when Aaron broke Babe Ruth's career home-run record on April 8, 1974.

1-2 PUNCH

The 752 total bases produced by the tandem of Hank Aaron and Eddie Mathews for the 1959 Milwaukee Braves was the highest by NL teammates since 1930.

BENCH BRUISES

Beyond his bevy of baseball records, Hall of Fame catcher Johnny Bench suffered 18 broken bones and seven broken cups.

CAL'S FAREWELL

In 2001, his final season, Cal Ripken Jr. was All-Star Game MVP for the second time. His homer, the second of his All-Star career, paced the AL to a 4–1 win in the Safeco Field

Eddie Mathews (left) and Hank Aaron hit a record 863 home runs during the time they were teammates with the Braves, from 1954 to 1966, and teamed up again after Mathews became team manager. This photo was taken in March 1974, a month before Aaron broke Babe Ruth's career home-run record. Mathews, his manager, manipulated the lineup so that Aaron could break the record at home in Atlanta. He did, on April 8, 1974. Dan Schlossberg

game. When he retired at season's end, he was one of seven men with 3,000 hits and 400 homers.

MACPHAILS FIND FAME

Executives Larry and Lee MacPhail, the only father-and-son tandem in the Baseball Hall of Fame, could be joined by two more generations: Lee's son Andy is president of the Cubs, while grandson Lee IV is scouting director of the Cleveland Indians.

First Hall Female

Effa Manley, general manager and co-owner of the Newark Eagles team in the Negro Leagues, became the first female member of the Baseball Hall of Fame in 2006.

Opening Day

Memorable moments from Opening Day games:

- 1900—Phils beat Braves, 19–17 in 10 innings, in highest-scoring opener
- 1910—William Howard Taft becomes the first president to throw out the first ball and watches Washington's Walter Johnson one-hit the A's, 3–0
- 1912—BoSox need 11 innings to top Yanks 7–6 in first Fenway opener
- 1923—Ruth homer helps Yanks top BoSox, 4–1, in Yankee Stadium bow
- 1925—Indians score 12 runs in eighth inning to win opener from Browns, 21–14
- 1925—Giants beat Dodgers, 7–1, in Brooklyn opener saddened by death of Dodgers owner Charles H. Ebbets earlier that morning at his Waldorf-Astoria apartment
- 1935—In NL debut, Babe Ruth's HR against Carl Hubbell helps Braves beat Giants, 4–2
- 1940—Cleveland ace Bob Feller no-hits White Sox, 1–0, at Comiskey Park
- 1946—Mel Ott hits last career homer versus Phils' Oscar Judd at Polo Grounds

Baseball Hall of Fame

Huge throngs swamped Yankee Stadium for the 1923 opener. More than 25,000 fans were turned away. *The Baseball Bulletin*

- 1947—Jackie Robinson breaks color barrier when he plays for Brooklyn at Ebbets Field
- 1950—Red Sox blow 9–0 lead to Yanks and lose 14–10 in Billy Martin's debut as player (he becomes first rookie to get two hits in an inning)
- 1958—At Seals Stadium, San Francisco, the Giants' Ruben Gomez blanks the Dodgers' Don Drysdale, 8–0, in first California contest
- 1961—Rookie Carl Yastrzemski gets first of 3,318 career hits for BoSox
- 1974—Atlanta's Hank Aaron hits three-run, first-inning homer off Jack Billingham in Cincinnati to tie Babe Ruth's record of 714 home runs
- 1975—Cleveland player/manager Frank Robinson not only becomes first black manager but also homers to lead 5–3 win over Yankees at Municipal Stadium
- 1985—Tom Seaver makes record 15th Opening Day start while working for the White Sox versus Milwaukee Brewers (Seaver adds a 16th Opening Day start later)
- 1988—Toronto's George Bell is first man to hit three home runs on Opening Day
- 1992—Baltimore's Rick Sutcliffe beats Indians, 2–0, in first Camden Yards game
- 1993—Ranger Nolan Ryan, 46, is oldest Opening Day starter

- 1999—Rockies beat Padres, 8–2, in Monterrey, Mexico—first opener not in the United States or Canada
- 2000—Cubs beat Mets, 5–3, at Tokyo Dome in Japan—first opener outside North America
- 2001—Blue Jays beat Rangers, 8–1, while starting season in San Juan, Puerto Rico

EQUAL OPPORTUNITY

President William Howard Taft, passing through St. Louis on May 4, 1910—a rare day when both the Cardinals and the Browns were playing at home—did not wish to offend either team. He managed to see parts of both games.

VEEP TOSS

Vice President Henry Wallace, substituting for President Franklin D. Roosevelt, threw the longest Opening Day first pitch by a politician in 1944. From his box seat, he threw it over the players' heads. The ball landed near second base, nearly 200 feet away.

Unpopular president Herbert Hoover risked the wrath of fans to throw out the first pitch on Opening Day 1929. Reprinted with permission, National Baseball Hall of Fame Library, Cooperstown, New York

SWITCH-PRESIDENT

Harry Truman was the first president to throw an Opening Day pitch left-handed and also the first ambidextrous president to do it. In 1950 he threw one ball as a lefty and another as a righty.

WORLDS APART

Richard Nixon and Ty Cobb attended the first game at San Francisco's Candlestick Park, on April 12, 1960. Not surprisingly, the Giants won on a wind-blown triple.

BUSH LEAGUES

Presidents George H.W. Bush, a left-handed first baseman, and George W. Bush, a right-handed pitcher, played college ball at Yale. The latter owned the Texas Rangers before getting into politics but failed to gain one position he really wanted: commissioner of baseball.

LONG TOSS

The longest first pitch on Opening Day was made by longtime Dodger Stadium peanut vendor Roger Owens. On the first day of the 1978 campaign, Owens threw a baseball from his second-deck territory to home plate. Known for remarkable control, the vendor could throw a bag of peanuts accurately from 65 rows away.

NIGHT SIGHT

The first Opening Day night game was played on April 17, 1950. The Cardinals beat the Pirates, 4–2, at Busch Stadium in St. Louis.

HEAVY HITTER

Don Drysdale was the only pitcher to hit two home runs on Opening Day.

APRIL FOOL

All three players who hit three homers in a game on Opening Day did it on April 4: Dmitri Young in 2005, Tuffy Rhodes in 1994, and George Bell in 1988.

LUCKY BROWNIE?

St. Louis Browns manager Luke Sewell believed that his luck improved when he kept infielders' gloves in the third-base coaching box while the team hit. Current rules prohibit leaving equipment on the field.

KINER'S KORNER

Ralph Kiner never stepped on a white line. "It didn't help or hurt me," he said. "I just didn't want to take any chances."

Opening Day is usually a festive occasion, but the serious faces of Dodgers players indicated some knew that the 1957 Ebbets Field lid-lifter would be Brooklyn's last.
Los Angeles Dodgers

PENNY PINCHER

Washington Senators first baseman Mickey Vernon picked up pennies he found on the field; he regarded them as omens of base hits to come. "I can't recall a time that I found a penny and did not get a hit," he said. "Why doesn't the manager throw pennies onto the field near first base? That's the catch. The penny had to be found by accident. You can't fool around with this superstition stuff and get away with it."

LUCKY NO. 9

Many experts considered Roger Maris "lucky" to hit 61 home runs in 1961—the only year he hit as many as 40. In 1967, however, Maris had a more likely encounter with Lady Luck. Wearing No. 9, he hit his first National League home run on May 9. The fan who caught it was sitting in row 9, seat 9. Maris was then with the Cardinals, a team with nine letters in its name.

AVOIDING NO. 13

Only the brave wear No. 13, but the Atlanta Braves do not. By executive decree in 1978, the No. 13 was banned throughout their entire major and minor league systems.

SUPERSTITIOUS SLUGGER

Hall of Fame first baseman Orlando Cepeda believed every bat had only one hit in it. When he got a hit, he would trash the bat he used and take another. He finished his career with 2,364 hits.

FIRST AND LAST
Philadelphia pitcher John Buzhardt, otherwise undistinguished during his brief career, was the winning pitcher at both ends of the Phils' 23-game losing streak in 1961. He wore uniform No. 23.

CHANGING LUCK
Some players tried to change bad luck by changing numbers; Roger Craig switched to No. 13 in his second year as a New York Met and lost 22 of 27 decisions after a 10–24 mark the year before. Jake Powell believed hairpins represented hits, collected 241 of them one season, and produced exactly that many hits for his team in the minors. Ron Northey, Pete Reiser, and Al Rosen were among several who made "X" marks at home plate before they batted.

SELECT COMPANY
Eleven major league managers have been honored with retired numbers, including Casey Stengel twice. They are Fred Hutchinson (Reds), Billy Meyer (Pirates), and Billy Martin (Yankees), all with No. 1; Tommy Lasorda (Dodgers), No. 2; Earl Weaver (Orioles), No. 4; Dick Howser (Royals), No. 10; Gil Hodges (Mets), No. 14; Walter Alston (Dodgers), No. 24; Stengel (Yankees and Mets), No. 37; and Danny Murtaugh (Pirates), No. 40. John McGraw, whose jersey was also retired, did not wear a number during his career.

TEXAS TRIBUTE
After losing his life prematurely because of a brain tumor, Johnny Oates was honored with the retirement of the No. 26 jersey he wore while managing the Texas Rangers from 1995 to 2001.

TIME TO QUIT
Some stars don't know when to quit. Babe Ruth and Carlton Fisk hit under .200 in their final seasons, Christy Mathewson failed to win a game, and Warren Spahn and Steve Carlton combined for 30 losses.

Bill Menzel

CHAPTER 10
SPRING INNINGS

BROOKS ROBINSON REMEMBERS...

I loved spring training. That was the best time of year for me. It was a relaxed time of year. You knew what you had to do to get in shape and get ready to play. They let you do what you wanted to do, but I liked to play a lot and that was one of the keys.

We used to come to spring training to get into shape, but now keeping in shape is a 12-month job. I never lifted a weight in my life. I ran a lot, trying to stay in shape that way, but never thought about baseball much during the winter. Because of the money involved in the game today, players have to stay in shape all year.

I played winter ball two years, in Colombia in 1955 and Cuba in 1957, but usually went back to Little Rock and got a job. I went to college one year at Little Rock University, got involved in the real estate business, and served five and a half years in the Arkansas National Guard. I also worked for a guy who manufactured Martin Hardcoating, which is put on the bottom of skis. That was about it.

CURRENT TRAINING SITES

Where the big-league clubs hold spring training today:

American League

- Baltimore—Fort Lauderdale, Florida
- Boston—Fort Myers, Florida
- Chicago—Tucson, Arizona*
- Cleveland—Winter Haven, Florida*
- Detroit—Lakeland, Florida
- Kansas City—Surprise, Arizona
- Los Angeles—Tempe, Arizona
- Minnesota—Fort Myers, Florida
- New York—Tampa, Florida
- Oakland—Phoenix, Arizona

Babe Ruth leaves for spring training in 1930. American League

- Seattle—Peoria, Arizona
- Tampa Bay—St. Petersburg, Florida*
- Texas—Surprise, Arizona
- Toronto—Dunedin, Florida

National League

- Arizona—Tucson, Arizona
- Atlanta—Lake Buena Vista, Florida
- Chicago—Mesa, Arizona
- Cincinnati—Sarasota, Florida
- Colorado—Tucson, Arizona
- Florida—Jupiter, Florida
- Houston—Kissimmee, Florida*
- Los Angeles—Vero Beach, Florida
- Milwaukee—Maryvale, Arizona
- Washington—Viera, Florida
- New York—Port St. Lucie, Florida
- Philadelphia—Clearwater, Florida
- Pittsburgh—Bradenton, Florida
- St. Louis—Jupiter, Florida
- San Diego—Peoria, Arizona
- San Francisco—Scottsdale, Arizona

*new location pending

THE "GOOD" OLD DAYS

Longtime manager and executive Branch Rickey attended his first training camp in Dallas as a rookie with the

1906 St. Louis Browns. There was no permanent camp, just a traveling road show to Fort Worth and Houston. Three of the 20 players had to be cut by Opening Day; when they were, the team had seven pitchers, three catchers, three outfielders, and four infielders. In camp everyone played except manager Jimmy McAleer, road secretary Lloyd Rickert, and trainer Kirby Samuels. There were no coaches, team doctors, scouts, or newsmen with the ballclub.

Red Sox roster book from the early 1950s, when the team trained in Sarasota. Boston Red Sox

TARGET PRACTICE

When John McGraw's New York Giants trained in Marlin Springs, Texas, the manager was not the only one who had to put up with the antics of Rube Marquard. The town's sheriff was also aware of the eccentric southpaw—especially on the night the star pitcher emptied his revolver into a billboard across the street from his hotel room. The lawman told McGraw to take the Giants out of town. "Look," said the manager, "I put this town on the map and I can rub it off just as easily." The sheriff thought for a moment, considered the economic benefits of hosting the Giants during the spring, and then relented—with assurances from McGraw that Marquard would quiet his nocturnal affairs.

SPRING WORKLOAD

During the days when the Yankees and Cardinals shared spring-training headquarters in St. Petersburg, Florida, some St. Louis players complained about the twice-daily workouts, as compared with the once-a-day workouts of the world champion Yankees. Manager Ray Blades responded that the Yankees' record should serve as an incentive. "You should want to be like the Yankees and work twice as hard," he insisted. Pepper Martin answered for the dissident players. "I got a jackass back in Oklahoma and you can work him from sunup 'til sundown and he ain't never gonna win the Kentucky Derby!"

The Chicago White Sox passed out this abbreviated media guide during 1952 spring training. Chicago White Sox

26 MILES ACROSS THE SEA
When Chicago Cubs owner William Wrigley Jr. bought compact Catalina Island in 1919, it had no electricity, running water, or paved streets. But Wrigley bought it for $700,000 with an eye toward making it spring-training headquarters for his team. He also purchased a ferry line, built a hotel, and added bungalows and a golf course. Except for the war years, when they were close to home because of wartime travel restrictions, the Cubs trained there from 1922 to 1951. They moved to mainland California in mid-March for exhibition play, with Los Angeles–based Wrigley Field their home base.

Winter Woes
"People always ask me what I do in the winter when there's no baseball. I'll tell you what I do. I stare out the window and wait for spring."
—Rogers Hornsby

NOT TOO STEEP
In 1937 Daytona Beach civic leaders offered the St. Louis Cardinals $5,000 to make the city their new spring-training home. They accepted.

This sign greeted visitors to Vero Beach, Florida, after the Brooklyn Dodgers won their only world championship in 1955.
Dan Schlossberg

TOBACCO ROAD

Baseball fan Erskine Caldwell, author of *Tobacco Road* and other classics, often traveled around Florida spring-training camps with his broadcasting friend, Ernie Harwell.

MUSIAL ON TRAINING

Hall of Famer Stan Musial, a dud in spring training as a rookie with the 1942 Cardinals, suggests preseason workouts are not accurate indicators of player potential. "I think there is a tendency to overrate pitchers and underrate hitters down there," he said. "In most of the parks, the background for a hitter is terrible, and you really notice the difference when you get home and see those doubled-decked stands."

FRENCH LICK FOLLIES

Because of wartime travel restrictions, both Chicago teams spent three springs

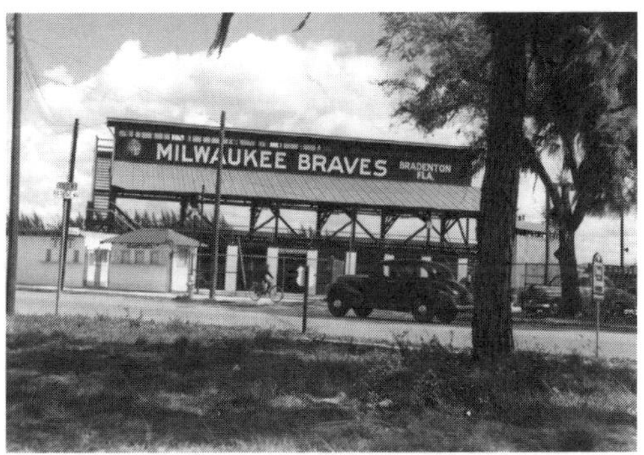

Shortly after moving their home city from Boston to Milwaukee, the Braves reported for spring training to the sleepy village of Bradenton, Florida.
Milwaukee Journal

A sure sign of spring is the palm trees that greet fans at Roger Dean Stadium, the only Florida facility shared by two teams, the Florida Marlins and the St. Louis Cardinals. Dan Schlossberg

training in French Lick, a Southern Indiana community 279 miles from the Loop. Both teams stayed in the French Lick Springs Hotel, a fancy 700-room property, and even used its ballroom as a makeshift field when inclement weather precluded outdoor exercises. The training regimen of the Cubs included five-mile hikes through wooded terrain.

NO KIDDING

A wire service once reported that actress Marilyn Monroe had joined husband Joe DiMaggio for a few days at spring training. The last paragraph said, "DiMaggio missed the workout."

TRAINING CAMP TRADE

One of the most unusual trades in baseball history occurred in 1951, when the New York Yankees and the New York Giants swapped training camps for one year only. The Giants trained in St. Petersburg, Florida, and the Yankees in Phoenix, Arizona, in 1951, met in the World Series that fall, then reverted to their original sites in 1952.

SPRING TO MILWAUKEE

The city of Milwaukee has twice won teams during spring training. On March 18, 1953, the Boston Braves announced their franchise would become the Milwaukee Braves that season—the first change in the baseball map since 1903. The Braves moved again, to Atlanta, after the 1965 season, but in March 1970, with little more than a week before Opening Day, the Seattle Pilots, a 1969 expansion team with financial woes, became the Milwaukee Brewers.

Dodgers players run their exercise routines at Holman Stadium in Vero Beach, Florida.
Dan Schlossberg

WHISTLE STOP

Veteran baseball executive Dallas Green on his first spring-training trip, in 1956: "Chris Short and I came by train. The train stopped in the middle of the road in Clearwater. When I got off, I said, 'What in the world have I gotten into?' That was a spring I'll never forget."

QUICK THINKING

A Southern restaurant owner once told Vic Power he didn't serve "Negroes." "That's okay," Power replied, "I don't eat Negroes. Give me some rice and beans."

SOME WELCOME MAT

Although the Tigers have trained in Lakeland, Florida, since 1934, not all members of the team felt welcome. It wasn't until 1962 that the Lakeland Holiday Inn agreed to admit black players.

THE BIKING COWBOY

The early Los Angeles Angels commuted from their Palm Springs spring-training hotel to their ballpark on bicycles. Owner Gene Autry, also known as "the Singing Cowboy," made a habit of leading the pack.

Musicians entertain fans between innings at Cracker Jack Stadium, spring home of the Atlanta Braves at Disney's Wide World of Sports. Dan Schlossberg

CAUGHT SHORT

Longtime baseball executive Donald Davidson, whose height was curtailed at 4' by a childhood case of polio, was the subject of considerable teasing. One spring, when a new guard was posted at the press gate of the Braves' spring-training camp, pitchers Warren Spahn and Lew Burdette warned the attendant that a midget had escaped from a nearby circus and was running around posing as a team official. When Davidson arrived, the guard refused him admittance. Davidson, a feisty character with a short fuse, kicked the recalcitrant guard in the shins and was about to start a major ruckus when the culprits admitted their ruse.

ROSE VERSUS REDS

In 1980, when Pete Rose played his first spring-training game against the Reds for the Phillies, the Phils allowed fans to watch behind roped-off sections of the outfield warning track.

STRIKEOUT ARTIST

Several major league pitchers have struck out four men in an inning, but Joe Niekro is the only one who had the

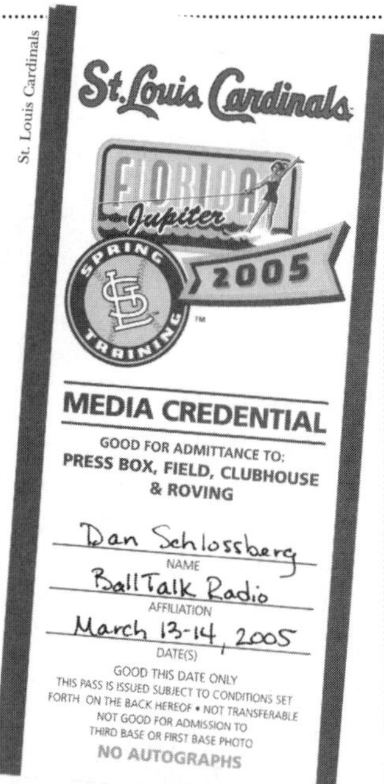

St. Louis Cardinals
St. Louis Cardinals
FLORIDA
Jupiter
SPRING TRAINING
2005
MEDIA CREDENTIAL
GOOD FOR ADMITTANCE TO:
PRESS BOX, FIELD, CLUBHOUSE
& ROVING
Dan Schlossberg
NAME
BallTalk Radio
AFFILIATION
March 13-14, 2005
DATE(S)
GOOD THIS DATE ONLY
THIS PASS IS ISSUED SUBJECT TO CONDITIONS SET
FORTH ON THE BACK HEREOF • NOT TRANSFERABLE
NOT GOOD FOR ADMISSION TO
THIRD BASE OR FIRST BASE PHOTO
NO AUTOGRAPHS

Cardinals manager Tony La Russa signs autographs for fans in Ft. Lauderdale.

Dan Schlossberg

ignominious distinction of fanning five. It happened in a spring-training exhibition game when Niekro's knuckler was so lively that Houston catcher Cliff Johnson twice missed third strikes, allowing runners to reach first base.

ALEX WATCHED CAL

Alex Rodriguez went to Orioles spring-training games in Miami to watch Cal Ripken Jr. play shortstop.

SOME COMEBACK

Among the replacement players during 1995 spring training was Jimmy Boudreau, who had last played professionally in 1986. After he struggled during an exhibition game, Pittsburgh broadcaster Steve Blass said, "He should have been better, pitching on 3,195 days' rest."

FAMILIAR FEEL

Tampa's Legend Field resembles Yankee Stadium in both appearance and approach. It has its own Monument Park, dancing groundskeepers, and Frank Sinatra musical sendoff after Yankees wins.

HUGGINS-STENGEL LIVES

Huggins-Stengel Field, where the Yankees once held spring training, still remains an integral part of the St. Petersburg, Florida, sports scene. Now used for various youth programs, the field still has dugouts, bullpen mounds, and a water tower behind home plate; monuments to former major league managers Miller Huggins and Casey Stengel; and a lake that has resident alligators (reputed to have chased Babe Ruth).

Chris Carpenter warms up for the St. Louis Cardinals before an exhibition game at Ft. Lauderdale against the Orioles. Dan Schlossberg

Pensive pitcher John Smoltz prepares for batting practice before a Braves game in Kissimmee, Florida. Dan Schlossberg

AL LANG FIELD
Al Lang Field, where the first exhibition game was played in 1914, features seagulls, sunshine, water views, old-time light towers, and proximity to Tropicana Field, regular-season home of the team that trains there, the Tampa Bay Devil Rays.

WATCH OUT FOR GATORS
Winter Haven's Chain of Lakes Park sits on the shores of Lake Lulu, inhabited by alligators that like to sun themselves on the shore during batting practice. The 7,900-seat park, which turned 40 in 2006, is the spring-training home of the Cleveland Indians.

FANS IGNORE SOUVENIR
Fans once refused to chase a home-run ball hit by Juan Gonzalez of the Texas Rangers in Port Charlotte, Florida. The ball landed in a pond where an eight-foot alligator had been sunning himself on the bank. After floating for 90 seconds, the ball sank.

ALWAYS READY
Tigers players keep fishing rods in their lockers and head for Lake Parker, Florida, after spring drills. The roar of motor boats from the lake can be heard during exhibition games.

SPRING IN BRADENTON
McKechnie Field, opened in 1923, is tucked into a neighborhood off 17th Avenue West in Bradenton, Florida. Foul balls sometimes hit passing cars.

SPRING-TRAINING HAZARD
Shawon Dunston was once stung by a scorpion in the Cubs' clubhouse at Scottsdale, Arizona.

BEDTIME STORY
Cleveland pitcher C.C. Sabathia said he had a sore back during

spring training because he "slept wrong." Asked about it, then-manager Charlie Manuel said, "I don't know. I don't sleep with him."

RIGHTY THROWS LEFTY
Chan Ho Park, a right-handed pitcher, raised a few eyebrows by throwing *left-handed* for a full 15 minutes. The test was designed by a back specialist.

WRONG HAT
Yankees owner George Steinbrenner, incensed that Andy Pettitte's son was wearing a Mets cap before a spring-training game, said Pettitte had to give it up—but could keep his son.

HAIRY SITUATION
After losing his cap *11 times in one inning* during a 2005 exhibition game, Seattle pitcher Felix Hernandez decided to get a haircut.

WHO NEEDS THEM ANYWAY?
Spring training has become such a big draw that ballpark traffic can influence the game. A contest between the Rockies and White Sox in 2005 was delayed 15 minutes because the umpires got caught in traffic.

BREAKING WIND
Jason Phelps homered in the eighth and ninth innings as Tampa Bay beat Detroit, 12–4, in Lakeland, Florida, on March

Orioles (batting) and Dodgers get ready for the season with a spring exhibition game at Holman Stadium, Vero Beach, Florida. Because the stadium has no dugouts, players sit on open benches with wet towels over their heads to avoid sunstroke. Dan Schlossberg

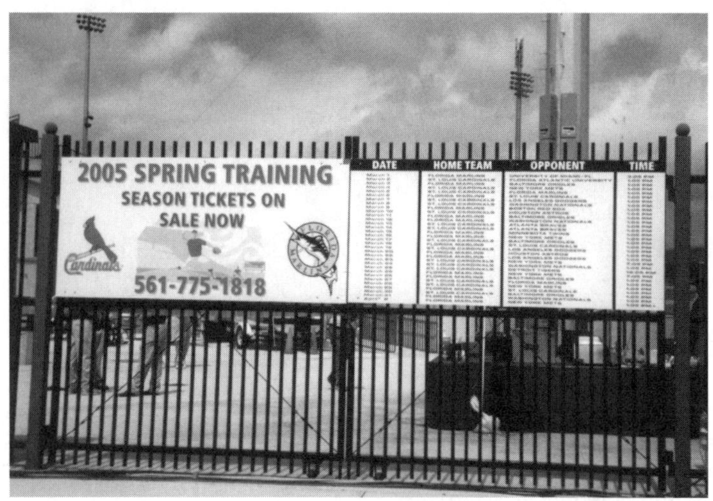

Schedules of the Marlins and Cardinals are posted outside the gates of Roger Dean Stadium in Jupiter, just north of the Palm Beaches. Dan Schlossberg

8, 2004. A 23-mile-per-hour wind helped. "If he hits like that," said then-manager Lou Piniella, "he'll get a lot of at-bats." Perhaps the pilot forgot that the Rays had a domed stadium, with zero wind.

O'Malley's Heart

The manmade, heart-shaped lake near Holman Stadium in Vero Beach was a valentine from Dodgers owner Walter O'Malley to his wife, Kay.

Springing Home

The Tampa Bay Devil Rays train five minutes from their home ballpark. But their website contains a section called, "Everything you need to know about your trip to Florida."

Grapefruit League Helps

Spring training in Florida generates half a billion dollars for the state's economy.

CHAPTER 11
SPECTACULAR SPECTATORS

BROOKS ROBINSON REMEMBERS...

Fans can be very vocal at the ballpark—especially if they don't like a player from the visiting team. But fans treated me very well on the road, even in New York. You know you're going to get booed a little bit, but I didn't mind. I don't remember anybody giving me a really hard time. Early in my career, I remember getting off the bus in New York and hearing, "Youse guys are gonna get it." And most of the time we did!

The organist in Anaheim played "Elephant Walk" when Boog Powell came to the plate for us and he didn't like it. They stopped doing it.

In Cleveland a fan sat in the right-field stands and beat a drum to death for nine innings. I never met him but I certainly heard him.

Our biggest fan in Baltimore was a taxi driver named Wild Bill Hagy. He started showing up around 1979, after I left. He sat in the upper deck and had his own section. He led the cheers and developed quite a rapport with the Orioles teams.

Nick Altrock and Al Schacht, longtime baseball clowns, stage a pregame boxing match, entertaining a crowd during the '30s.

FAN INTERFERENCE
Cincinnati ground rules in 1884 permitted outfielders to pursue batted balls that bounced into the bleachers. Pittsburgh's Elmer Smith, chasing a two-out drive by George "Germany" Smith, was physically assaulted by several fans—one of whom finally made his point by pulling a gun. Not surprisingly, the Reds won, 7–6.

TAFT TARDY?
President William Howard Taft is widely credited with creating the traditional seventh-inning stretch. It is said that when he stood to stretch his legs at a 1910 game, the crowd stood as a sign of respect. Some historians disagree, saying the seventh had been considered a "lucky inning" long before Taft reached the White House. According to the *Buffalo Express* of May 13, 1892, "The crowd came to its feet in the lucky seventh but it did no good."

PIONEER PROMOTER
Frank Bancroft, business manager of the Cincinnati Reds from 1892 to 1921, was the first baseball official to promote the game heavily. He staged the first home-plate

wedding, led major league squads to Cuba, and arranged baseball Olympics, featuring long-distance throwing, races, fungo hitting, and home-run derbies. A one-time field manager in the early days of the National League, Bancroft had a background as advance man for the circus and vaudeville tours.

Ripley's
Believe It or Not!
PRESIDENT WILLIAM HOWARD TAFT IN 1910, IN A BASEBALL GAME BETWEEN THE WASHINGTON SENATORS AND PHILADELPHIA ATHLETICS, STARTED THE PRESIDENTIAL CUSTOM OF THROWING OUT THE FIRST BALL

BEWARE OF LIGHTNING
Lightning plays no favorites. Five fans were killed and 25

hurt when lightning struck a crowd watching a minor league game in Mobile, Alabama, on May 27, 1906.

THE DENVER NIGHTINGALE

"Take Me Out to the Ballgame," written in 15 minutes by vaudeville entertainer Jack Norwood, was popularized by Billy Murray, a baseball fan whose nickname was "the Denver Nightingale." After his initial recording in 1908, Murray sang the song an estimated 20,000 times before his death in 1954. To this day, the song trails only "Happy Birthday" and "The Star-Spangled Banner" in frequency of performance.

NO SOUVENIRS

Prior to 1916, fans who caught baseballs hit into the stands were required to return them. New Chicago Cubs ownership that year let fans keep such balls as a goodwill gesture, though such policy did not become universal until the 1920s.

RED SOX RECORD

The largest crowd to see the Red Sox play in Boston came not to Fenway Park but to Braves Field, borrowed from the National League as the site of the 1916 World Series. The Sox drew 42,620 as they won the World Series in five games over the Brooklyn Dodgers. The score of the October 12 clincher was 4–1.

CHEAP DATE

Brooklyn fans in 1920 ate nickel hot dogs and read nickel programs. Schoolchildren got

A month after he died, Lou Gehrig was honored at a special July 4 memorial game in 1941. His No. 4, retired that day, became the first of many jerseys retired by the Yankees over the years.

bleacher seats for a quarter apiece on Friday afternoons.

FOWL FOUL

During baseball's early years, fans routinely returned baseballs hit into the stands. In 1923, however, a 12-year-old Phillies fan in Baker Bowl refused. Whisked off to jail, where he spent a night, he sued the team and won, giving fans the right to keep future fouls.

FELLER'S PRIZE

Hall of Fame pitcher Bob Feller was only 10 years old when he obtained a ball autographed by Babe Ruth and Lou Gehrig. But he got it the hard way. "In 1928 Ruth and Gehrig came to Des Moines with their barnstorming teams and my father took me to see them," he said. "They were selling autographed balls for $5 apiece to raise money for the crippled children's hospital in Des Moines. I bought a ball with money I earned from catching gophers. For every pair of claws, you got a dime in bounty at the county treasurer's office. I got my 50 gophers in a couple of weeks and was able to get the ball. It's probably my most prized trophy—more than anything I earned myself."

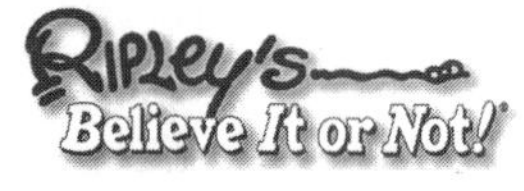

Believe It or Not!
THE ODDS of A BASEBALL FAN BEING HIT BY A BALL AT A MAJOR LEAGUE GAME ARE 300,000 to 1.!
NY

LOUDMOUTH TANDEM

Jimmie Dykes was so distracted by the heckling of the Kessler brothers in 1932 that the Philadelphia Athletics had to trade him. Sitting on opposite sides of the field, the Kesslers were so abusive that A's pilot Connie Mack took them to court—but lost.

FAIR TRADE?

Babe Ruth's home run in Detroit on July 13, 1934, was his 700th, a number never reached before. Wanting to keep the ball as a memento, the Yankee slugger contacted the fan who caught it, Lennie Bieleski, and agreed to trade it for a better seat, another ball autographed by Ruth, and $20.

BABE'S DOGS

Babe Ruth often ate hot dogs during games. When he didn't think his batting turn would come up, he'd stay in right field, walk to the hot dog vendor, and eat with the fans.

BABE'S LAST BLAST

Although he retired from baseball in 1935, Babe Ruth hit his last Yankee Stadium home run in 1942! It happened on August 23, when 69,136 fans gathered for a doubleheader between the Yankees and Washington Senators and a special between-games exhibition that featured Ruth batting against long-retired Hall of Fame pitcher Walter Johnson. Ruth's presence

ON MOTHER'S DAY IN 1939, CLEVELAND INDIANS PITCHER **BOB FELLER** HURLED A BALL TO A CHICAGO BATTER THAT WAS FOULED OFF INTO THE STANDS and **STRUCK HIS OWN MOTHER!**

Bill Veeck was only 30 years old when he became president of the Cleveland Indians in 1946. Within two years, he had integrated the American League.
American League

raised a record $85,000 for the Army-Navy Relief Fund, but he also left a lasting memory. Catcher Benny Bengough and umpire Billy Evans watched Ruth smack the third pitch from Johnson into the lower right-field stands, once known as "Ruthville" because of the slugger's frequent deposits.

BABE WHO?

Not all members of the Society for American Baseball Research deserve to belong; four of them omitted Babe Ruth when asked to list baseball's best 100 players.

LONG-LIVED FAN

Michigan fan Stanley Tyrkus had his picture taken with Lou Gehrig in 1935 and Cal Ripken Jr., the man who broke Gehrig's record for consecutive games played, in 1996. Both shots were taken at Tiger Stadium in Detroit.

BROWNOUT

Only 88,113 fans turned out to watch the last-place St. Louis Browns during the 1935 season.

DIZZY'S LAST GAME

Colorful Dizzy Dean, Cardinals star of the 1930s, had been retired six seasons when the St. Louis Browns reactivated him for one game as a publicity stunt in 1947. Dean, then a popular St. Louis broadcaster, was not only out of condition but also overweight. But he still had his baseball instincts; he pitched four scoreless innings against the Chicago White Sox, lined a hit to left, and later slid into second while on the base paths. When the 36-year-old right-hander got up limping at second, his wife, Pat, leaned over the dugout rail and hailed Browns manager Muddy Ruel. "He's proved his point," she said. "Now get him out of there before he kills himself!" In the four-inning stint that closed his career, Dean yielded three hits and one walk.

"CADDIE DAY"

Free Fenway Park admission for Boston golf caddies resulted in a hail of golf balls directed at the visiting Philadelphia Athletics during a 1949 promotion-gone-awry. Two caddies started the barrage but hundreds joined them, forcing both teams off the field. After the caddies ran out of balls, the groundskeepers retrieved them and play resumed.

MINORS DRAW MILLIONS

Before the advent of television, minor league baseball consisted of 438 cities in 59 leagues. Attendance that same year, 1949, was 42 million, another record.

RECORD WATCHER

Like players, fans set some impressive records. Dr. Seth Hawkins of St. Paul, Minnesota, claimed that he attended major league games in all 54 parks used between 1950 and 1996 *and* that he saw 13 players collect their 3,000th hit.

Manager Zack Taylor with 3'7", 50-pound midget Eddie Gaedel. Wearing No. ⅛, Gaedel pinch hit for Bill Veeck's Browns against Detroit. He walked on four pitches, then left the game. American League

THOMSON THRILLED TORRE
Joe Torre played for the Braves, Cards, and Mets and managed the same three teams before moving on to the Yankees. But the native New Yorker grew up as a fan of the New York Giants who was thrilled by Bobby Thomson's "shot heard 'round the world." He still calls the 1951 Thomson blast the biggest home run of all time.

UNIFORM TOSS
After the St. Louis Browns played their last game, manager Marty Marion went to the upstairs clubhouse at Sportsman's Park, peeled off his jersey, and threw it to kids waiting in the street below. Not anticipating the future development of the baseball memorabilia hobby, Marion thought there was no future need for a Browns uniform.

SOME GIRLFRIEND
A jilted girlfriend shot Cubs shortstop Billy Jurges twice during an altercation in his hotel room. The incident, fictionalized in Bernard Malamud's *The Natural,* faded from view when the player failed to press charges against Violet Popovich Valli. She later became a Chicago stage act.

YOGI MUSEUM
The Yankee Stadium scoreboard in the Yogi Berra Museum, in Little Falls, New Jersey, is a replica of the $300,000 electronic board that made its debut in the Bronx in 1959. When installed, it was the largest and most elaborate in the majors, measuring 113 feet in width and 45 feet in height while rising 75 feet above the center-field bleachers. Depicted on the museum's replica are

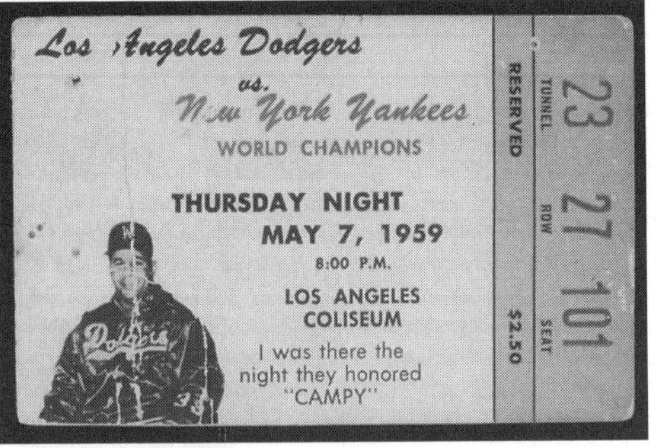

When the Dodgers hosted the Yankees in an exhibition game honoring Roy Campanella, a three-time MVP paralyzed in a winter car crash, a record 93,103 fans attended. The game was played May 7, 1959, at the Los Angeles Coliseum, home of the Dodgers during their first four years in Los Angeles.

Teams in tight pennant races often print postseason tickets in advance. When they don't make it, the tickets become known as "phantoms" and are considered hot collectibles. Chicago White Sox

the scores of Yogi Berra Day, held on September 19, 1959.

PLAYER MUSEUMS
Beyond the Baseball Hall of Fame, several top stars have their own museums. They include Yogi Berra (Little Falls, New Jersey), Ty Cobb (Royston, Georgia), Bob Feller (Van Meter, Iowa), Cal Ripken Jr. (Aberdeen, Maryland), Babe Ruth (Baltimore), and Ted Williams (St. Petersburg, Florida). There is also a Negro Leagues Museum in Kansas City, Missouri.

MARVELOUS MINNY
The Minnesota Twins, formerly known as the Washington Senators, led the American League in attendance in each of their first 10 seasons, 1961–70.

FATEFUL DAY
The future Mrs. Roger Clemens was an infant when her mother took her to see the ill-fated Dallas motorcade of President John F. Kennedy on November 22, 1963.

CROSLEY REPLICA
High school and amateur teams in a Cincinnati suburb play games on a Crosley Field

Brock Gets Gift

"I don't remember [my first] card as much as I do the gift for being on the card. No one had ever given me a gift in baseball before, so that was very rewarding. I got a $25 gift certificate and I used it to buy a radio."

—Lou Brock

replica constructed by a farmer. Built from the original blueprints, the park—located in Blue Ash, Ohio, 15 miles from the original site—includes the actual outfield dimensions, including the embankment that served as a warning track for outfielders. Lineups from the last Reds game at Crosley, on June 24, 1970, are preserved on the replica scoreboard. The complex includes an original Crosley Field ticket booth and some of the original seats.

Towering Atlanta outfielder Dale Murphy, twice Most Valuable Player in the National League, also stands tall in the eyes of autograph seekers. In this spring-training scene, the affable athlete balances his own glove under his elbow while using his hands to field as many requests as he can handle. Dan Schlossberg

MAGIC MOMENT

Every October 13, Pittsburgh fans party on the spot where Bill Mazeroski's ninth-inning, Game 7 home run won the 1960 World Series for the Pirates. They share hot dogs and soda and listen to taped replays of the game. A plaque marks the spot where the ball cleared the wall, parts of which still stand behind the Law School Building at the University of Pittsburgh, next to Schenley Park. Visitors can still see the 436-foot and 457-foot markers, plus a row of imbedded sidewalk bricks that trace the outline of the wall, razed with the rest of the ballpark in 1971.

10-CENT BEER NIGHT

The Cleveland Indians lost a game by forfeit on June 4, 1974, when fans inebriated during 10-Cent Beer Night poured onto the field and attacked Texas right fielder Jeff Burroughs, other Rangers players, and umpire Nestor Chylak. Six fans were arrested.

FOWL PLAY

Ted Giannoulas, who began his act as the San Diego Chicken in 1974, launched baseball's trend toward lovable furry mascots by making people laugh and bringing more families to the ballpark. His popularity zoomed so fast that he went from an original salary of $2 an hour to nearly $1,000 a week. But how did his mother feel about her son running around in a chicken suit? "She thinks I'm a doctor in Wisconsin," said Giannoulas.

THE KISSING BANDIT

Amply endowed Morganna Roberts, a one-time exotic dancer, established a new career as "the Kissing Bandit," playing the part of a lovesick fan who interrupted games by jumping fences to kiss unsuspecting players. The gimmick, once an unpaid publicity stunt for Morganna's act, became a career when she began booking herself as an attraction for minor league teams.

DISCO DEMOLITION

Master promoter Bill Veeck was the victim of one of his own gags when fans ran wild during "Disco Demolition Night" festivities at Comiskey Park in 1979. A mass record-burning in the outfield, plus the unruly fans, made the field unplayable for the second half of a scheduled doubleheader. The umpires forfeited the game to the visiting Detroit Tigers.

Honus Wagner T-206 tobacco card in the National Baseball Hall of Fame and Museum's collection. Milo Stewart Jr./National Baseball Hall of Fame Library, Cooperstown, New York

KEY BASEBALL CARD DATES

- 1881—First cards produced
- 1900—Cards issued with cigarettes
- 1930—Goudey Co. packages cards with gum
- 1948—Bowman Co. issues major set
- 1951—Topps Co. puts out pair of 51-card sets

- 1952—Prototype for future cards issued by Topps
- 1981—Fleer, Donruss challenge Topps monopoly

A NIGHT TO REMEMBER

When the Pawtucket Paw Sox and Rochester Red Wings met for an International League game at McCoy Stadium in Pawtucket on April 18, 1981, none of the 1,740 fans anticipated watching history in the making. After a 30-minute power failure delayed the start of the game, the AAA farm teams of the Boston Red Sox and Baltimore Orioles battled to a 2–2 tie that was suspended after 32 innings and a time of eight hours and seven minutes. Although 19 fans remained at the point of suspension, 5,756 showed up for completion of the historic game on June 23. It took only one more inning for the Sox to win, 3–2. Participants included future Hall of Famers Wade Boggs (Pawtucket) and Cal Ripken Jr. (Rochester).

SWEET MUSIC VIOLA

Minnesota pitcher Frank Viola, a New York skeptic by birth and by nature, noticed that he pitched his best games when a Metrodome fan displayed a large banner that read "Frankie Sweet Music Viola." The lefty not only went 15–0 in "banner" games during the 1987 regular season but also won World Series MVP honors by winning the first and last games—after giving tickets to banner man Mark Dornfield.

DANGEROUS LIAISONS

Although baseball tickets stipulate that teams are not responsible for bats or balls that fly into the stands, a

Fans who collected this 1956 Sandy Koufax card had no idea he would blossom into a superstar or that the Dodgers would leave Brooklyn. A bonus baby who had to be kept on the big-league roster, Koufax took the spot of another left-handed pitcher, future manager Tommy Lasorda.

The Topps Company

Mickey Mantle baseball cards are among the game's most coveted collectibles. The Topps Company

Detroit jury ordered the Tigers to pay $1 million to a 10-year-old girl whose hand was hurt by an airborne bat fragment in 1994.

Dog Days of August

Fans who believe baseball is going to the dogs got a convincing argument at Chicago's Comiskey Park on August 28, 1996. With 320 canines watching the White Sox that day, special events included dog music and movies, relay races, parades, performances, Frisbee catching, and even a costume contest. Trees, hydrants, and other props added to the atmosphere, which also included grooming and veterinary tips for owners. One question: What exactly is "dog music"?

Helping Hand

With the Orioles ahead, 4–3, in Game 1 of the 1996 ALCS at Yankee Stadium, New York's Derek Jeter hit a long eighth-inning drive. As Baltimore right fielder Tony Tarasco readied to catch it, 12-year-old Jeffrey Maier reached out and deflected it into the stands. Umpire Rich Garcia, oblivious to the apparent fan interference, ruled it a home run that tied the game. New

Bob Sheppard joined the Yankees as public-address announcer in 1949 and quickly won a reputation as the team's poet laureate. Reprinted with permission, National Baseball Hall of Fame Library, Cooperstown, New York

York won, 5–4, in 12 innings and took the series, four games to two.

WISHFUL THINKING

Be careful what you wish for: you just might get it. The Milwaukee Brewers and the Cincinnati Reds learned that lesson in 1997, when weather spoiled weather-related promotions. On June 8 the Reds gave their first 7,500 fans under age 14 packaged fishing rods—props the ground crew used to pose for photos on the infield tarp. Because of the steady downpour, the game never started. Two weeks later, the Brewers and the Kansas City Royals were flooded out on "Umbrella Night." Fans were to receive free umbrellas, but they should have gotten boats: water was chest-high at Milwaukee County Stadium following seven inches of rain.

FANS SEE RED

Six people were arrested at Cincinnati's Cinergy Field after a fight in the stands spilled into the visiting team's dugout, delaying an April 28, 1998, game. The alcohol-related, front-row fight got the Phillies' attention when a man fell just short of their bench during the eighth inning. Police needed pepper spray to end the hostilities.

SON OF COORS

A $2.7 million replica of Coors Field, built especially for youth baseball, opened in the Denver suburb of Lakewood, Colorado, on July 7, 1998, the date the All-Star Game was played at Coors. The youth field, named All-Star Park, was 90 percent the size of the original.

BEANIE BABY BABY

After the Cincinnati Reds refused to hand a female fan a Beanie Baby during a 1998 team giveaway, the woman threatened to sue. She said she deserved the toy bear, reserved for fans 14 and under, because she was pregnant.

SHORT-LIVED PRIZE

Spawn creator Todd McFarlane spent $3 million to buy the ball Mark McGwire hit in 1998 for his 70th home run—only to see the record fall to Barry Bonds three years later.

USHER TO OWNER

White Sox co-owner Eddie Einhorn once worked in old Comiskey Park as an usher.

GIANT FREE-FOR-ALL

The fan frenzy to grab free souvenir baseballs is just as frenetic in McCovey Cove as it is at AT&T Park. After a splashdown, vessels converge on the target while warding off swimmers and trained water dogs. A boat belonging to former Candlestick Park groundskeeper Joseph Figone was rammed by another, also in hot pursuit of the first regular-season home run in San Francisco Bay. The array of craft includes powerboats, sailboats, dinghies, rowboats, kayaks, charters, and even homemade inflatables of various sizes and descriptions. Getting a ball into the bay requires a poke of more than 420 feet—over the wall, over two rows of seats, and over a public pier.

Fans filter into Yankee Stadium for a day game early in the 1996 season. The giant bat was the idea of Joe Garagiola Jr., later general manager of the Arizona Diamondbacks.

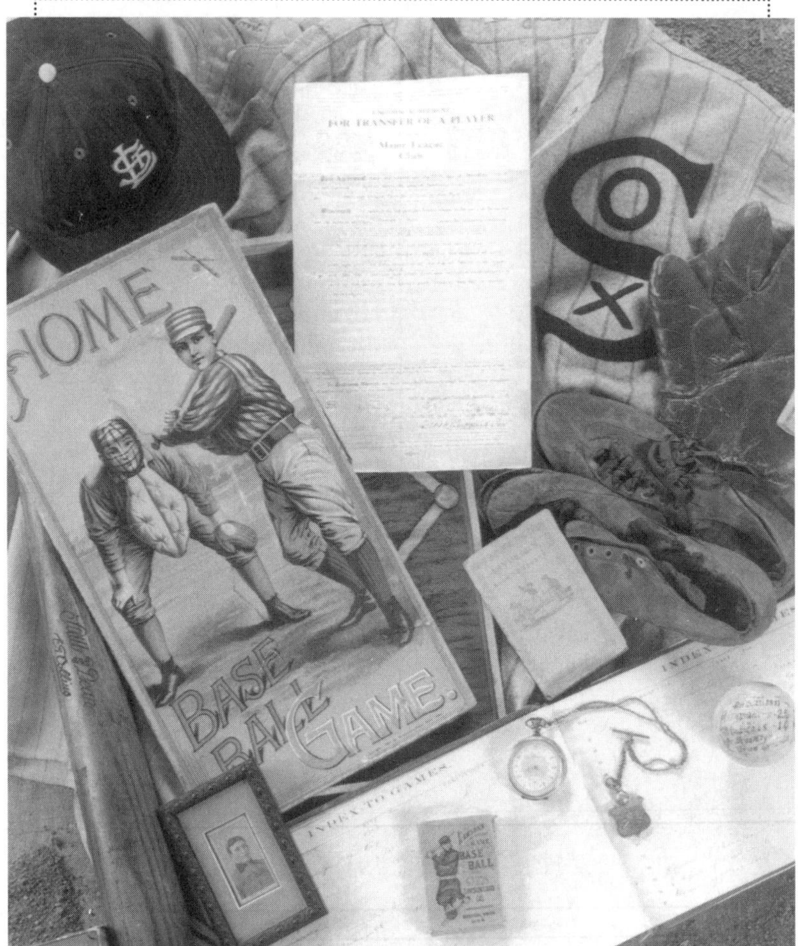

Given the chance to acquire the top 20 percent of Barry Halper's 50-year memorabilia collection, the Hall of Fame picked some of the above (from top left, clockwise): a St. Louis Browns cap worn by Satchel Paige; a uniform shirt worn by Joe Wood, Boston Red Sox; Joe Jackson's jersey and glove; Honus Wagner's spikes; *Boys and Girls Book of Sports,* 1839; Henry Chadwick's 1872 National Association scorebook; a trophy ball from Haymakers-Mutuals game at Brooklyn's Union Grounds, May 25, 1871; a watch awarded to Fred Parent, Boston Pilgrims, by the *Boston Globe,* 1903; Lawson's Patent Baseball Game, 1884; a Honus Wagner T-206 baseball card; a Stall and Dean bat, an E.T. Collins model; an original box, Harwood League ball, c. 1860; and a transfer agreement for Babe Ruth from the Boston Red Sox to the New York Yankees, 1920.

Baseball Hall of Fame

BARRY'S TREASURE TROVE
The collection of the late Barry Halper, acquired over 50 years, once included 400 bats, 1,000 uniforms, 1,800 balls, 4,000 photographs, 5,000 personal papers, and 30,000 cards. Virtually everything was autographed. The collection went on public display in 2002 after Major League Baseball bought the best 20 percent for $7.5 million, then donated it to the Baseball Hall of Fame. Another 80,000 items were auctioned by Sotheby's. Among items that went to Cooperstown were Shoeless Joe Jackson's bat, George Brett's can of pine tar, and uniforms worn by Ty Cobb and Satchel Paige.

FRANK FACTS
Baseball fans consumed 27.5 million hot dogs at major league parks in 2004, according to the National Hot Dog and Sausage Council.

TIGER TIES
Atlanta pitcher John Smoltz has family ties in Detroit: his grandfather spent 38 years on the Tiger Stadium ground crew, while an uncle placed numbers on the hand-operated scoreboard. More recently, the teenaged Smoltz caught a hunk of turf dug up by celebrating fans who stormed the field after the Tigers beat the Padres to win the 1984 World Series.

NO FANS TODAY
Mike Veeck, son of Bill, proved the apple doesn't fall far from the tree during a zany minor league publicity stunt. One day after his Charleston, South Carolina, Riverdogs drew a record crowd of 7,885, Veeck decided to play the first five innings of the next game while keeping the stands empty. The idea was to record a paid attendance of zero—and break the record-low "crowd" of 12 (Chicago versus Troy on September 17, 1881). Fans were allowed through Charleston's gates after the fifth inning, once the game was official.

LONG ODYSSEY
New Hampshire fans Bill Craib, age 27, and Sue Easler, age 23, visited all 178 parks used by professional baseball teams in 1991.

SHUFFLING OFF TO BUFFALO
The 1991 Buffalo Bisons drew 1,240,951 fans, a minor league record, and led the minors in attendance for 12 straight years.

Working out team schedules is especially difficult because leagues and divisions have different seasons and interleague play must be taken into account. The 2001 season was interrupted for six days in September after the terrorist attacks in New York and Washington, D.C., on September 11. Major League Baseball

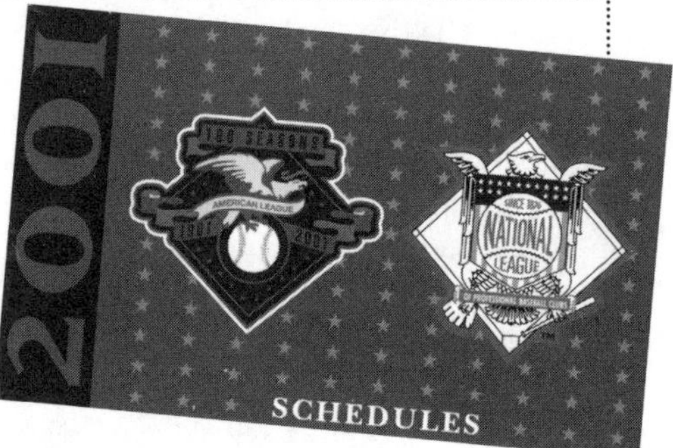

MARTIAL ARTIST
It's a good thing Randy Myers is versed in the martial arts. During a 1995 game at Chicago's Wrigley Field, the left-handed relief pitcher was attacked on the mound by a 27-year-old fan. The two rolled on the ground before security separated them. The fan was fined, ordered to perform community service, and banned from Wrigley for a year. No soup for him!

PETTING ZOO
Chicago White Sox fans can bring their pets to the ballpark, which includes a kennel.

FAN TARGETS
Chili Davis, Tony Phillips, and Albert Belle were among the players who had physical confrontations with fans in the 1990s. Davis and Phillips received $5,000 fines from the American League, while Belle was penalized too many times to list here.

FAN FRIENDLY
To keep fans happy, many clubs have added extras to their ballparks. Detroit's Comerica Park has a carousel, Ferris wheel, and tavern with a 70-foot bar, while Chase Field in Phoenix has a pool and hot tub that occupy 385 square feet of beyond-the-fence ballpark real estate. The Toronto Blue Jays run a lottery on weekends and both San Francisco and San Diego provide Internet access.

NICKEL A HEAD
Bob Feller: "I had it in my contract that I'd get a nickel a head for every fan over 500,000 we drew in Cleveland during the year. Made me want to go out and drag people off the street into the ballpark."

SILENT NIGHT

Fans didn't cheer at the Charleston Riverdogs game on July 14, 2003. They didn't even talk. Broadcaster Dan Lehv worked from an outside-the-park lift hovering above the center-field fence. The "Silent Night" promotion was the brainchild of team president Mike Veeck, son of Hall of Fame owner and innovator Bill Veeck.

CUSTODY OF BALL?

The two fans who claimed ownership of Barry Bonds's record 73rd home-run ball were ordered by a judge to sell it and split the profits. Alex Popov gloved it for an instant, then lost it to Patrick Hayashi in a struggle.

KNOTHOLE GANG REDUX

Fans can see three innings of any Giants game free via a viewing area behind the right-field wall. The gimmick was created by team owner Peter Magowan, who remembered a Norman Rockwell painting of kids watching a game through a knothole in a fence.

HUNGRY FANS

The average Veterans Stadium crowd consumed 9,700 hot dogs, 10,000 sodas, 9,000 beers, 2,300 pretzels, and 1,000 orders of French fries. During the life of the ballpark (1971–2003), the team averaged 24,498 fans per game and topped 50 thousand 99 times.

THE POWER OF PAFKO

Because Andy Pafko was card number one in the 1952 Topps set, it's hard to find the card in mint condition today. As a

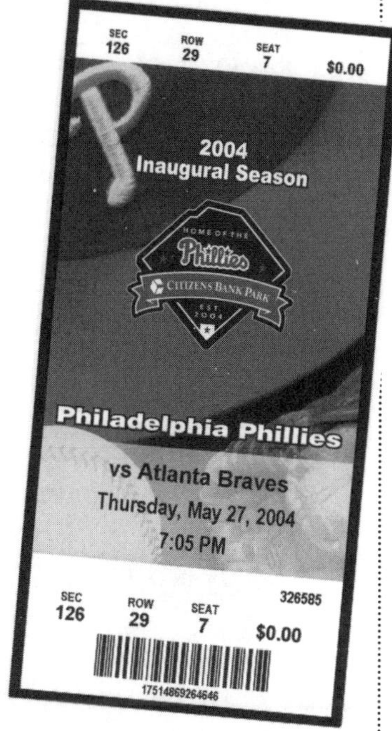

The Philadelphia Phillies pleased their fans in 2004 by opening two new ballparks—one in Clearwater, Florida, and another in the City of Brotherly Love. Philadelphia Phillies

result, a mint version sold at auction in 2000 for $83,870, more than Pafko earned in any single season. Pafko's 1954 card, No. 79 in the series, is worth only 25 cents.

SY OF RELIEF

Working at home, Sy Berger wrote the backs of the 307-card set that Topps issued in 1952. He had to double-check statistics because numerous sources were in disagreement.

WHO KNEW?

Topps executive Sy Berger once dumped thousands of unsold 1952 Mickey Mantle cards into the Atlantic Ocean. Years later, a 1952 Topps Mickey Mantle card in mint condition sold for $121,000.

The Society for American Baseball Research (SABR) consists of nearly 7,000 writers, researchers, educators, and rabid fans. The group produces publications, holds annual and regional conventions, and has become so influential that it has persuaded baseball authorities to change numerous long-standing records. Society for American Baseball Research

TOPPS FEES RISE

Players once received $5 for signing and $250 when their Topps card was issued. The compensation later doubled to $500.

NOT IN THE CARDS

Notable Topps error cards:

- 1957 Hank Aaron—reversed negative
- 1959 and 1964 Lew Burdette—show righty as lefty pitcher
- 1969 Aurelio Rodriguez—actually Angels batboy
- 1974 Padres—15 cards say "Washington, Nat'l League"
- 1985 Gary Pettis—picture is of his teenage brother
- 1988 Al Leiter—player pictured is Steve George

JORDAN CARDS JUNKED

Fleer destroyed the 90,000 Michael Jordan cards it made in 1994 because it didn't like the way his picture came out. Jordan took a hiatus from basketball to spend the summer with the Double A Birmingham Barons in the Chicago White Sox system.

The Grandstand Theater at the National Baseball Hall of Fame and Museum.
Milo Stewart Jr./National Baseball Hall of Fame Library, Cooperstown, New York

Because surviving Jordan cards are scarce, their value has shot past $1,200.

BIG BAD BALL

Harry Caray's Restaurant, a Chicago institution, bought the Steve Bartman ball at auction for $113,824 and then blew it up as a publicity stunt. It happened in February 2004.

FANS VERSUS PLAYERS

Are baseball fans becoming more brazen? Or just more boozed? Consider these incidents:

- 2002—Two fans (father and son) jump Kansas City Royals first-base coach Tom Gamboa during a game at U.S. Cellular Field, Chicago
- 2000—A fan at Wrigley Field in Chicago grabs the hat of Dodgers catcher Chad Kreuter, who takes off in pursuit with several teammates, some of whom invade the stands
- 1999—Astros right fielder Bill Spiers suffers a bloody nose, whiplash, and a welt under his left eye after a fan attacks him during a game in Milwaukee
- 1995—Cubs pitcher Randy Myers knocks down a fan who charged the mound

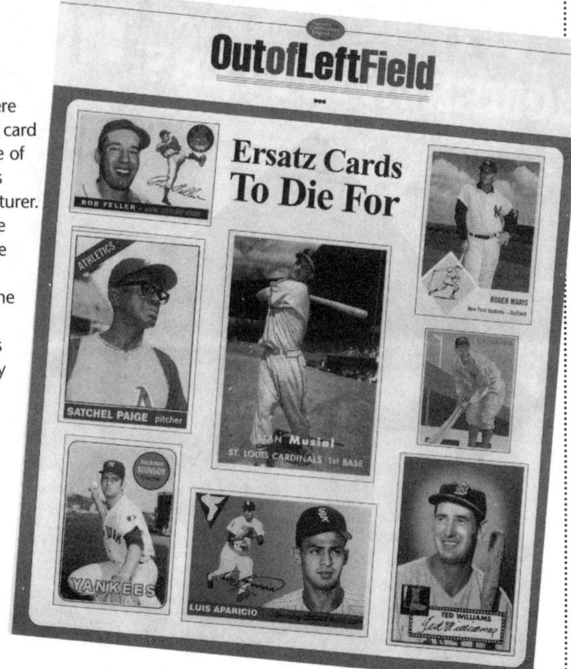

Many top stars were not included in all card sets, often because of exclusive contracts with one manufacturer. Those on this page existed only on the pages of *Sports Collectors Digest,* the Iola, Wisconsin, tabloid that covers the baseball hobby world. *Sports Collectors Digest*

- 1984—Fans join Braves-Padres brawl in Atlanta
- 1972—Baltimore's Don Buford, waiting in the Comiskey Park on-deck circle, KO's a drunken fan who charged him

THE SINGING USHER

Ed Hoffman, known as "the Singing Usher" at Anaheim's Edison Field, is the father of All-Star Padres closer Trevor Hoffman and former Dodgers manager Glenn Hoffman.

FIVE FAMOUS FANS

If fans had a Hall of Fame (or perhaps a Hall of Shame), the five charter members could be:

- Hilda Chester—Rang two cowbells from seat in Ebbets Field bleachers
- Mary Ott—Umpire Bill Klem threatened to eject "the Horse Lady of St. Louis"
- Gus Miller—Newsstand owner and usher was unabashed cheerleader for Pirates

- Patsy O'Toole—"All-American earache" cheered Depression-era Tigers
- Lollie Hopkins—Prewar Boston fan used megaphone to voice her opinions

THE KING OF PITCHERS

Softball barnstormer Eddie Feignor entertained fans of three generations—pitching well past the age of 80. The star performer of a four-man team called The King and His Court, Feignor threw 930 no-hitters during his 60-year career. His stunts included pitching blindfolded and throwing from second base.

FLORIDA FROLICS

The Three-Quarter Century Club, a softball league with a minimum age of 75, was founded in St. Petersburg, Florida, in 1930 by retired actress Evelyn Barton Rittenhouse. Two teams, the Kids and the Kubs, play three times a week between November and April. The Kids wear blue caps and the Kubs wear red caps. Otherwise, players from both teams wear white shirts, sweaters, long-duck trousers, bow ties, and sneakers. One player lasted until age 102, when the Civil War bullet lodged in his bicep started to bother him.

HEFTY TAG

A rare 1909 Honus Wagner card sold for $1.265 million in 2000.

TAKING FENWAY HOME

Fans bought pieces of the 2004 Boston Red Sox world championship. With Fenway Park scheduled for resodding, the team sold off 9-by-18-inch sections of sod for $150 apiece.

HOME SWEET HOME

Randy Johnson, who threw a perfect game for the 2004 Diamondbacks, can't break those Arizona ties. His Yankees contract guarantees him six premium seats at D'back games for the first five years after his retirement as an active player.

Relaxed Fans?

"For the parents of a Little Leaguer, a baseball game is simply a nervous breakdown divided into nine innings."

—Earl Wilson

BLANKET STATEMENT

Blankets given to fans by the Los Angeles Dodgers in 2005 contained incorrect lists of championship Dodgers clubs. According to the blankets, the team won World Series in 1962 and 1966. Not true. The 1962 Dodgers lost a pennant playoff to San Francisco, while the 1966 club suffered a surprising Series sweep by the Baltimore Orioles.

FINAL REST

Babe Ruth and Billy Martin are buried in the same place, Gate of Heaven Cemetery in Hawthorne, New York, 25 miles north of Yankee Stadium.

ROLE REVERSAL

When John Lennon met Jack Klugman (also known as the sloppy sportswriter Oscar Madison) on the set of TV's *The Odd Couple,* the former Beatle asked for *his* autograph.

HALL OF ICHIRO

Ichiro Suzuki's dad displays his son's memorabilia in a four-story brick building that costs Japanese fans $8 to enter.

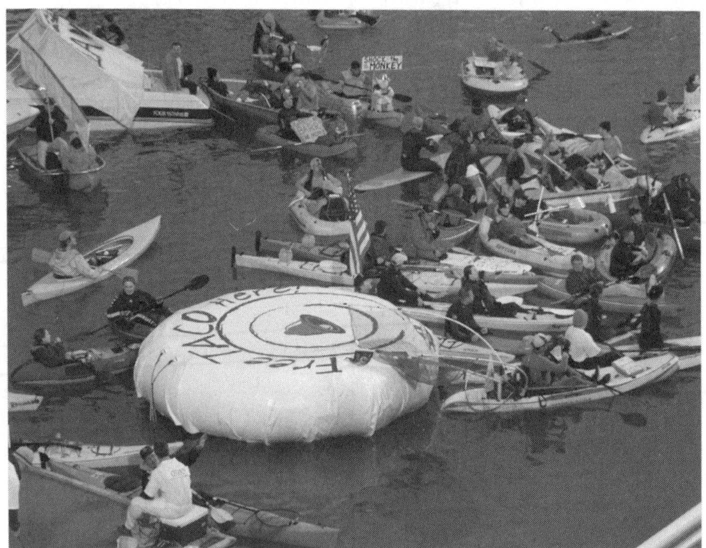

Vessels of every size and description patrol the waters of San Francisco Bay in search of souvenir baseballs hit over the fence by Barry Bonds. His primary splashdown site took on the name "McCovey Cove" after a former feared left-handed Giant, Willie McCovey.

Bill Menzel

WE *KNEW* HE COULD CATCH

Baseball fan Jeffrey Maier, forever remembered for turning a Derek Jeter fly ball into a home run in the 1996 ALCS opener, went on to break the Wesleyan University record for career hits.

MUSTARD TOO?

After a food fight broke out in the stands during their weekly $1 weenie promotion, the Minnesota Twins restricted customers to five hot dogs.

SPEECHLESS IN SEATTLE?

Former Microsoft employee Anthony Ercolano once sued the Seattle Mariners for threatening to confiscate his season tickets. The M's had warned him to tone down the frequency and volume of his heckling or forfeit his two $32,000 Diamond Club seats.

WELLS AND THE BABE

Pitcher David Wells, an unabashed fan of Babe Ruth, has a million-dollar memorabilia collection in the basement of his Clearwater, Florida, home. The collection includes a game-worn Ruth cap the pitcher purchased for $35,000 and wore for an inning in one of his starts.

ULTIMATE OLD TIMER

Negro Leagues legend Buck O'Neil batted twice in a 2006 Northern League game at age 94! Activated for the game by the Kansas City T-Bones, O'Neil walked both times. He passed away several months later.

Tube Steaks Best

"A hot dog at the ballpark is better than a steak at the Ritz."
—Humphrey Bogart

Ed and Allison Lucas formed their own double-play tandem on March 10, 2006, when they became the first couple to be married at home plate in Yankee Stadium. Although he lost his sight while playing baseball at age 12, Ed became a college graduate, grandfather, sportswriter, and broadcaster with many close friends in major league clubhouses and press boxes.

CHAPTER 12
EXPANSION AND BEYOND

BROOKS ROBINSON REMEMBERS...

Every time you go through expansion, you're going to get weaker pitching, with Triple A pitchers in the major leagues. The funny thing is, I had more trouble hitting against the first two expansion teams—Washington and Los Angeles—than any other staffs. I thought I would hit better against those guys, but it never worked out that way.

The overall pitching in baseball became weaker with the first expansion and never really recovered. Even when there were signs of recovery—like Bob Gibson's great ERA in 1968—baseball officials reacted by lowering the mound. They wanted to give the hitters a better chance.

Adding the wild-card, another product of expansion, gave more teams a better chance, and kept interest alive in more cities late in the season. I think it took a while for the wild-card to become a positive factor, but it's been a big plus for baseball. The game drew 75 million fans in 2006, a record, and the minors drew another 41 million, a record for them. Fans follow the wild-card standings every day in the paper and it creates more interest.

Interleague play also energizes the fans. Some rivalries, like Yankees-Mets or White Sox–Cubs, are better than others, but it's been a good way to stimulate interest in the game. It's like the designated hitter. People who come to the ballpark after watching football and basketball want to see things happen. Thanks to the DH, there are more hits, more home runs, more RBIs, and more runs scored. It may be harder for hitters to learn all the pitchers with interleague play, but good scouting helps. There are guys on every team who have seen those pitchers before. And hitters report back to the dugout during the game and warn their teammates how hard a guy throws or how his curveball breaks.

There were many different commissioners during the expansion era, but I had no favorites. As players, we always felt the owners hired the commissioners so what chance did we have? I'm sure they tried to be fair and impartial, but they knew what they had to do to keep the game the way it was. I considered Bowie Kuhn, Fay Vincent, and Bud Selig my friends. I think they all did what they thought was right.

I think the owners and players now see eye-to-eye more than they ever have. Looking back at the eight work stoppages, it upsets me now because the players have gotten just about everything they could get. I just don't think the owners were that smart in my day. Their philosophy was that the reserve clause had been there for 100 years and that's the way it was going to be. But the players felt no one should have a lifetime contract. They wanted the right to say what they do or where they go. Someone stuck behind Johnny Bench or Mike Schmidt should have an out.

Marvin Miller found a loophole in the Basic Agreement and was able to get it upheld by an arbiter, Peter Seitz. The owners fired him and went to court but lost there, too. Then they reached an agreement with the union that players needed six years of service time in the major leagues before they became eligible for free agency. If all players had become free agents at once, or every other year, it would have been a lot more chaotic.

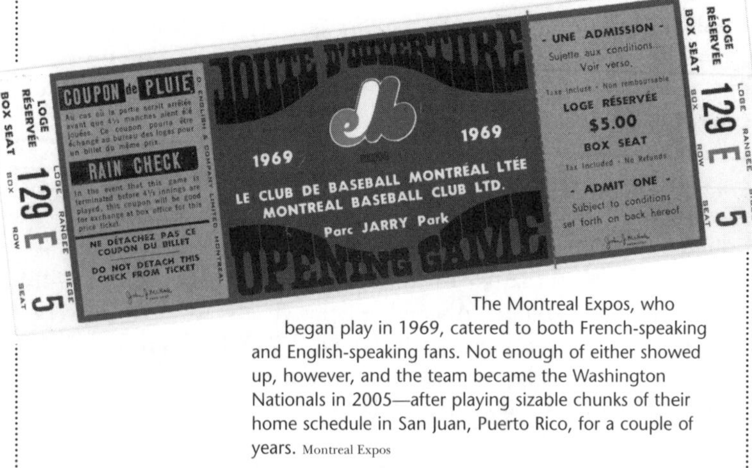

The Montreal Expos, who began play in 1969, catered to both French-speaking and English-speaking fans. Not enough of either showed up, however, and the team became the Washington Nationals in 2005—after playing sizable chunks of their home schedule in San Juan, Puerto Rico, for a couple of years. Montreal Expos

CONTINENTAL QUINTET
Talk of a third major league, the Continental League, forced reluctant major league owners to expand in 1961–62. All five original cities of Branch Rickey's proposed league, announced in 1959, eventually received franchises: Denver, Houston, Minneapolis–St. Paul, New York, and Toronto. Rickey, a former Brooklyn GM, had targeted New York as his key objective.

GENE'S PICK
At the "Welcome Home" banquet given for the original 1961 L.A. Angels, owner Gene Autry told the crowd that Casey Stengel was his first choice as manager. When Casey rejected the offer, Autry said, he settled for Bill Wrigley. The only problem was that the manager's real name was Bill *Rigney*.

STAYING POWER
Bill Rigney lasted longer than any expansion manager: nine

EXPANSION PICKS

Year	Team	First Draft Choice
1960	Los Angeles Angels	Fred Newman, P, Boston
	Washington Senators	Dick Donovan, P, Chicago
1961	Houston Colts	Joey Amalfitano, 2B, San Francisco
	New York Mets	Bob Miller, P, St. Louis
1968	Kansas City Royals	Roger Nelson, P, Baltimore
	Seattle Pilots	Don Mincher, 1B, California
	Montreal Expos	Manny Mota, OF, Pittsburgh
	San Diego Padres	Ollie Brown, OF, San Francisco
1976	Seattle Mariners	Ruppert Jones, OF, Kansas City
	Toronto Blue Jays	Bob Bailor, SS-OF, Baltimore
1992	Colorado Rockies	David Nied, P, Atlanta
	Florida Marlins	Nigel Wilson, OF, Toronto
1997	Arizona Diamondbacks	Brian Anderson, P, Cleveland
	Tampa Bay Devil Rays	Tony Saunders, P, Florida

EXPANSION MARKS

Year	Team	Won	Lost	Pct.	Pos.#	Attend.
1961	Los Angeles Angels*	70	91	.435	8	603,510
1961	Washington Senators†	61	100	.370	9	597,287
1962	Houston Colts‡	64	96	.400	8	924,456
1962	New York Mets	40	120	.250	10	922,530
1969	Kansas City Royals	69	93	.426	4W	902,414
1969	Seattle Pilots§	64	98	.395	6W	677,944
1969	Montreal Expos	52	110	.321	6E	1,212,608
1969	San Diego Padres	52	110	.321	6W	512,970
1977	Seattle Mariners	64	98	.395	6W	1,338,511
1977	Toronto Blue Jays	54	107	.335	7E	1,701,052
1993	Colorado Rockies	67	95	.414	6W	4,483,350
1993	Florida Marlins	64	98	.395	6E	3,064,847
1998	Tampa Bay Devil Rays	63	99	.389	5E	2,261,158
1998	Arizona Diamondbacks	65	97	.401	5W	3,600,412

* Became California Angels in 1966 and Anaheim Angels in 1997.

†Became Texas Rangers in 1972 .

‡ Became Houston Astros in 1965.

§ Became Milwaukee Brewers in 1970.

Final place in league standings.

years with the original Los Angeles Angels (1961–69).

FROSTY CASEY

Casey Stengel, who called the Mets' home field "the Polar Grounds," might have been thinking about the team's ice-cold play when he said it.

UP IN FLAMES

Sherman "Roadblock" Jones lived down to his middle name. Scheduled to start the second game in Mets history, he decided to light a cigarette as the team plane headed to St. Louis. The matchbook caught fire, burning the pitcher's face, and canceling his start. Too bad "Roadblock" was a smoker:

he lost his first four decisions and, on May 9, his spot on the 1962 big-league roster.

GROW A BEARD
Evans Kileen lost his shot at a pitching job with the 1962 Mets after he cut his thumb shaving. The pitcher couldn't throw a decent curveball after the accident.

DOUBLE AARON
Brothers Hank and Tommie Aaron homered in the same inning for the Milwaukee Braves on July 12, 1962.

WITTY WAGNER
Leon Wagner, who hit 211 home runs, also owned a clothing store. Its slogan was, "Buy your rags from Daddy Wags."

THREE ALOUS
The three Alou brothers produced successive groundball outs in the bottom of the eighth inning of a 13–4 San Francisco victory over the New York Mets on September 22, 1963. In the same game, Matty Alou, Jesús Alou, and Felipe Alou also became the lone fraternal trio to appear in the same outfield at the same time.

MONSTER VERSUS MANTLE
Dick "the Monster" Radatz fanned Mickey Mantle 12 times in 16 at-bats. The imposing Red Sox reliever won or saved 118 of Boston's 224 victories during his first three years with the team (1962–64).

HANK'S STRANGEST HOMER
Three years after pitching a perfect game on Father's Day 1964, future Hall of Famer Jim Bunning yielded the only inside-the-park home run ever hit by Hank Aaron.

HITLESS WONDER
Jim Maloney pitched a pair of extra-inning no-hitters for the 1965 Reds, beating the Cubs 1–0 in 10 innings before losing to the Mets by the same score in 11 innings. Solo homers decided both games.

AVOIDING THE MINORS
Since the 1965 advent of the amateur draft, the only draftees who never played in the minors were Dave Winfield and Bob Horner. Outfielder Rick Monday was the top pick in the first draft in 1965.

MAYBE TRY PRAYER?
Don Drysdale was forced to pitch the 1965 World Series

opener because Sandy Koufax was observing the Jewish holiday of Yom Kippur. Drysdale was on the wrong end of an 8–2 score against Minnesota when Dodgers manager Walter Alston trudged to the mound. Before he could say anything, Drysdale said, "I bet you wish I were Jewish, too."

Ronnie Joyner
Roger Maris
THE NEW YORK YANKEES RETIRED ROGER'S NUMBER "9" IN 1984!
MUCH OLBLIGED!
ROGER
ROGER EUGENE MARIS SHOWED A FLAIR FOR DRAMA WHEN HE WAITED UNTIL THE LAST GAME OF THE 1961 CAMPAIGN TO POLE HIS RECORD SETTING 61ST LONG BALL OF THE SEASON! CAPTURING BASEBALL'S MOST COVETED SINGLE SEASON RECORD INSTANTLY ENSURED THAT ROGER'S NAME WOULD FOREVER BE MENTIONED ALONGSIDE OTHER GREATS OF THE GAME, BUT ROGER'S LEGACY WENT MUCH DEEPER THAN THE HOMER RECORD! ROGER, BORN ON SEPTEMBER 10, 1934, IN HIBBING, MINNESOTA, MOVED WITH HIS FAMILY TO FARGO, NORTH DAKOTA, AS A BOY, AND IT WAS THERE THAT HE GREW INTO A GREAT ALL-AROUND ATHLETE! A STANDOUT FOOTBALL PLAYER WHO ONCE SET A NATIONAL HIGH SCHOOL RECORD BY SCORING FOUR TOUCHDOWNS IN ONE GAME ON KICKOFF RETURNS, ROGER GAVE UP A SCHOLARSHIP TO PLAY FOOTBALL AT THE UNIVERSITY OF OKLAHOMA TO PURSUE A CAREER IN BASEBALL! ROGER QUICKLY ASCENDED THE MINOR LEAGUE LADDER THANKS IN PART TO HIS MANAGER AT KEOKUK, FORMER BIG LEAGUER JO-JO WHITE, WHO TAUGHT HIM TO PULL THE BALL -- SOMETHING THAT WOULD SERVE HIM WELL IN LATER YEARS AS A LEFT-HANDED POWER HITTER AT YANKEE STADIUM!
JOYNER
BLEACHER BUMS BEWARE!
ROGER SPENT HIS EARLY YEARS WITH THE INDIANS AND ATHLETICS, BUT IT WAS WITH THE PINSTRIPERS THAT HE WOULD ESTABLISH HIMSELF AS ONE OF THE MOST DOMINANT PLAYERS OF THE FIRST HALF OF THE 1960s! AN ALL-STAR WHO WON 2 MVP AWARDS, TWO RBI TITLES, ONE HOME RUN CROWN, AND A GOLD GLOVE, ROGER MARIS HELPED THE YANKEES KICK START A NEW DYNASTY THAT WON FIVE CONSECUTIVE A.L. PENNANTS FROM 1960-64! ROGER ENDED HIS CAREER IN ST. LOUIS WHERE HE HELPED THE CARDS TO PENNANTS IN 1967 AND '68!
ROGER HIT 275 HOME RUNS IN HIS CAREER, PLUS AN ADDITIONAL SIX IN WORLD SERIES PLAY! HIS FIRST CAREER CIRCUIT BLAST WAS A BIG ONE -- A GAME-WINNING GRAND SLAM IN THE 11TH INNING TO LEAD THE INDIANS TO VICTORY ON APRIL 18, 1957!
GET USED TO IT, FELLAS, THERE'S MORE TO COME!

FREAK INJURIES

- Curt Simmons sliced off a toe while mowing his lawn.

- Tony Gwynn closed the door of his Porsche on his middle finger.
- Oddibe McDowell cut his hand buttering a dinner roll.
- Wade Boggs suffered bruised ribs when he fell while donning cowboy boots.
- Jeff Juden lost playing time after a new tattoo became infected.

Marvin's Detractors
Marvin Miller's election as executive director of the Major League Baseball Players Association in 1966 was far from unanimous. Owners campaigned against him, warning players that unionizing would ruin baseball, and convinced four Arizona-based spring-training teams—the Cubs, Giants, Indians, and Angels—to vote against him. But Miller prevailed, winning the support of the 16 teams that trained in Florida and finishing with 489 votes in favor and 136 against.

Year of Yaz
Red Sox outfielder Carl Yastrzemski had a remarkable year in 1967. Leading his club to a photo-finish pennant against 100-to-1 odds, Yaz won the Triple Crown with a .326 batting average, 44 home runs, and 121 runs batted in. He led in hits, runs, total bases, and slugging average. Down the stretch, he poked 10 hits in his last 13 at-bats, including four in the pennant-clinching finale against Minnesota and three the previous day.

Last Brownie
Don Larsen, better known for pitching the only perfect game in World Series history (for the Yankees against the Dodgers in 1956), was also the last active player who performed for the St. Louis Browns. Larsen's career began with the Browns in 1953, their last year, and ended with the Cubs in 1967.

King and His Court
Softball sensation Eddie Feignor, who toured with his four-man team well into his eighties, struck out six major league stars during a two-inning exhibition stint in 1967: Willie Mays, Willie McCovey, Harmon Killebrew, Brooks Robinson, Roberto Clemente, and Maury Wills.

Double Trouble
Rival pitchers have twice hurled back-to-back no-hitters in the

same series. It happened first on September 17, 1968, when Gaylord Perry of the San Francisco Giants no-hit the St. Louis Cardinals the day before Ray Washburn of the Cards no-hit the Giants. On April 30, 1969, Jim Maloney of the Cincinnati Reds pitched a hitless game against the Houston Astros one day before Houston's Don Wilson no-hit the Reds.

HUNTER'S HITS

Catfish Hunter had three hits and three RBIs while pitching a 4–0 perfect game against Minnesota for Oakland in 1968. A's owner Charlie Finley once gave him a $5,000 bonus for his hitting.

CLASSICAL CLOSER

During his heyday as closer for the St. Louis Cardinals, Al Hrabosky parlayed a scowl and a Fu Manchu mustache into a reputation as "the Mad Hungarian"—and entered games to the strains of Franz Liszt's *Hungarian Rhapsody No. 2.*

DIAMOND DISPUTES

The baseball season has been interrupted eight times by labor-management problems:

- 1972—Players strike for 13 days (nine in regular season)
- 1976—Owners lock players out of spring training (17 days)
- 1980—Players strike for one week during spring training

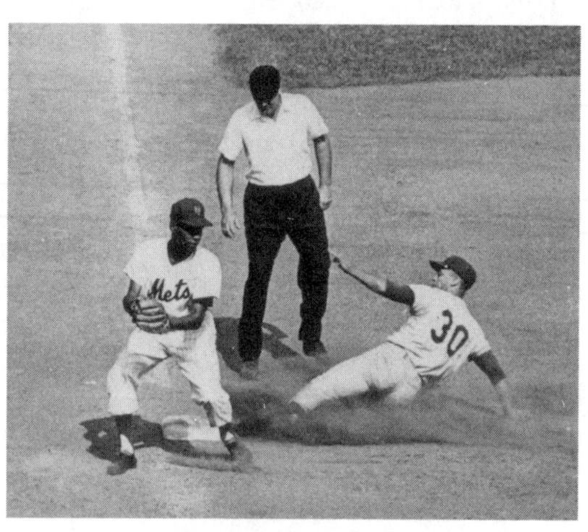

Maury Wills slides into third ahead of the throw. The wily Wills, more than anyone else, reintroduced the stolen base as a key offensive weapon.
Reprinted with permission, National Baseball Hall of Fame Library, Cooperstown, New York

Pete Rose posted 10 200-hit seasons, played five different positions in the All-Star Game, tied a National League mark with a 44-game hitting streak, and broke Ty Cobb's record for career hits. But his path to Cooperstown was blocked when Hall of Fame directors ruled suspended players ineligible. Rose, who would have been a certain first-time selection in 1992, was banned for life in 1989 for violating Major League Rule 21. The star player, who spent his first 16 years with Cincinnati and later managed the club, had been under investigation for allegedly betting on baseball games. Less than a year after his suspension, he spent five months in jail for income-tax evasion. Reprinted with permission, National Baseball Hall of Fame Library, Cooperstown, New York

- 1981—Players strike for 50 days during season
- 1985—Players strike for two days during season
- 1990—Owners lock players out of spring camps (32 days)
- 1994—Player strike ends season August 12 (232 days)
- 1995—Continuing strike shortens season to 144 games

Out of Order

Retrosheet.org reveals that Dwight Evans batted out of order *in his first at-bat.* It happened on September 16, 1972, when the Boston Red Sox were hosting the Cleveland Indians. With the Sox up by 9–0 in the sixth, Evans and Cecil Cooper entered the game as pinch runners and stayed in the game but batted in the wrong sequence in the eighth. No protest was made, and the Sox went on to win, 10–0.

Designated Hebrew

When sportswriter Dick Schaap asked Ron Blomberg what it was like to be the first DH, the slugger said, "Whaddya mean? Designated Hebrew?" The first Jewish star to play for the Yankees, Blomberg became the first designated *hitter* on April 6, 1973—walking with the bases loaded in his first at-bat. The bat he carried to the plate was quickly carted off to Cooperstown, where it became the only bat displayed because of a walk.

SURPRISE SLUGGER

Mark Whiten of the Cardinals not only hit four homers in a game against the Reds on September 7, 1993, but also tied Jim Bottomley's 1924 single-game record of 12 runs batted in.

NASTY NOLAN

Nolan Ryan whiffed 19 men in a game three times in the same season, with the 1974 Angels.

NO PITCH COUNT?

Nolan Ryan once threw 259 pitches in a game. The 1974 contest went 12 innings.

Though American League pitchers didn't bat after the advent of the DH rule in 1973, Vida Blue won a 1971 MVP award that made him the last AL MVP who was also a switch-hitter. Oakland Athletics

WALK MEISTER

How much better would Nolan Ryan's records be if he had better control? He led his league in bases on balls eight times, three more than any other pitcher.

WHIFF WHIZ

Nolan Ryan won a record 16 strikeout crowns, one more than Walter Johnson. Randy Johnson (13) and Roger Clemens (12) are the only other pitchers with at least a dozen.

MIGHTY MIKE

Mike Marshall pitched for nine teams in 14 seasons but proved himself the most durable reliever in baseball history. Working for the 1974 Los Angeles Dodgers, the right-hander went 15–12 with 21 saves and a 2.42 earned-run average but worked *208 innings* in *106 games,* both records for relief pitchers. Able to throw four types of screwballs, Marshall threw at least 100 innings four years in a row from 1971 to 1975.

WILHELM ON MARSHALL

After Mike Marshall worked 106 games for the Dodgers in 1974, veteran bullpen star Hoyt

THE '75 ROOKIE RACE

Teammates Fred Lynn and Jim Rice of the AL champion Boston Red Sox staged the closest Rookie of the Year race in 1975. Lynn led the league in runs scored, doubles, and slugging percentage; was second in batting; and third in runs batted in. But Rice, his fellow outfielder, almost matched him. Their statistics:

	G	AB	R	H	HR	RBI	SB	BA
Lynn	145	528	103	175	21	105	10	.331
Rice	144	564	92	174	22	102	10	.309

Wilhelm said, "If somebody had come along 15 years ago and told me a guy would someday work 100 games while throwing a fair amount of fastballs, I'd have said it was a ridiculous statement. In fact, I'd have said it was about as ridiculous as the breaking of Babe Ruth's lifetime home-run record!"

SALARY SANITY

At the 1976 advent of free agency, the average salary was $50,000 and the top salary was $500,000.

LONG-LIVED TIGERS

Detroit's double-play tandem of Lou Whitaker and Alan Trammell was together 18 years, longer than any other double-play combination. They played second and short, respectively, from 1977 to 1994, a total of 4,459 games.

THANKS, DOC

Dr. Sidney Gaynor was team physician for the Yankees before, during, and after the time Casey Stengel's clubs won 10 pennants in 12 years. Gaynor's tenure lasted from 1948 to 1976.

BLEEDING DODGER BLUE

Steve Garvey and Don Sutton, stars on the 1978 Dodgers team that won the NL pennant, got into a pushing-and-shoving match at Shea Stadium after an argument escalated. Teammates had to pull them apart after the struggling players fell to the floor.

Ron Blomberg changed baseball history on April 6, 1973, when he became the first designated hitter. Batting sixth for the New York Yankees on Opening Day in Fenway Park, he walked with the bases loaded in the top of the first inning, providing the Hall of Fame with the only bat ever displayed as the result of a walk. The first prominent Jewish Yankee later chronicled his career in a 2006 book called *Designated Hebrew: The Ron Blomberg Story.* Sheldon Stone collection

HOW SALARIES ROSE

Free agency escalated salaries immediately. The 1976 average salary was $51,000, but that figure jumped to $77,000 in 1977 and $100,000 in 1978.

EQUAL OPPORTUNITY PITCHER

Phil Niekro's 21–20 record in 1979 gave him the National League lead in both wins and losses—the only time that happened in the 20th century.

THE NIEKROS

Phil and Joe Niekro had more wins (579), more losses (478), and more combined years in the majors (46) than any other brothers who pitched in the majors.

NO KNUCKLER FOR KNUCKSIE

Knuckleballer Phil Niekro threw only one of his trademark pitches—striking out Jeff Burroughs for the last out—during his 300th win on October 6, 1985. He said later he wanted to see if he could win a game without throwing a knuckler.

FRATERNAL WINNERS

The Niekros (Phil and Joe) and the Perrys (Gaylord and Jim) were the only brother tandems to win 20 games each in the same season.

PITCHER BATS EIGHTH

Steve Carlton once batted eighth, ahead of shortstop Bud Harrelson, for the 1979 Phillies.

BUT HE'S A PITCHER!

Mercurial Mike Marshall, a Dodgers reliever who doubled as a kinesiology professor at Michigan State, was once arrested *for his hitting*. He had

refused a police order to stop showing college players how to hit. The cops thought the out-of-the-park balls hit by Marshall might injure students or cause property damage.

Ronnie Joyner
KING HENRY
AARON
HANK HIT THE FIRST OF HIS 755 HOME RUNS -- A SOLO SHOT -- OFF OF CARDINALS PITCHER VIC RASCHI ON APRIL 23, 1954 AT OLD SPORTSMAN'S PARK IN ST. LOUIS!
I THINK THIS FELLA'S GOIN' PLACES!
HENRY LOUIS "HANK" AARON WAS BORN ON FEBRUARY 5, 1934 IN MOBILE, ALABAMA! HANK WAS PLAYING SEMI-PRO BASEBALL AT THE AGE OF 15 BEFORE PLAYING TWO YEARS WITH THE INDIANAPOLIS CLOWNS OF THE NEGRO LEAGUES! IN 1952 THE MILWAUKEE BRAVES PAID THE CLOWNS A MERE $7,500 TO ACQUIRE HANK -- THE MAN WHO WOULD ONE DAY OWN THE ALL-TIME BIG LEAGUE HOME RUN RECORD!
JOYNER
HANK WORE NUMBER 5 IN HIS FIRST SEASON BEFORE SWITCHING TO HIS FAMOUS NUMBER 44! THAT NUMBER TURNED OUT TO BE A GOOD ONE FOR HANK AS HE LED THE LEAGUE IN HOME RUNS 4 TIMES -- WITH 44 HOMERS IN THREE OF THOSE YEARS! HANK WAS A CLUTCH PLAYER IN POST-SEASON PLAY! HE HIT A COMBINED .364 WITH 20 HITS AND 3 LONG BALLS IN THE '57 AND '58 WORLD SERIES! HE BATTED .357 WITH 3 ROUND-TRIPPERS IN THE 3-GAME 1969 LCS! HAMMERIN' HANK WAS REWARDED FOR HIS UNMATCHED PLAY BY BEING ELECTED TO EVERY ALL-STAR GAME DURING HIS ENTIRE CAREER SPANNING 1954-1976!
IT'S ALL YOURS, KID!
715
HANK BECAME "KING HENRY" WHEN HE HIT HOME RUN NUMBER 715 OFF OF AL DOWNING ON APRIL 8, 1974! THAT BLAST CROWNED HIM THE NEW CAREER HOME RUN KING DE-THRONING THE LEGENDARY BABE RUTH!

SWEET STROKE

George Brett is the only man who won batting crowns in three different decades. In 1980, his best season, he hit .390 while collecting 118 RBIs in 117 games.

Though saddled by bad ballclubs most of his career, knuckleballer Phil Niekro won 318 games and combined with Joe Niekro to win more games than any other brother combination.
The Topps Company

GWYNN WAS GREAT
In his 20-year career with the San Diego Padres, perennial All-Star Tony Gwynn hit .338, won eight NL batting crowns, collected 3,141 hits, and had more consecutive .300 seasons (19) than anyone in baseball history. The only National Leaguer with as many batting crowns was Honus Wagner.

POWER PLANT
Mike Schmidt won eight home-run crowns and led the NL in slugging five times and RBIs four times while winning 11 Gold Gloves at third base. The three-time MVP, who spent his entire career with the Philadelphia Phillies, was elected to the Hall of Fame in 1995.

VERSATILITY HELPS
Pete Rose is the only player to start at least 500 games at five different positions. Any challenger to his career hits record would have to average 212.8 hits per season for 20 years.

BASE PATH BANDITS
Montreal speed merchants Ron LeFlore and Rodney Scott stole 160 bases, a two-man record, for the 1980 Expos. Also that season, LeFlore, an ex-con, became the first man to lead both leagues in steals.

THE FOUR KINGS
Four players shared the AL home-run crown during the strike-shortened 1981 season: Tony Armas Sr., Dwight Evans, Bobby Grich, and Eddie Murray.

MEXICAN MARVEL
Left-handed screwball specialist Fernando Valenzuela, elevated from the Mexican League to the Dodgers in 1981, became

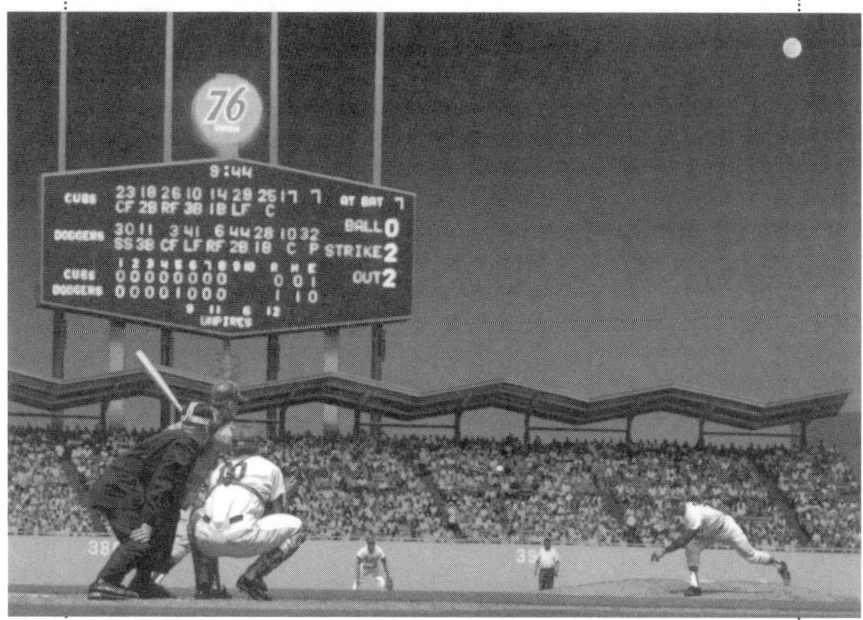

Before arthritis forced him to retire in 1966, Sandy Koufax pitched four no-hitters, including this perfect game against the Cubs on September 9, 1965. Copyright 1996 by Bill Purdom. Reprinted with permission, Bill Goff, Inc./GoodSportsArt.com.

the only Cy Young Award winner to win a Rookie of the Year Award in the same season. The first NL rookie to start the All-Star Game, he hurled eight shutouts while winning 16 games, three of them in postseason play.

Down to the Wire

From 1978 through 1982, at least one of the divisional races was decided on the last day of the regular season or in a divisional playoff. In 1978 the Yankees beat the Red Sox in a sudden-death playoff for the AL East flag. In 1979 the Pirates needed a win or an Expos loss to clinch the NL East on the final day (they got both). The 1980 NL West race was decided when the Astros rebounded from three straight defeats by the Dodgers to win a one-game playoff. In the East, the Phils avoided a playoff with an 11-inning win over the Expos. The Royals won the second half of the 1981 split season when they won the opener of a makeup doubleheader at Cleveland. In 1982 the Brewers rebounded from three straight losses to beat the Orioles on the last day, finishing first in the AL East by a game. The Braves also kept a one-game margin, winning the NL West when the Dodgers lost to the Giants (the Braves lost to the Padres but still finished first).

Happy He Wasn't

"Baseball owners are the toughest set of ignoramuses anyone could ever come up against. Refreshingly dumb fellows. Greedy, shortsighted, and stupid."

—Commissioner Happy Chandler after owners fired him in 1951

WILD PITCHERS

Three pitchers made six wild pitches in a game, the modern-era mark: J.R. Richard and Phil Niekro, both in 1979, and Bill Gullickson, in 1982.

SLUGGER SANDBERG

Ryne Sandberg's game-tying homers off Bruce Sutter in the ninth and tenth innings on June 23, 1984, made him a strong candidate for both the MVP award and the Hall of Fame. His 5-for-6 night in a 12–11 Cubs win over the Cards included a career-best seven runs batted in. In his career, Sandberg was the only player with a 200-hit season, a 50-steal season, and a 40-homer season.

RYNE FOR RYNE

Ryne Sandberg was named after Yankees reliever Ryne Duren. According to the 1984 National League MVP, "My parents went to a game in Minneapolis and the next day they noticed his name in a newspaper article."

FINE FIRST FRAME

In 1985 Phillies outfielder Von Hayes became the first man to hit two home runs in the first inning. The Phils beat the Mets, 26–7.

FAT TUB OF GOO?

Dubbed a "fat tub of goo" by David Letterman on late-night TV in 1985, Terry Forster retired from baseball as the owner of the highest batting

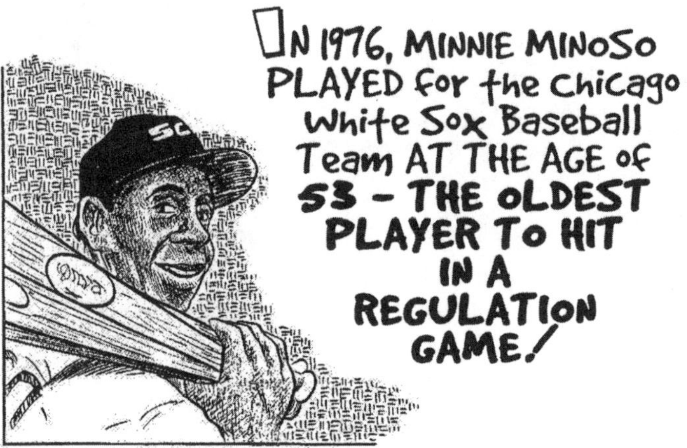

average by a man who appeared in 500-plus games. Forster, a left-handed relief pitcher, hit .397 lifetime, including .526 (10-for-19) in 1972. Held to 78 at-bats by the advent of the designated hitter, plus the fact managers preferred him to pitch rather than pinch hit, Forster appeared in 614 games in 16 seasons.

IN 1976, MINNIE MINOSO PLAYED for the Chicago White Sox Baseball Team AT THE AGE of 53 - THE OLDEST PLAYER TO HIT IN A REGULATION GAME!

DON'T BLAME

Bobby Lowe and Bob Horner, Braves who played in different cities a century apart, are the only men to hit four home runs in a game their team lost. Lowe did it for Boston in 1894, Horner for Atlanta in 1986.

BONDS BATTED FIRST

Future slugger Barry Bonds was Pittsburgh's primary leadoff man for the first four years of his big-league career, 1986–89.

PHIL'S FORMULA

Late-blooming knuckleballer Phil Niekro won a record 121 games after his 40th birthday—after winning only 31 times before age 30.

CHEAP LABOR

Pete Rose earned 11 cents a day in the machine shop of the

Marion, Illinois, federal prison in 1990. His sentence included five months in the penitentiary for tax evasion, three months in a halfway house, 1,000 hours of community service, and counseling for gambling addiction. He was also fined $50,000.

GRIFFEYS GO DEEP

Ken Griffey Jr. was on deck when his father hit a home run against Angels starter Kirk McCaskill on September 14, 1990. "He got the green light on 3–0 and hit it out," said the younger Griffey. "When he got to home plate, he said, 'That's how you do it, son.'" So he did—making the Griffeys the only father-and-son tandem to produce consecutive home runs.

Down on Owners

"Welcome to the den of village idiots."

—Baltimore owner Edward Bennett Williams to Commissioner Peter Ueberroth in 1984

Native Texan Nolan Ryan, who pitched for the Astros and, late in his career, the Rangers, never seemed to slow down. He kept accumulating strikeouts and no-hit games well into his 40s, finally retiring after a record 27 seasons in the majors. The Topps Company

RAINES REIGNS

Tim Raines and Tim Raines Jr. joined the Griffeys as the only father-and-son tandem to play together, with the Baltimore Orioles in 2001. Unlike the Griffeys, however, the son did not have anything approaching the ability of the father. His tenure in the majors was short-lived.

STEALING PAYS

Otis Nixon stole six bases, tying the major league mark held by

Sinkerballer Orel Hershiser, star right-hander of the Los Angeles Dodgers, completed the 1988 season by throwing a record 59 consecutive scoreless innings, one more than the 1968 record of Don Drysdale. He then went on to win MVP honors in both the National League Championship Series and the World Series. In his last 13 outings, including postseason play, Hershiser went 9–0 with three no-decisions, one save, and a 0.59 ERA. He was a unanimous choice for the NL's Cy Young Award. Los Angeles Dodgers

Eddie Collins, for the Braves against the Expos on June 16, 1991.

HOOPS HEROES

Baseball players who also played pro basketball: Danny Ainge, Frankie Baumholtz, Gene Conley, Chuck Connors, Dave DeBuscherre, Dick Groat, Mark Hendrickson, and Ron Reed.

SOME DAY OF REST

Without ace closer Rob Dibble, who had asked Reds manager Lou Piniella for a day off during the 1991 season, the Reds lost a key game. When Dibble told reporters he was fine, Piniella flew out of his office and into the player's face. Punches followed in front of the pitcher's locker.

YANKEE PANKY

The $5.3 million annual average of Danny Tartabull's free-agent deal with the Yankees in 1992 paid him $392,592 every 12 games—more than Lou Gehrig's total career income of $386,400. In other words, Tartabull made more money in 17 *days* than Gehrig made in 17 *seasons.*

SELIG'S SWITCH

Allan H. "Bud" Selig, owner of the Milwaukee Brewers, became acting commissioner in September 1992, full-time commissioner six years later, and eventually had his tenure extended through 2009—even though he passed the usual retirement age of 70 in 2004. Although he introduced numerous innovations, including interleague play and wild-card winners, Selig's stay was controversial from the start. Judge Kenesaw Mountain Landis had the longest tenure of any baseball commissioner: 23 years.

Ageless Wonder

Nolan Ryan not only won four strikeout crowns after turning 40 but also pitched his seventh no-hitter at age 44 in 1991—18 years after his first one. The oldest man to throw a no-hitter and the only one to pitch no-hitters for three different teams, Ryan was 46 when he recorded his final strikeout.

Ryan's Records

When he retired late in the 1993 campaign, Nolan Ryan held or shared 53 records, including 27 seasons as a major league player, 19 low-hit games, 2,795 walks, and most strikeouts in a season (383) and career (5,714). His six 300-strikeout seasons were also a record, along with his average of K's per nine innings in a season (11.48) and career (9.55). A challenger to Ryan's career strikeout mark would have to average 285.7 whiffs for 20 years to forge a tie.

After 12 years as a starter, Dennis Eckersley moved to the bullpen in 1987 and promptly became baseball's most dominating closer. In 1990 he converted 48 of 50 save opportunities, had a 0.61 ERA, and had more saves than base runners allowed (41 hits and four walks in 73⅓ innings). Two years later he won the Cy Young Award and Most Valuable Player honors after posting the second 50-save campaign in baseball history (Bobby Thigpen of the White Sox had saved 57 games in 1990). Oakland Athletics

The Colorado Rockies produced single-game and single-season attendance records in 1993, their first season, because they played home games in enormous Mile High Stadium. Colorado Rockies

FACT SHEET
THE COLORADO ROCKIES

National League Expansion Team, officially announced June 1991
Manager: Don Baylor

Record-Breaking Facts:

•All time major league single season attendance record: (4,483,350)

•Largest opening day crowd and largest crowd for a single game: 80, 227, April 9, 1993

•Largest attendance for a four-game series: 251,521, July 22–25, 1993

•National League season attendance record: 3,617,863 reached on August 30, 1993

•Fastest team to reach 1, 2, 3 and 4 million attendance levels

•National League batting title Andres Galarraga, with batting average of .370

First Game: April 5, 1993, at Shea Stadium, against the New York Mets

Last Game: October 3, 1993, against the Atlanta Braves in Atlanta

First Home Game: April 9, 1993, against the Montreal Expos
Attendance: 80,227 (a major league record for opening day)
Outcome: 11–4, Rockies
First Hit at Home: A home run, by Eric Young

Season ticket holders came from 33 states, Puerto Rico and Japan

BIRTHDAY BOYS

The MVPs of both major leagues in 1994, Jeff Bagwell (NL) and Frank Thomas (AL), shared the exact same birthday: May 27, 1968.

BAGGING AWARDS

Jeff Bagwell was the only member of the Houston Astros to win Rookie of the Year or MVP honors. He won both, though not in the same season.

LABOR CRISIS

The 232-day player strike that started August 12, 1994, was baseball's eighth work stoppage. The walkout wiped out the World Series, caused $800 million in lost revenue, and angered many fans whose

The crowd may be cold, but the Rockies are hot! In the first game at Denver's Coors Field, on April 26, 1995, Colorado captures a 14-inning, 11–9 victory on a three-run home run by Dante Bichette. The Rox overcame one-run deficits in the ninth, thirteenth, and fourteenth innings as 47,228 freezing fans watched in the thin air of the Mile High City.

allegiance to the game stayed shaky for years. Only an injunction issued by U.S. District Court Judge Sonia Sotomayor convinced owners to let players return under work rules that prevailed prior to the strike. A new agreement was reached 18 months later.

GOOD STICK TOO

Atlanta pitcher Greg Maddux twice enjoyed seasons in which his batting average exceeded his earned-run average. In 1994 he hit .222 while posting a 1.56 ERA. Four years later he hit .240 while pitching to a 2.22 ERA. Mike Hampton of the Astros duplicated the Maddux feat in 1999, when he hit .311 and kept his ERA at 2.90.

BIG PAYOFF

The 1995 New York Yankees were the first team to have an average player salary of more than $2 million per year. Two years later baseball's average annual salary had reached $1,385,548.

BEST OFF THE BENCH

John Vander Wal of the 1995 Colorado Rockies had a record 28 pinch-hits, including seven doubles and four home runs, in 72 at-bats. His pinch-hitting average that year was .389.

BATTING BARRAGE

The Chicago White Sox and the Detroit Tigers combined for 12 home runs in a game at Tiger Stadium on May 28,

1995. The 12 homers in that game totaled 4,645 feet, nearly seven times the height of Detroit's 740-foot Renaissance Center, the tallest building in town.

50-HOMER SEASONS

Before Albert Belle hit 50 home runs in 1995, major leaguers had reached the 50-homer plateau only 18 times. In the seven seasons from 1995 to 2001, players topped the 50-homer mark 16 times and topped 60 six times, three times more often than in the preceding century.

TURN IT DOWN

Cleveland teammates Kevin Mitchell and Chad Curtis tangled in the clubhouse after an argument about loud music.

NOMO'S NO-NO

Hideo Nomo threw the only no-hitter at Coors Field, in 1996. He also is among the handful of pitchers to hurl hitless games in both leagues.

KEN'S CLOUTS

San Diego slugger Ken Caminiti homered from both sides of the plate in the same game four times—a major league record—in 1996. He later became the first San Diego Padre ever voted Most Valuable Player in the National League.

NEW PITCH

During the 1996 season, Barry Larkin beat Bob Patterson with a home run. But Patterson beat Larkin with the best postgame quip. "It was a cross between a

BASEBALL WORK STOPPAGES

1972	Players strike for 13 days (9 in regular season)
1976	Owners lock players out of spring training (17 days)
1980	Players strike for one week during spring training
1981	Players strike for 50 days during season
1985	Players strike for two days during season
1990	Owners lock players out of spring camps (32 days)
1994	Player strike ends season August 12 (232 days)
1995	Continuing strike shortens season to 144 games

screwball and a change-up," he said. "It was a screw-up."

LONG DAY'S NIGHT

The Rockies and Padres played a *three-hour inning* in 1996. The July 12 game at Denver's Coors Field featured four pitching changes, two rain delays, an on-field fight, an ejection, and 11 runs, all by Colorado.

TIGERS IN TATTERS

The five-man Detroit pitching rotation combined for fewer wins during the 1996 season than Denny McLain managed all by himself in 1968. McLain had 31 wins that year, two more than the '96 Tigers starters.

For more than five years, there was no commissioner of baseball. The game was run by an executive council of owners headed by Allan H. "Bud" Selig, chief executive of the Milwaukee Brewers. Unable to settle the 1994 player strike, Selig had the job of canceling the World Series. Major League Baseball

FELIPE FLIPPED

Mild-mannered Montreal manager Felipe Alou was thrown out of a game on his birthday in 1996.

FRUSTRATED FRANCO

Julio Franco's rocket off the Camden Yards scoreboard on July 28, 1996, resulted in a force-out. The ball was hit so hard that Bobby Bonilla had time to play the carom and fire the ball to second ahead of the sliding Albert Belle.

KING GEORGE

In his first 25 years as majority owner of the Yankees, George Steinbrenner changed managers 20 times, general managers 15 times, pitching coaches 37 times, and media relations directors 12 times. He had highly publicized battles with Billy Martin, Reggie Jackson, Dave Winfield, and even fan-favorite Yogi Berra, whose estrangement from the team lasted 14 years. On the other hand, Steinbrenner's teams won world championships in

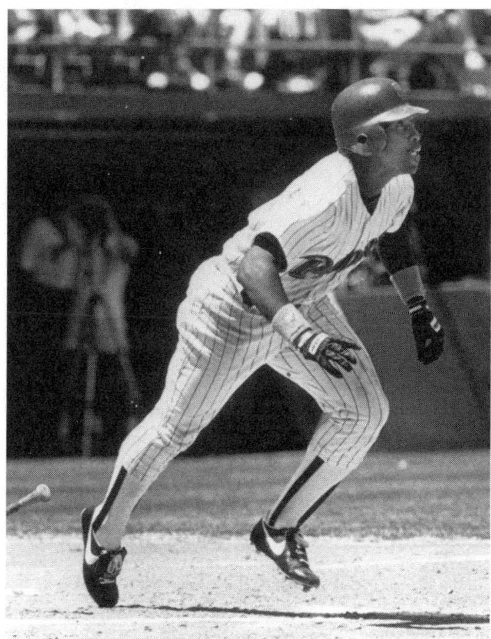

When Tony Gwynn won his eighth batting title in 1997, he tied Honus Wagner's mark for the most times leading the National League in that department. The longtime star right fielder of the San Diego Padres also became the first player to win four straight NL batting crowns since Rogers Hornsby won six in a row from 1920 to 1925. Gwynn's .394 average in 1994 was the closest anyone has come to .400 since Ted Williams hit .406 in 1941. He got the ninth five-hit game of his career on April 29, 1998. San Diego Padres

1977, 1978, and 1996—more than any other club during the 25-year span that started with the time of his purchase, on January 3, 1973.

NO RICKSHAW?

Rick Aguilera, a star relief pitcher for years, suffered an embarrassment of sorts in 1996. He got tendinitis from carrying his wife's luggage.

CARRY-ON BAG

After pitcher Dennis Martinez hurt his arm heaving luggage onto the team bus, the *Baltimore Sun* said he fell victim to "Samsonitis."

GREAT COOKIES

The employee who carried cookies and water to umpires after five innings of A's games was none other than Debbie Fields, who later parlayed that experience into the Mrs. Fields baking empire.

MOVING MAN

In 1997 Mark McGwire became the first man to hit at least 20 homers in the same season for two different clubs.

HISTORIC HITS
While Paul Molitor is the only man whose 3,000th hit was a triple, Wade Boggs is the only man whose 3,000th hit was a home run.

WADE'S WHITEWASH
During his scoreless inning of relief for the Yankees against the Angels in 1997, third baseman Wade Boggs threw 16 knuckleballs and a 74-mile-per-hour fastball.

DANNY'S DAMAGE
Danny Tartabull suffered such a severe injury fouling a Pedro Martinez pitch off his foot in the 1997 season opener that he batted only five more times before calling it a career at age 34.

SAYONARA, MIKE
Former Red Sox star Mike Greenwell was in his second week with Japan's Hanshin Tigers in May 1997 when he fouled a ball off his foot and broke it in six places. He retired a few weeks later at age 33.

DISTORTED PRIORITIES
Bud Selig made seven times more money as acting baseball commissioner in 1997 than Bill Clinton did as president of the United States.

Though Sammy Sosa was runner-up to Mark McGwire in a pair of record-smashing home-run races, he one-upped the Cardinals slugger by winning an MVP award (1998) and becoming the first man to top 60 in successive seasons (1999). Sosa, who once shined shoes in his native Dominican Republic for 35 cents a pair, was paid $9 million in 1999, when he led the majors with 397 total bases and 89 extra-base hits.

STAN'S THE MAN
Stan Javier hit the first homer in interleague play.

NO GOPHERS
Flame-throwing reliever Mark Wohlers faced 840 hitters from

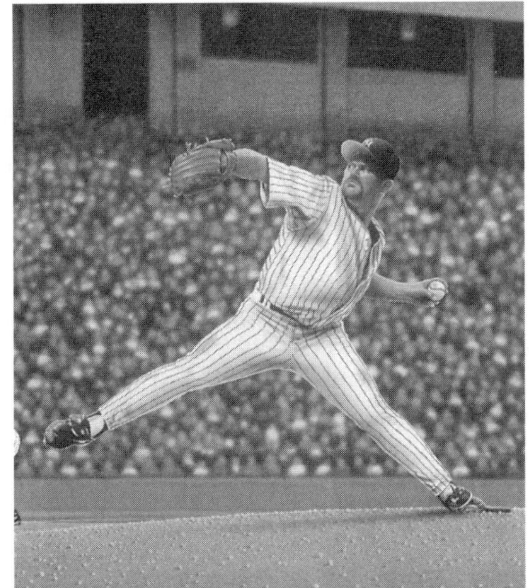

Portly but perfect, lefty David Wells thrilled a Beanie Baby Day crowd at Yankee Stadium with a 4–0 perfect game against the Minnesota Twins on May 17, 1998. Wells, who fanned 11, got help from second baseman Chuck Knoblauch, who snared a Ron Coomer smash in the eighth. Copyright 1998 by Bob Novak. Reprinted with permission, Bill Goff, Inc./ GoodSportsArt.com.

1997 to 2001 without ever yielding a home run on the first pitch.

HEY MISTER, WANT A WATCH?
When Roger Clemens signed with the Toronto Blue Jays, Carlos Delgado wore his preferred No. 21. The pitcher persuaded Delgado to take No. 25. The price of that persuasion included a good Presidential Rolex valued at $15,900.

WRIGHT ANSWER
After walking three batters and hitting another in the first inning of a 1998 game, Colorado pitcher Jamey Wright blamed his poor start on listening to CDs in the clubhouse too long before warming up.

MARCH ON MARIS
With three sluggers in hot pursuit of the Roger Maris home-run record in 1998, the Baseball Hall of Fame mounted a "March on Maris" exhibit that featured a game-by-game scoreboard showing the 1998 exploits of Mark McGwire, Sammy Sosa, and Ken Griffey Jr., matched against the 1961 pace of Maris.

Pitching Strategy

"It would be hard to go back to the four-man rotation. It would be even more risky to pitch guys on the fourth day all year long if they had multiyear contracts when you owed them money in the future. You don't want to hurt a guy and then have to pay him when he can't perform. Every decision we make in baseball today is based on a different set of conditions than when I played [from 1964 to 1977]. Most of them are regarding money—and wanting to make sure your money is well-spent."

—Larry Dierker

NEW NAME, BAD ARM

During his days as manager of the Milwaukee Brewers, Phil Garner had a pitcher with a tender arm. He told the pitcher not to pitch winter ball in his native Puerto Rico, but the pitcher protested that he needed the money. Garner arranged for the Brewers to pay the pitcher not to pitch. A month later, however, Garner went to Puerto Rico on a scouting mission. His biggest discovery was the same left-hander, pitching under an assumed name. He even had a new "winter league family" off the field.

NO KNOCK ON WOOD

With an NL-record 20 strikeouts against the Astros on May 6, 1998, Cubs rookie Kerry Wood tied the nine-inning mark of Roger Clemens, who did it twice for the Boston Red Sox.

SIZZLING SAMMY

Sammy Sosa is the only player to hit 20 home runs in a month. He did it in June 1998 while playing for the Chicago Cubs.

QUICK CLINCH

The 1998 New York Yankees were the first team in major league history to clinch a postseason berth in August.

RIPKEN RESTS

When Ryan Minor replaced Cal Ripken Jr. in Baltimore's starting lineup on September 20, 1998, it marked the first time since May 30, 1982, that Ripken's name was not listed in the Orioles' batting order.

The Yankees toast pitcher David Cone after his perfect game against the Montreal Expos at Yankee Stadium on July 18, 1999. The 36-year-old right-hander needed only 88 pitches in baseball's 16th perfect game. Among the witnesses were Don Larsen, author of the only perfect game in World Series history, and 1956 battery mate Yogi Berra, welcomed back into the Yankees family after a 14-year estrangement. The event also coincided with the 59th birthday of Yankees manager Joe Torre.

BIG MAC

Mark McGwire broke in with a bang (a rookie-record 49 homers in 1987) and never stopped. The first man with four straight 50-homer seasons won four home-run crowns, two in each league, and hit a record 135 over a two-year span in 1998–99. Giving a hint of things to come, he hit 71 home runs in his first 162 games with the Cardinals.

REDBIRD RIPPER

On April 23, 1999, Fernando Tatis of the St. Louis Cardinals became the only man in major league history to hit two grand-slam home runs in the same inning. His victim on both occasions was Chan Ho Park of the Los Angeles Dodgers.

SURPRISE NO-HITTER

Jose Jimenez, a rookie with a sorry record, carved a niche in baseball history by throwing a no-hitter against Arizona ace Randy Johnson in Phoenix on June 25, 1999. The first hitless game by a Cardinal in 16 years was decided when St. Louis scored a single run in the ninth. Jimenez then reverted to form, lost his spot in the rotation, and soon was back in the minors.

CHIPPER SWITCHER
Chipper Jones hit 45 home runs, an NL record for a switch-hitter, en route to National League MVP honors in 1999.

Mazzone's Credo

"I believe in throwing more often, with less exertion, and emphasizing touch, changing speeds, spin, and control. The thing I was most proud of [in Atlanta] wasn't the 20-game winners we had or the Cy Young Award winners. It was our health record. People said we couldn't throw as much as we did and be successful, but we did it. I liked proving people wrong."

—Leo Mazzone

Chipper Jones won National League MVP honors in 1999 after hitting 45 home runs, a National League record for a switch-hitter. Seven years later when Houston's Lance Berkman duplicated that record, Jones tied a Paul Waner mark by poking extra-base hits in 14 consecutive games. Bill Menzel

LEAVING HIS MARK
From 1996 to 1999 Mark McGwire *averaged* 61 home runs and 132 RBIs per year. At his peak in 1998–99, he blasted 135 homers and drove in almost 300 runs—figures never reached by Babe Ruth, Hank Aaron, or Willie Mays.

ELUSIVE CROWN
Nine of the twenty-six players who produced 3,000 hits never won a batting crown. They are Lou Brock, Eddie Collins,

THE HOME RUN KINGS

	BONDS	MCGWIRE	MARIS	RUTH
Year	2001	1998	1961	1927
Games	153	155	161	151
HR	73	70	61	60
RBIs	137	147	142	164
Average	.328	.299	.269	.356
Slugging Pct.	.863	.752	.620	.772
Walks	177	162	94	137
At-bats	476	509	590	540
ABs per HR	6.5	7.3	9.7	9.0

Rickey Henderson, Paul Molitor, Eddie Murray, Rafael Palmeiro, Cal Ripken Jr., Dave Winfield, and Robin Yount.

CONSISTENCY COUNTS

Eddie Murray is the only member of the 500 Home Run Club who never hit 40 in a season.

YEN FOR POWER

Japan's single-season home-run record is 55, achieved by Sadaharu Oh, Tuffy Rhodes, and Alex Cabrera.

GOPHER VICTIM

Ferguson Jenkins, always around the plate, could not always keep the ball in the park. He led his league in home runs allowed seven different times, a major league record.

SALARY SPIRAL

The highest-paid players of their time:

- 1947—Hank Greenberg $100,000
- 1977—Mike Schmidt $500,000
- 1980—Nolan Ryan $1,000,000
- 1982—George Foster $2,000,000
- 1990—Kirby Puckett $3,000,000
- 1991—Roger Clemens $5,000,000
- 1999—Kevin Brown $15,000,000

Chapter 13
The 21st Century

Brooks Robinson Remembers...

Baseball is certainly the most resilient sport there is. Check the papers and see how many people are coming to ballparks—both major league and minor league. I love football and basketball, but I think every person has a baseball memory. Not everyone has a football or basketball memory. Baseball is so ingrained in our society that people are compelled to go to games. There's more publicity, more TV and radio coverage, and more writers, and that makes people want to come out to the parks.

Just the chance to see anyone approach Hank Aaron's record for career home runs is a big story. To me, Aaron, Willie Mays, and Mickey Mantle were the three best players I ever saw. I would have a hard time separating them.

I don't think we'll ever change the records, no matter who does what. If some of the players suspected of substance abuse eventually reach the Hall of Fame, I would be inclined to put something on their plaques that says, "Played in the Steroid Era."

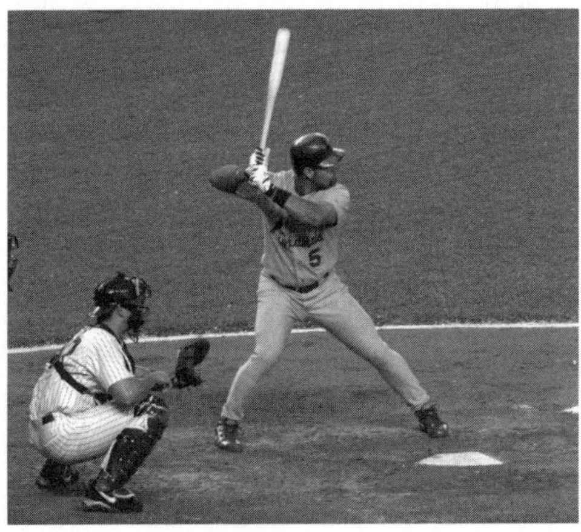

A rare player capable of carrying a club on his back, Albert Pujols projected the St. Louis Cardinals into postseason play in five of his first six seasons. The 2005 NL MVP is the only player in baseball history to hit .300 with 30 homers and 100 RBIs in each of his first six seasons. Bill Menzel

HOW BASEBALL HAS CHANGED

Major changes in baseball since the 1994–95 player strike:

- Interleague play—New rivalries kindled in several cities
- Realignment—Milwaukee moves from AL to NL
- Three-division format—More winners, including wild-card
- Expansion—Arizona and Tampa Bay added in 1998
- New ballparks—More than a dozen have opened
- Talent pool—Many more players arrive from Latin America and Asia
- Publicity—Every game is found on TV, radio, or Internet
- Parity—Revenue sharing, luxury tax make teams more equal
- Power—Explosion of 50-plus homer seasons, increased offense
- Minors revival—Better ballparks, cheap seats spark comeback

"WANT ME TO DO *WHAT*?"

During her tempestuous tenure as owner of the Cincinnati Reds, Marge Schott once ordered GM Bob Quinn to clean up after Schottzie, her St. Bernard, had "an accident" in the team's executive office.

IMPOSING IMPORTS

Ichiro Suzuki of the Mariners and Hideki Matsui of the Yankees are lefty-hitting outfielders who won three MVPs apiece in Japanese baseball before signing three-year contracts to play in the United States. Ichiro, who won seven batting titles in Japan before signing with Seattle in 2000, later became the first player to have at least 200 hits in each of his first four seasons.

THE ROOKIE

Jim Morris was out of baseball for *10 years* before he attended a Tampa Bay Devil Rays tryout on a dare from the Texas high school players he coached. A survivor of four arm operations and 203 innings of pro ball, Morris managed to throw 98 miles an hour and work his way to the majors, where he pitched 21 games without a decision in 1999–2000. The story of the 35-year-old physics teacher was later made into a movie, *The Rookie.*

SCOTT FREE

Scott Sheldon of the Texas Rangers may have played all nine positions for the team on September 6, 2000, but he made a putout only as a catcher. No balls were hit to him at any of the eight other spots.

RICK'S STICK

After an impressive rookie season in 2000, Cardinals southpaw Rick Ankiel suddenly lost his control in the NL playoffs. He spent most of 2001 in the low minors, where he doubled as a DH and hit 10 home runs.

SAVING SAN DIEGO

Trevor Hoffman was the first pitcher to post four straight 40-save seasons.

JAPANESE IRON MAN

Before retiring at the end of the 2001 campaign, Cal Ripken Jr. played in 2,632 consecutive games. But he needed 2,216 of those to break the Iron Man mark of Japanese star Sachio Kinugasa.

SWIFTY RICKEY

Rickey Henderson remains the only man with more than 1,000 steals (1,406).

RUN COLLECTORS

During the postwar era that began in 1946, the only men to post seasons with at least 160 RBIs were Manny Ramirez (1999) and Sammy Sosa (2001).

A former AL batting king and 40/40 performer with Seattle, A-Rod pounded a personal-peak 52 homers, a Texas club record and the most ever hit by a shortstop. Copyright 2000 by Bill Purdom. Reprinted with permission, Bill Goff, Inc./GoodSportsArt.com.

SLAMLESS SAMMY

Sammy Sosa hit 246 home runs before hitting one with the bases loaded.

WHEN BONDS WENT BUST

Slumps can hit anyone at any time. In 2001, the year he hit 73 home runs, Barry Bonds started with three hits in his first 29 at-bats, giving him a batting average of .103.

50 FOR BARRY

The only 50-homer season Barry Bonds ever had came in 2001, when he hit a record 73.

A hero in Japan, Ichiro Suzuki accepted a huge offer from the Seattle Mariners and became an instant star in the U.S. majors. The fleet leadoff man was American League MVP and Rookie of the Year in 2001, three years before setting a new standard with 262 hits. Bill Menzel

UNREDEEMED BONDS

Barry Bonds broke the single-season home-run mark, hitting his 71st and 72nd, in the longest nine-inning game ever played up to that point. His Giants lost to the Dodgers, 11–10, in four hours and 27 minutes on October 5, 2001.

LONG-DISTANCE DIALER

The total distance of the 73 home runs Barry Bonds hit in 2001 was 23,809 feet—the equivalent of 71,427 cheeseburgers lined up in a single row. The San Francisco outfielder's home-run trots, added together, stretched 4.98 miles, or 26,280 feet.

BARRY-METRIC PRESSURE

During his 73-homer season in 2001, Barry Bonds homered once every 6.52 at-bats and every 9.10 plate appearances. He also had an .863 slugging percentage and .515 on-base percentage.

FOUR FOR 50

More than two players had 50-homer seasons in the same year only twice, in 1998 (Mark McGwire, Sammy Sosa, Ken Griffey Jr., and Greg Vaughn) and 2001 (Barry Bonds, Sosa, and Luis Gonzalez).

HOME-RUN MACHINE

Mark McGwire retired after the 2001 season with a career home-run ratio of one per 10.61 at-bats, the best ever. Babe Ruth ranks second at one per 11.76 at-bats, with Barry Bonds third at one per 13 at-bats (entering 2007).

MARK'S FAST FINISH

Mark McGwire hit more home runs (254) in his final five seasons than Joe Torre, Robin Yount, Ted Simmons, Hack Wilson, and Roberto Clemente hit in their whole careers.

TOWERING TANDEM

The Arizona pitching punch of Randy Johnson and Curt Schilling posted an imposing .800 winning percentage in 2001. The 13th teammate tandem since 1920 to win at least 50 games in a season, they went 52–13 with a 2.52 ERA and 768 strikeouts (postseason figures included). None of the other pitching pairs matched that percentage.

RANDY AS VIDA

As a kid, Randy Johnson pretended he was Vida Blue while throwing tennis balls at his garage door.

HOLY STICKS

Superstitious outfielder Luis Gonzalez, who hit 57 home runs for Arizona in 2001, sends his bats to church. The habit started in 1993, when Gonzalez was with the Houston Astros. Aware that a chapel service was taking place in a room near the clubhouse, Gonzalez slid his bats into the room and asked someone to bring them back. He got a hit that day, finished the year at .300, and continued to slide his bats into the back of the chapel room—despite the strange looks he often got from chapel leaders.

ROOKIE RECORDS

In 2001 Albert Pujols compiled 360 total bases and 194 hits, both records for a National League rookie, and was the first player since Ted Simmons in 1973 to lead the Cardinals in the Triple Crown categories of batting, home runs, and RBIs.

TOTAL BASES ACES

With 402 total bases in 2001, Colorado's Todd Helton became the first player to top 400 in consecutive seasons. But he wasn't the NL leader: Sammy Sosa had 425, most in the majors since Stan Musial's 429 in 1948.

ROOKIE RAVE

In his first season with the Seattle Mariners (2001), Ichiro Suzuki led the majors in fan balloting for the All-Star Game, became the first man since Jackie Robinson in 1949 to lead the majors in both batting and stolen bases, and joined Fred Lynn as the only players to win MVP and Rookie of the Year awards in the same season.

JAPAN'S TANDEM

Japan's Osaka Kintetsu Buffaloes gave rivals double trouble in 2001 when Tuffy Rhodes (55) and Norihiro

Nakamura (46) combined for 101 home runs.

Peak Salaries

- $25,000,000. Alex Rodriguez, Rangers, 2001
- $15,000,000. Kevin Brown, Dodgers, 2000
- $14,000,000. Gary Sheffield, Dodgers, 1998
- $10,000,000. Albert Belle, White Sox, 1997
- $9,000,000. Cecil Fielder, Tigers, 1995
- $7,000,000. Ryne Sandberg, Cubs, 1993
- $6,000,000. Bobby Bonilla, Mets, 1992
- $5,000,000. Roger Clemens, Red Sox, 1992
- $4,000,000. Jose Canseco, Athletics, 1991
- $3,000,000. Kirby Puckett, Twins, 1990
- $2,000,000. George Foster, Mets, 1980
- $1,000,000. Nolan Ryan, Astros, 1980

"The Cooler"

Texas players called Alex Rodriguez "the Cooler" because teams that acquired him always cooled off.

Pro and Con

Scott Hatteberg (Boston Red Sox) was the first player to hit a grand slam and hit into a triple play in the same game (2001).

Missed Crown

Rafael Palmeiro is the only 500-homer hitter who never led his league in home runs.

Slammin' Sammy?

Sammy Sosa hit 63 home runs for the 2001 Cubs but did not deliver a single grand slam.

Best in a Pinch

Dave Hansen (2000 Dodgers) and Craig Wilson (2001 Pirates) share the single-season mark for pinch-homers (7), while Cliff Johnson holds the career record of 20.

Pain in the Neck

Pittsburgh shortstop Jack Wilson strained his neck when he bumped heads with outfielder Craig Wilson during pregame stretching exercises. He was removed in the fourth inning with a tingling sensation, then sat out two more games.

No Triple Threat

John Olerud, never known for his speed, rarely legged out a three-base hit. But he did manage to hit for the cycle—a feat that includes a triple—in both leagues. Both times, in

1997 and 2001, those were his only triples of the season.

TOP TANDEM

On June 6, 2002, Atlanta Braves aces Greg Maddux and Tom Glavine became the first teammates since New York Giants legends Christy Mathewson and Joe McGinnity with career records at least 100 games over .500.

TOP POSTWAR TANDEMS

During their time as teammates with the Braves, Greg Maddux and Tom Glavine won 347 games, the second-highest 10-year total of any two teammates in the postwar era. The only better tandem, also with the Braves, was Warren Spahn and Lew Burdette with 372 wins from 1953 to 1962.

TOUGH OPPONENT

Even though he was the first man to win four straight Cy Young Awards, Greg Maddux was never able to strike out eight-time batting champ Tony Gwynn.

CONTROL WHIZ

Greg Maddux once went nine straight seasons while averaging fewer than two walks per nine innings pitched.

Shawn Green had himself a career in one day during the 2002 season, collecting a record 19 total bases in a 6-for-6 performance that included four home runs, a double, and a single. Green, then playing for the Dodgers, victimized the Brewers in Milwaukee. The Topps Company

MODEL OF CONSISTENCY

Greg Maddux won at least 15 games 17 years in a row, a major league record that ended in 2005.

SUPER SMOLTZ

During his short-lived but brilliant stint as closer for the Atlanta Braves, John Smoltz pitched in a record 73 consecutive games that his team won.

Though constantly enveloped in controversy, Barry Bonds belted a record 73 home runs in 2001 and won his second batting crown three years later with a career-best .362 mark. He also set records that year for on-base percentage (.609), walks (232), and intentional walks (120). Bonds tied a Hank Aaron record with his eighth 40-homer season and had an .812 slugging percentage. Bill Menzel

GOOD COMPANY
John Smoltz and Hall of Famer Dennis Eckersley are the only pitchers with 20 wins in one season and 50 saves in another.

LEAGUE'S TOUGHEST OUT
Eight-time NL batting king Tony Gwynn was the toughest out for John Smoltz, the longtime Atlanta starter.

LONGTIME TEAMMATES
Tom Glavine and John Smoltz were teammates 14 straight years before Glavine bolted the Braves via free agency to sign with the New York Mets.

DOG FOOD WITH BITE
Pitcher Matt Mantei, recovering from elbow surgery, suffered a setback when he cut his hand opening a can of dog food just prior to the start of 2002 spring training.

WHIFFS DON'T MEAN WINS
Fanning 20 men in nine innings doesn't guarantee victory. Randy Johnson learned that lesson in 2001, when he fanned 20 Reds in the first nine innings of an 11-inning game on May 8. Johnson, who yeilded only three hits and no walks, left after nine innings with the score tied but got no decision, as Arizona won, 4–3, in 11 innings.

GREEN RAIN
How Dodgers outfielder Shawn Green amassed a record 19 total bases at Milwaukee on May 23, 2002:

- First inning: double to right field on 1–2 pitch
- Second inning: home run to right field on 1–1 pitch
- Fourth inning: homer to right-center field on 1–1 pitch
- Fifth inning: homer to left field on 1–0 pitch

- Eighth inning: single to center field on 1–0 pitch
- Ninth inning: homer to right-center field on 1–0 pitch

TOTAL TERROR

Just weeks after hitting four home runs in a game and collecting a record 19 total bases early in the 2002 season, Dodgers outfielder Shawn Green hit four *consecutive* home runs against the Angels over a two-game span. Green and Mike Schmidt are the only players to have a four-homer game and a separate streak of four consecutive home runs, but Green is the only one to do it in the same season. Only 13 other players have hit four home runs in a game.

GREEN EXPLOSION

Shawn Green's 6-for-6 performance against Milwaukee in 2002 included four home runs, a double, and a single, helping Los Angeles win, 16–3. The 29-year-old outfielder, who tied a modern-era mark with six runs scored, even got a standing ovation from fans at Miller Park. One year earlier, Green set Dodgers records with 49 home runs and 125 runs batted in.

EMPTY RECORD

Nobody was on base for any of the four home runs Mike Cameron hit for Seattle in a 2002 game.

The Topps Company

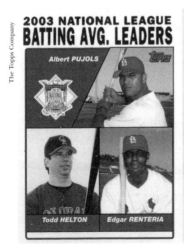

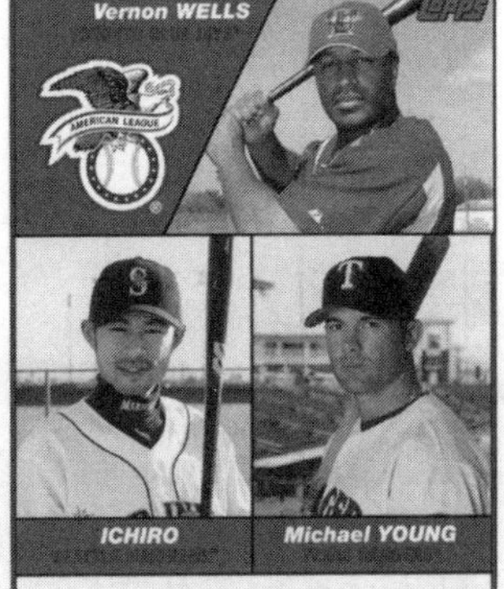

2003 AMERICAN LEAGUE
HITS LEADERS
Vernon WELLS
ICHIRO
Michael YOUNG

World Series artifacts from the 2004 world champion Boston Red Sox in the National Baseball Hall of Fame and Museum's collection.
Milo Stewart Jr./National Baseball Hall of Fame Library, Cooperstown, New York

CARDS LOSE KILE
St. Louis pitcher Darryl Kile, who died in his Chicago hotel room at age 33 in 2002, had never been on the disabled list during his 11-year career. From his June 22 demise until season's end, the Cards matched Kile's uniform number with 57 wins.

EARRING DELAY
A game was delayed in 2002 while Manny Ramirez crawled on his hands and knees in search of a $15,000 diamond earring he lost on a headfirst dive into third base.

SET THE ALARM
Baltimore outfielder Marty Cordova missed a day game because his face was burned a day earlier when he fell asleep in a tanning booth.

HUGE TURNOVERS
The 2002 Indians and Padres used a record 59 players each, three more than the 56 used by the 2000 Padres and 1915 Philadelphia A's.

DELAYED REACTION
Major league players and owners failed to prohibit the use of performance-enhancing drugs until 2002—a dozen years after Congress banned all known anabolic steroids.

EQUAL OPPORTUNITY
In 2002 Al Leiter became the first pitcher to beat all 30 major league teams.

WRIGHT IS WRONG

After eight years in the minors, Ron Wright made his big-league bow with the 2002 Seattle Mariners. He fanned in his first at-bat, bounced into a triple play in his second, and then rapped into a double play. Three at-bats, six outs, end of career—Wright returned to oblivion.

NO TRIP TO TOKYO

Because of security concerns after the American invasion of Iraq in 2003, the Oakland-Seattle series that would have opened the 2003 season in Tokyo was scrapped.

DISAPPOINTING DEBUT

In 505 regular-season starts with the Braves, Tom Glavine lost only one game by a 13-run deficit. Then he lost his first start for the Mets (2003) by a score of 15–2.

NAMES DON'T HELP

Among 2003 Opening Day starters who failed to win were Greg Maddux, Pedro Martinez, Randy Johnson, and Tom Glavine, who had combined for 14 Cy Young Awards in previous seasons.

GAGNE'S STREAK

Not counting a blown save in the 2003 All-Star Game, Dodgers closer Eric Gagne converted a record 84 straight opportunities—including 55 straight during the 2003 regular season. His ERA after the All-Star Game that year was 0.24.

ACCIDENTAL CLOSER

Eric Gagne became a closer by accident. Jim Tracy, then managing the Dodgers, moved him from the starting rotation to the late-inning spot after bids for free agents Troy Percival and Billy Koch were rejected. The original plan was for Gagne to join a closer-by-committee with Paul Quantrill and Giovanni Carrara, but the Canadian-born right-hander soon staked a solo claim to the job.

MUELLER THE MASHER

In 2003 Bill Mueller of the Red Sox became the first man to hit grand slams from both sides of the plate in one game. The slap-hitting third baseman turned the trick on July 29, 2003, at The Ballpark in Arlington.

SLAMMIN' ROBIN
Robin Ventura was the first player to hit a grand slam in both games of a doubleheader.

BOBBY TAUGHT BARRY
The young Barry Bonds was taught to hit left-handed by his father Bobby because Bobby knew the big leagues needed left-handed hitters.

SOLE MEMBER
Barry Bonds is the only player with 400 home runs and 400 stolen bases.

RESPECTED HITTER
At age 39 in 2003, Barry Bonds had more intentional walks (60) than strikeouts (55).

FIVE-YEAR FEAST
Barry Bonds hit the most home runs over any five-year span, with 258 from 1999 to 2003. That total included 73, a single-season record, in 2001.

GRAND-SLAM LEADERS

• Lou Gehrig	23
• Manny Ramirez*	20
• Eddie Murray	19
• Willie McCovey	18
• Robin Ventura	18
• Jimmie Foxx	17
• Ted Williams	17

* Active player.

BABE BEAT BARRY
Though Barry Bonds bested Babe Ruth's mark of 714 career homers, Ruth produced four times more seasons of 50-plus home runs (four to one).

BARRY AND SAMMY
During his best decade, 1995 to 2004, Barry Bonds hit 444 home runs, a figure that ranked second during that span to Sammy Sosa (479). No other player topped 400 in the same time frame.

BARRY THE BAT KING
Two years after becoming the oldest man to win a National League batting crown, Barry Bonds did it again. He was 40 when his .362 mark in 2004 led the NL, giving him his second batting title. That was also the season he parlayed 232 walks (120 of them intentional) into a .609 on-base percentage. All three figures were major league records. Bonds capped the 2004 campaign with his seventh MVP award and fourth in succession. No one else has won more than three.

HOT AND LATE
Barry Bonds hit more home runs after his 35th birthday than Roger Maris hit during his entire career.

MINIMUM WAGE
Baseball's minimum salary rose to $300,000 in 2003, with cost-of-living adjustments included for additional years. Players with contracts split between the majors and minors get at least $50,000.

TIMELY CLOUT
Kevin Millar's game-winning home run for the Red Sox on March 31, 2003, came in the sixteenth inning. No previous player had ever hit a home run so late in the game so early in a season.

IMPRESSIVE IMPORT
Hideki Matsui is the only Yankee to hit a grand slam in his Yankee Stadium debut. He did it on April 8, 2003.

SWEET AND SOUR
Yankees outfielder Hideki Matsui, who came to the U.S. majors from Japan in 2003, swings hot and cold: he loves hot baths and green-tea ice cream.

After winning two American League MVP awards, Juan Gonzalez succumbed to hamstring problems that curtailed his career. The Topps Company

INSTANT JOLT
Yankees second baseman Alfonso Soriano hit a record 13 leadoff homers in 2003.

KOREAN CLOUTER
Samsung Lions first baseman Seung-Yeop Lee hit 56 home runs, a record for any professional team in Asia, during the Korean Baseball Organization's 135-game season in 2003. Sadaharu Oh (1964), Tuffy Rhodes (2001), and Alex Cabrera (2002) had previous 55-homer seasons in Japan.

Roger Clemens and Randy Johnson proved that life begins at 40. Though both men pitched for several teams late in their careers, both refused to let age hamper their production. Between them, they won a dozen Cy Young Awards and excelled in postseason play. The Topps Company

PERSON POWER

When Robert Person hit a triple and a home run in the same game for the 2003 Phillies, he became the first pitcher in team history to collect seven RBIs in a game. The Phils beat Montreal, 18–3.

THREE GENERATIONS

Three generations of Hairstons played in the big leagues: Sam Hairston, son Jerry Hairston Sr., and grandsons Jerry Hairston Jr. and Scott Hairston. The Boones are baseball's only other three-generation family, with Ray Boone, Bob Boone, and brothers Bret and Aaron Boone.

TUNNEL VISION

Seattle pilot Lou Piniella and several of his players suffered from smoke inhalation when their team bus caught fire in Boston's Ted Williams Tunnel on May 20, 2003.

PLAYING WITH ZEAL

In 2003 Todd Zeile became the first man to homer for 10 different teams.

SPRY SOUTHPAWS

Warren Spahn (1963) and Jamie Moyer (2003) are the only left-handed pitchers to post 20-win seasons after their 40th birthdays.

CARLOS THE JACKER

Carlos Delgado clouted four straight homers for the Blue Jays during a 10–8 win over Tampa Bay at the Toronto SkyDome on September 25, 2003. He victimized three different pitchers and four different pitches in producing his fifth three-homer game, one short of the record shared by Sammy Sosa and Johnny Mize.

DELGADO'S BOOK

Carlos Delgado began keeping a written record of his at-bats after watching Albert Belle do the same thing. Delgado's book includes pitch sequence and selection.

OFF THE TRACK

Brawny slugger Carlos Delgado keeps his legs in shape by riding a bicycle. But it isn't always easy. When he played in Toronto, Delgado crashed when his bicycle wheels got wedged between streetcar tracks and the street. "It was kind of wet and I slipped," he said later. "Nothing happened other than a couple of scratches here and there."

STRANGE CLAUSE

After coming to the National League via free agency, Carlos Delgado signed a contract that included a $50,000 bonus for finishing second to Barry Bonds in the MVP voting, but nothing for finishing second to any other potential winner.

KILLER CARLOS

Carlos Delgado not only produced his 10th straight 30-homer season in 2006 but also became the first man to have 30-homer seasons with three different teams in as many seasons (Toronto in 2004, Florida in 2005, New York Mets in 2006).

PAYROLL MISMATCH

The 2003 World Series showed that money can't always buy happiness. The Florida Marlins, with a payroll of $52 million, defeated the New York Yankees, whose players earned $185 million.

GESUNDHEIT

Sammy Sosa wound up on the Chicago Cubs' disabled list in

2004 after wrenching his back while sneezing.

ONE-SIDED GAME
Cleveland's 22–0 defeat of the Yankees on August 31, 2004, matched the score of the most lopsided shutout of all time.

CLEVER KID
During his youth in the Dominican Republic, 2004 American League MVP Vlad Guerrero had to play with sticks for bats and rag-wrapped lemons for balls.

BARRY'S BONANZA
How Barry Bonds impacted the baseball record book in 2004:

- Highest on-base percentage in a season (.609)
- Most bases on balls in a season (232)
- Most intentional walks in a season (120)
- Most intentional walks in a nine-inning game (four)
- Most walks in a career (2,302)
- Most intentional walks in a career (604)
- Most times leading a league in intentional walks (10)
- Most consecutive NL seasons with 30-plus homers (13)
- Most career multihomer games in NL (68)
- Highest career slugging average in NL (.611)

FATHER-SON CYCLE
Gary Ward (1980 Twins) and Daryle Ward (2004 Pirates) are the only father-and-son tandem to hit for the cycle.

BUSH AT BUSCH
Secret Service agents disguised as ballplayers sat in the Milwaukee and St. Louis dugouts when President George W. Bush threw out the first pitch of the 2004 season at Busch Stadium. One agent asked a real Brewer what to do if a kid asked for an autograph. He was told just to sign and not say anything.

LOOK WHO'S TALKING
President George W. Bush once told Joe Garagiola Jr., "I'm always suspicious of guys who've got a famous father."

RING-A-DING
Texas right fielder Carl Everett was hit in the head with a thrown cell phone during the team's 12–2 loss to the Oakland A's at Ameritech Field on April 19, 2004. Everett was struck four days after a fan attacked umpire Laz Diaz at U.S. Cellular Field in Chicago.

RANDY'S HANDY

Randy Johnson's perfect game against the Atlanta Braves on May 18, 2004, was the 17th in baseball history. The 40-year-old Arizona lefty, who pitched a no-hitter for Seattle against Detroit in 1990, became the oldest man to pitch a perfecto. He threw 117 pitches and had 13 K's—second-best total ever posted in a perfecto. Only Sandy Koufax, with 14 in 1965, had more.

ROUGH 'N RANDY

Over the eight-year span that ended in 2004, Randy Johnson *averaged* 231 innings pitched and 307 strikeouts per season.

RAPID RANDY

Randy Johnson is the only pitcher to post four straight 300-strikeout seasons.

ALL AS FOR A'S

The 2004 Oakland A's won 20 games in a row for a new American League record.

OAKLAND MÊLÉE

Texas reliever Frank Francisco was arrested in Oakland on September 13, 2004, after he threw a chair into the stands in the ninth inning. He was charged with aggravated assault after the thrown chair broke the nose of 41-year-old fan Jennie Bueno, a mother of three and season-ticket holder. The fight apparently started after Oakland fans heckled Texas players during the game.

Only three men saved more games in a season than Mariano Rivera did in 2004. The Panamanian right-hander saved 53 games, a Yankees franchise record, in a career-best 74 appearances, and joined Eric Gagne as the only men with two 50-save seasons. Rivera failed to convert save opportunities only four times. He was the World Series MVP in 1999.

Bill Menzel

HIT MAN

Ichiro Suzuki collected a record 262 hits for the 2004 Seattle Mariners. That figure topped the 257 that George Sisler compiled for the 1920 St. Louis Browns.

SURPRISE SWITCH

Jeff Moorad moved from labor to management in 2004 when he agreed to become general partner of the Arizona Diamondbacks. Both the Commissioner's Office and the Players Association initially opposed the switch, which left 75 players without an agent but brought the team a $20 million investment.

HIS SUN ALSO RISES

White Sox pitcher Freddy Garcia likes to see the sun come up. In 2004 he went 9–0 during the day but only 4–11 at night.

PAINFUL PENALTY

The Cubs slapped slugger Sammy Sosa with a fine of $87,400, a single day's pay, for arriving late and leaving early on the last day of the 2004 season. The team had been eliminated from playoff contention the previous day.

OLDSTERS HANG ON

Players are lasting longer these days. The 2004 season was the first one that featured more than 100 players over the age of 35.

GROUNDHOG DAY

The 2004 Kansas City Royals were the only team to produce three straight identical scores while scoring in double digits. They won 10–4 three games in a row.

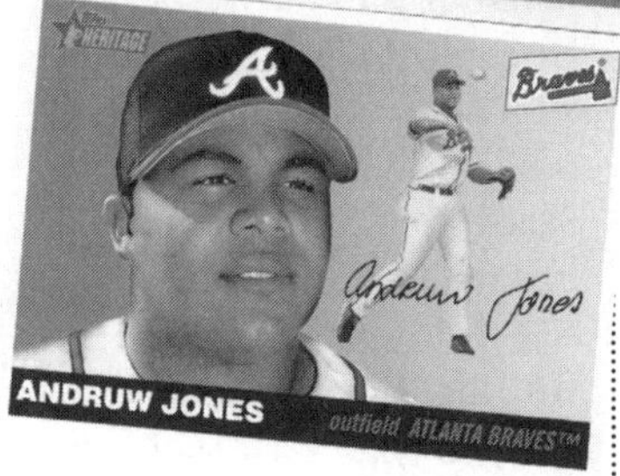

The Atlanta Braves streaked to 14 straight divisional crowns, a pro-sports record that extended through 2005, on the strength of shrewd scouting and player development. Among athletes discovered by Atlanta scouts were switch-hitting Chipper Jones, who won an MVP award following a 45-homer season, and smooth-fielding Andruw Jones, a Curacao native who finished second in the 2005 MVP voting after a 51-homer campaign. The Topps Company

PREDICTABLE PEDRO

The .760 winning percentage Pedro Martinez posted as a

member of the Boston Red Sox was the best any pitcher with a minimum 100 decisions ever recorded. The Dominican right-hander went 117–37 with the BoSox from 1998 to 2004.

FLYING LEAP
Tagg Bozied has a great baseball name but uncertain future following his ill-advised celebratory leap onto home plate after a game-winning grand slam for the 2004 Portland Beavers. The San Diego farmhand was so enthusiastic that he ruptured his patellar tendon and missed the last six weeks of the season.

BUT HE COULD FIELD
The .239 batting average by Oakland shortstop Bobby Crosby in 2004 was the lowest ever by a nonpitching AL Rookie of the Year.

HORSING AROUND
The four-year, $45 million contract that brought free-agent slugger Troy Glaus to the Arizona Diamondbacks for 2005 contained a clause giving his wife up to $250,000 for equestrian expenses.

FATEFUL FLINGS
Some ballplayers shouldn't try other sports. Prior to the 2005 season, Lance Berkman, Rocco Baldelli, and Jeff Conine suffered off-season injuries playing flag football, Wiffle Ball, and paddleball, respectively. Both Berkman and Baldelli injured a knee while Conine hurt his shoulder.

REGGIE'S HAUL
Reggie Sanders spent the 2004–05 off-season training with old Russian cannonballs weighing up to 100 pounds apiece. Hauling the balls was his trainer's idea; he thought it would increase the athlete's strength, agility, and *explosiveness.* He must have been right, since Sanders gave St. Louis one of his best years in 2005.

SLUGGERS FOR RENT
Manny Ramirez, Mark McGwire, and Rafael Palmeiro are the only players to hit at least 200 home runs for two different teams.

COLORFUL CARDINAL
On March 17, 2005, during Congressional hearings into alleged baseball steroids abuse, former slugger Mark McGwire

refused comment. A writer said later that McGwire wore a green tie and a red face.

No Jumping
The first contract signed by Joey Gathright with the Tampa Bay Devil Rays forbade him from jumping over cars. The scout who signed the outfielder had seen him do just that before he ever saw him play baseball.

Never Say Die
The 2005 New York Yankees, trailing Tampa Bay by eight runs in a June 21 game, exploded in the eighth for 13 runs and won the game, 20–11.

Last-Minute Rally
The Cleveland Indians rallied for an 11-run ninth inning, giving them a 13–7 victory, against the Kansas City Royals on August 9, 2005. Three Royals errors in the ninth contributed to the carnage—and the team's 11th straight loss.

Slam in Debut
Jeremy Hermida of the Florida Marlins became the first player to hit a grand slam in his first at-bat on August 31, 2005.

Pitcher Hits Seventh
When good-hitting Florida pitcher Dontrelle Willis batted seventh on September 22, 2005, it was the first time any pitcher had done that since Steve Renko of Montreal on August 26, 1973.

Sluggers Missed Series
Members of the 500 Home Run Club without a World Series appearance: Ernie Banks, Ken Griffey Jr., Eddie Murray, Rafael Palmeiro, and Sammy Sosa.

Power at Short
Ernie Banks and Miguel Tejada are the only shortstops to hit three home runs in a game more than once.

Gagne Got Burned
Players can play while appealing suspensions, but it's not always a good idea. Dodgers closer Eric Gagne, under suspension for razzing an umpire from the dugout, yielded home runs to Chipper Jones and Andruw Jones—the first two batters he faced in 2005.

Bad Beginning
Chicago Cubs outfielder Adam Greenberg had a rude welcome to the big leagues: he was hit in

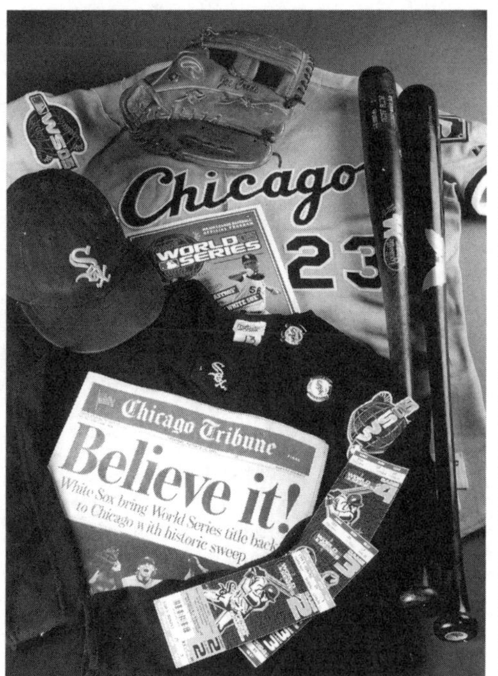

Artifacts donated to the National Baseball Hall of Fame following the Chicago White Sox's 2005 World Series victory include (clockwise from top left) road jersey worn by Series MVP Jermaine Dye, glove worn by Joe Crede, bat used by Geoff Blum to provide the game-winning home run in Game 2, White Sox press pins, World Series tickets, newspaper accounts of the Series, warm-up fleece worn by Manager Ozzie Guillen, cap worn by Freddy Garcia during Game 4, and a World Series program. Milo Stewart Jr./National Baseball Hall of Fame Library, Cooperstown, New York

the head by the first pitch ever thrown to him. Pinch hitting in Miami during the 2005 campaign, with his parents looking on, Greenberg was dizzy for weeks. After coming off the disabled list, he eventually went to the minors but has not returned to the big leagues. For all his trouble, he did not even receive an official at-bat.

STRENGTH IN NUMBERS
Sammy Sosa and Rafael Palmeiro of the 2005 Baltimore Orioles were the first pair of teammates with 500 home runs.

SAGGIN' SAMMY
The Baltimore Orioles paid Sammy Sosa $17 million in 2005 for hitting .221 with 14 homers, 45 RBIs, and a .295 on-base percentage. The only man with three 60-homer seasons went unsigned for 2006.

CURTAIN CALL
During the 2005 season, Rafael Palmeiro testified before

Congress in March, took part in an anti-steroids teleconference in July, and incurred an August suspension for violating baseball's drug policy. He also managed to deliver his 3,000th career hit.

OH, DEER

Tired of waiting for the elevator in his apartment building, Colorado shortstop Clint Barmes decided to walk up four flights of stairs. He didn't make it. Carrying deer meat given to him by teammate Todd Helton, Barmes slipped and fell, fracturing his collarbone. The injury, which cost him three months of the 2005 season, deprived him of a strong shot at the National League's Rookie of the Year award.

STINGY ON THE ROAD

Yankees closer Mariano Rivera yielded only one run on the road during the entire 2005 season. It was a home run by Eduardo Perez of Tampa Bay on August 16.

NO DIVINE DEBUT

Joey Devine is the only pitcher to yield grand slams in his first two major league games. He did it as a rookie with the 2005 Atlanta Braves.

A rare combination of speed and power made leadoff man Jose Reyes the ideal catalyst for the lineup of the 2006 New York Mets. Bill Menzel

INJURIES OF THE YEAR

If they gave such prizes, the following would have been contenders in 2005:

- White Sox outfielder Jermaine Dye missed four games after he was bitten by spiders in his Cleveland hotel room
- Padres pitcher Jake Peavy needed a tetanus shot after cutting his left hand taking out the garbage
- Cubs ace Carlos Zambrano suffered elbow pain from typing too many emails to his family in Venezuela
- Rockies shortstop Clint Barmes missed 78 games after breaking his

collarbone in a fall on his apartment house stairs

THE FIVES HAVE IT

On 5/5/05, the key hit in the Mets' 7–5 win over the Phillies was a fifth-inning, two-run double by a batter wearing No. 5, David Wright, and playing a position (third base) listed as number five on the scorecard. Need we add that Wright was batting fifth?

THAT MARIS MARK

The North Dakota State Senate unanimously approved a resolution requesting that Baseball Commissioner Bud Selig reinstate Roger Maris's 61 home runs in 1961 as the single-season record. The mark had been passed six times since, but the steroids scandal prompted questions. Maris grew up in Fargo, where he was a high school baseball and football star.

JUAN GONE

Two-time MVP Juan Gonzalez finished his career in 2005 with a one-at-bat season. Batting for Cleveland in the first inning on May 31, Gonzalez hit a grounder—and tweaked a spring-training hamstring strain that kept him sidelined all year. His last previous at-bat had been on May 21, 2004, as a member of the Kansas City Royals. Back problems limited him to 33 games that season.

SCOTT'S IRE

On May 2, 2005, Scott Eyre of the Giants gave up a run without allowing a hit, a walk, or a hit batsmen. Catcher Mike Matheny failed to catch strike three on Shawn Green, who reached first safely. With Eyre out of the game, Green scored on a double by Tony Clark.

HARPER HARPOONED

Tampa Bay reliever Travis Harper yielded nine earned runs, four of them on homers, in two-thirds of an inning at Yankee Stadium on June 21, 2005. The Yanks won, 20–11.

ROGER'S RICHES

Roger Clemens became the best-paid pitcher in baseball five different times:

- 1989—Boston Red Sox ($2.5 million)
- 1991—Boston Red Sox ($5.38 million)
- 1997—Toronto Blue Jays (12.375 million)
- 2000—New York Yankees ($15.45 million)
- 2005—Houston Astros ($18 million)

300-Game Winners Meet
The 2005 pitching matchup of Roger Clemens and Greg Maddux marked the NL's first battle of 300-game winners since 1892. But four *former* NL pitchers with 300-plus wins battled another ex-National Leaguer, Don Sutton, in American League matches of 300-game winners. Those games—pitting Sutton against Phil Niekro twice and Steve Carlton and Tom Seaver once each—occurred during the 13½-month stretch from June 28, 1986, through August 4, 1987.

Heavy Hitters
Three 500-homer men appeared in the same game for the first time on June 10, 2005, when the Reds (Ken Griffey Jr.) hosted the Orioles (Sammy Sosa, Rafael Palmeiro).

Potent in a Pinch
Lenny Harris collected a record 212 pinch-hits in a career that ended in 2005.

Painful Closer
Seattle closer Eddie Guardado saved 36 games in 2005 while pitching with a fully torn rotator cuff.

Busy Surgeon
Dr. James Andrews performed 1,128 Tommy John surgeries from 1988 to 2005.

What a Relief
John Franco, who retired in 2005, pitched more games without a single starting assignment than any other pitcher (1,119).

Devil Ray Thinking
After finishing last seven times in eight seasons, Tampa Bay general manager Chuck LaMar actually said the following: "The only thing that keeps this organization from being recognized as one of the finest in baseball is wins and losses at the major league level."

Chip off the Old Block
Future National League MVP Chipper Jones was five years old when he learned to switch-hit while playing backyard games at his central Florida home with his schoolteacher dad, Larry Wayne Jones Sr. Chipper holds the single-season NL record for home runs by a switch-hitter (45 in 1999) and shares the major league record, with Paul Waner, for most consecutive games with an extra-base hit (14 in 2006).

THE MOLINA TROIKA
Three Molina brothers were big-league catchers for different teams in 2006: Benjie in Toronto, Jose in Anaheim, and Yadier in St. Louis.

MUST BE HUNGRY
Major league players consume 300,000 bags of sunflower seeds per season.

2006 TICKET PRICES
Average ticket prices in 2006 reached as high as $46.46 at Boston's Fenway Park and as low as $13.71 at Kansas City's Kauffman Stadium. The only team besides Boston above the $30 average was the Chicago Cubs, at $34.30. The compact size of the ballparks in Boston and Chicago was certainly a factor, since tickets were hard to get for both ballparks.

WELL-PAID PLAYERS
The average player salary in 2006 was $2.85 million. More than 400 players earned seven-figure salaries, and the major league minimum was $327,000—$77,000 a year more than the best contract of Hank Aaron's career.

Julio Franco switched teams because the New York Mets were willing to give him a two-year contract *at age 47*. The Dominican first baseman proved to be a stabilizing influence inside the clubhouse as well as a productive pinch-hitter.
Bill Menzel

LOWEST PAYROLL
At the beginning of the 2006 season, 12 major leaguers made more money than the entire 25-man roster of the Florida Marlins.

AN INTERNATIONAL GAME
Foreign players have a major presence in 21st-century baseball. Of 813 players on 2006 Opening Day rosters and disabled lists, 223 were born outside the United States. The Dominican Republic had the most (85), followed by Venezuela (43), Puerto Rico (33), Canada and Mexico (14

The final cornerstone in the 2006 New York Mets juggernaut was the arrival of Carlos Delgado, secured in an off-season swap with the Florida Marlins. Having Delgado's booming bat in the number four lineup spot proved enormously beneficial to both Carlos Beltran, batting ahead of him, and David Wright, hitting behind him. Bill Menzel

each), Japan (9), Cuba (6), South Korea (5), Panama (4), Taiwan (3), Australia and Colombia (2 each), and Aruba, Curacao, and Nicaragua (1 each). The Mets had the most foreign-born players (15), just ahead of the Dodgers (14) and Angels (13).

COMEBACK CITY

More than 11,006 fans packed Zephyr Field for the 2006 opener of the New Orleans Zephyrs, Triple A affiliate of the Washington Nationals. The field, used as a National Guard rescue operations center in the wake of Hurricane Katrina, suffered severe damage in the August 2005 storm, but owner Don Beaver spent more than $2 million to repair it. Before the first pitch, players tossed the crowd their warm-up jackets. They read, "Proud to Call New Orleans Home."

WINNIE THE PUJOLS

Albert Pujols, first baseman for the St. Louis Cardinals, hit 14 home runs in April 2006 to set a record for the first month of the season.

CRACKED HALO

Angels pitcher Chris Bootcheck landed on the 15-day disabled list after straining a hamstring while running from the bullpen to join an on-field brawl in May 2006.

SWING IN THE PINK

More than 50 players used pink bats during Mother's Day games in 2006 to show support for the Susan G. Komen Breast Cancer Foundation. Players and other uniformed personnel wore pink wristbands and ribbons to show breast-cancer awareness.

AGED OUTFIELD

The San Francisco Giants fielded the oldest outfield in baseball history early in the 2006 season: Barry Bonds (41) in left, Steve Finley (41) in center, and Moises Alou (40) in right. The trio comprised the game's first all-40 outfield.

230 BURGERS TO GO

Like Woody Allen in the movie *Bananas,* Angels traveling secretary Tom Taylor rounded up 230 White Castle hamburgers at 3:45 in the morning. While the team plane sat on a Detroit tarmac in a weather delay, Taylor discovered the fast-food restaurant was open. He called in his order to disbelieving workers, who eventually acquiesced.

TRAVIS TREMORS

Travis Hafner of the 2006 Cleveland Indians hit a record five grand slams before the All-Star break. He finished the year with six, tying Don Mattingly's single-season mark.

NOW TOP THIS

Subbing for slugger Travis Hafner, Cleveland rookie Kevin Kouzmanoff hit a grand slam *on the first pitch he saw in the major leagues.* It happened in Texas on September 2, 2006, when Hafner—author of a record-tying six slams during the 2006 season—was sidelined by injury. Kouzmanoff joined Jeremy Hermida of the Florida Marlins (2005) and Bill Duggleby of the Philadelphia Phillies (1898) as players who poked a grand slam in their first at-bat. Bobby Bonds is the only other player to hit a grand slam in his first game.

60-HOMER SLUGGERS

In the first 125 years of professional baseball, two men hit 60 or more home runs in a season. In the last nine years, the 60-homer barrier has been crashed seven times—three of them by Sammy Sosa. Also topping 60 were Barry Bonds, with a record 73; Mark McGwire twice, with 70 and 65 in successive seasons; and second-year slugger Ryan Howard in 2006. Historians may determine whether the assault is the result of smaller parks, inferior pitching, livelier balls, or substance abuse by players.

LOBSTER PARADE

After he hit his 41st homer for the 2006 Boston Red Sox in August, DH David Ortiz received a gift from the governor of a neighboring New England state: 41 Maine lobsters. The gift was actually an invitation from Governor John Baldacci, who had heard Ortiz state in an interview that he had never been to Maine and wasn't sure where it was.

LONG NIGHT
The 14–11 Yankees victory at Boston's Fenway Park in the second game of a day-night doubleheader on August 18, 2006, consumed four hours and 45 minutes—making it the longest nine-inning game in major league history. With 10 pitching changes and 437 pitches thrown, the lengthy duration was no surprise.

TAXI TROUBLE
Mets pitchers were injured in taxicab crashes two years apart: Tom Glavine in 2004 and Duaner Sanchez in 2006.

RACE TO SECOND
Luis Gonzalez makes it a habit to touch second base on his way to and from his position in left field. In Los Angeles, however, he has to race to get there after the third and sixth innings, when the groundskeepers change the bases.

Yankees shortstop Derek Jeter has been a perennial MVP candidate since reaching the majors in 1996. This Topps card was painted in the style of the company's 1953 set. Copyright 1999 by James Fiorentino. Reprinted with permission of Bill Goff, Inc./GoodSportsArt.com.

BASEBALL ARTIST
Vernon Wells III plays center field for the Toronto Blue Jays. His father, Vernon Wells Jr., paints portraits of major leaguers. Selling price is $6,000 to $20,000.

PRINCE ALBERT
Albert Pujols of the Cardinals is the only man ever to hit .300 with 30 homers and 100 RBIs in each of his first six seasons.

WHAT'S IT ALL ABOUT, ALFIE?

In 2006 Alfonso Soriano of the Washington Nationals became the first player not named Bonds to have at least four seasons with 30 home runs and 30 stolen bases. The father-and-son tandem of Bobby and Barry Bonds had turned the trick previously.

40-40 GUYS

Barry Bonds, Alex Rodriguez, Jose Canseco, and Alfonso Soriano enjoyed 40/40 seasons.

MVP MONOPOLY

Barry Bonds, with seven, is the only man to win more than three MVP awards.

COMPLETING THE CYCLE

Kenji Johjima (Mariners) became the first Japanese catcher in the majors in 2006—41 years after Masanori Murakami became the first Japanese import to play in the American big leagues. A Japanese player from every position has now appeared in the U.S. majors.

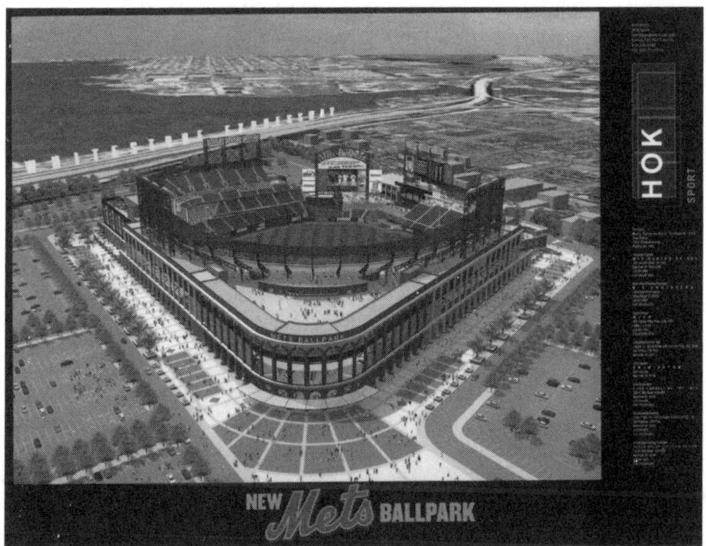

Elements of Ebbets Field, including the rotunda and pedestrian plaza, will be a hallmark of the new Mets ballpark, scheduled to open in Queens in 2009 near the current Shea Stadium. New York Mets

FATHERS AND SONS

An All-Star team of active players whose fathers also played big-league ball:

Position	Player
C	Jason Kendall (son of Fred)
1B	Adam LaRoche (son of Dave)
2B	Josh Barfield (son of Jesse)
SS	Bobby Crosby (son of Ed)
3B	Aaron Boone (son of Bob)
OF	Barry Bonds (son of Bobby)
OF	Gary Matthews Jr. (son of Gary)
OF	Ken Griffey Jr. (son of Ken)
P	Tony Armas Jr. (son of Tony)
P	Brian Bannister (son of Floyd)
DH	Moises Alou (son of Felipe)

NOT PAYING ATTENTION

Nearly three dozen players have contract clauses calling for bonuses if they win MVP honors in the Division Series—the only postseason series for which *no MVP award is given.*

WHERE JUNIOR LEARNED

According to his father, Ken Griffey Jr. learned to play baseball under the stands of Yankee Stadium. The senior Griffey threw batting practice to his promising young son while winding down his own career as a player.

CINCY SIZZLER

A double by Ken Griffey Jr. was the first hit at Cincinnati's Great American Ballpark, which opened in 2003.

A NEW ALOU

Two generations of Alous have played and managed in the majors, but Christia Alou is the first nonuniformed family member to get involved. The sister of Moises Alou and daughter of Felipe hoped to parlay her University of Maryland law degree into certification as one of fewer than a dozen female player agents.

ROGER THE STREAKER
Roger Clemens is the only pitcher ever to win at least 16 games in a row twice.

MAUER'S MARK
Minnesota catcher Joe Mauer, the American League's surprise batting champion in 2006, gave hint of things to come when he proved his ability as a contact hitter during his high school career in St. Paul. He struck out exactly once as a schoolboy star. Once.

HANDS OFF
Slick-fielding Phillies center fielder Aaron Rowand is superstitious. He won't let anyone else slip a hand into his Rawlings Pro Preferred glove.

RANDOLPH'S ROLE MODEL
Mets manager Willie Randolph, formerly a second baseman with the Yankees, credits the late Billy Martin as his inspiration. "I loved the way he played the game, the way he loved to attack the opponent, the way he loved to take advantage of every opportunity," Randolph explained.

HOFFMAN TOPS SMITH
Trevor Hoffman passed Lee Smith as the career saves leader during the final week of the 2006 season, helping San Diego stay alive in its bid for a postseason berth.

PASSING HENRY
Barry Bonds became the lifetime leader in National League home runs late in the 2006 campaign. He topped Hank Aaron, who hit 733 in the NL before hitting 22 more as a designated hitter for the Milwaukee Brewers, then in the American League.

About the Author

Dan Schlossberg is the author of 32 baseball books and thousands of articles about the game. In 2006 he coauthored autobiographies of Ron Blomberg and Milo Hamilton, wrote baseball articles for the in-flight magazines of United Airlines and U.S. Airways, and covered spring training, the All-Star Game, the winter meetings, and other special events for *Ball Talk,* a syndicated radio show for which he is cohost and managing editor.

Originator of the baseball-themed-cruise concept in 1981, Schlossberg has created, coordinated, and hosted more than two dozen baseball-themed cruises. He has contributed to dozens of preseason baseball annuals and written player biographies for every card company, including Topps and Upper Deck.

Also a travel writer, Schlossberg is president of the North American Travel Journalists Association, travel editor of ConsumerAffairs.com, columnist for *Travel World International,* contributing editor for the *Travel with Kal* radio show, and former president of the Working Press Association of New Jersey. His reports on travel have appeared in AAA publications and have aired on XM Satellite Radio's Lifestyles Channel 155.

The 1969 Syracuse University graduate has been a writer/editor for American Express, the Associated Press, *The Bergen Jewish News,* Motor Club of America, and the University of Medicine and Dentistry of New Jersey. He claims Passaic, New Jersey, as his hometown but currently lives in Fair Lawn.

For more details, see www.DanSchlossberg.com.